D RAW

KENYA HARA

Lars Müller Publishers

DRAW

Kenya HARA

With clumsy line drawings, I delve into the unknown

Kenya HARA

I'm not skilled at sketching. When I think of great artists like Leonardo da Vinci, Tomitaro Makino, or Hokusai Katsushika, I'm embarrassed to even show my work. However, once I started editing my collected sketches, I became surprisingly engrossed. It took me just two weeks to write and edit this book, from the end of 2023 to the beginning of 2024. Upon realizing that these materials required editing, I eagerly anticipated the task.

From March to July 2023, I held a solo exhibition at the National Art Museum in Poznan, Poland. It was a spacious venue, so it became a comprehensive overview of my past work. This was a commemorative exhibition for the Jan Lenitsa Award. During this time, Lars Müller, a Swiss graphic designer and publisher with whom I've worked in the past, saw the 100-plus hand-drawn pencil sketches on display, and suggested that I compile them into a book – not as a collection of artwork, but rather to provide insight for other creators on how a designer works with hand-drawn sketches in the age of artificial intelligence (AI).

It's easy to imagine that many jobs we consider creative will be taken over by AI in the near future. However, when this happens, we may realize that the parts of the job AI can handle are not the creative aspects, and we'll be happy to give those to AI, and perhaps, supported by AI, we can then spend our days diligently sketching away. Lars Müller may have shared a similar perspective.

Sketching is the process of taking a vague idea floating in your mind and bringing it into the dimension of this physical world. I believe that the ideas that come and go in our minds arise from a vast pool of dazzling images that far exceed our imaginations. While AI is believed to be capable of accessing more data than humans can, is this really true? The images we create when we are in an expressive state are probably not based on the experiences of a single individual; they seem to include the memories of all humanity since time immemorial, and even the memories of the creatures we were before we evolved into humans. We know that in the process of developing their human form, human fetuses take on the characteristics of fish and amphibians, but we do not know what kind of imagination lies dormant in the part of the brain buried in the layers of time, nor the new cortex. Upon closer inspection of these sketches, we recognize that they emerge in a precise narrowing down from all possible forms, and in the finishing process, they converge with high precision in a certain direction, closing the gap between extremely minor differences. While AI can be a reliable thinking partner, I intuitively think that we cannot rely on it to create images. As living beings, we are born into this universe and have spent our lives imagining. Most of the things we imagined were based on hypothetical reasoning, beyond logic and empirical rules, or, in other words, "what if" thinking, based on leaps of reason and thinking outside the box. Semiotician Charles Sanders Pierce called this form of thinking "abduction," which differs from both deduction and induction insofar as it is not based on either logic or empirical rules. I also wonder if our brains generate unpredictable, unexpected, and out-of-schedule phenomena, as exemplified by the mathematical concept of "repellers" in René Thom's catastrophe theory.

Sketching is the process of bringing these "what if" images from one's mind into the outside world, as accurately and directly as possible. The mind is a multidimensional sea of chaos, swirling with absurdities and inconsistencies. Sketching is the task of bringing what is conceived in the mind into conformity with the harsh reality of the laws of physics, three-dimensionality, and the scale of the human body.

In a later chapter, I will describe how I took a croquis class after I finished graduate school at an art university. I believe my motive was not to improve my drawing skills but to acquire the skill or know-how to smoothly externalize excitements or ideas that arose in my mind. Even if an image shines brightly in my mind, if I don't have the skill to bring it outside in a fresh manner, the image that sprang to life will immediately wither away and die. At the same time, we must avoid viewing sketching as something that aims toward improvement, for instance, at producing a good drawing. If this is the case, sketching becomes an art form and thus is liable to turn into an object of enjoyment or appreciation. Since the line is constantly in contact with the unknown imagination, it should have no room for mastery. The normal state of sketching is rather instability. Using the motion of the hand, an organ directly connected to the brain, the sketcher, trembling inside, gingerly traces the boundary between the body and the universe.

Design is the process of creating an external environment. Living organisms draw inspiration from their surroundings to generate images and change the form of their environment. Sometimes it's something ordinary and unexpected. Groundbreaking ideas are often hidden in the daily life of any living creature. Taking humans as an example, the idea of the right-angled shape, the rectangle and the square, was revolutionary. We have divided the organic earth into squares / rectangles and created right-angled buildings, houses, corridors, vertical elevators, rectanglular paper, furniture, and computers, all modeled using the rule-based grid. Of course, the right-angled parallelogram is just one of the images created by humans, but it is a product of the human race, resulting from our con-sciousness of vertical and horizontal, which in turn stems from our bilaterally symmetrical body – a body that stands up, in constant defiance of gravity. In other words, the rectangle is one of the masterpieces of the human imagination. Perhaps the traces of countless sketches brought this shape into being in this world. Since it is quite difficult to find a natural rectangle or square in the organic universe, it is fair to say that Homo Sapiens' creations are quite original in their own way.
Buildings and products surround us and it's safe to assume that all shapes have originated through a similar process, such as that of the rectangle, and have been established through many iterations. This applies to vessels, knives, glasses, toilet paper, macaroni, housing, clothing, etc. Creation is the infinite repetition of the

process of finding materials in the environment and giving them form through imagination. The basic form remains constant, although trends do effect some changes. However, as living creatures, we never stop exploring hypothetical "what if" scenarios. It's important to note that new doesn't necessarily mean good. Just as we continually strive for the ideal form of housing as a space for eating and sleeping, finding creative solutions within the familiar is crucial. This is where the intelligence of design comes into play.

I believe I will continue pondering throughout my life the theme of how design shapes the environment in which people live. I identify myself as a designer in the sense of "someone who lives with design at my side."

As a design professional, my role is to continuously generate "what ifs" in response to real-life issues. Whether it's designing packaging, identification, advertisements, or exhibitions, I have continued to approach every challenge with a "what if" mindset, imagining new ideas and solutions. This book captures some of the "what if" ideas that I've recorded. Every job represents a conclusion I came to while on a deadline, and I don't consider each one to be the correct answer, but these many sketches are the vestiges of the imaginative leaps I made along the way.

Although each of my sketches deals with a specific issue, when viewed on a somewhat broader scale, they all suggest the direction of my future work. The time of a generation of individuals may be as short as the twinkling of a star, but I hope you can see in it a vector of life – the power to move toward a specific direction. There must be something in "I" that encompasses "we," and I hope my work is also oriented in that direction.

My mentor at university, Shutaro Mukai, once said, "Form is life's gesture to the universe." It is in this sense, I think, that gestures are clearer in my sketches than in my finished work.

1983—2000

Dangling a fishing line into my inner self

I started working as a designer during my graduate studies, although it wasn't a direct path. I had learned design as a theoretical skill at Musashino Art University's Department of Science of Design, but I lacked the confidence to start working immediately. I needed some time to figure things out. Eventually, I was offered a job at the workplace of a designer who had taught me at the university, and that's how I got started.

My mentor at university, Nobukuni Takada, was a graphic designer who primarily worked in editorial design.

Attracted by the atmosphere of a meticulous and honest workplace, I entered the world of book design and encyclopedia diagrams. After about a year of working there, I began working in the design office of Takada's friend, Eiko Ishioka. Impelled by an urge to experience first-hand the work done at Eiko Ishioka's studio, work which epitomized the fashion and commercial worlds of the 1980s and the golden age of Japan's economy, I told Takada of my wish to work there. My charitable mentor kindly put in a good word for me. The work was far more demanding than I had imagined, and my theory-heavy design sense was no match for it. And so every day, I was subjected to Ms. Ishioka's sharp criticisms and scolding, like a *loofah* being tested with a *katana*, and without any means of resistance, I was cut to pieces and rolled around, exposing my dumb cross sections. In fact, I was astounded by Ms. Ishioka's sketches. For example, a front-view drawing of a bride dressed in a white kimono riding a 750 cc Suzuki Katana motorcycle, or the drawing of a half-naked man with tattoos all over his body, even his shaved head, sitting in zazen, with a small SONY television set placed a few meters away. She was able to conceive of extraordinary scenes and then draw them accurately in fine detail. I was blown away by these alluring drawings.

Although I found Ms. Ishioka's work exceptional, I left my job after completing my graduate studies. Having to resign was quite frustrating, but it helped me understand the hard work and dedication required to attain the highest level in one's career.

As soon as I graduated, I entered Nippon Design Center, and forty years later, I'm still working at the same company. The corporate culture of working at one's own pace, which is more like a school than a private office, suits me, and it is in this environment that finally been able to spread my wings and find the rhythm of my work.

When I first joined the company, I used to go to a croquis sketching class on the weekends. If I think about it now, rather than cultivating excellent drawing skills, this class trained me to instantaneously release the images I hold in my soul. My first efforts were aimed at "drawing well," perhaps due to the tension I felt because the subject was a nude woman. However, gradually I became less interested in form and balance and more interested in expressing in my sketchbook the impulses and emotions I felt when I looked at the subject. In the end, I drew neither with Conte crayons nor with pencil, but by striking an ink-stained cloth against the paper. In this way, little by little, I learned how to pull the things inside my mind out into the open.

The first images in this book are drawings I made around 1990. These are not dynamic like croquis sketches, but rather sketches that carefully extracted images of objects I had floating in my mind. They date from the time when I was trying to learn my nature as a designer, as if dropping a fishing line into myself to see what I would catch. This was when I had just begun work on the Takeo Paper Show for the fine paper company Takeo, for whom I created three pieces a year which resembled art posters. This work is not geared toward marketing, but work in which I express my feelings and intuitions just as they are. Without looking at anything, without referencing anything, while I'm sketching whatever shape comes up in my mind, it mysteriously coalesces into a particular form. And while at first I thought these must have been expressions of my own memories, gradually I began to think they may be things that contain some of humanity's distant memories.

Around the same time, I was asked to handle package design for Nikka Whisky Distillery. The first product was Nikka Cidre, a sparkling alcoholic beverage made from apples, but gradually I was asked to handle spirits with a high alcohol content, such as brandy and whisky. In addition to the labels and typography, I began to become interested in the shape and texture of the bottles as well. I sensed the attraction of the elegant gleam of the amber spirits, aged in wooden barrels, as glimpsed through their thick bottles. What I felt was the excitement of a sense of disquietude, which stemmed from something like magic or sorcery, rather than the lineage of modernism.

At that same time, I also received advertising work from the veteran copy-writer, Yusuke Kaji. The rough sketches for Japan Michelin Tire were done around 1990. Yusuke Kaji was more of a scholar of branding than a copy-writer. He always advised me to maintain my composure and grace, even when a big client had me at its mercy. He taught me to uphold my dignity as a creator. He had the ability to come up with countless ideas overnight, and was skilled at expressing his unique rhetoric.

I think my work on books for Issey Miyake's im product and the booklet for the Aichi Expo came after that. I was trying to create something like a story as I imagined the flow of a book's layout. This was the period in which I began to add the sensibility of an editor to my work.

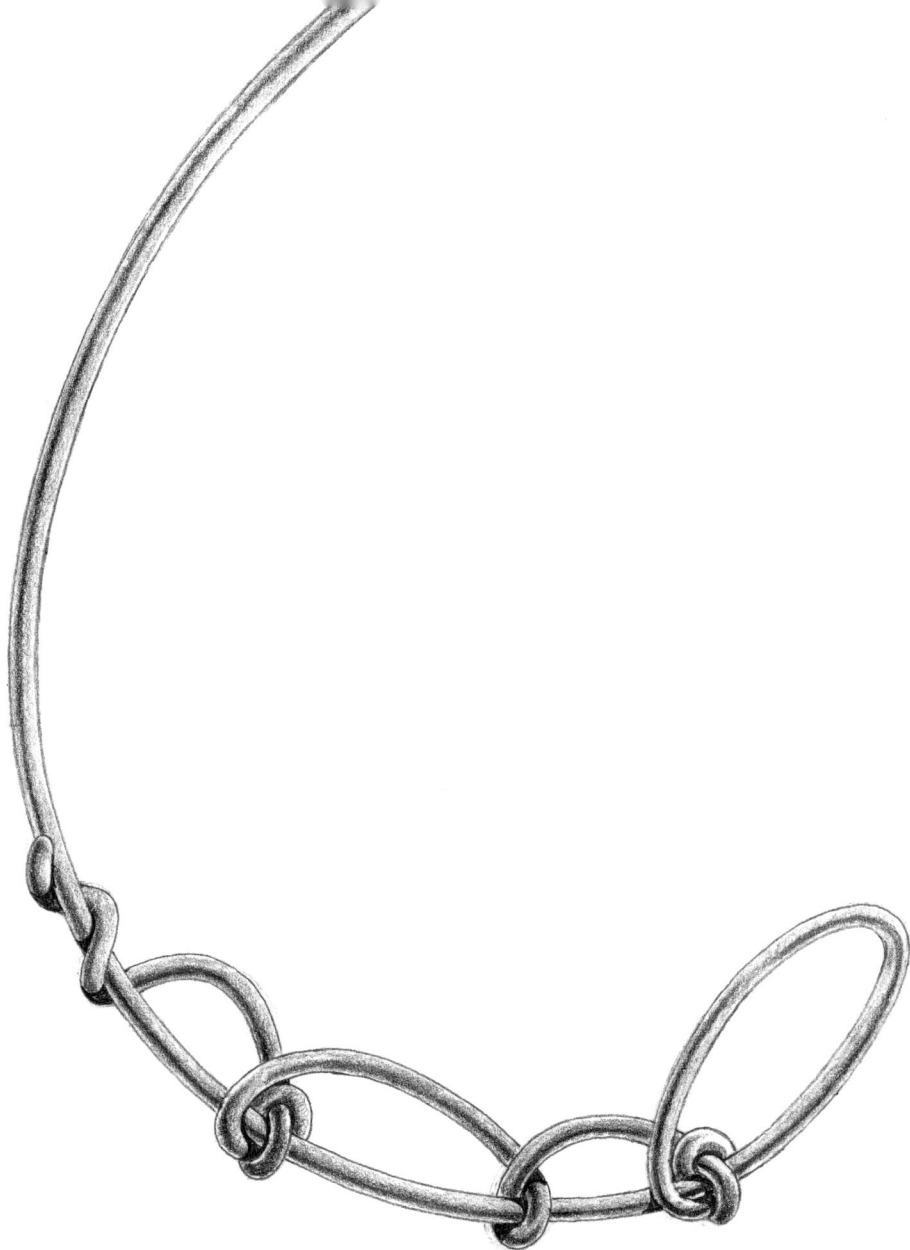

I drew what came into my head, as if exploring the qualities that define me.

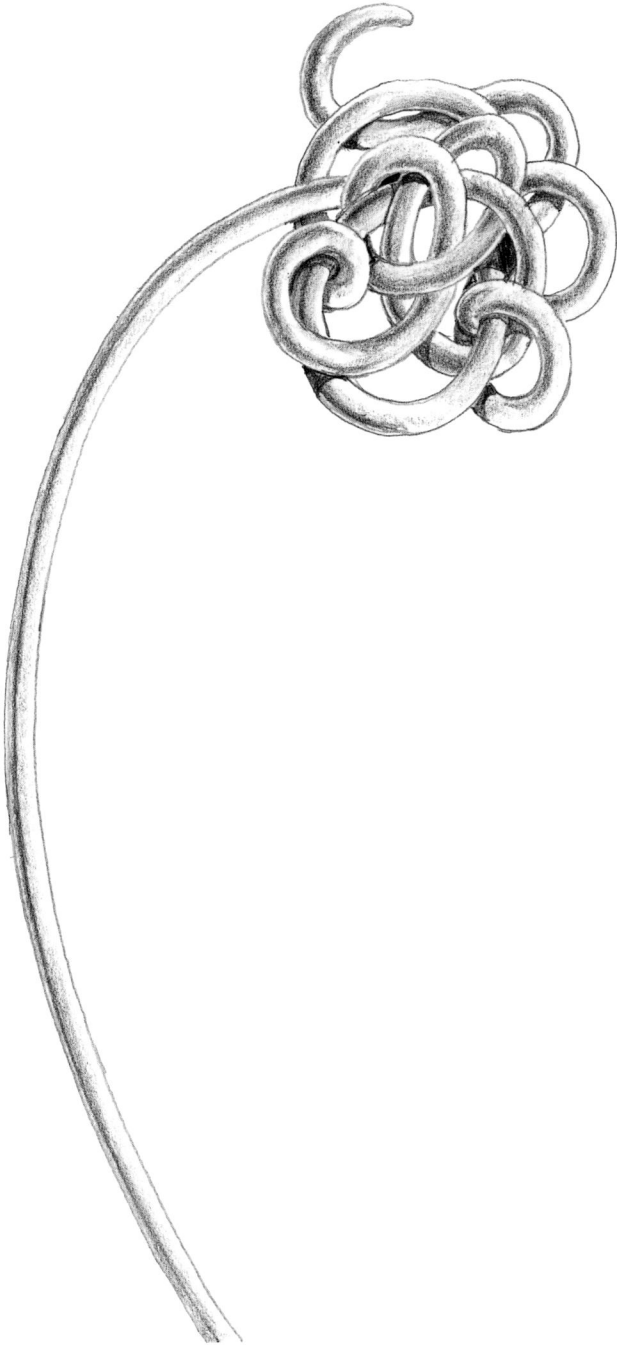

1983—2000   Dangling a fishing line into my inner self

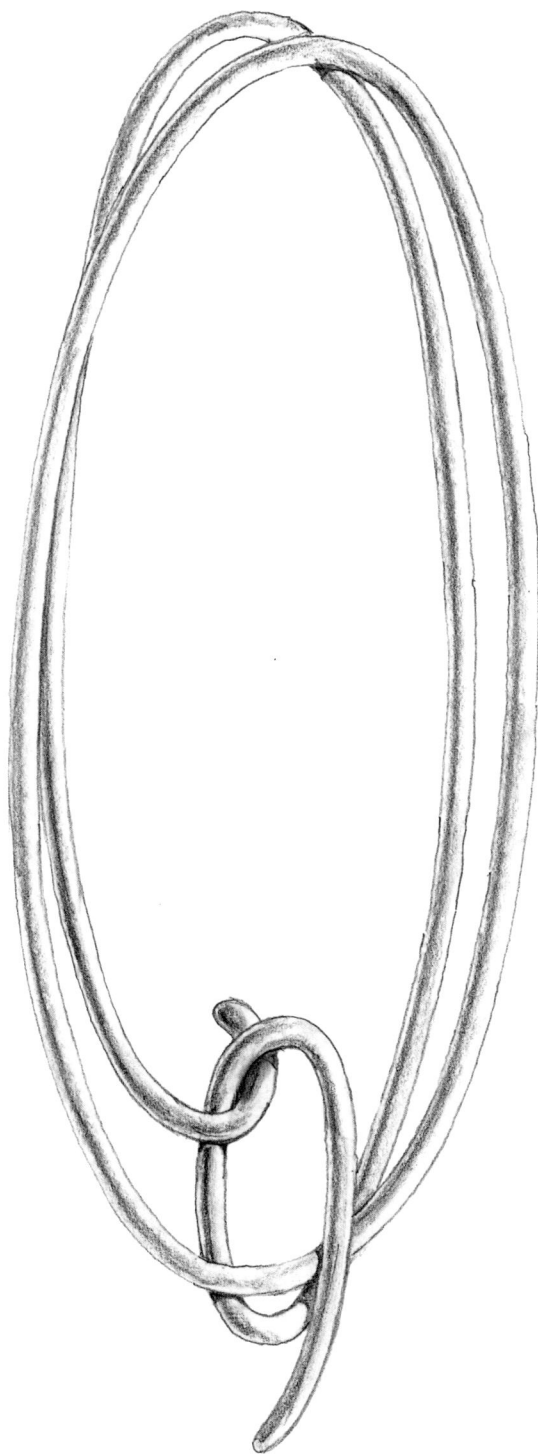

1983——2000   Dangling a fishing line into my inner self

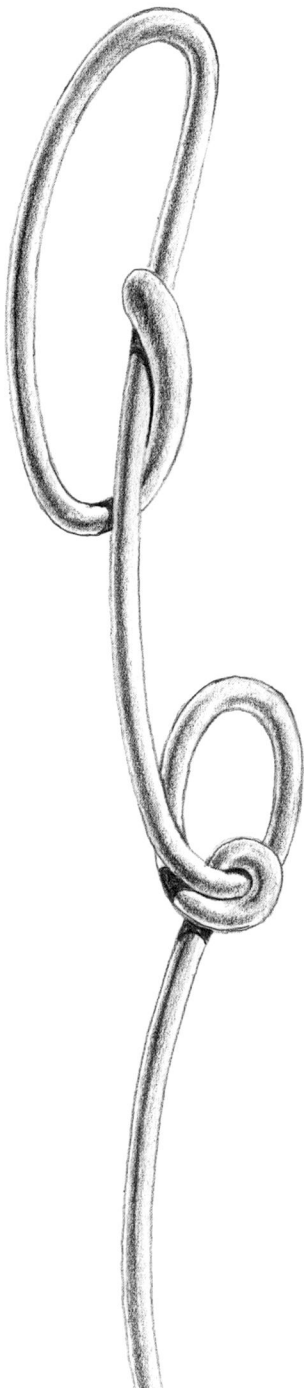

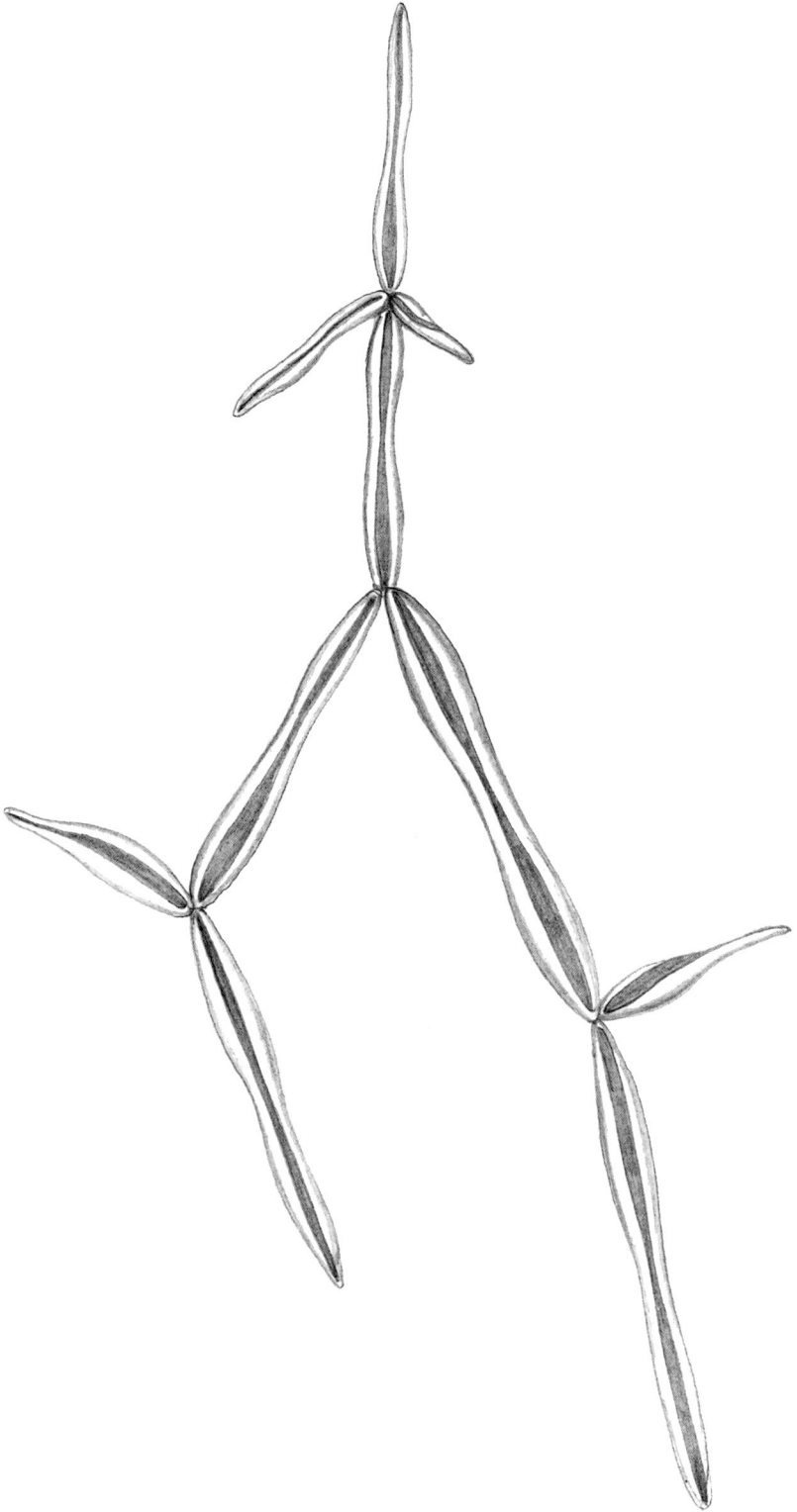

1983——2000   Dangling a fishing line into my inner self

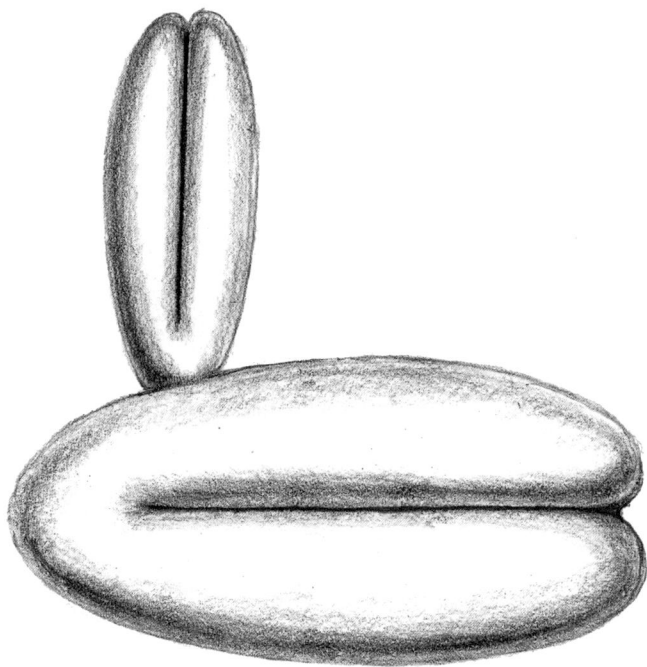

The elastic trough resulted from folding a taut shape in two, bearing a mysterious smile.

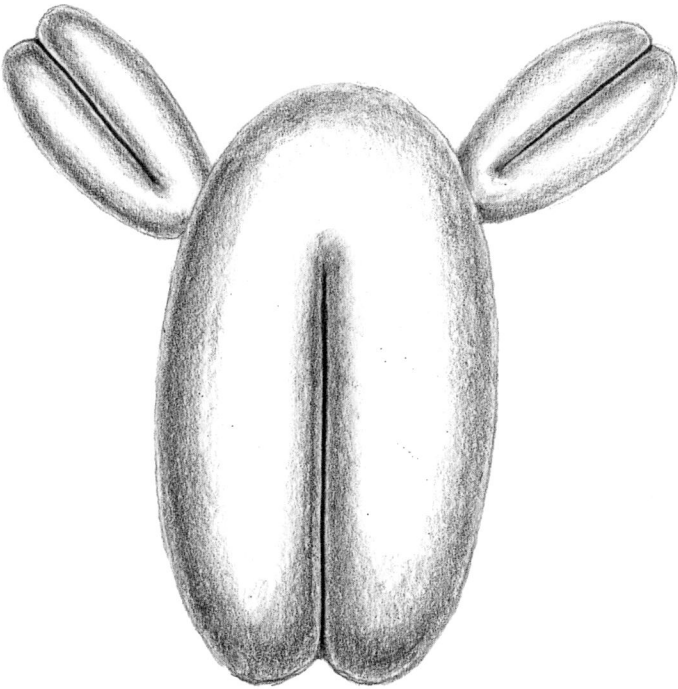

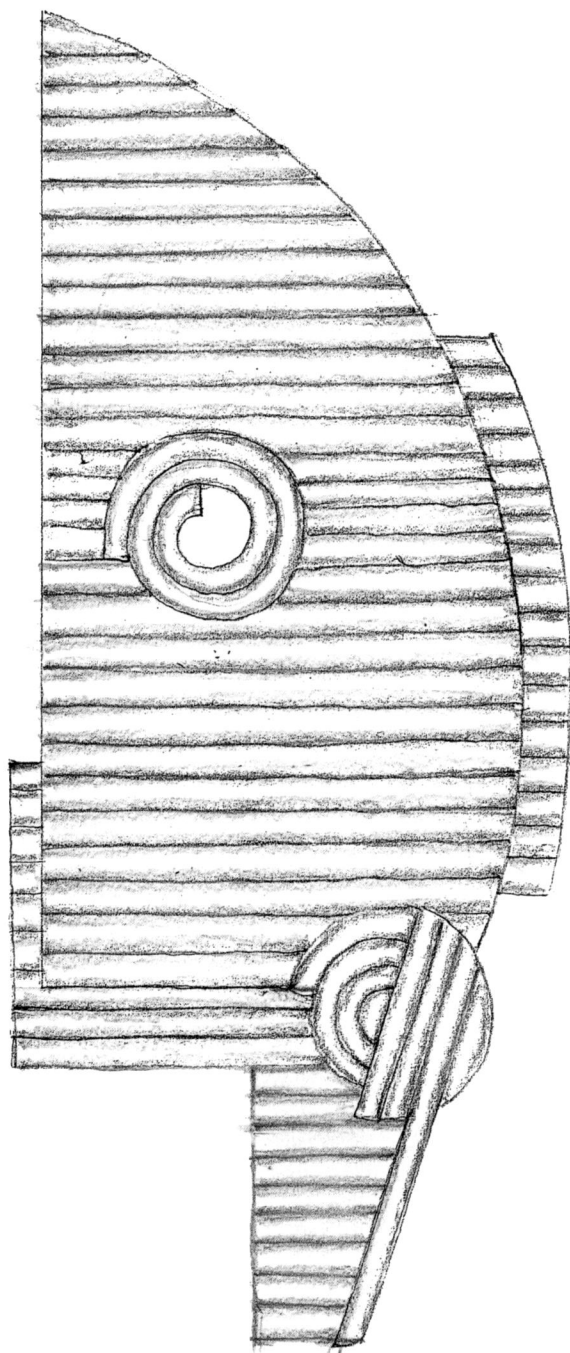

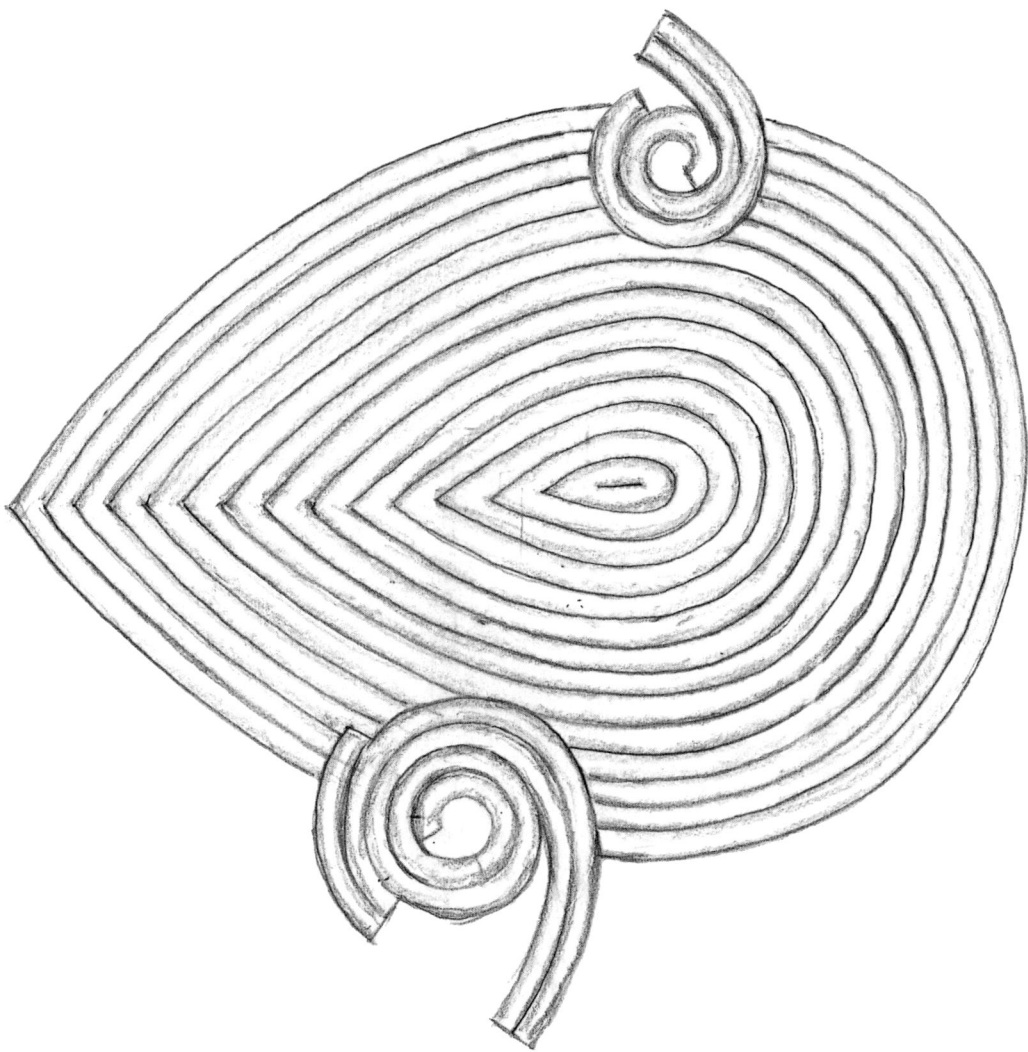

1983—2000   Dangling a fishing line into my inner self

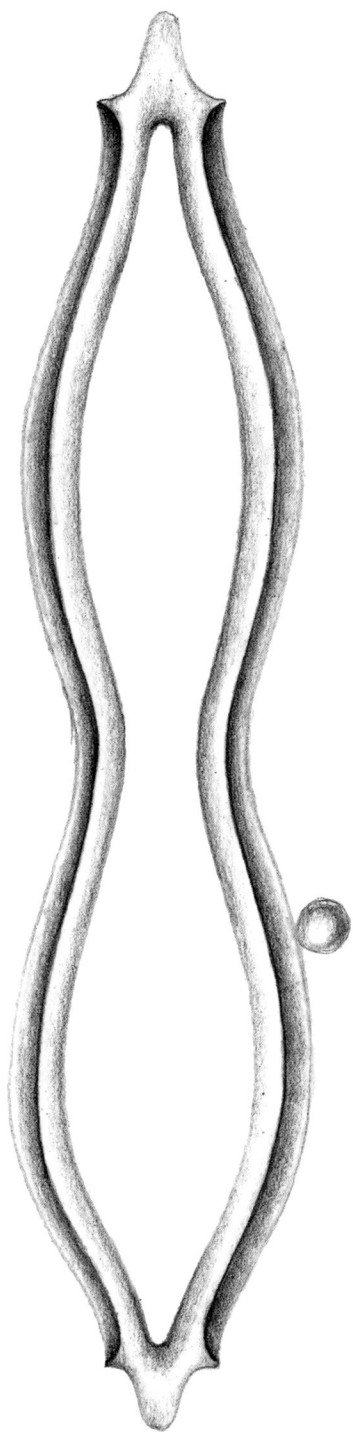

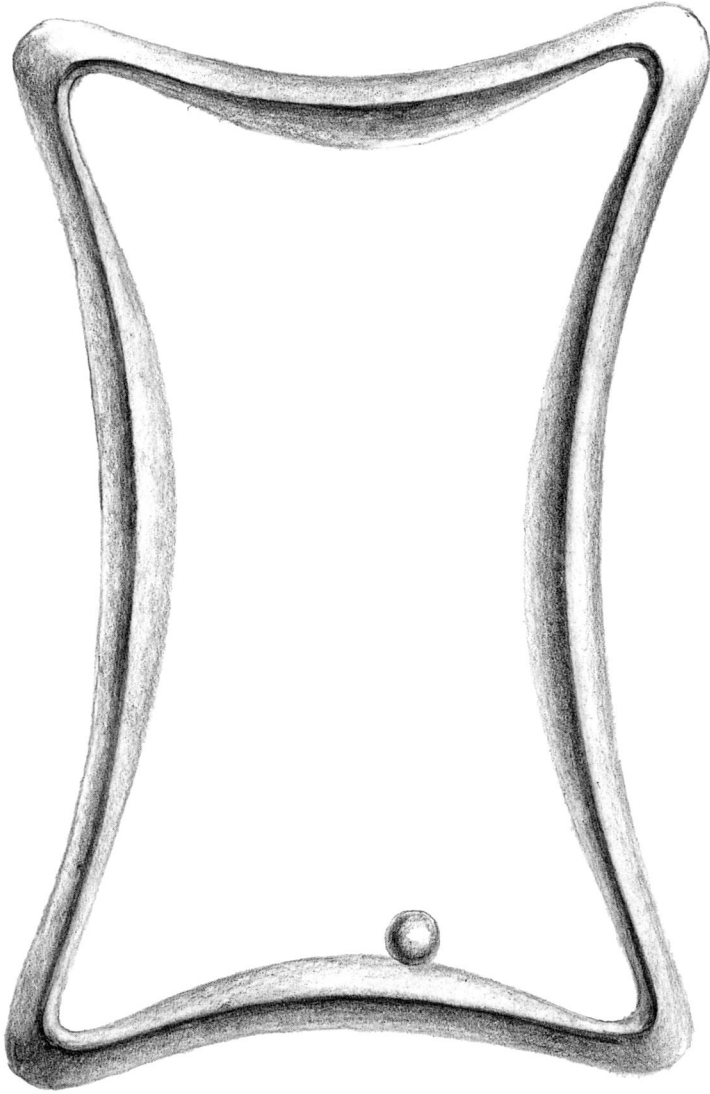

This shape emerged from my impressions and memories of seeing Italian church windows.

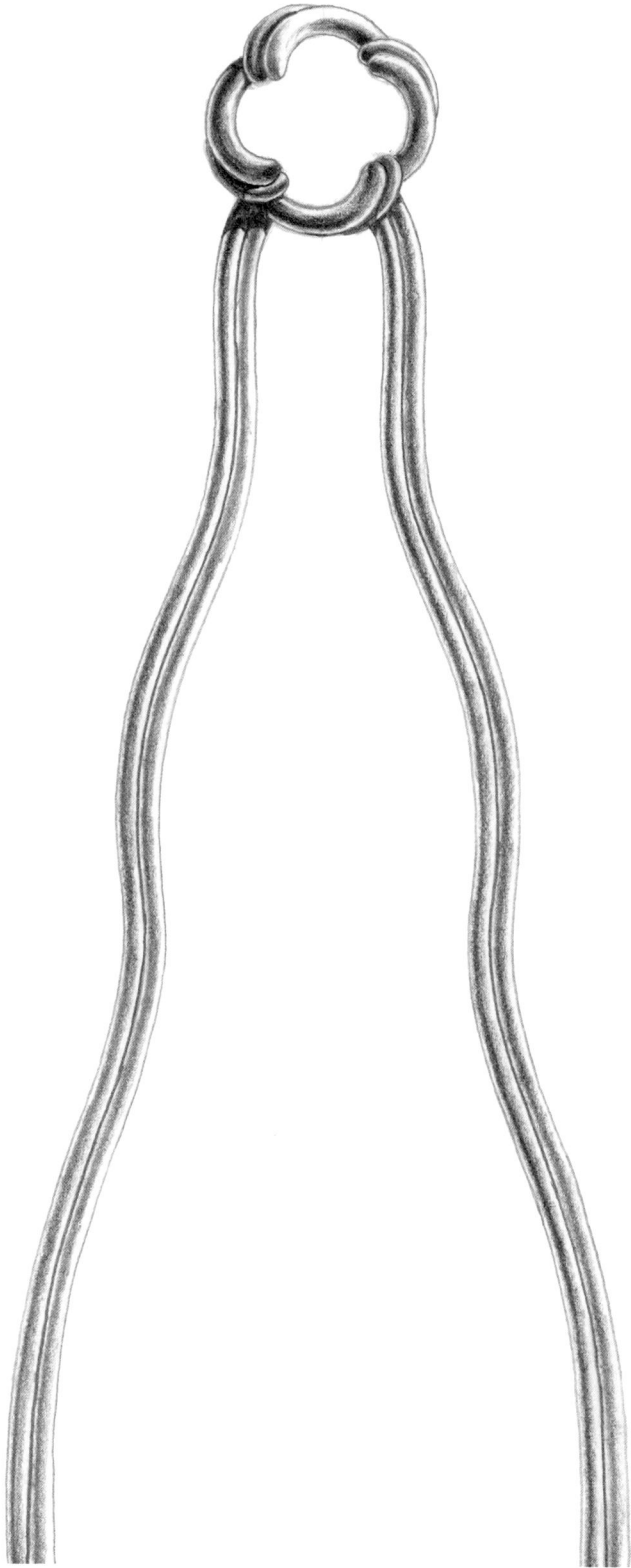

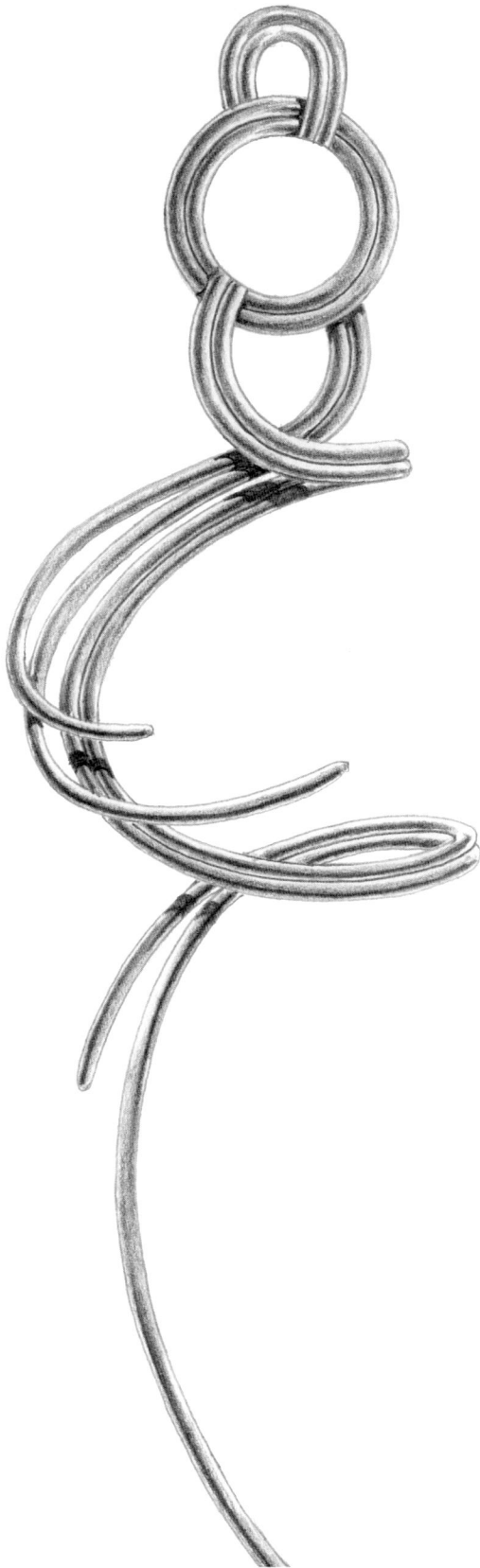

1983—2000   Dangling a fishing line into my inner self

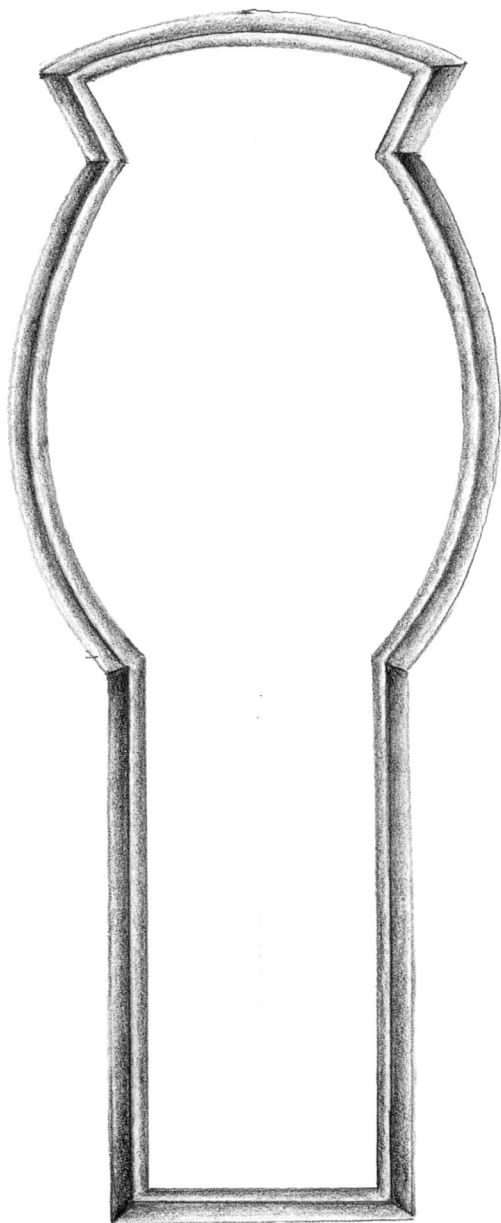

Prototypical forms: mirrors, keyholes, and picture frames.

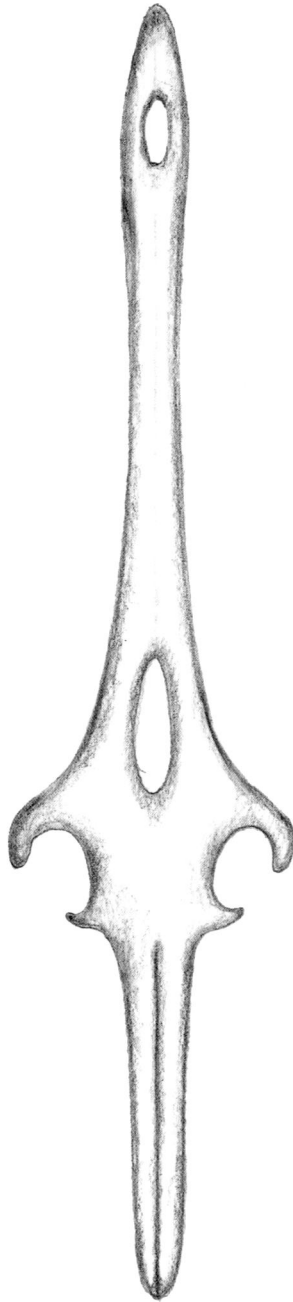

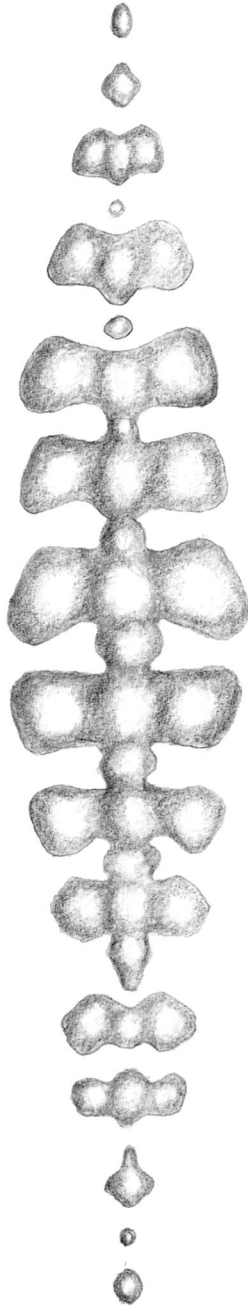

I felt like I had found something viable,
but it too plainly resembled bones; I couldn't make it into a piece of work.

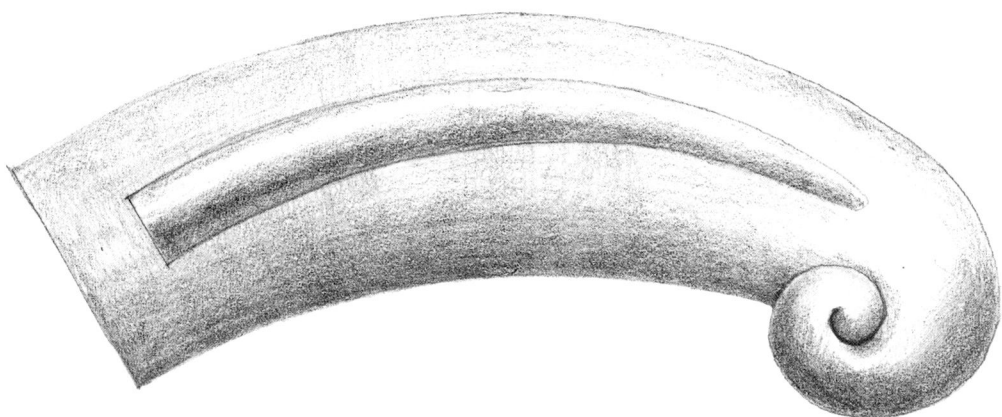

The excavation of images explores ancient layers of memory.
It connects to humanity's distant recollections.

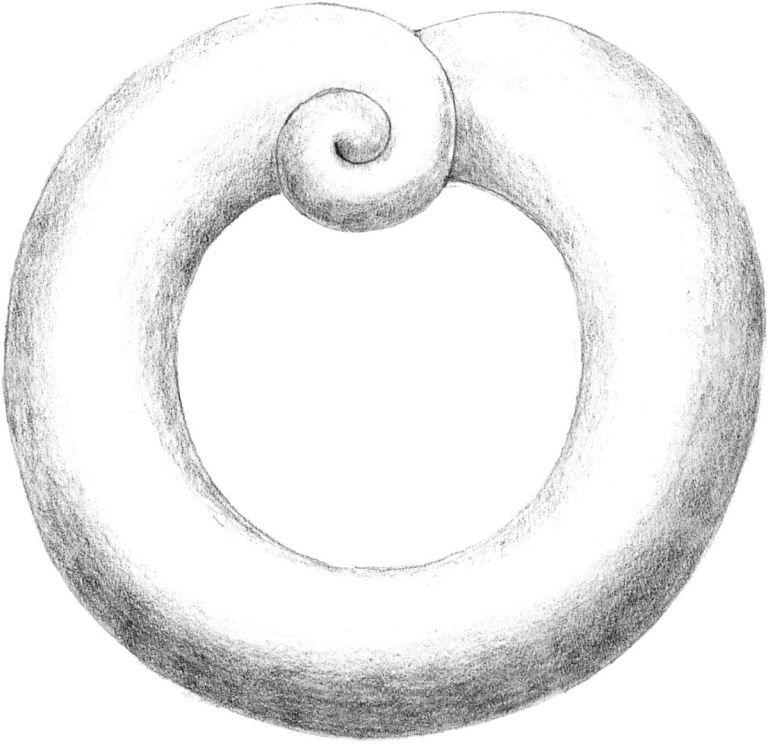

1983—2000   Dangling a fishing line into my inner self

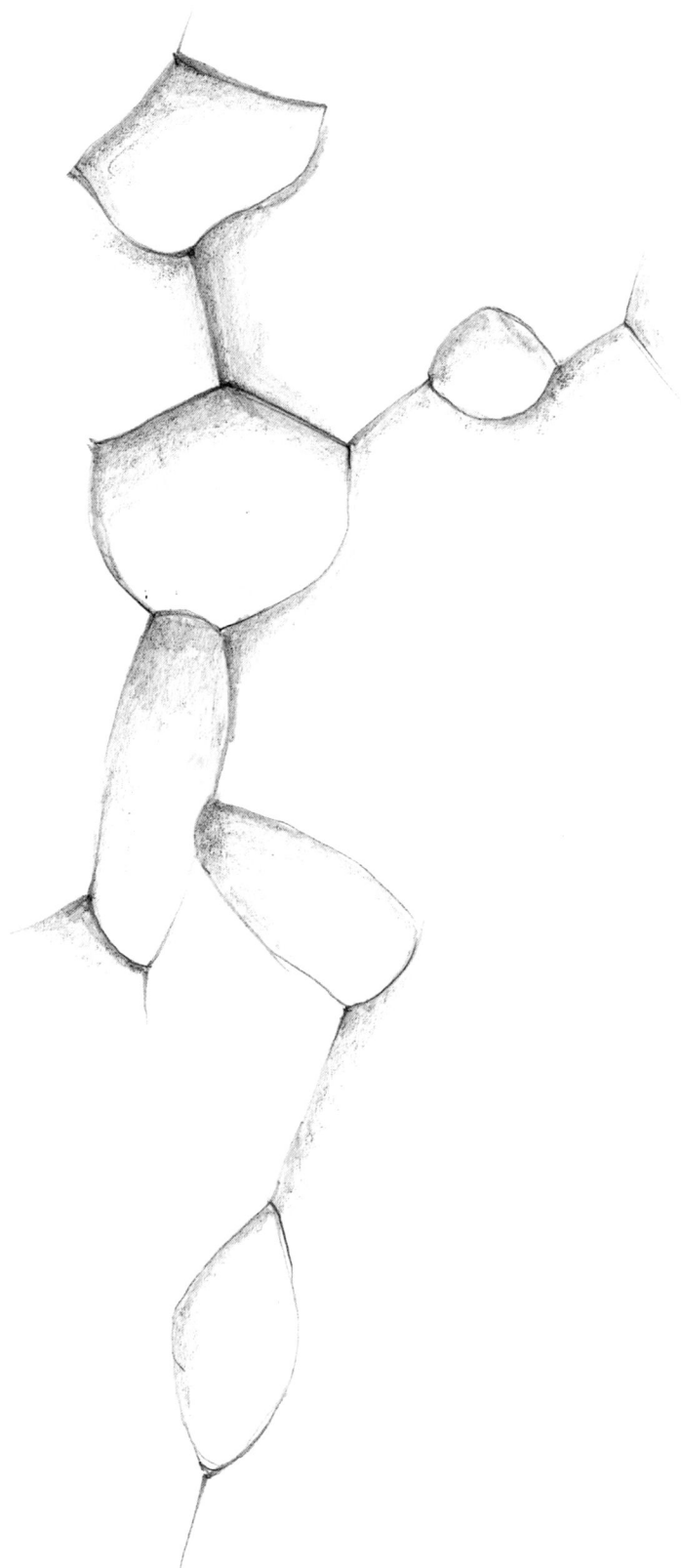

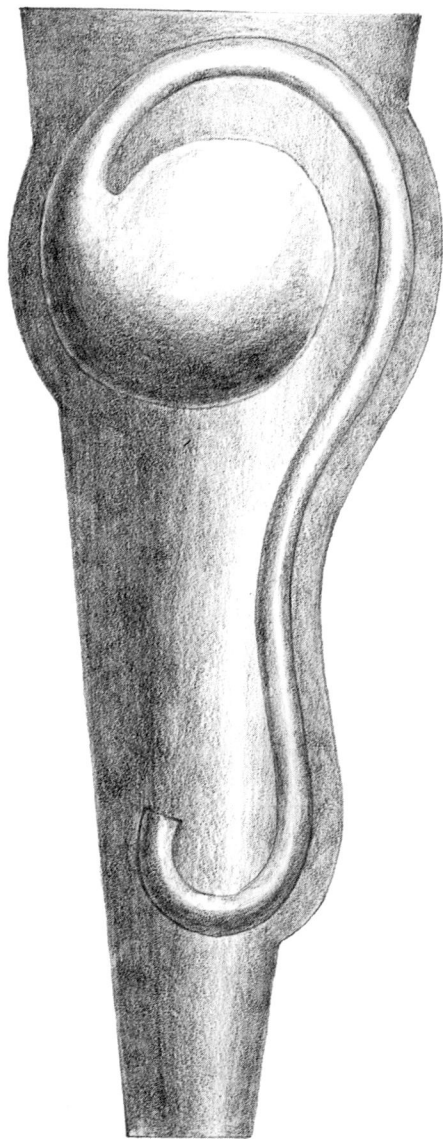

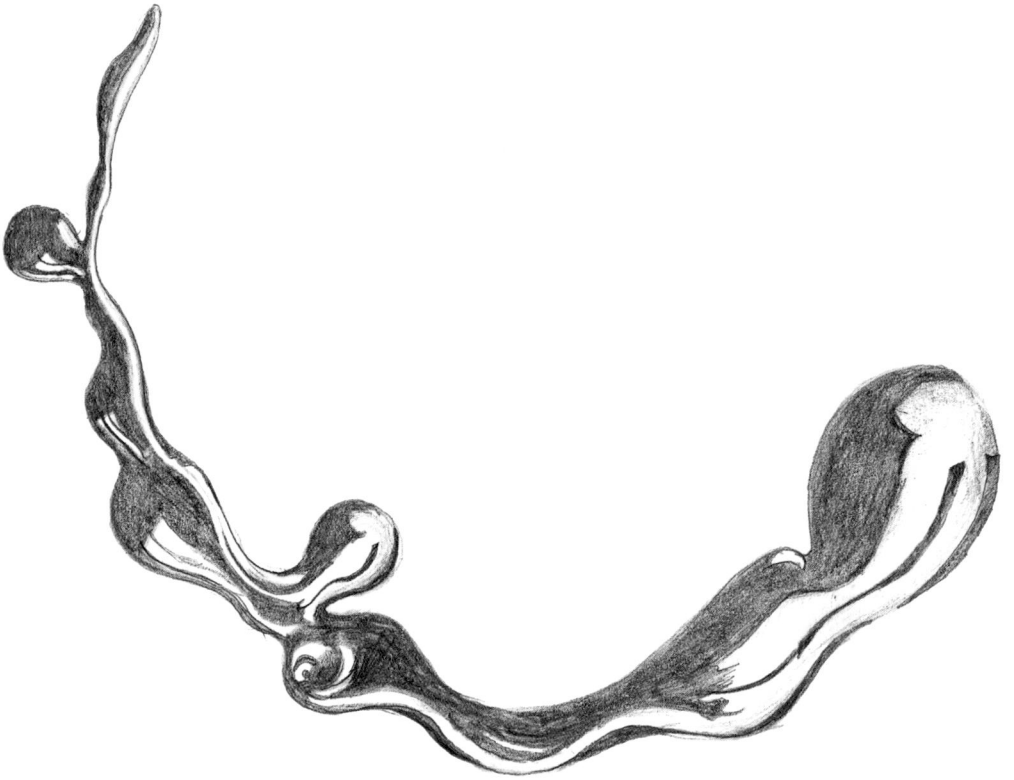

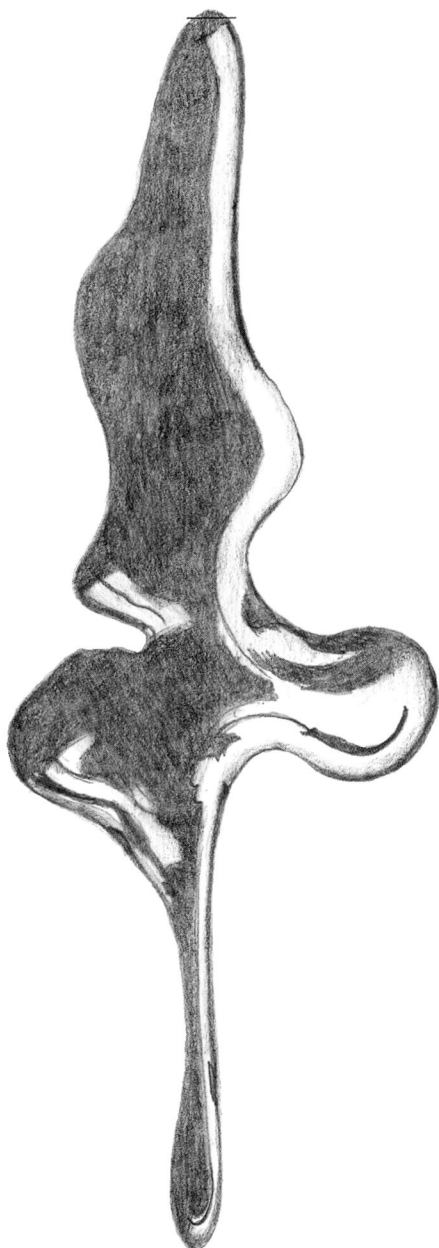

1983—2000   Dangling a fishing line into my inner self

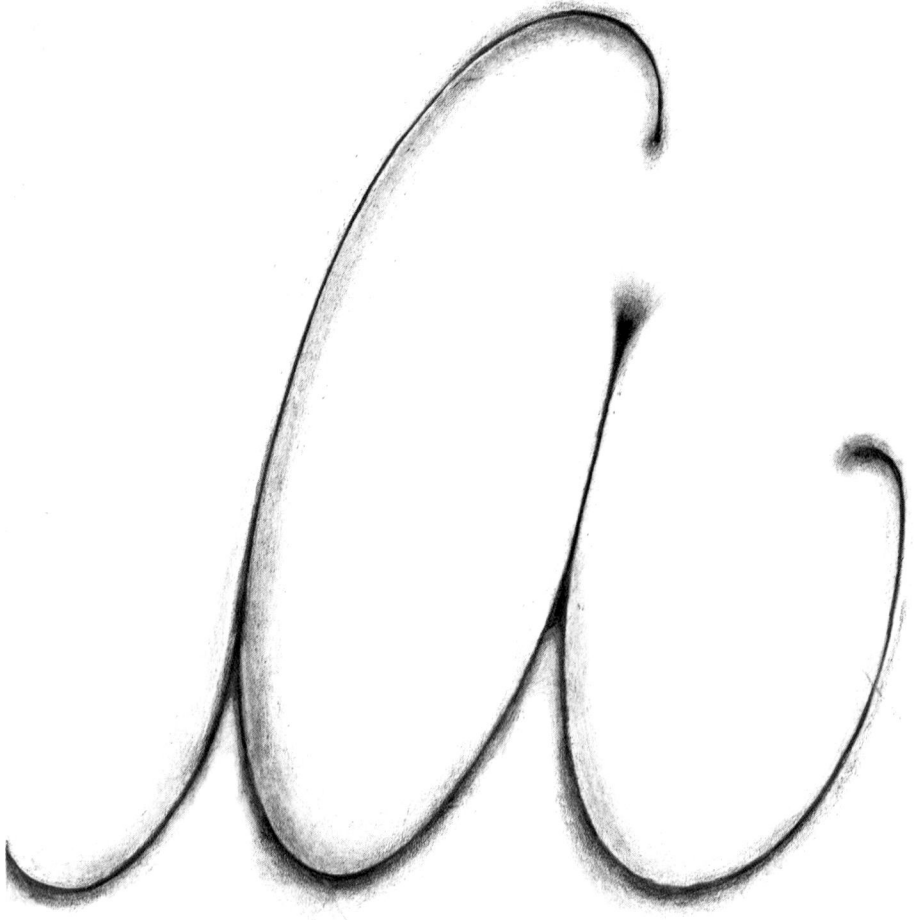

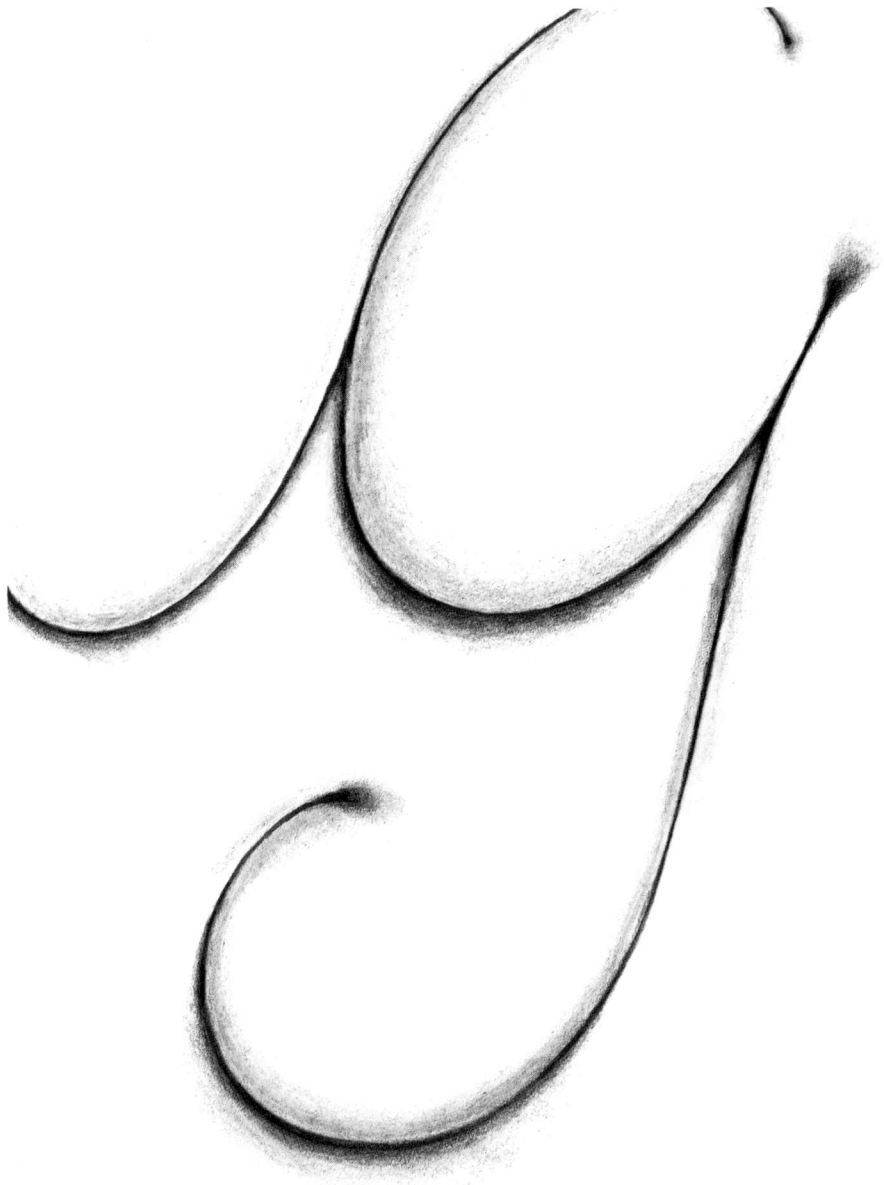

1983—2000   Dangling a fishing line into my inner self

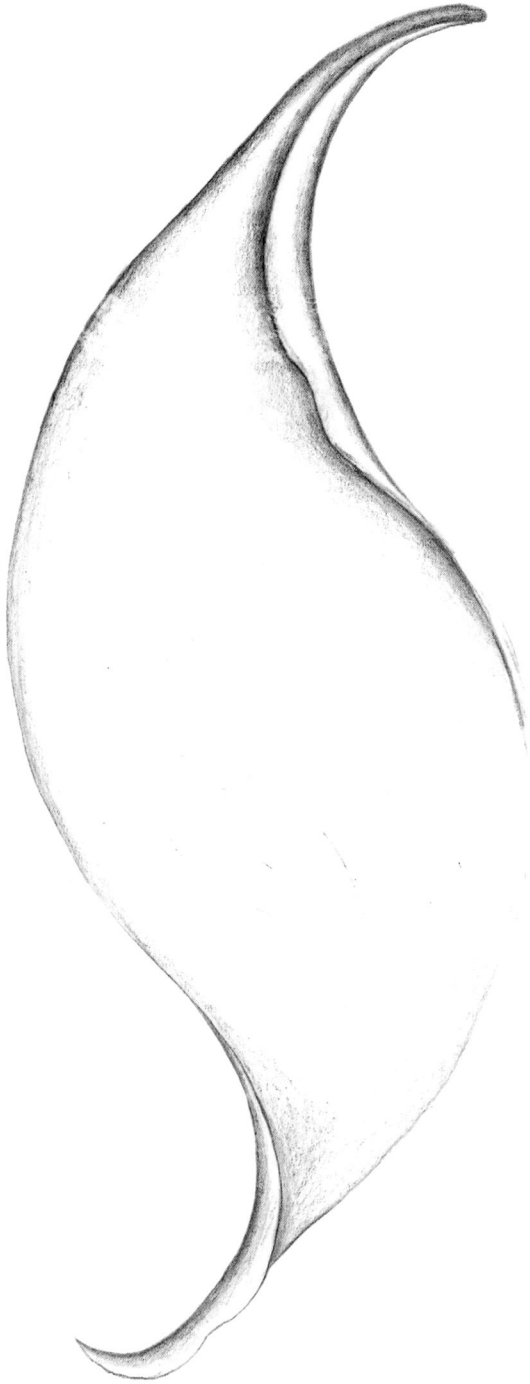

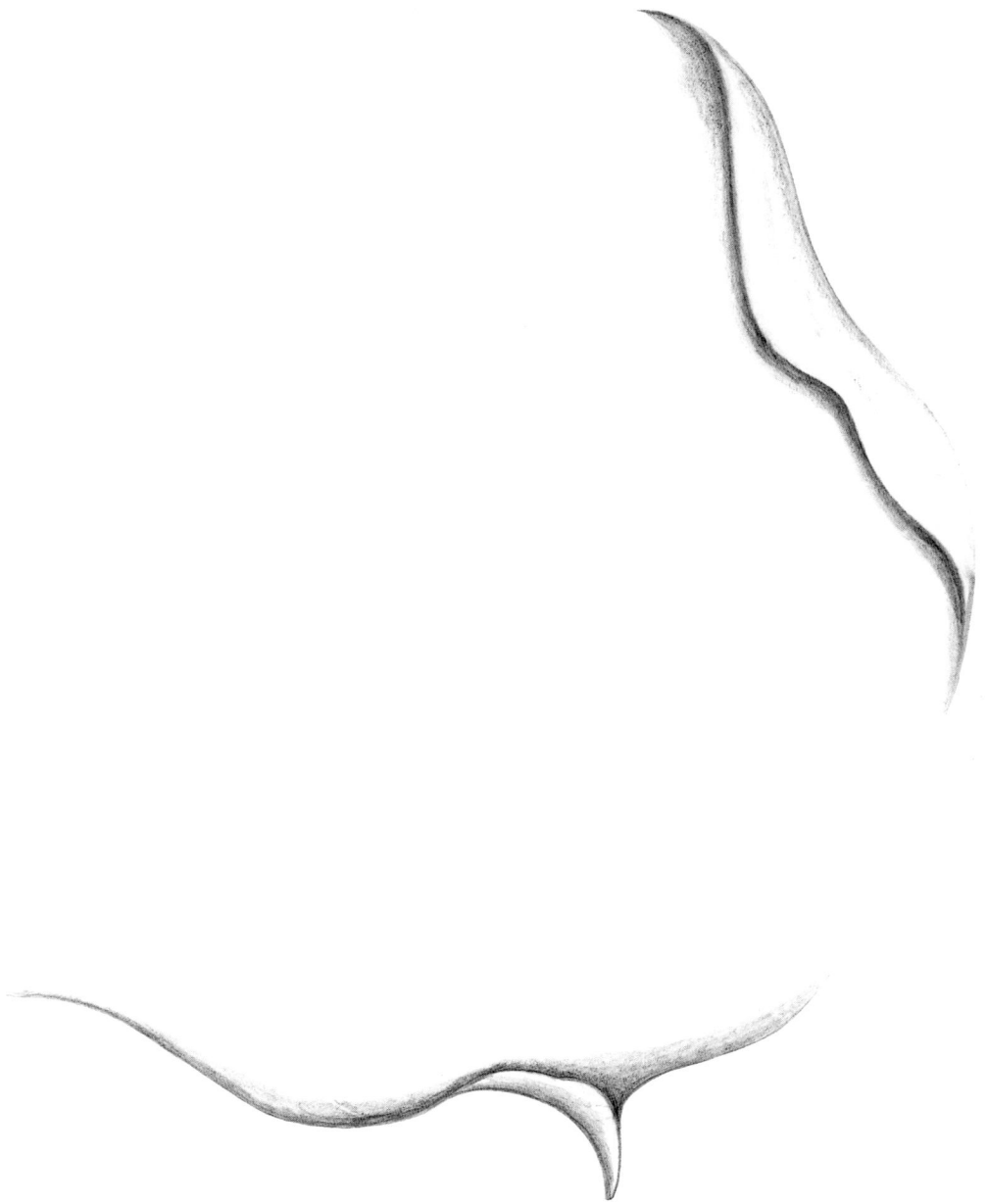

1983—2000 Dangling a fishing line into my inner self

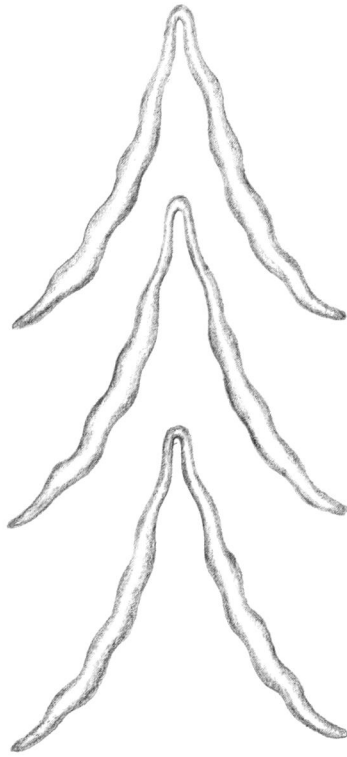

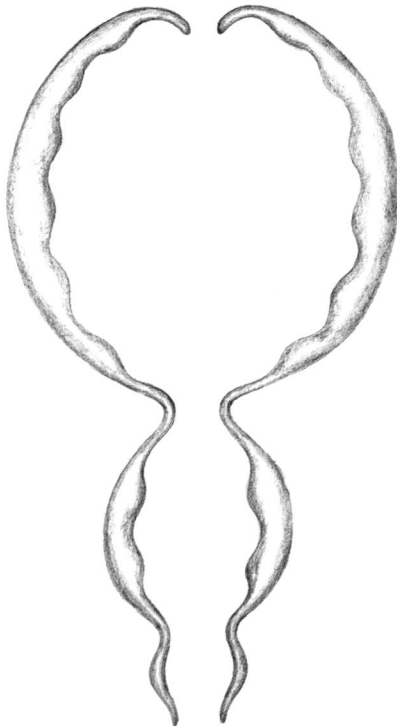

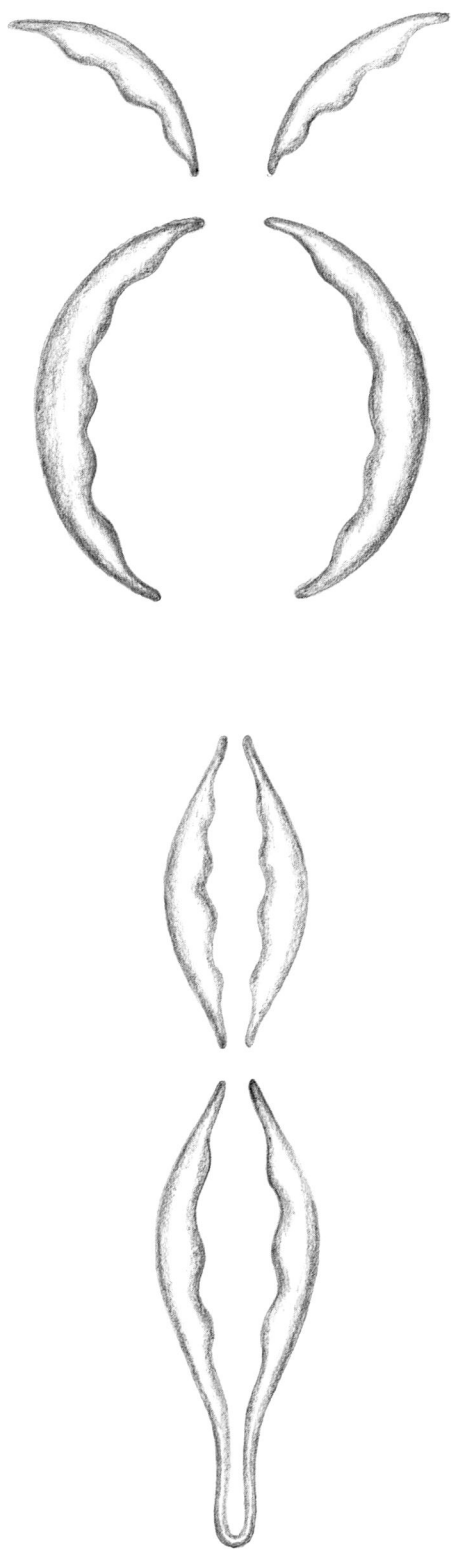

1983—2000   Dangling a fishing line into my inner self

The front and back cover of the *Japan Graphic Designers Association Yearbook*; this represents the satisfaction and joy of achievements.

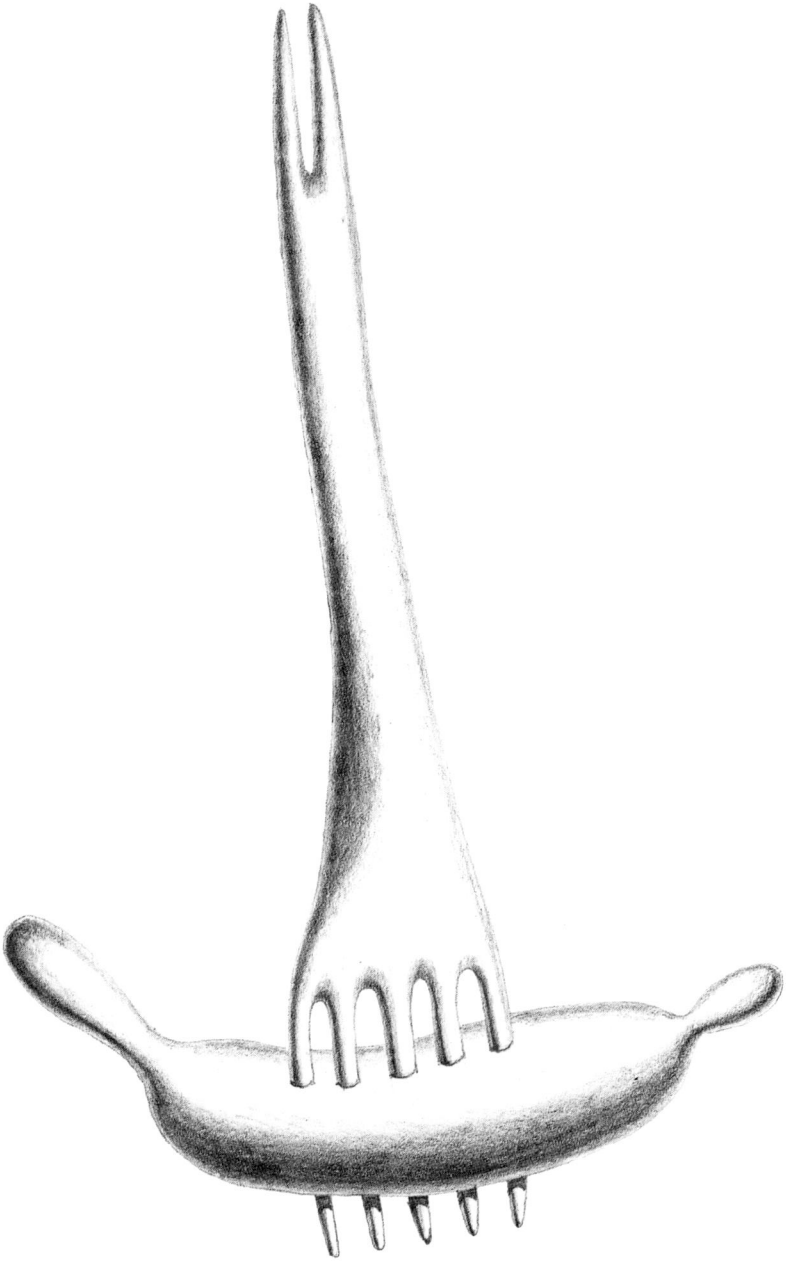

1983—2000   Dangling a fishing line into my inner self

一冊の本

2001

1

朝日新聞社

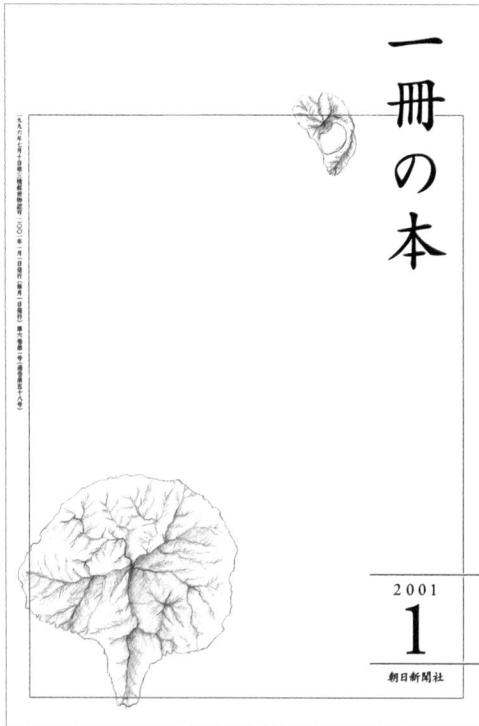

一冊の本

2001

1

朝日新聞社

Sketches for the cover of Asahi Shimbun's monthly book magazine *A Book*, ongoing since 1996 with quarterly themes.

一九九六年七月十日第三種郵便物認可　二〇〇一年一月一日発行（毎月一日発行）　第六巻第一号（通巻第五十八号）

一冊の本

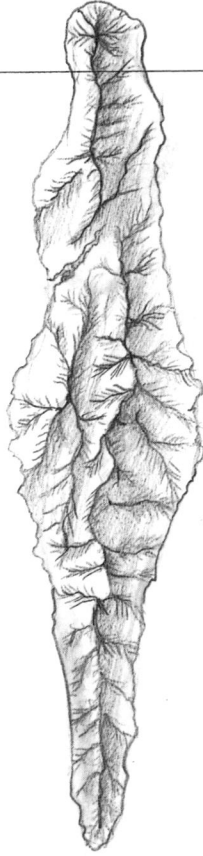

2001

1

朝日新聞社

1983—2000　Dangling a fishing line into my inner self

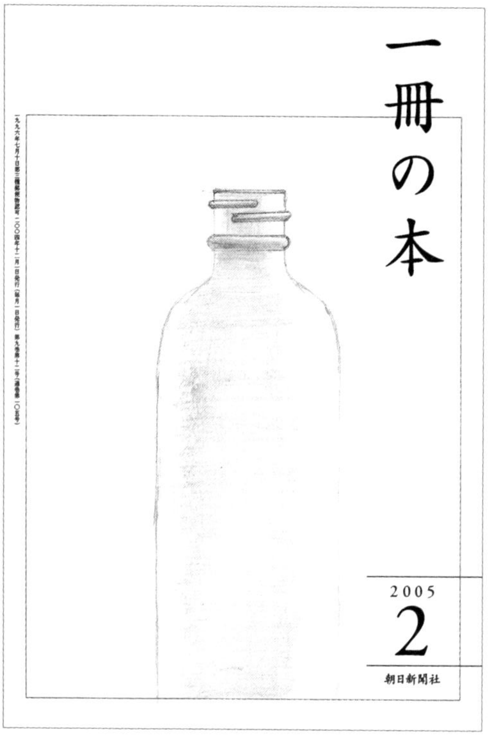

The texture of the screw portion of a glossy white bottle.

一冊の本

一九九六年七月十日第三種郵便物認可 二〇〇四年十二月一日発行（毎月一日発行）第九巻第十二号（通巻第一〇五号）

2005
2

朝日新聞社

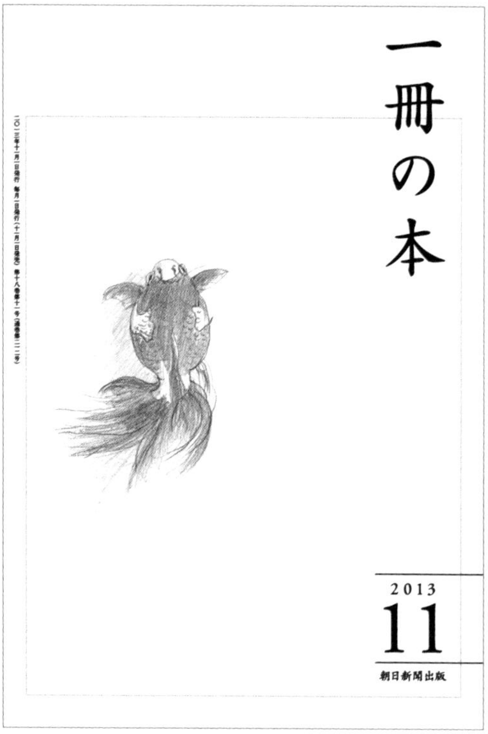

一冊の本

2013
11
朝日新聞出版

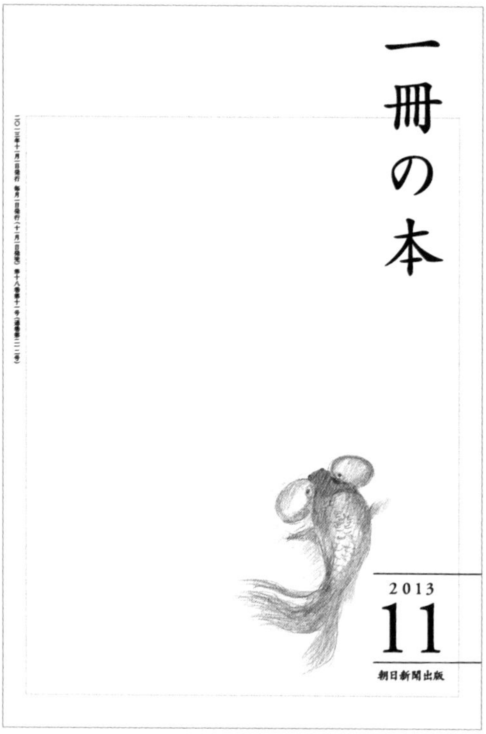

一冊の本

2013
11
朝日新聞出版

一冊の本

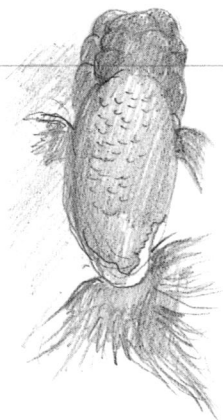

二〇一三年十一月一日発行　毎月一日発行（十一月一日発売）　第十八巻第十一号（通巻第二一二号）

2013

11

朝日新聞出版

1983—2000　Dangling a fishing line into my inner self

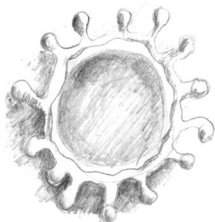

一冊の本

二〇一三年十一月一日発行　毎月一日発行（十一月一日発売）　第十八巻第十一号（通巻第二二三号）

2013
11
朝日新聞出版

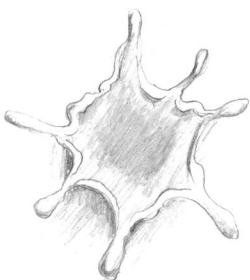

一冊の本

二〇一三年十一月一日発行　毎月一日発行（十一月一日発売）　第十八巻第十一号（通巻第二二三号）

2013
11
朝日新聞出版

二〇一三年十一月一日発行　毎月一日発行(十一月一日発売)　第十八巻第十一号(通巻第二一二号)

一冊の本

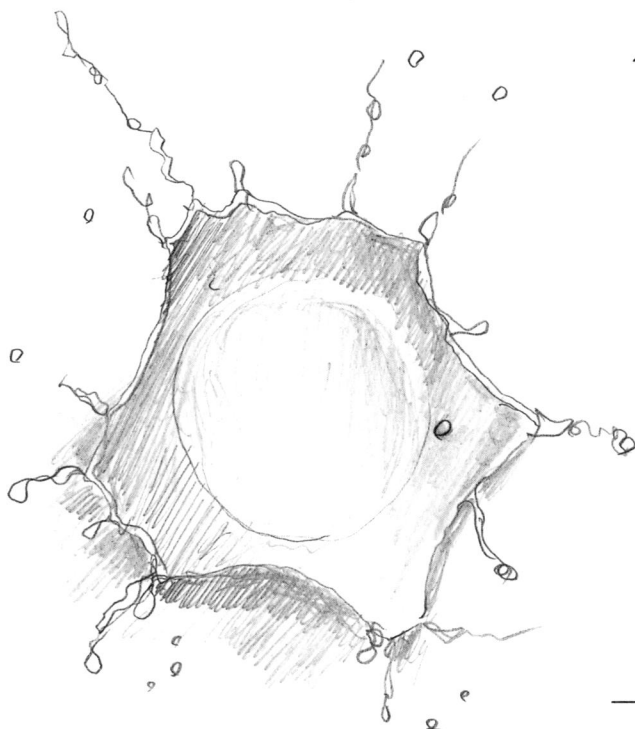

2013

11

朝日新聞出版

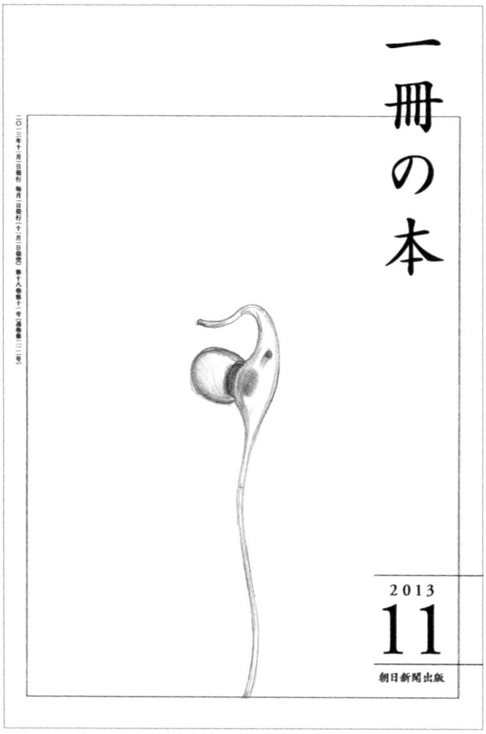

一冊の本

二〇一三年十一月一日発行　毎月一日発行（十月十日発売）　第十八巻第十一号（通巻第二二一号）

2013
11
朝日新聞出版

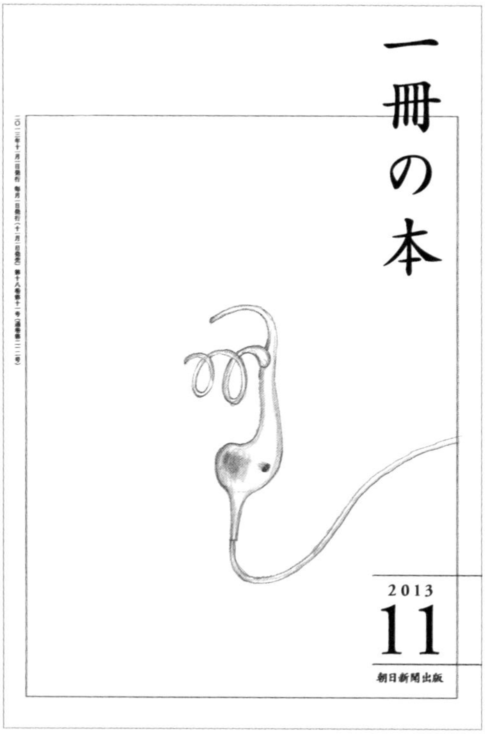

一冊の本

二〇一三年十一月一日発行　毎月一日発行（十月十日発売）　第十八巻第十一号（通巻第二二一号）

2013
11
朝日新聞出版

一冊の本

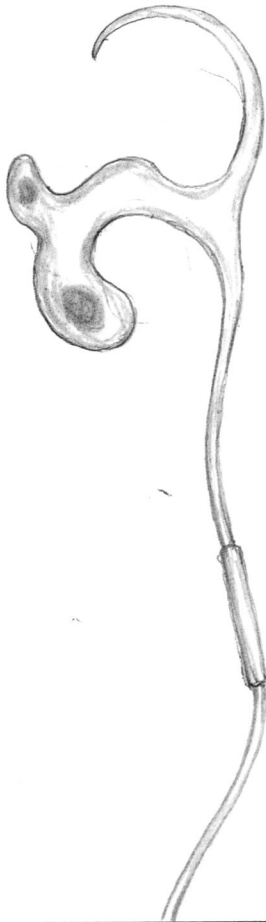

二〇一三年十一月一日発行　毎月一日発行（十一月一日発売）　第十八巻第十一号（通巻第二一二号）

2013
11

朝日新聞出版

1983——2000　Dangling a fishing line into my inner self

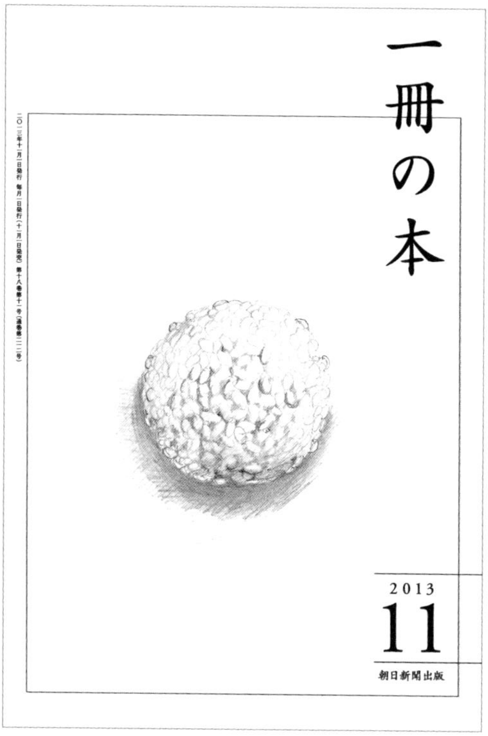

一冊の本

2013
11
朝日新聞出版

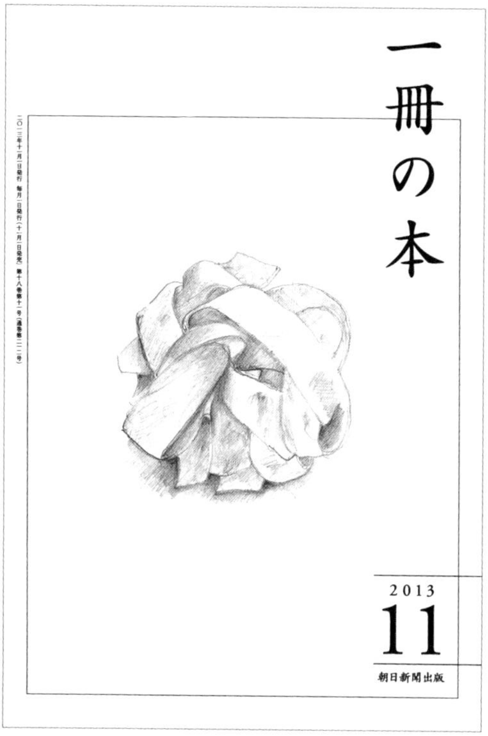

一冊の本

2013
11
朝日新聞出版

一冊の本

二〇一三年十一月二日発行　毎月一日発行（十一月二日発売）　第十八巻第十一号（通巻第二一二号）

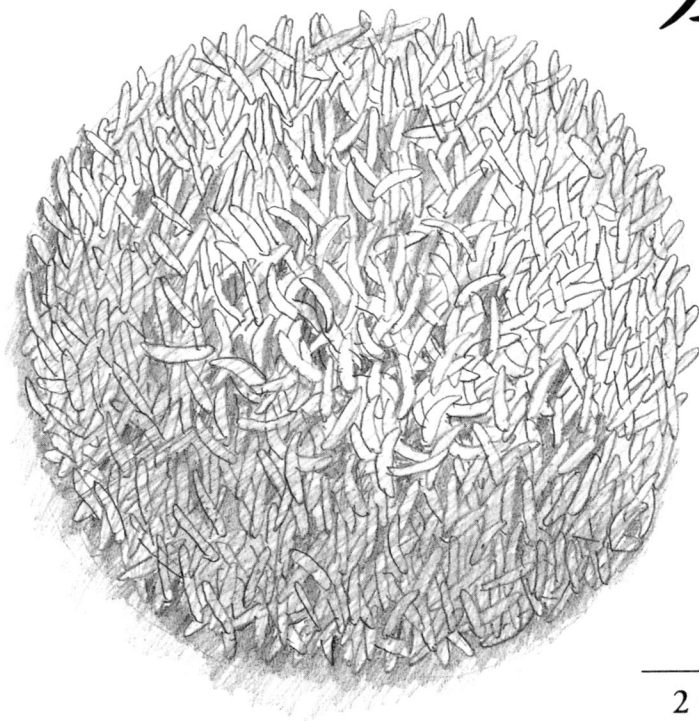

2013
11

朝日新聞出版

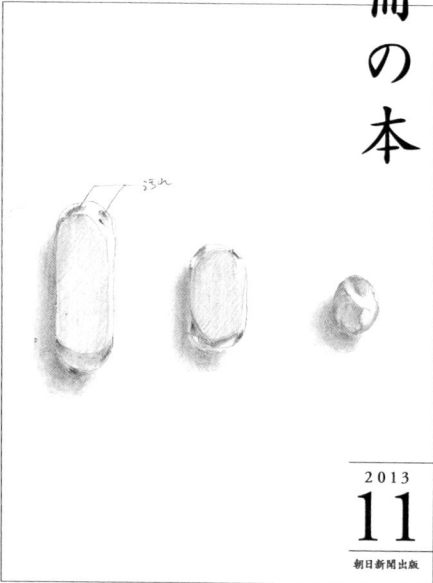

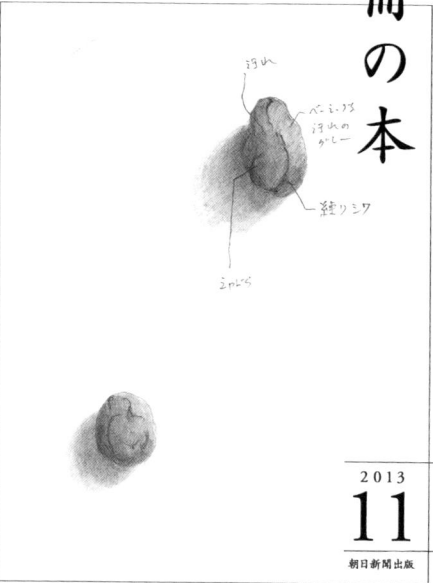

一冊の本

二〇一三年十一月一日発行　毎月一日発行（十一月一日発売）　第十八巻第十一号（通巻第二一二号）

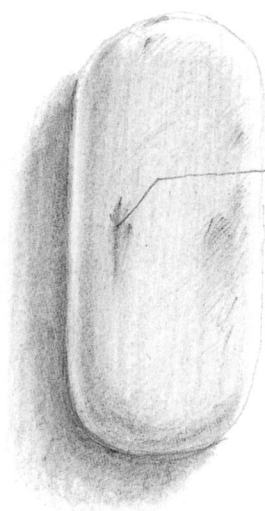

軽度の汚れ

2013
11
朝日新聞出版

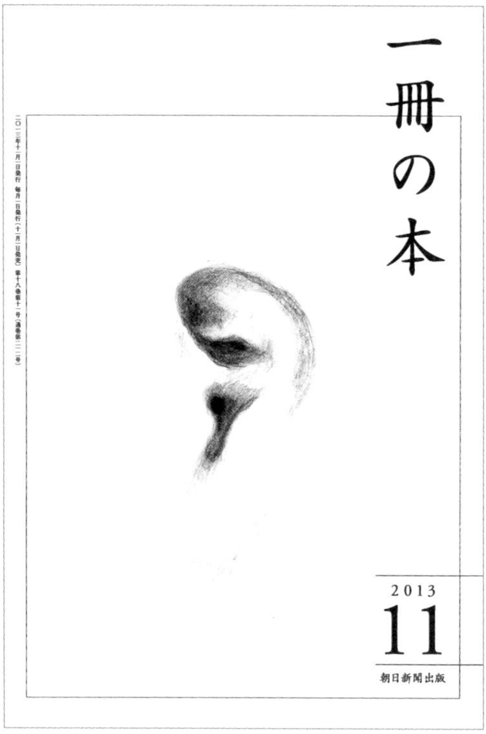

一冊の本

二〇一三年十一月一日発行 毎月一日発行(十一月一日発売) 第十八巻第十一号(通巻第二一〇号)

2013
11
朝日新聞出版

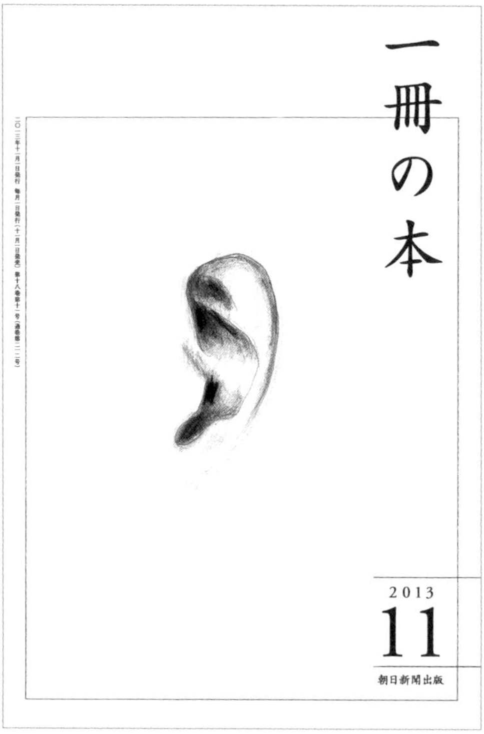

一冊の本

二〇一三年十一月一日発行 毎月一日発行(十一月一日発売) 第十八巻第十一号(通巻第二一〇号)

2013
11
朝日新聞出版

一冊の本

二〇一三年十一月二日発行　毎月一日発行（十一月一日発売）　第十八巻第十一号（通巻第二一二号）

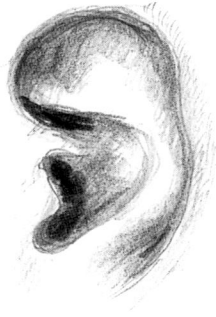

2013
11

朝日新聞出版

1983—2000　　Dangling a fishing line into my inner self

Nikka Cidre marked my first foray into package design.

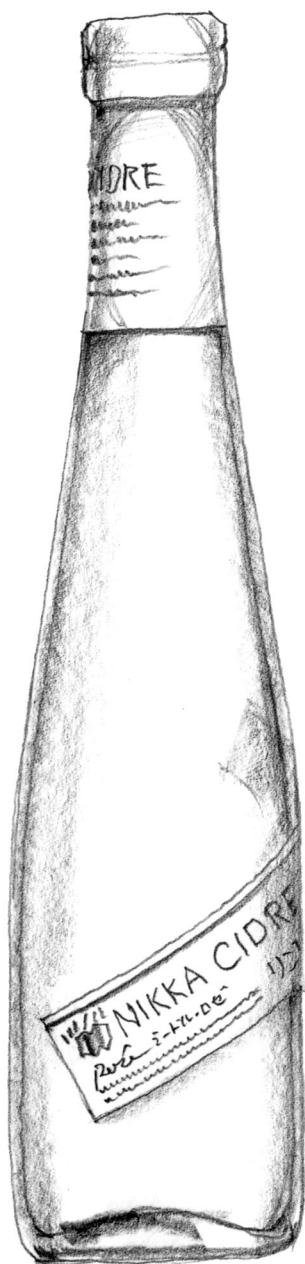

1983—2000   Dangling a fishing line into my inner self

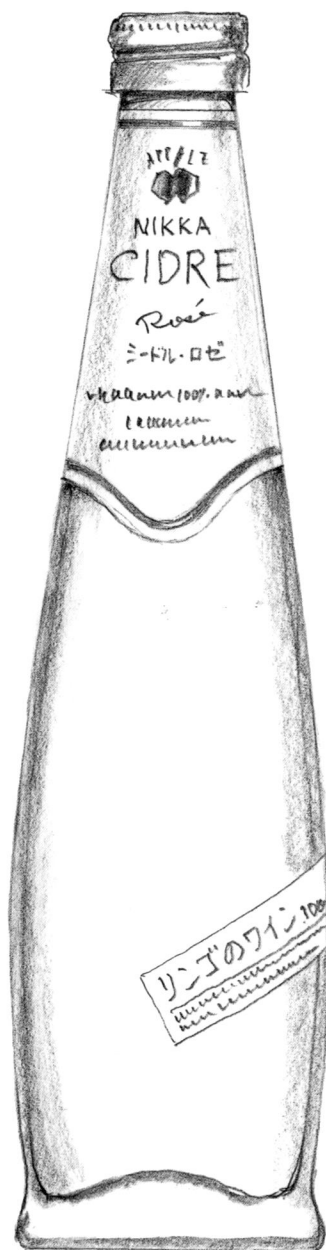

1

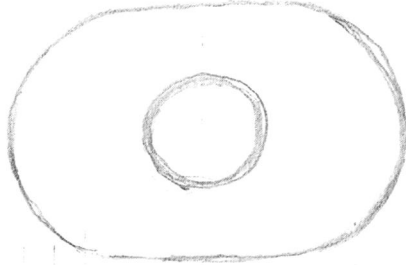

Super Nikka 12 Year Miniature Bottle:
The goal was to create a shape that had personality, though the scale was small.

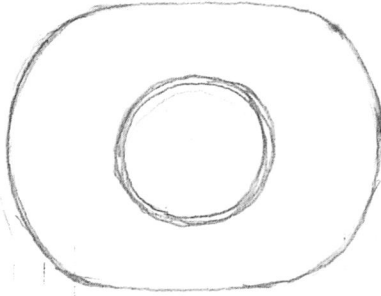

3

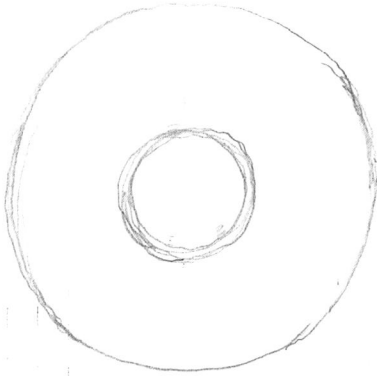

Rare Old
Super
NIKKA WHISKY
12

5

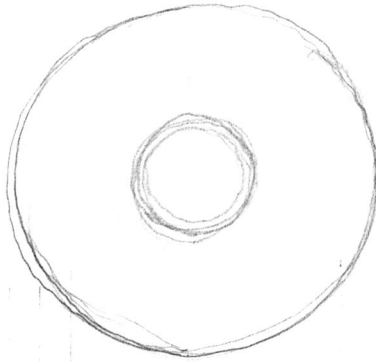

White frosted bottles; the surface is treated with sulfuric acid.

1983—2000   Dangling a fishing line into my inner self

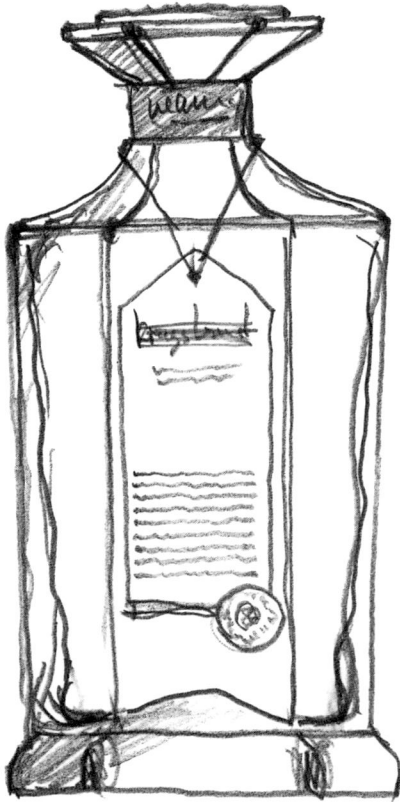

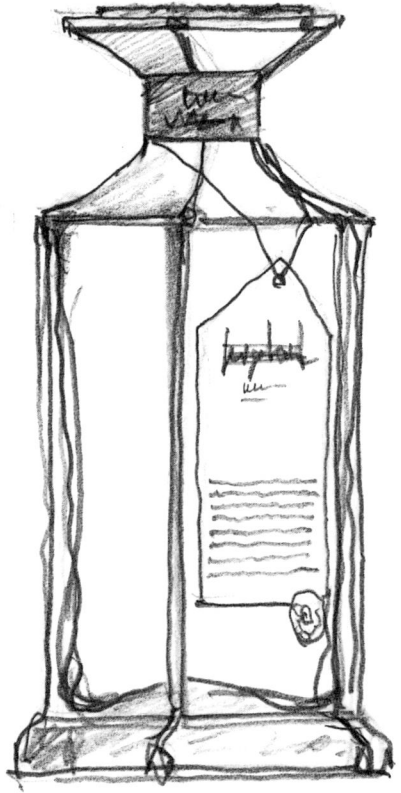

I wanted to give the bottles for high-grade spirits an almost spellbinding appeal, which deviated from modernism's rationalism.

Whisky's appeal is in its shimmering amber color, visible through the thick bottle.

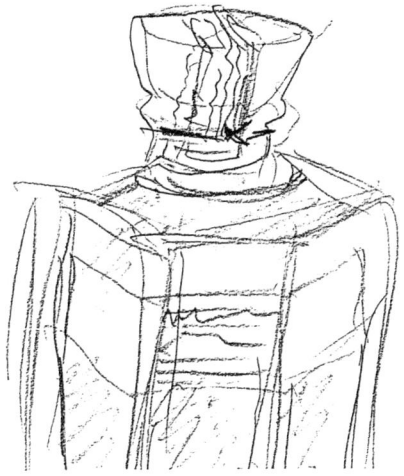
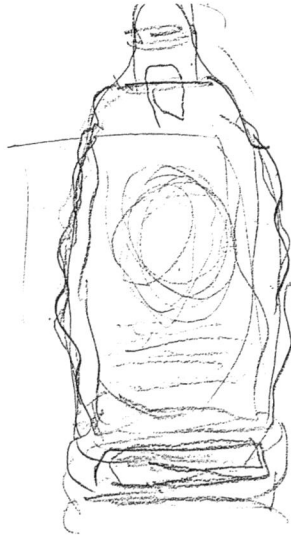

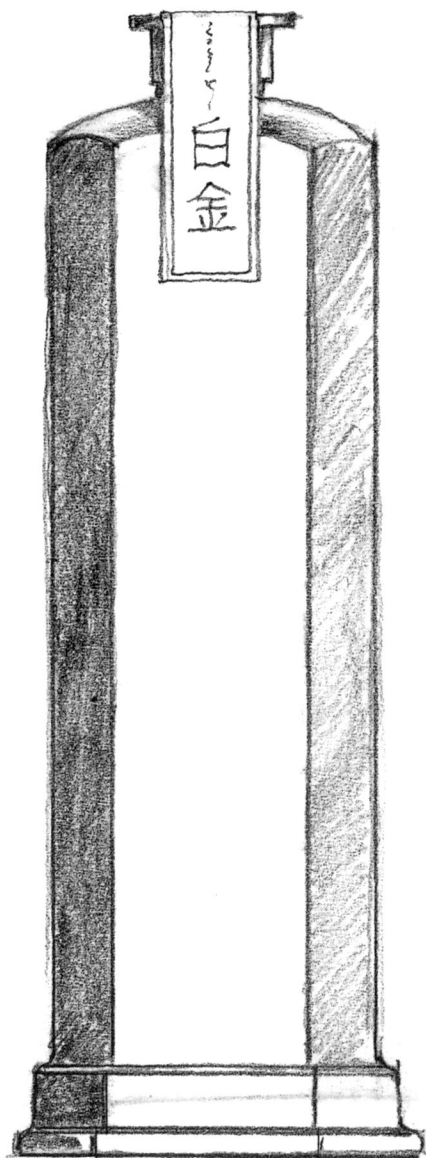

Sarah Marie Cummings, director of Obuse-do, suggested stainless steel for this packaging.

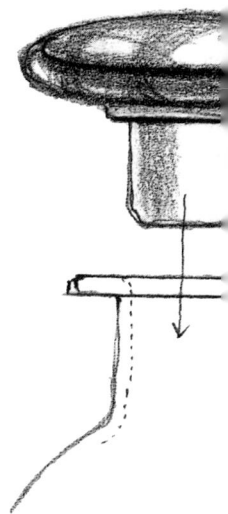

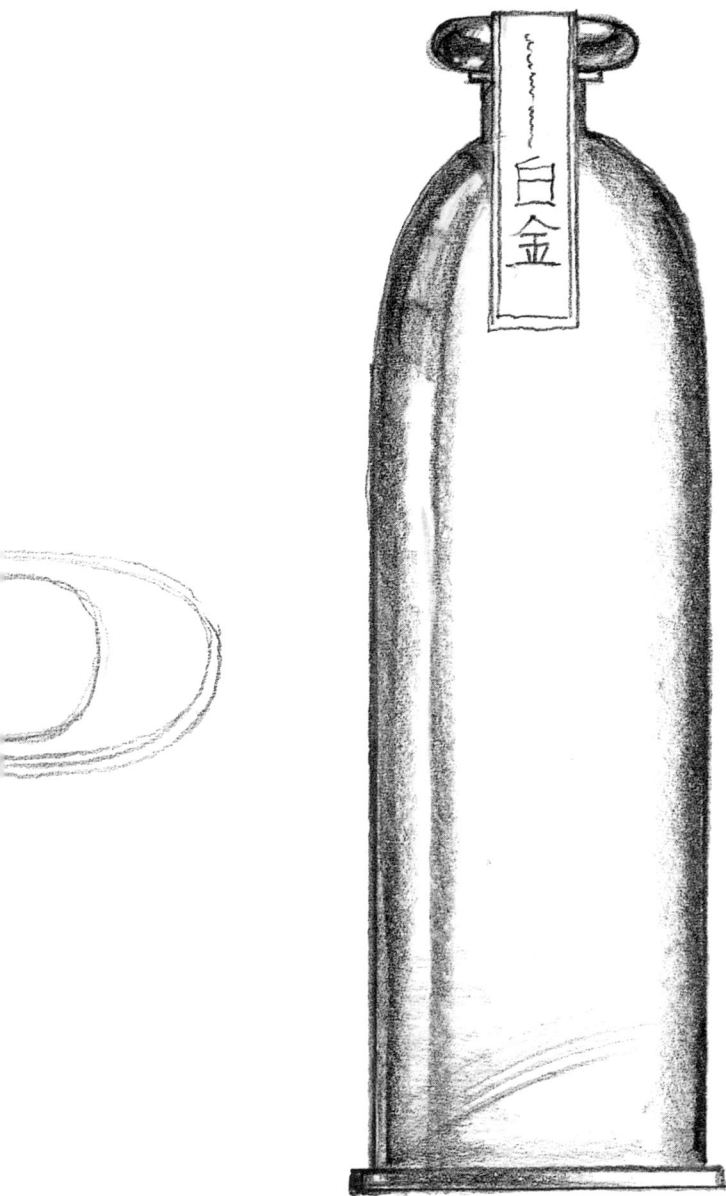

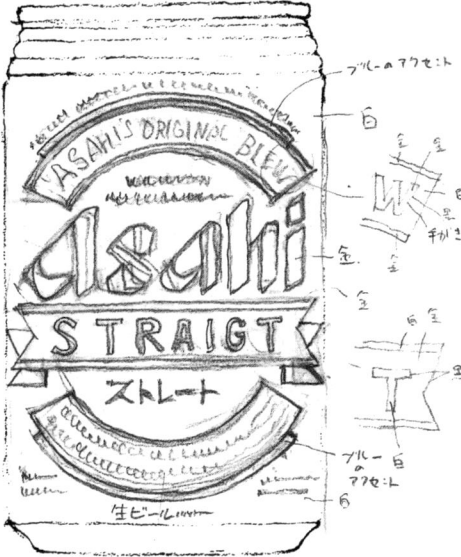

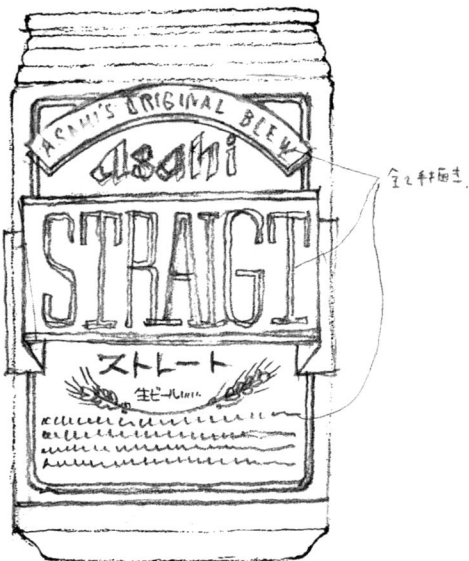

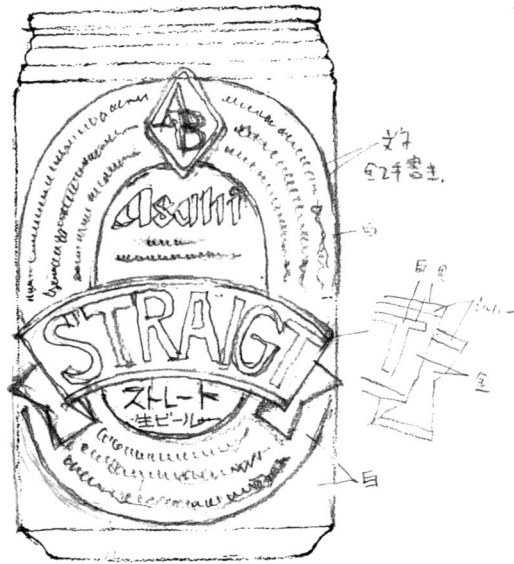

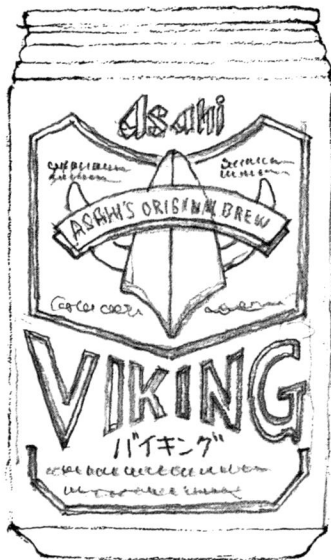

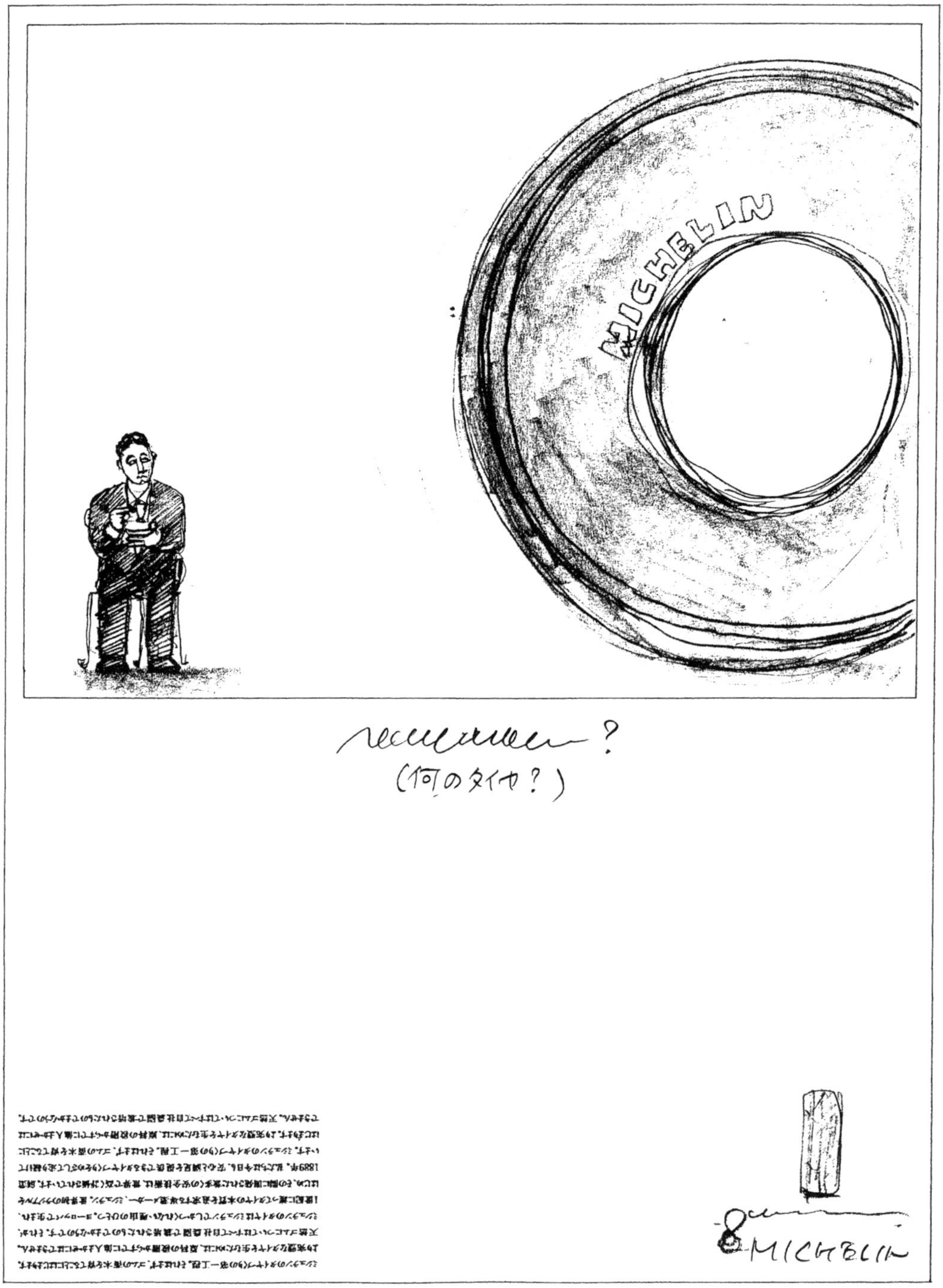

My advertising work benefited greatly from
the expertise of Yusuke Kaji, a copywriter and brandologist.

何のタイヤ？

MICHELIN

もう少し早く気が付けば…。

タイヤの危険を見張るMTMシステム。
世界で初めてミシュランが開発──。

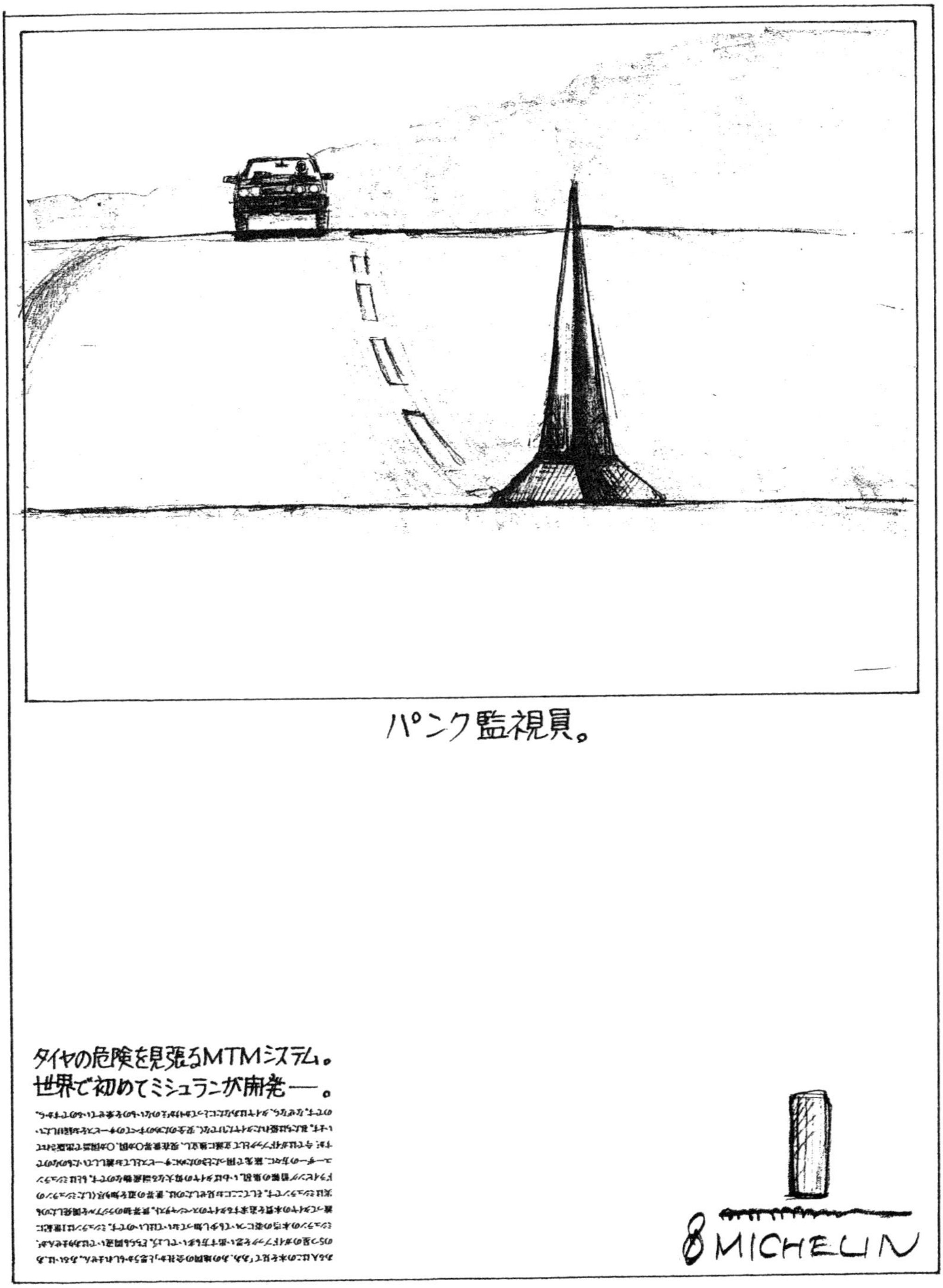

パンク監視員。

タイヤの危険を見張るMTMシステム。
世界で初めてミシュランが開発——。

8 MICHELIN

Sketching out ideas was refreshing and, at the same time, painful.

クルマ先」進国ヨーロッパで
70%のシェアを誇るタイヤメーカーがある。

MICHELIN.

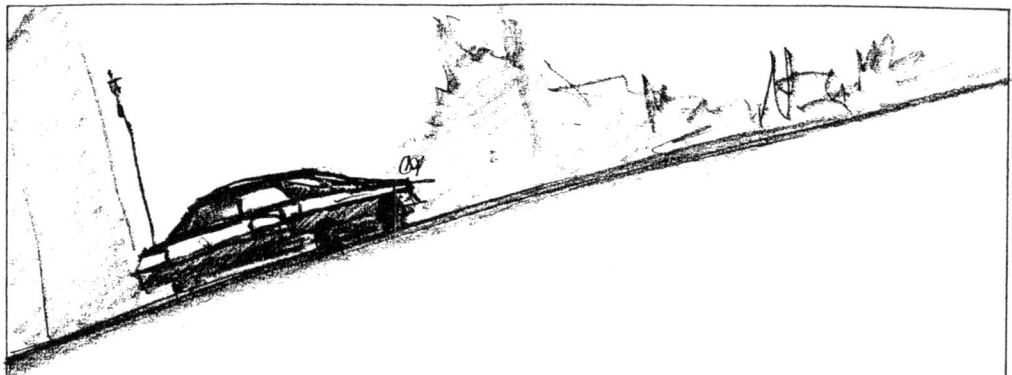

お気づきかもしれませんが、フェラーリ 抜かれている。

MICHELIN

お気づきかもしれませんが、メルセデスがはいている

MICHELIN

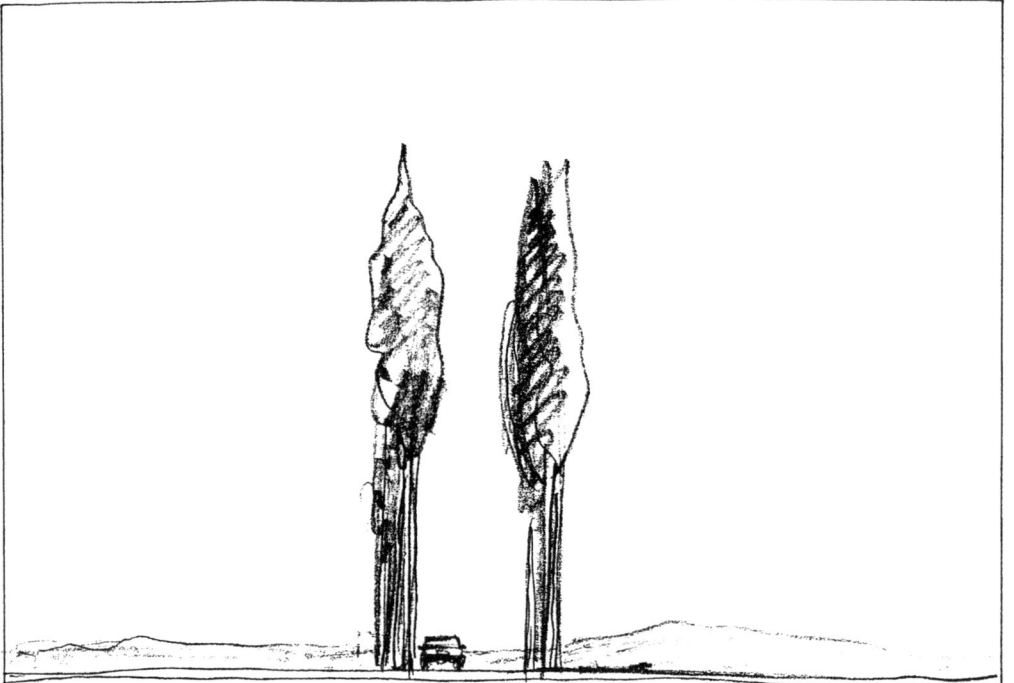

クルマ先進国のヨーロッパで
70%のシェアを誇るタイヤメーカーがある。

8 MICHELIN

クルマ先進国のヨーロッパで
70%のシェアを誇るタイヤメーカーがあ。

MICHBLIN

曲りくねったハイヴェイ.
車のシッソウ感.

免許は持っていなくても、ミシュランには乗っているはずです。

MICHELIN.

運転免許を持っていなくても、ミシュランに乗ってくれはずです。

THE TIER
MICHELIN

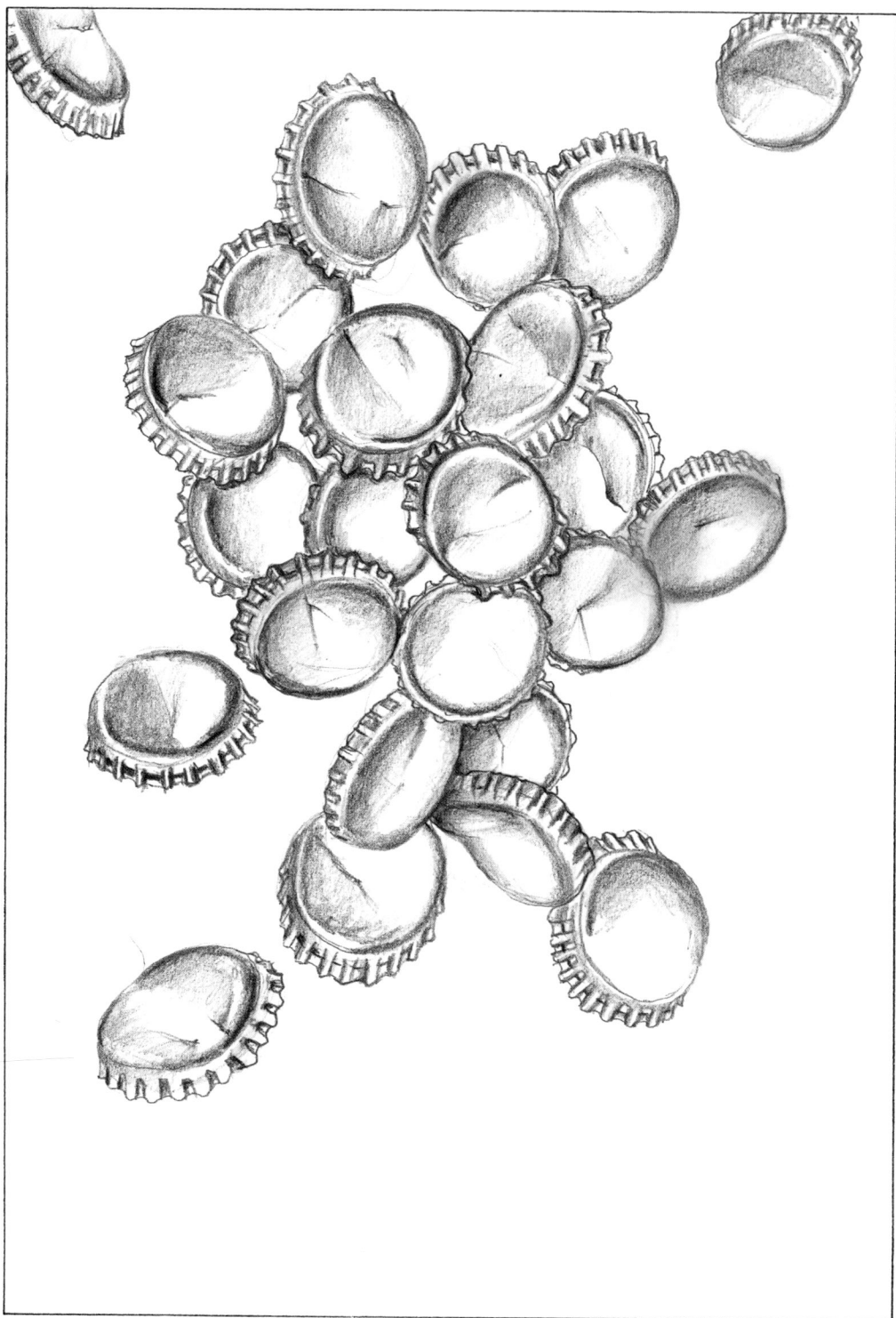

In addition to this beer cap proposal, there was one featuring edamame,
a common snack enjoyed with beer.

1983—2000   Dangling a fishing line into my inner self

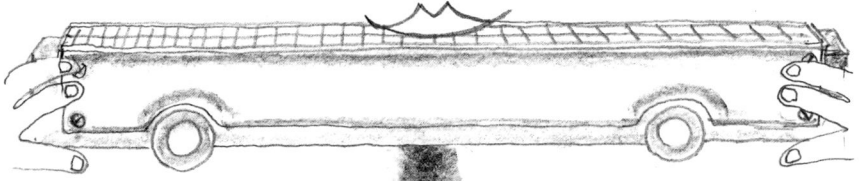

CO2

Play well for the Earth.

UNFCCC-COP3-KYOTO

The 3rd Session of the Conference of the Parties to the United Nations Framework Convention on Climate Change

Poster for COP3, where the Kyoto Protocol was adopted in 1997.
The drawing on the right was produced.

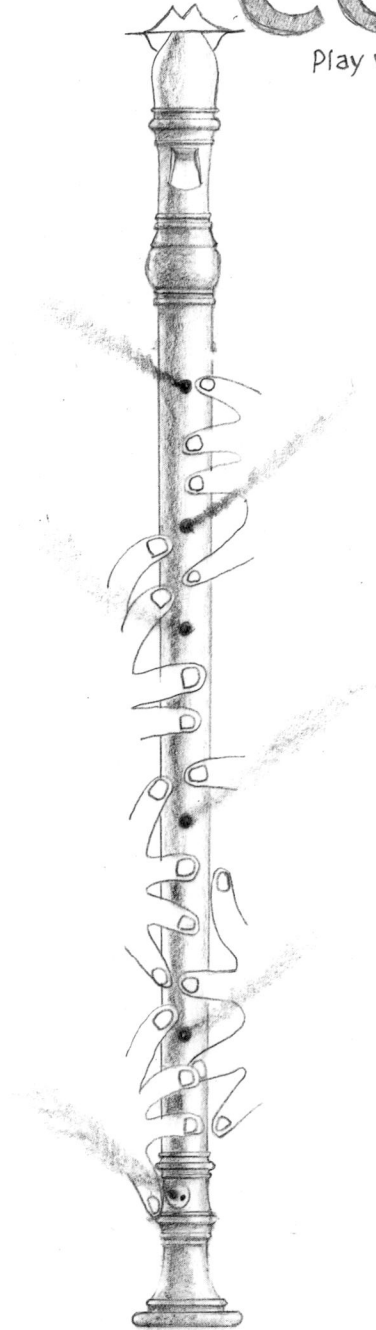

CO$_2$
Play well for the Earth.

UNFCCC-COP3-KYOTO

The 3rd Session of the Conference of the Parties to the United Nations Framework Convention on Climat Change

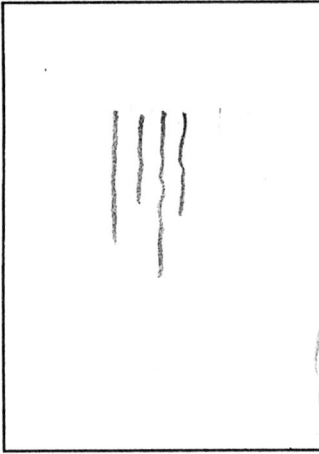

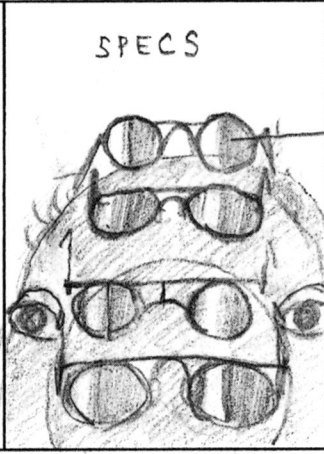

33

32 Ⓛ

SPECS

サングラス

3

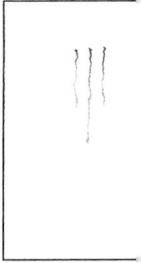

9

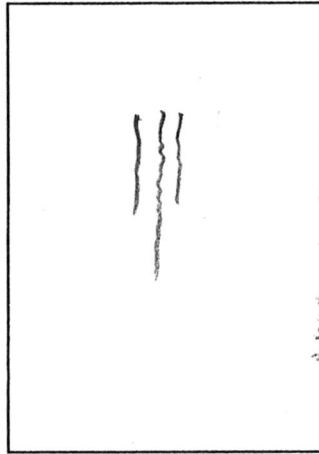

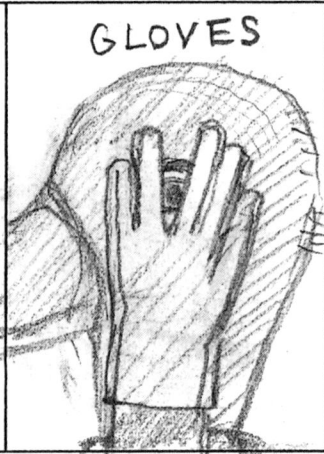

GLOVES

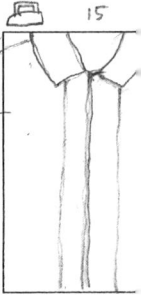

15

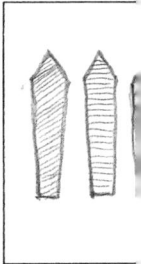

21

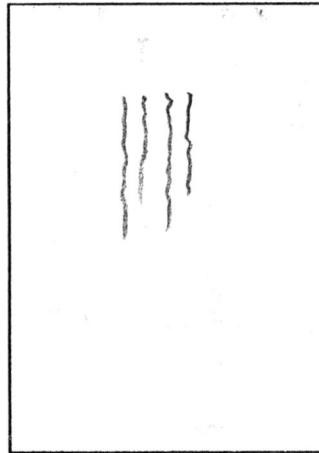

43

42 Ⓛ

SHOES

ひげをセーターの中に入れてしゃがんでいる

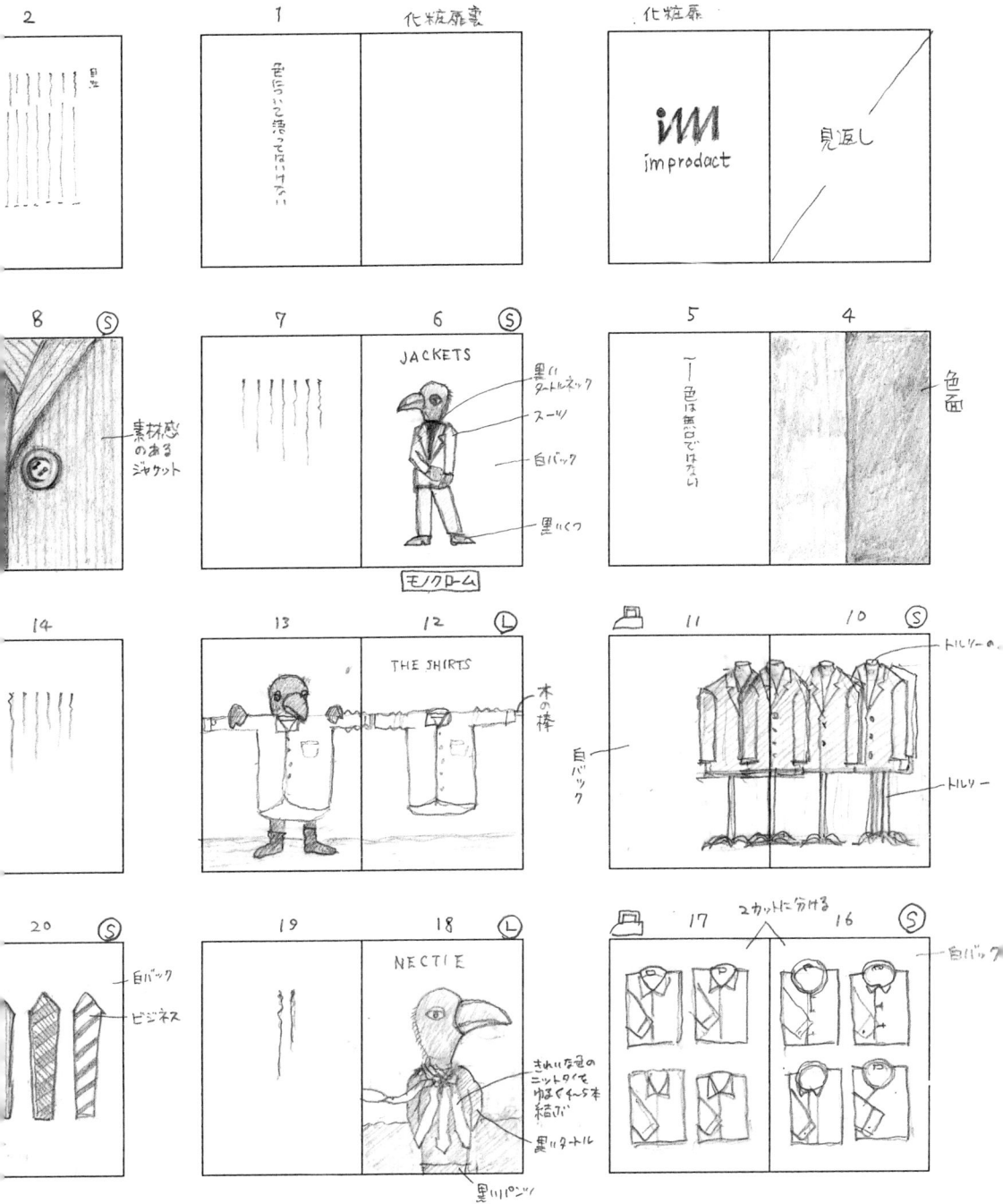

Book on the brand "im product" (developed in the late 1970s–80s).
I created a story, "Don't Talk about Colors," featuring the crow from Aesop's fables.

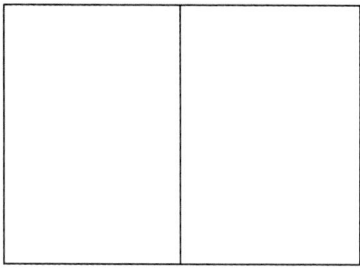

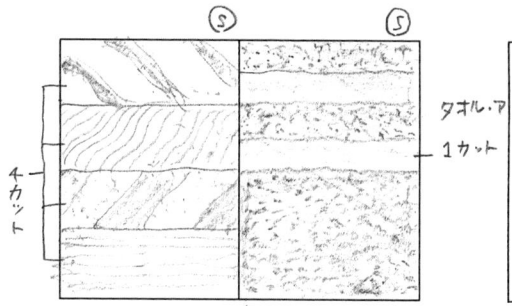
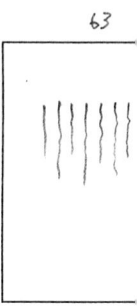

タオル・ア

1カット

4カット

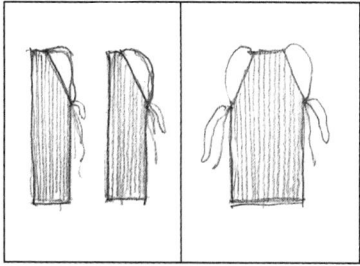

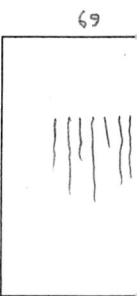

APRON

グリーン
(仕社の背

デニムのコ
(ガーデニ

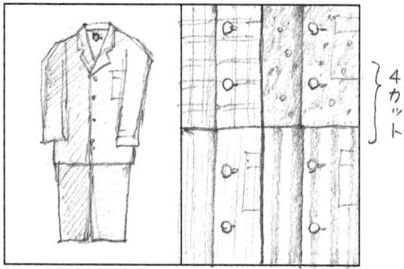

SLEEP

4カット

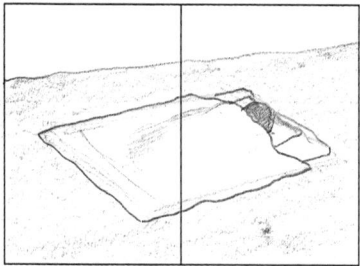

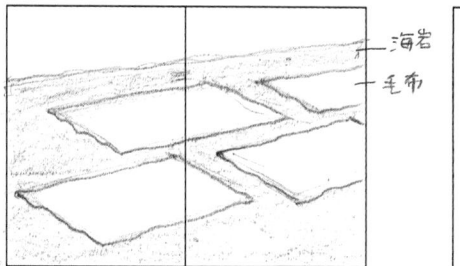
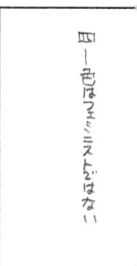

海岩

毛布

四一色ほつとミストがはない

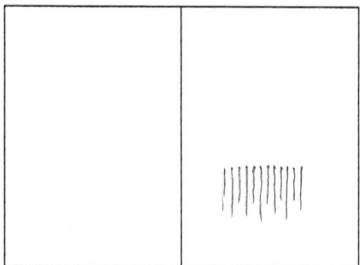

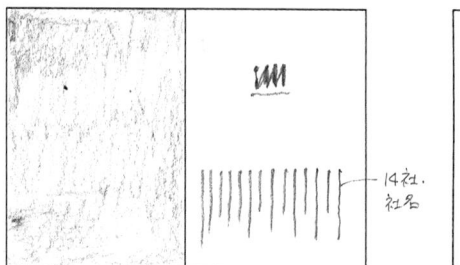
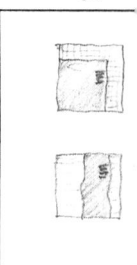

14社.
社名

62 Ⓛ

KNIT

61

三一色には故郷がある

60

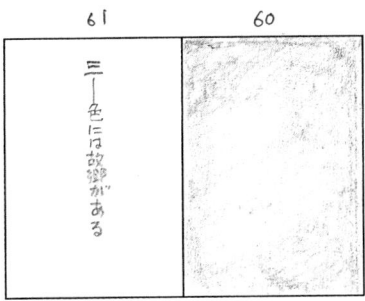

59　58 Ⓛ

流木

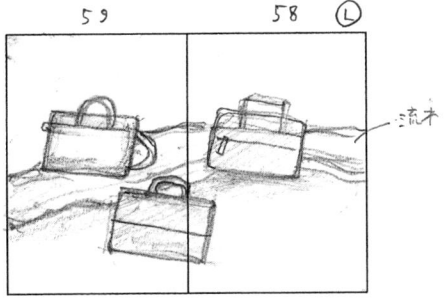

68 Ⓛ

NDERWEAR

67 Ⓢ　66 Ⓢ

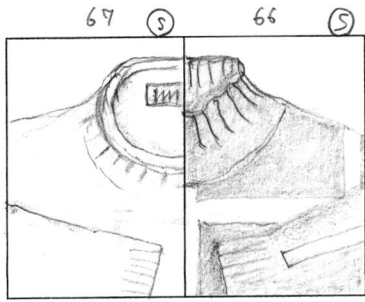

65　64 Ⓢ

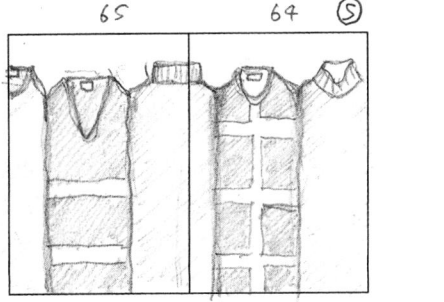

Eノクローム

74 Ⓛ

SOCKS

73　72 Ⓛ

海辺の岩場に干す。

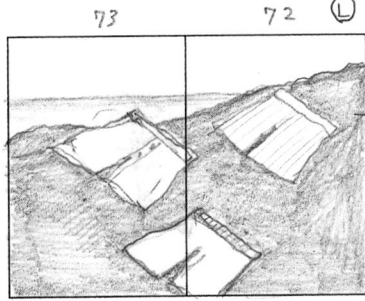

71 Ⓛ　70 Ⓛ

ロープ

木の洗濯

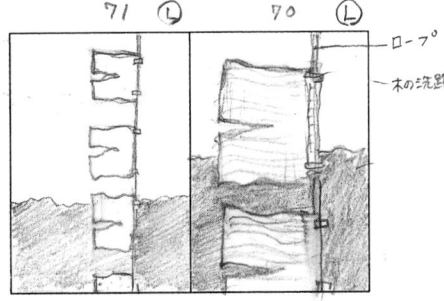

籠のようにたな

80

79　78

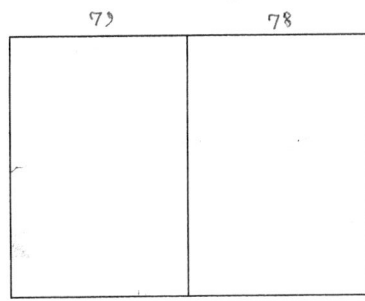

77　76 Ⓛ

ホルター
あみハ?
クリケット
スティッ
（平たい

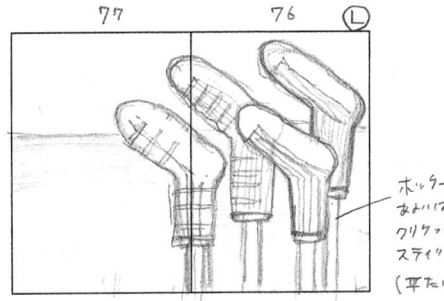

86 Ⓢ

85　84

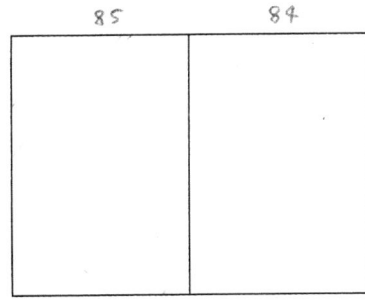

83　82 Ⓛ

HANDKERCHIEF

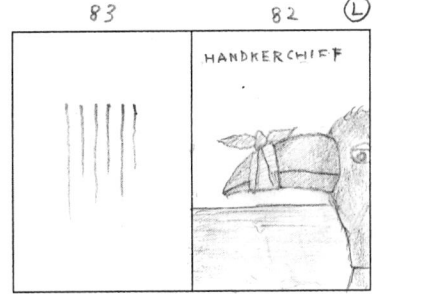

1983—2000　Dangling a fishing line into my inner self

'99 2005 WORLD EXPOSITION, JAPAN パンフレット、ページ展開。

置かれた卵
=
生み出す工場（トポス）
=
中のトポス型建築
・=
ングなの（まだ生れていない）
EXPO計画

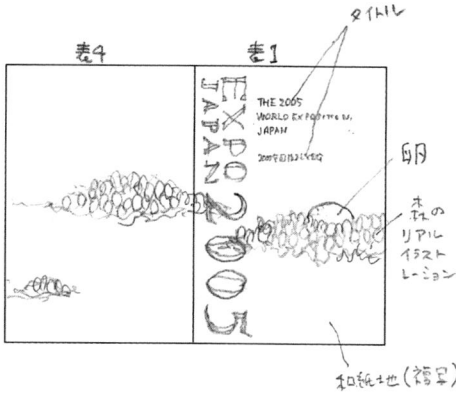

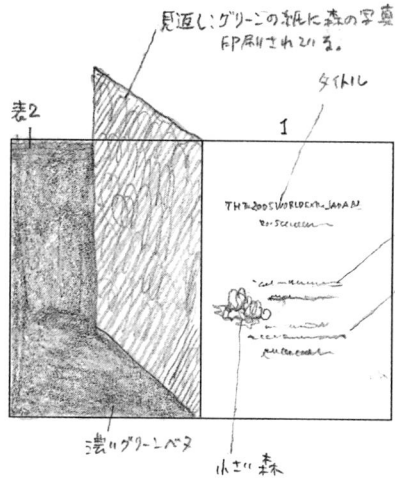

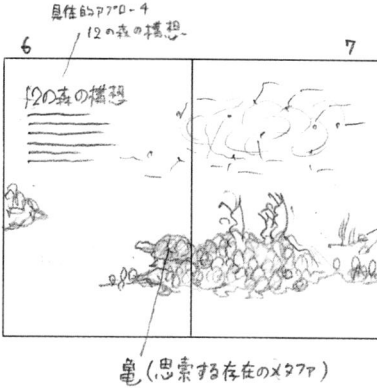

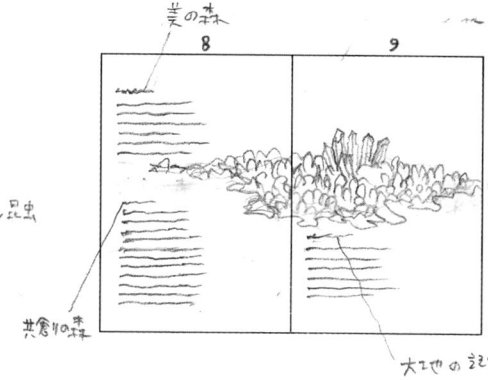

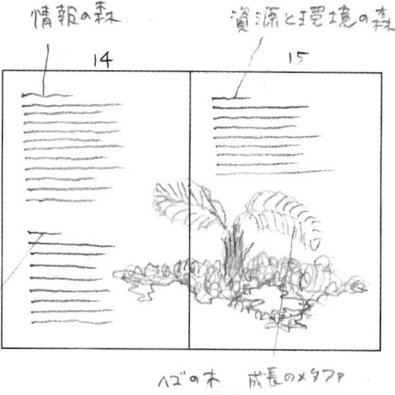

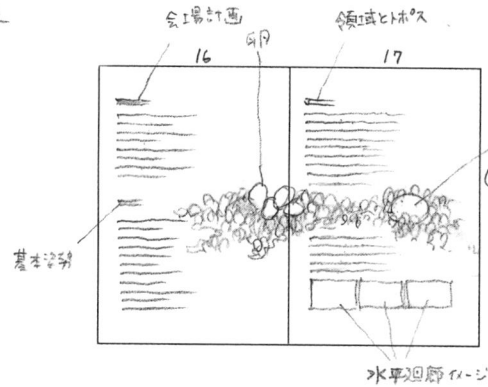

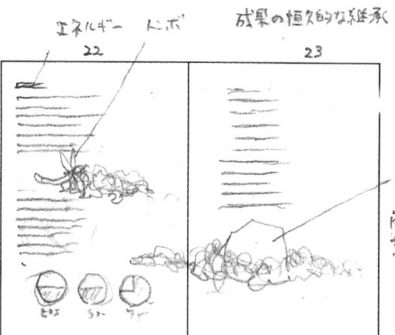

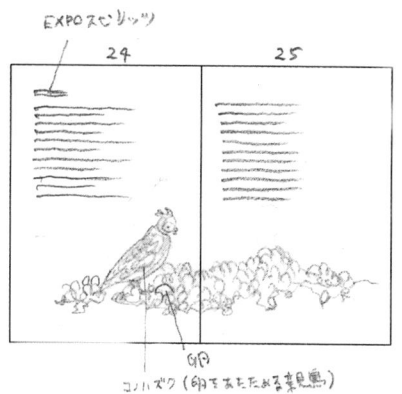

表4　表1　タイトル

EXPO JAPAN 2005

THE 2005
WORLD EXPOSITION,
JAPAN
2005年9月15日～

卵

森の
リアル
イラスト
レーション

和紙地（裾写）

見返しグリーンの紙に森の写真
FP刷りされている。

表2　タイトル　1

THE 2005 WORLD EXPO JAPAN
2005年9月15日～

濃いグリーンベタ　小さい森

具体的アプローチ
12の森の構想

6　7

12の森の構想

昆虫

亀（思索する存在のメタファ）

美の森

8　9

共創りの森

大エやの記

情報の森　資源と環境の森

14　15

宇宙の森

ヘゴの木　成長のメタファ

会場計画　卵　領域式トポス

16　17

基本骨格

水平回廊イメージ

エネルギー　トポ　成果の恒久的な継承

22　23

鉱物

成果の結晶

EXPOスピリッツ

24　25

卵
コノハズク（卵をあたためる夜見鳥）

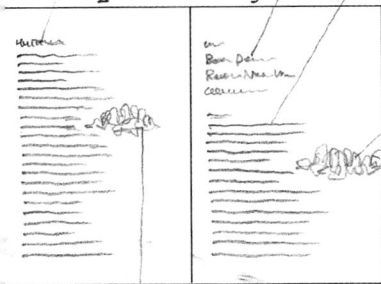

2005年EXPO構想の宣言 / あるいは目的

2 3

テーマ 理念

森林

森

問題提起型

実験場

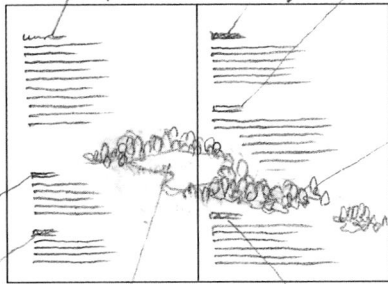

2005 EXPOの特徴

成果の継承く 参加型

4 5

森

池

会期、場所を超えた展開、

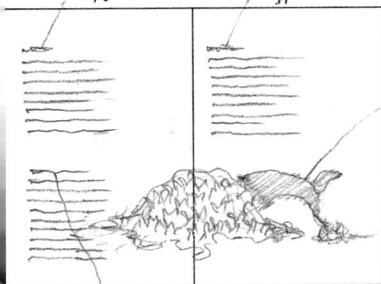

生命の森 技芸の森

10 11

くじら、生命のダイナミズムのメタファ

学びと遊びの森

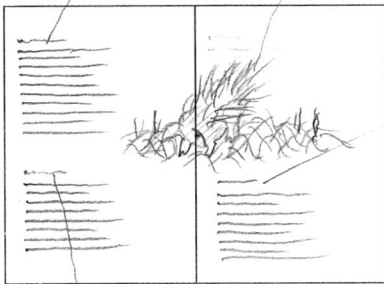

聖なるものの森 山嵐、荒ぶる自然のメタファ

共の器の表

鎮魂の森

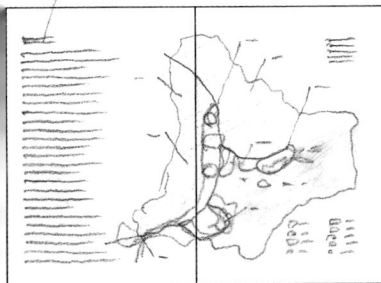

会場計画案

18 19

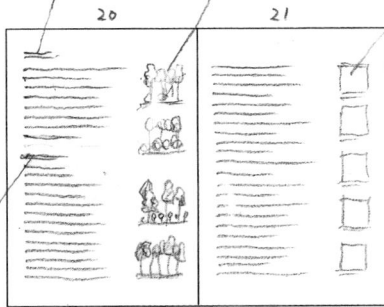

環境プログラム 森林報告の事例

20 21

海上の森 photo

自然環境

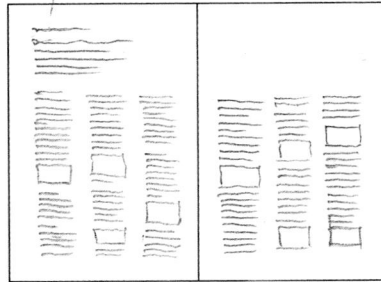

万博の歴史

26 27

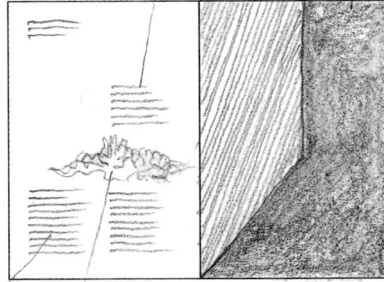

引用図版解説

28

見返し：グリーンの紙に森の写真が淡く印刷されている。

表3：裏…グリーンベタ

奥付

森

1983—2000　Dangling a fishing line into my inner self

2000—2010

Encountering competitions, encountering work,
and awakening to the possibilities of exhibitions

Whenever there was a symbol mark competition for a huge event, I enthusiastically entered it. The dedicated efforts of graphic designers at this stage makes the world much
more enjoyable. For the 2005 Aichi Expo and the 2008 Beijing Olympics competitions,
I explored the circular pattern. I was also in the middle of designing the symbol mark
of the Jingdezhen Imperial Kiln in China, a design that spirals out from the center, as if
trying to express the generation of all creation reflected in the undulations of arabesques
and clouds. Decoration is an innate human instinct, and it's somehow uplifting to surrender
to the rhythm of the work in creating forms.

For the 2005 Aichi Expo, I had a vision of the event set in a forest, so I sketched countless
rhythms and movements of life. Shapes flooded out. Eventually, ideas for rotating bodies,
branching structures, and other forms converged into the shape of a water droplet. Although my submissions for both the Aichi Expo and the Beijing Olympics were runners-up,
when I look back on these sketches, I feel something significant was retained in this work.

I started working as MUJI's art director in 2002. Looking back at my early sketches, I
notice how tense and stiff my approach was. I suppose that's how I viewed MUJI at the
time, and I was trying to dramatize undramatic angles: straight on, directly beside, and
directly overhead. A MUJI exhibition was held in Milan in conjunction with the 2004
Milano Salone. I created sketches for photographs to be used in a concept book for the exhibition. The sketches included a black lava background from Izu Oshima, a dried Japanese
pampas grass field, and a beach scene. These sketches were designed to reflect MUJI's
minimalist philosophy and echo the main visual's horizon.

I made the house sketches while studying various settlements around the world in
search of the original form of a "home." These sketches included imaginary dwellings,
carved from a baobab tree or a giant rock. Based on these sketches, I filmed on location
in Morocco and Cameroon.

I planned and drew the commercial as a one-take video. I tried to distance myself from
current trends and focus on timeless values. Even today, I believe these storyboards
would come across clearly.

The corporate ad with the tagline "Let's be gentle" features a close-up of a hand. We can't
help but admire hard-working hands. Humans must have a deeply held sense that fingertips
without any ornate decorations are beautiful in themselves. I was searching for the type of
hand that conveys the joy of the beautiful bare hand. The production of MUJI's message
involved extensive global research. We need the conceptual macro view in relation to
the detail-oriented micro view of the thousands of MUJI products. When MUJI opened
stores in Italy, Turkey, China, and the United States, we shot images of MUJI paper bags
in the streets of the relevant cities. MUJI effortlessly circulates worldwide, just like
water. Hence the text, "LIKE WATER."

Around this time, I began to receive requests for architectural concepts from friends over-
seas. A friend with a large plot of land on the island of Lombok in Indonesia asked me for

advice on what facilities to build there. Without hesitation, I drew a sketch for him. The architecture, spanning horizontally, can be extended to any degree, and is based on the idea of inserting an artificial plane into the rolling terrain to emphasize the undulations of nature. During this time, I also sketched what I considered an ideal facility for blending our modern lifestyle, in which there is less of a boundary between work and rest, into nature.

I got to know a Chinese Zen monk, who asked me to come up with a design for an accommodation facility for a Zen temple under her jurisdiction. I made a site visit to Wuhan and left sketches with the client. I was also asked by the government of the city of Jingdezhen (known as the Porcelain City) to conceptualize a ceramics museum. I drew inspiration from the climbing kilns and fragments of unglazed saggars (ceramic box-like containers used to protect pieces during firing). I then asked the architect Hiroshi Naito to bring my idea to life, and presented the basic concept to the government. While none of my ideas were directly realized, similar buildings have been constructed in Jingdezhen in recent years, so we can assume that they have captured the imagination of the local people.

During this time, I became involved in several projects disseminating information in the form of exhibitions. The Ministry of Economy, Trade, and Industry commissioned me to plan and conceive the "SENSEWARE" exhibition twice, in 2007 and 2009. The show aimed to explore the applications of advanced Japanese fibers with creators from various fields. It traveled to Paris, Milan, Tokyo, and Holon, Israel.

In 2009, architect Shigeru Ban and I created an exhibition called "JAPAN CAR." It was held at the Science Museums in Paris and London. While a design museum was under consideration, after talking it through with design department heads at several Japanese companies, we concluded that an exhibition planning engine would be more effective than a facility to house collections. We then decided to plan a series of Japanese industry-themed exhibitions and send them out to the world. The first attempt was "JAPAN CAR," a large-scale event with the participation of seven major Japanese car manufacturers. Even today, I believe it was an exhibition that captured the essence of Japanese cars, and can contribute to the world.

A sketch of the symbol mark for the 2005 Aichi Expo, depicting the pulsation of everything in the universe. The human race has found numerous eternities in the *ensō*, the never-ending movement of a circle with neither beginning nor end. The following sketches represent a glimpse of that.

These sketches are for the symbol of Jingdezhen Imperial Kiln,
which specializes in restoring ceramics from the Ming and Qing dynasties.

People undulate like gently curving hieroglyphics in
this sketch for the Beijing Olympic symbol.

Sketches for the Expo 2005 Aichi symbol, contemplating the wisdom of nature.

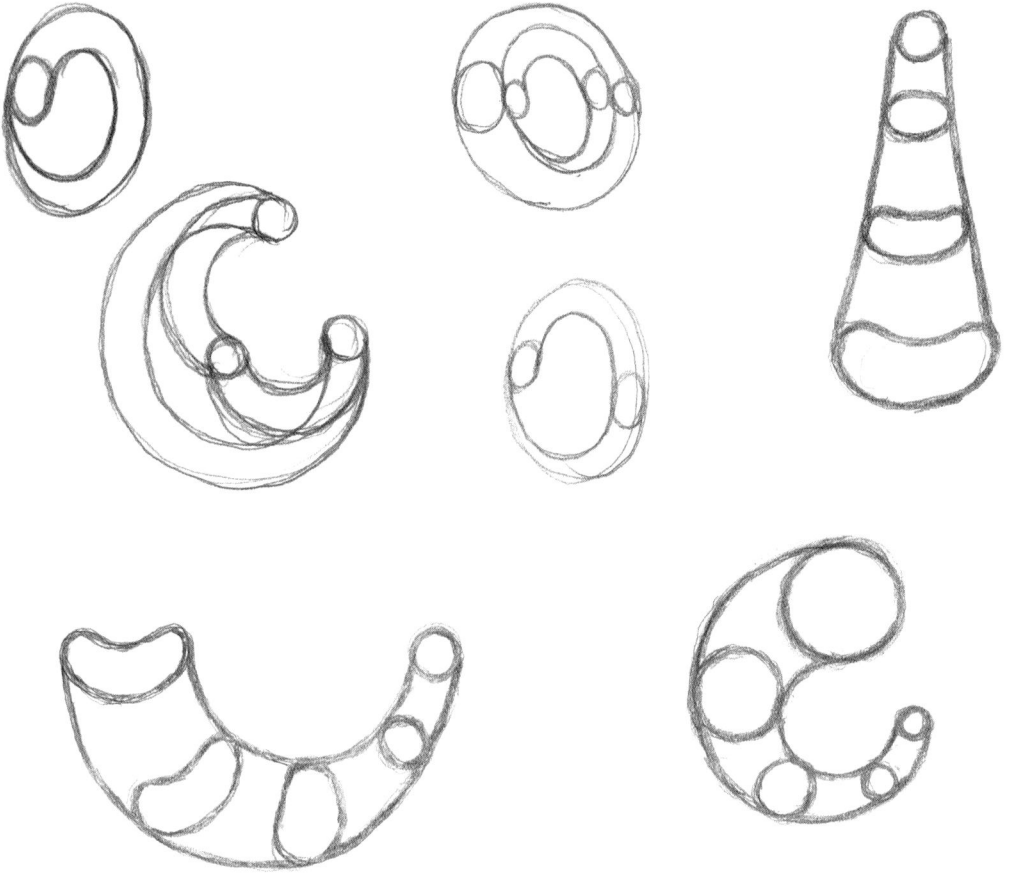

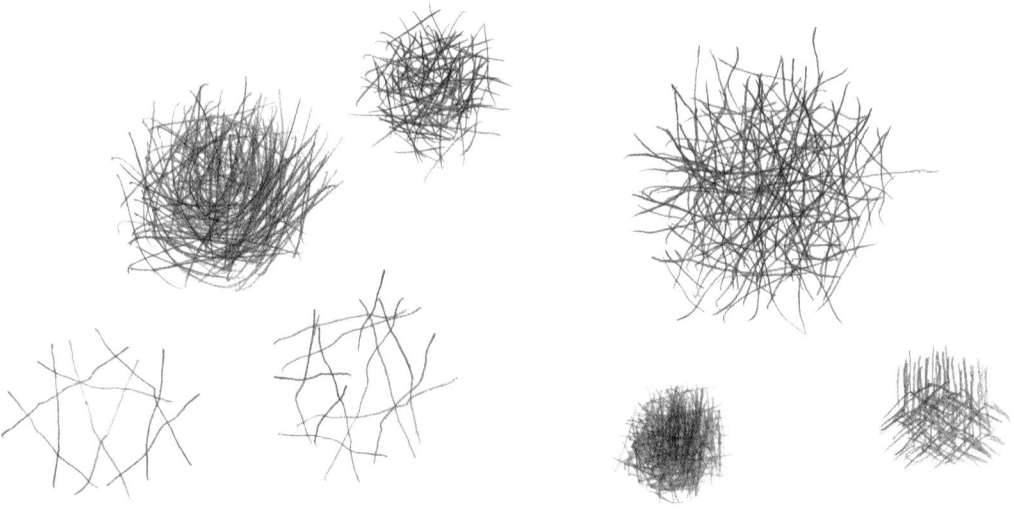

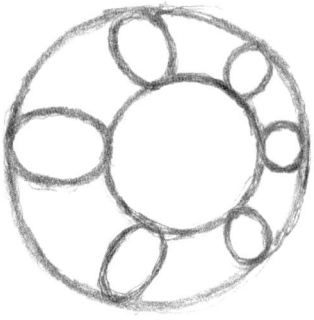
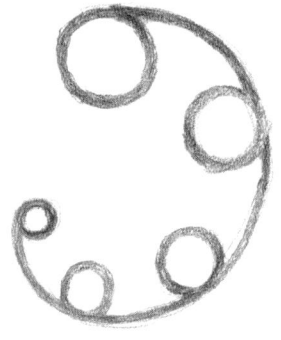

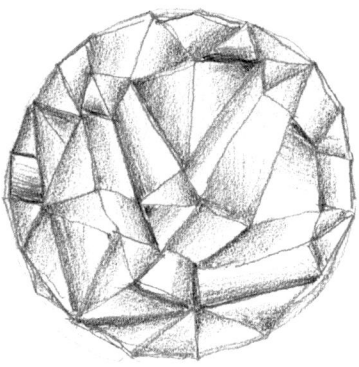
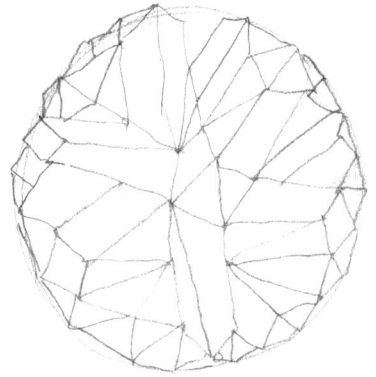

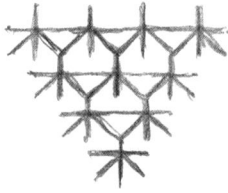

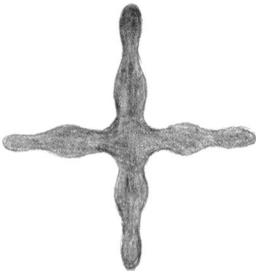

木の枝　インテラクション

シンボルの生む

レプリカの生式
＝
瀬戸の産業（たくさん生みだし、大量にシンボルマークのレプリカを生産 する）。

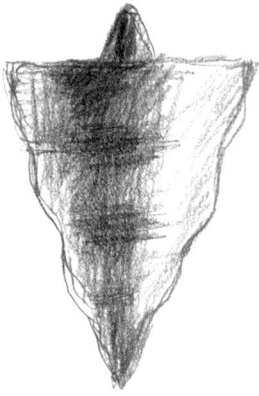

回転させる

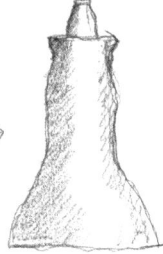

symbol B.

symbol A

木の枝

瀬戸を つくる
人の土を
象形の教習

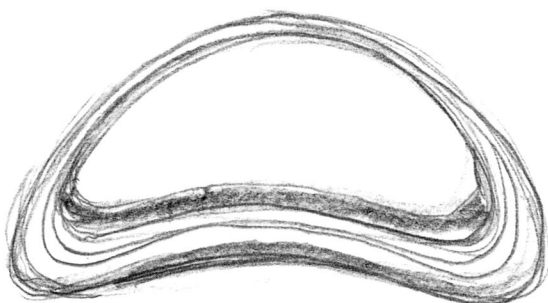

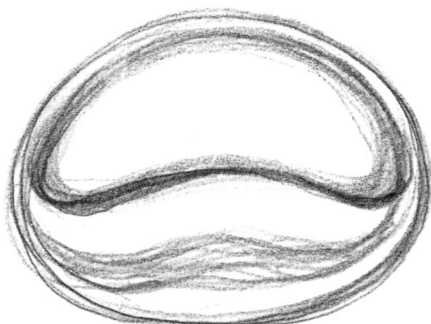

After passing through the forms of all of the things in the universe,
these sketches crystallized into the form of a single water drop.

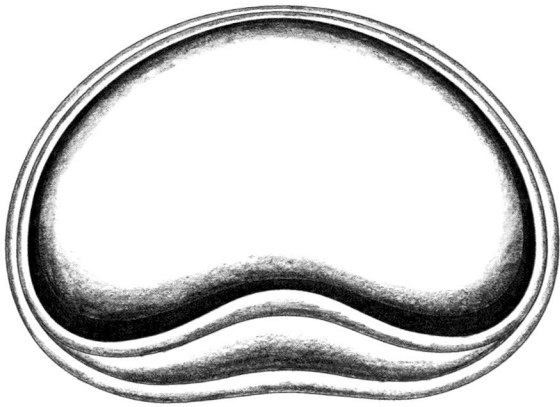

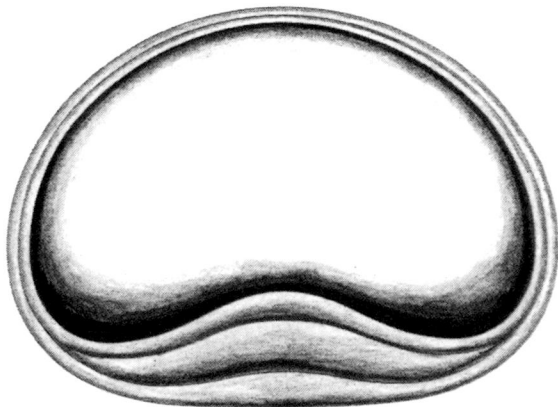

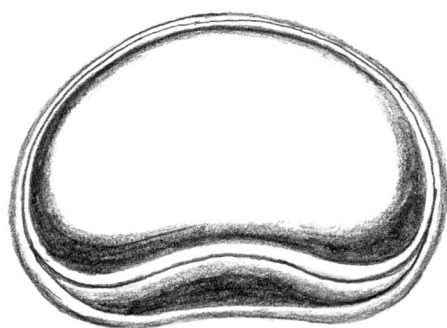

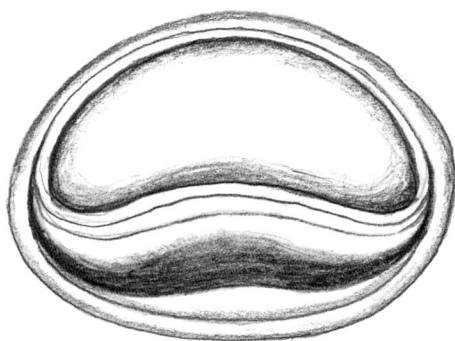

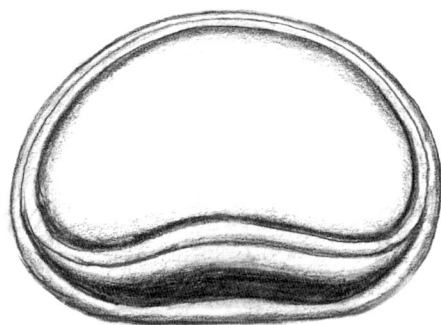

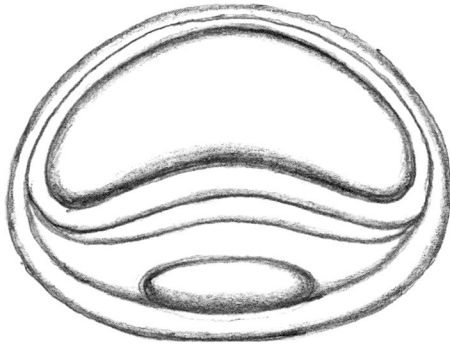

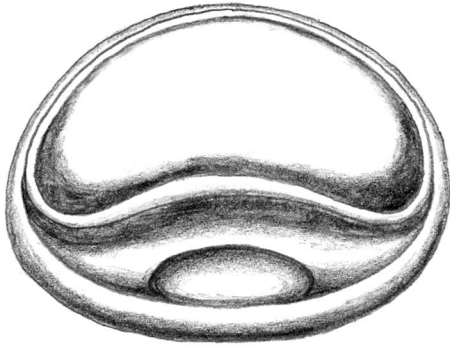

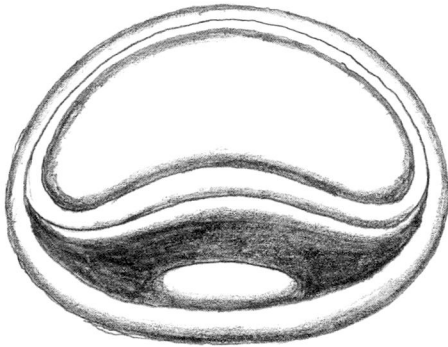

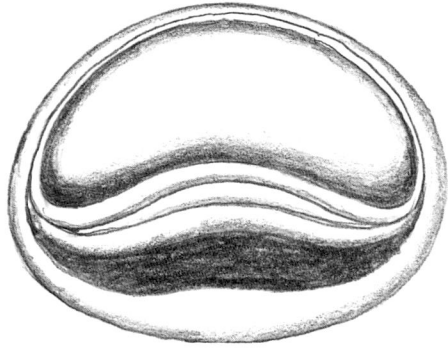

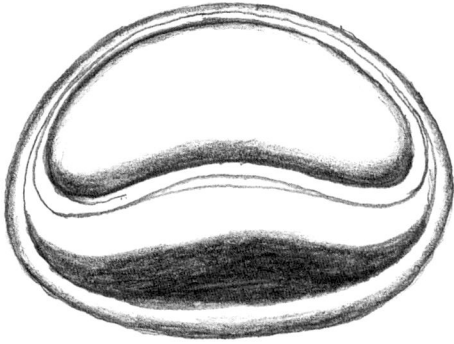

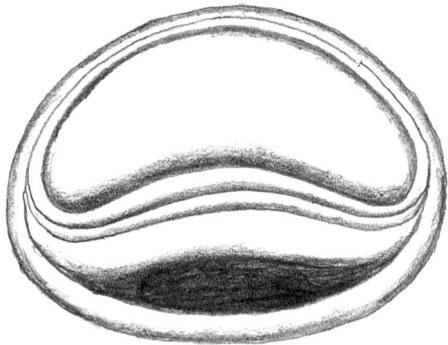

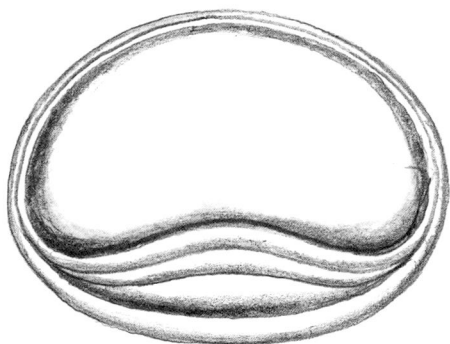

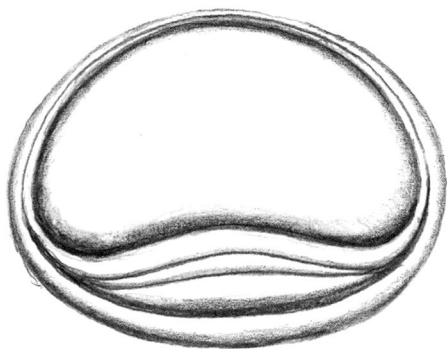

The final image: a drop of water encompassing infinite motion.

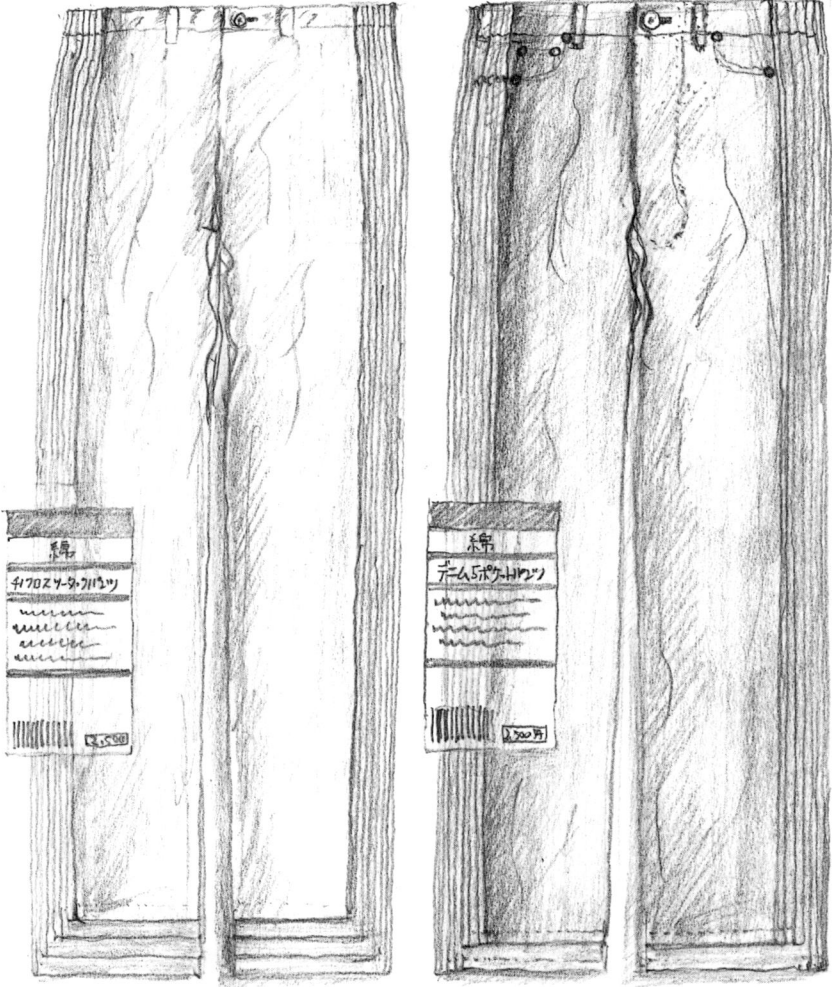

70 · 73 · 76 · 79 · 82 · 85 · 88 · 91

綿
チノクロスワーク・パンツ

綿
デニム5ポケットパンツ

73 · 77 · 81 · 85

77 · 85

Work for MUJI around 2003. The interpretation is very rigid,
but this likely reflected my impression of MUJI at that time.

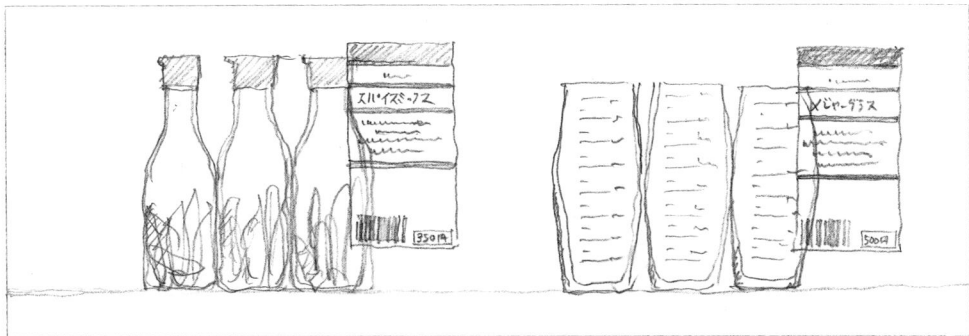

窓上変形ワイド　H355×W1060

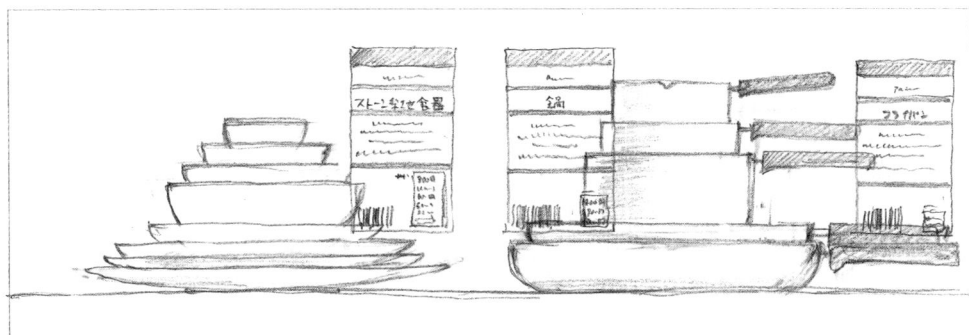

窓上変形ワイド　H355×W1060

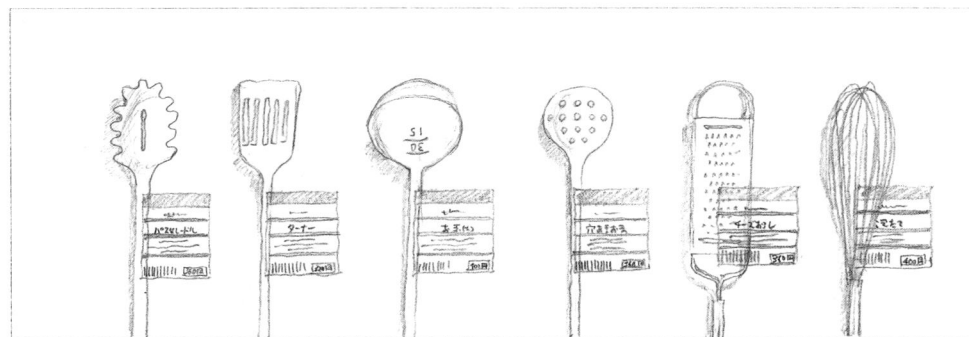

窓上変形ワイド　H355×W1060

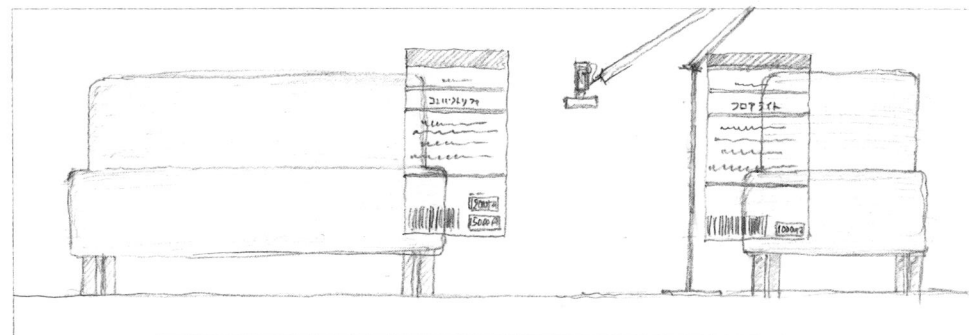

窓上変形ワイド　H355×W1060

2000—2010　Encountering competitions, encountering work, and awakening to the possibilities of exhibitions

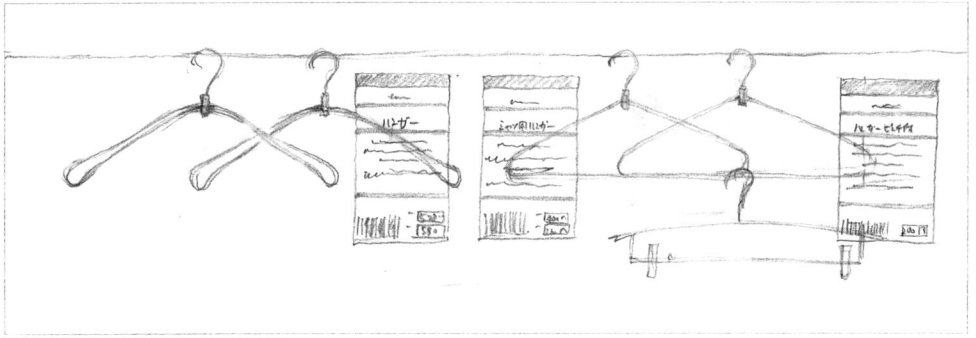

窓上変形ワイド　H355×W1060

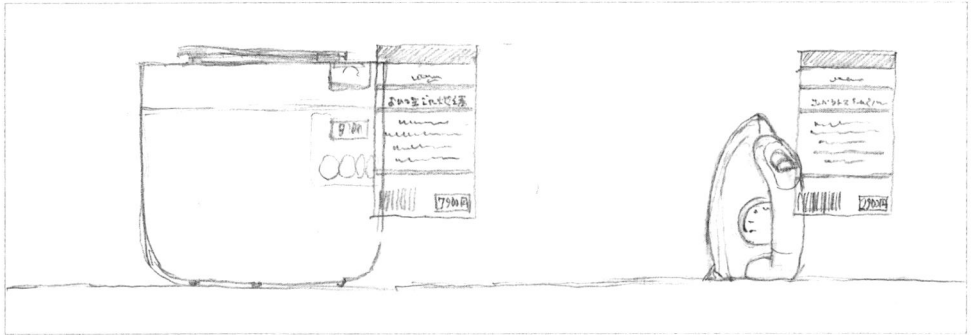

窓上変形ワイド　H355×W1060

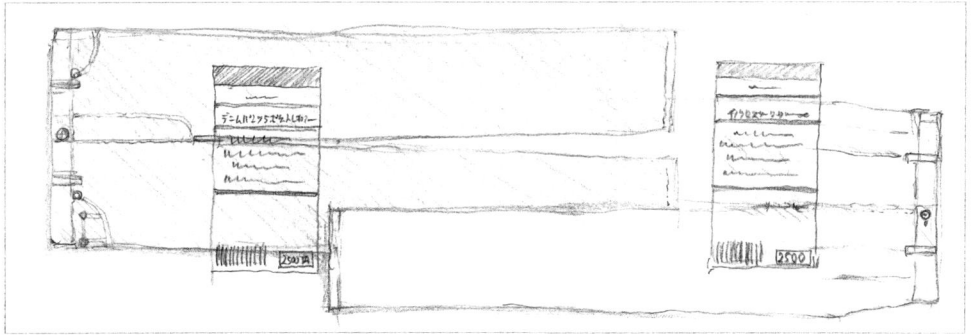

窓上変形ワイド　H355×W1060

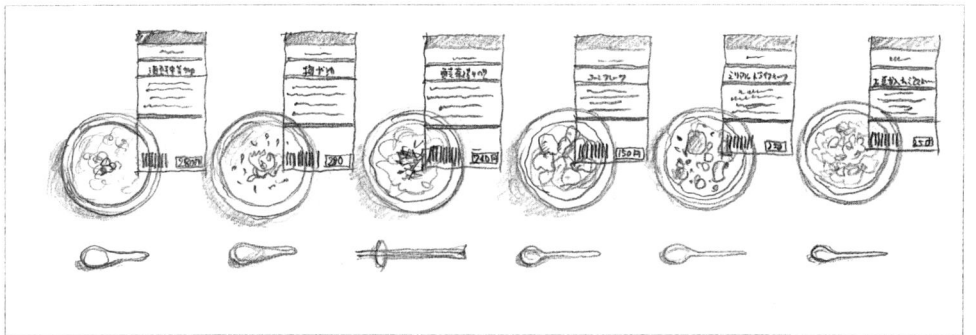

窓上変形ワイド　H355×W1060

窓上変形ワイド　H355×W1060

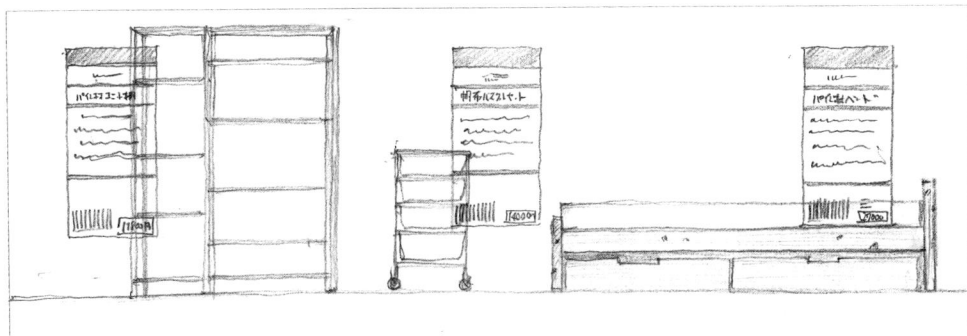

窓上変形ワイド　H355×W1060

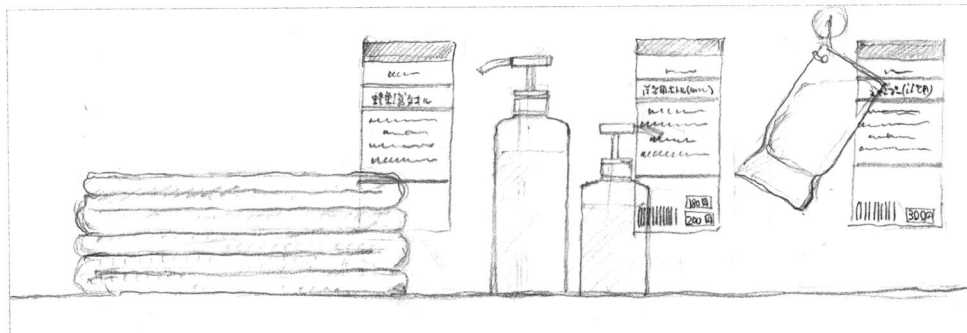

窓上変形ワイド　H355×W1060

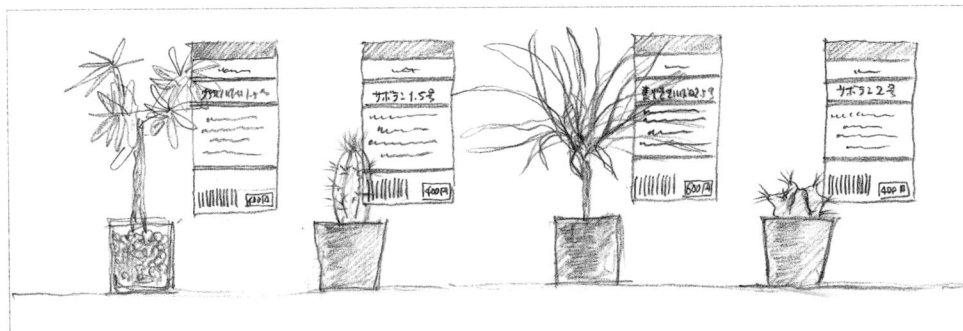

窓上変形ワイド　H355×W1060

2000—2010　Encountering competitions, encountering work, and awakening to the possibilities of exhibitions

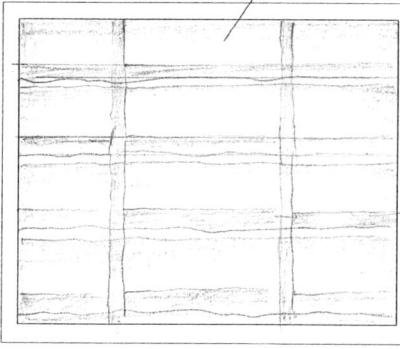

8 PP アップ

9

〈PP. 収納〉

黒い王。砂利

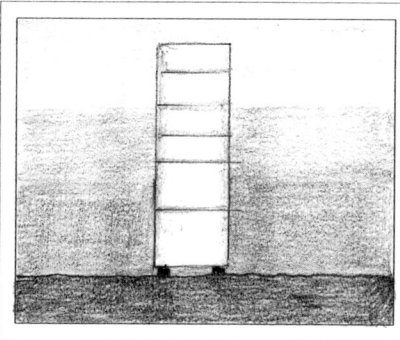

10

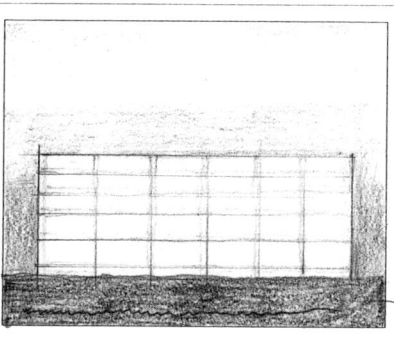

11

〈PP. 収納〉

空.海.浜のボク
グラデーション

堤防のような所

12

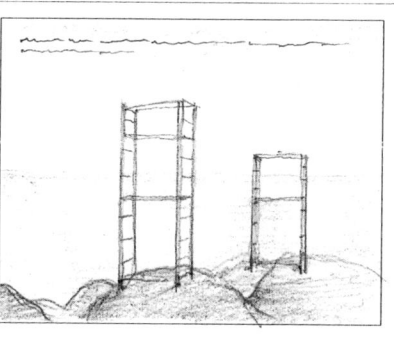

13

〈スチール棚〉

← 水平線

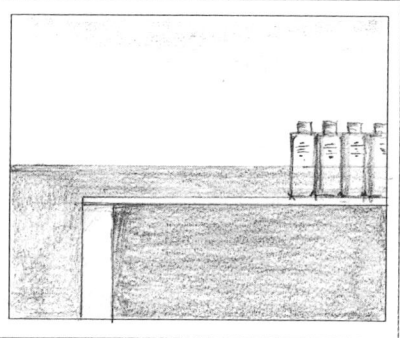

14

15

〈アルミ.テーブル〉
〈ペット.化粧水〉

← 水平線

18 19

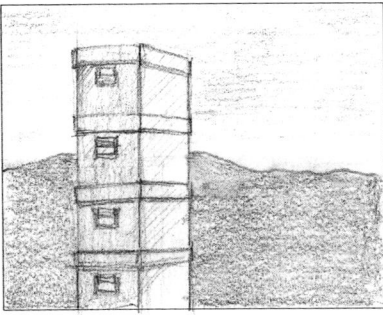 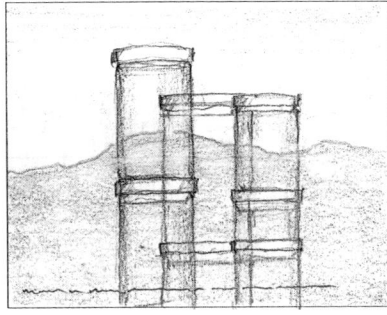

〈トタン収納〉
〈ガラスキャニスター〉
（フタは白プラスチック）

← 山のスカイライン

20 21

〈アルミ角型ハンガー 150ピ〉
〈アルミハンガー、シャツ用〉

← 水平線

22 23

 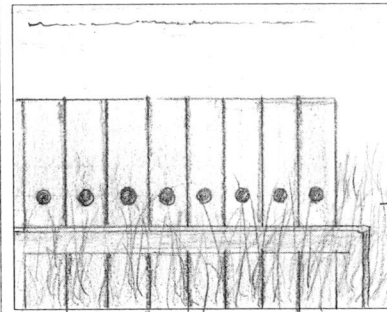

〈再生クラフトファイル〉
〈スチール棚〉

→ 枯れススキのような茂み

24 25

〈ヌメ革、革張リソファ〉

→ 枯れススキのような茂み

MUJI corporate advertisement.
I thought of MUJI not as a group of thousands of products but as a form of living.
I journeyed to Morocco and Cameroon to find the reality of houses not designed by architects.

♪ ゆっくり回転（自転）しながら
右端から しょう油さし 登場

同様に 自転しながら
きゅうすが登場

同様に 皿、丼類
（アンバランスに積まれているので
自転しているのがわかる）

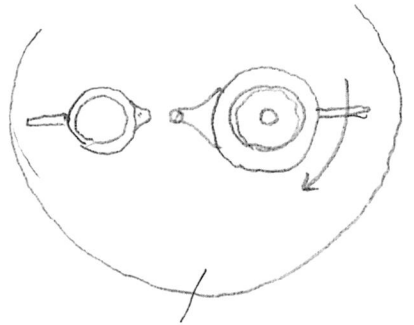

この台ごと回転している

洋の器 ポットとミルクピッチャー 登場
洋の器はペアになって回転している
ワルツを踊るように。

コーヒーカップのペア 登場

ティーカップと マグカップのペア登場

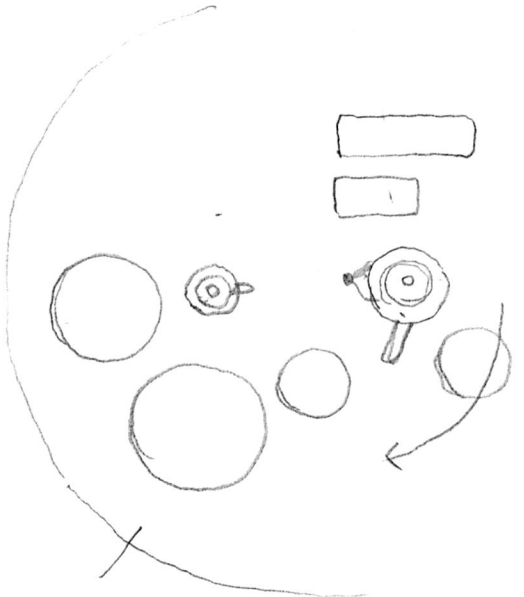

大きな台にのせて
グループごと回転

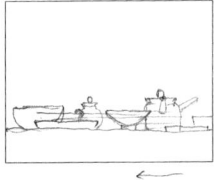

Na
和の器 集合で登場
（ぜんとこ）なりました

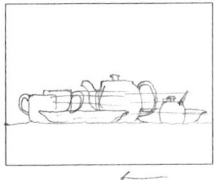

洋の器、集合で登場

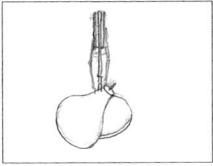

♪～

うなじの美しい踊り子
あるいは トップモデルのような
自信に満ちたポーズ

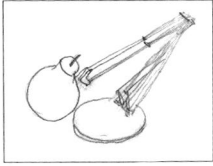

台ごと ゆーっくりと回転している

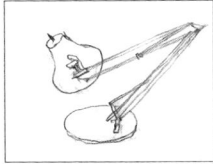

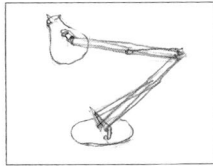

上へゆっくりと首を持ちあげる
首すじのラインが美しい

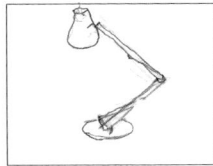

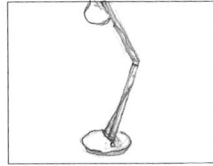

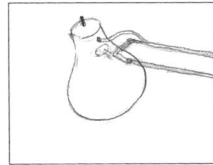

上ち向へのみ 引っぱり
動きをつける。

伸びきったポーズを決める

大きな回転台の中央で
ゆ～っくりと回るそライト

カメラ寄って首すじのアップ
—きれいだなーと
観ている人に感じさせてから
Na
しぜんとこうなりました。

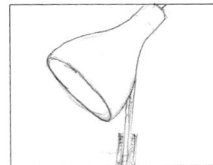

顔が見えそう！というところで
ロゴ入る。

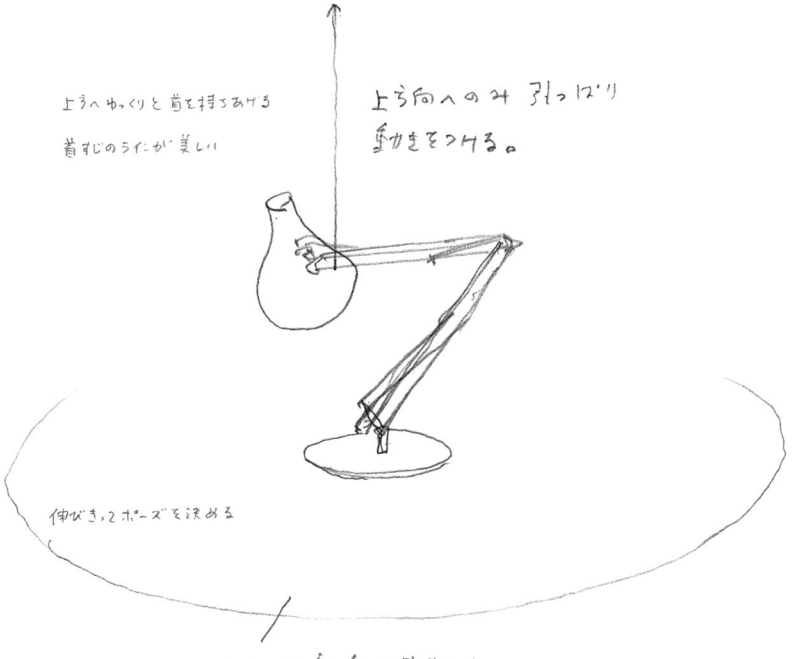

A storyboard for a MUJI commercial. This was intended as a one-take video.

駅構内の時計が
無印の掛時計になっている。

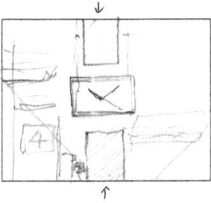

時計の上下から
ベルトが接近

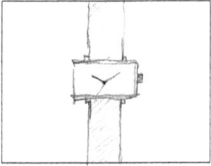

腕時計になる

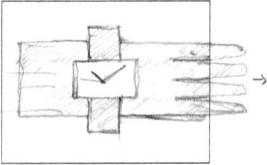

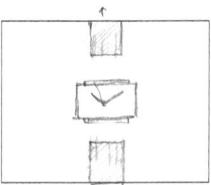

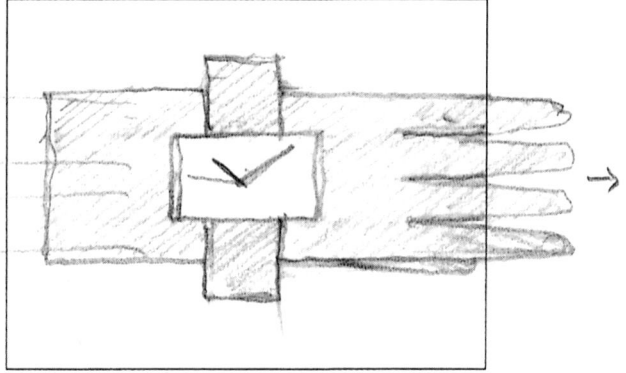

置き時計になる
メガネとカレンダー配置

Na 時計、徐々にアップに…。
自然とこうなりました。

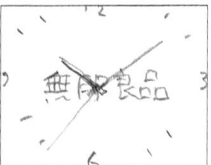

ロゴ．F.I．

Distance yourself from trends. The copy reads, "What happens naturally."

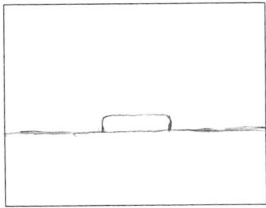

白い台の中から
頭をのぞかせている何か。

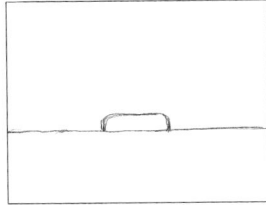

しばらくそのまま動かない。

焼きあがった

ポン！とトーストのようにとび出す。

次々にとびだす。
ふっくらボディソファ

Na

是

自然と：

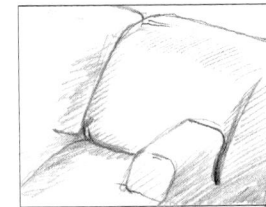

カメラ回り込んで
ソファの形を
見せて止める。
ロゴ、T.I、

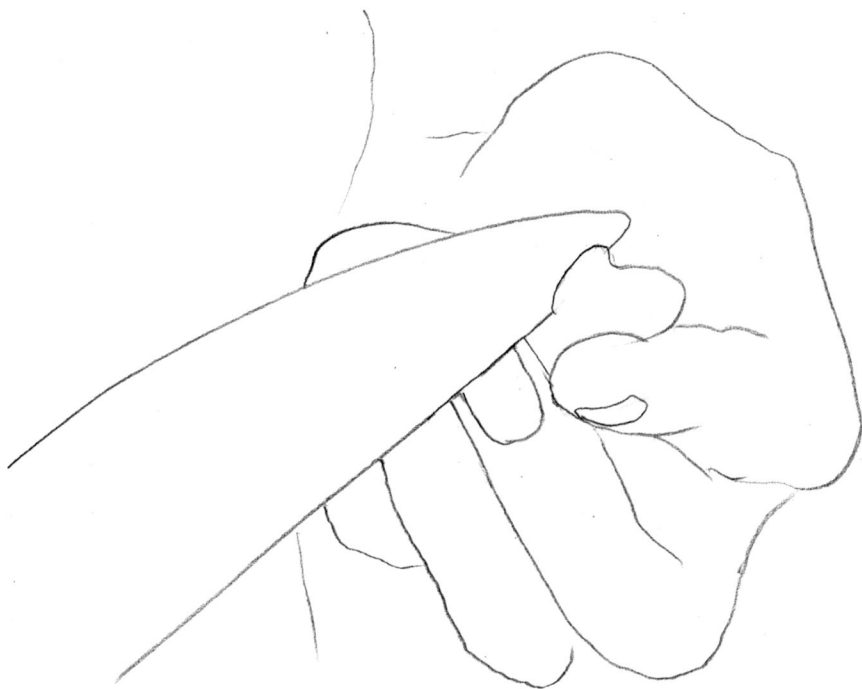

Rough sketches for MUJI's corporate campaign, "Let's be gentle."
I was trying to capture the beauty of working hands and fingers.

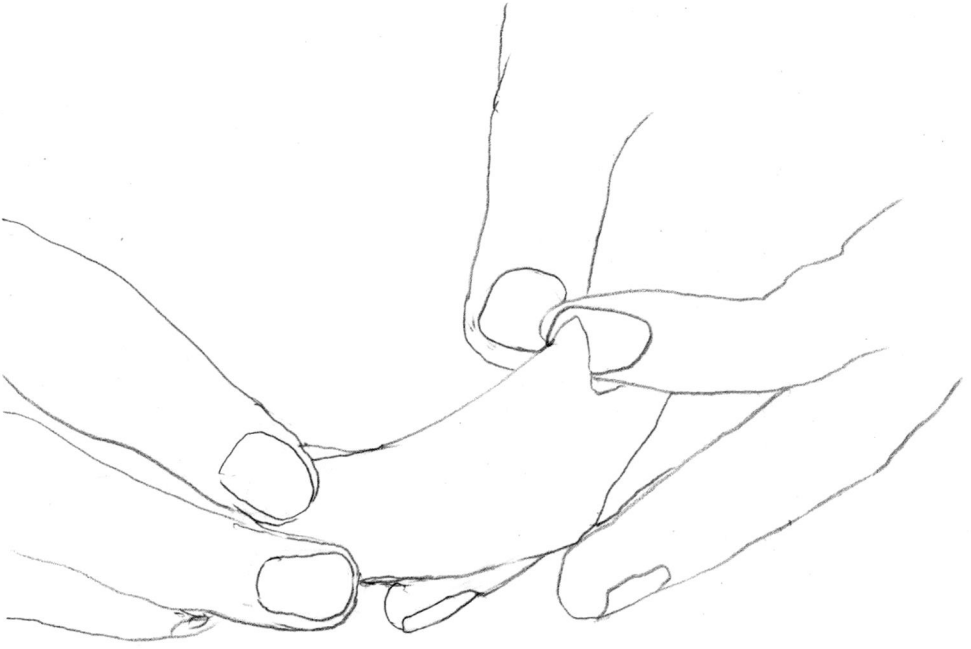

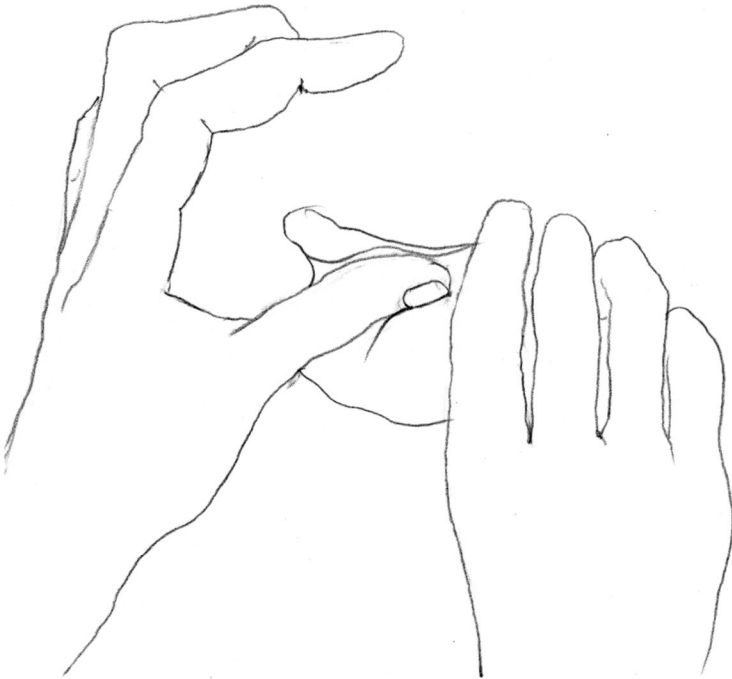

Sketches for a corporate campaign for MUJI, which had begun to open shops worldwide at this time.
The copy reads "Like Water": blending like water into the living climate of every country.
The piece was filmed on location in New York, Rome, Istanbul, and Beijing.

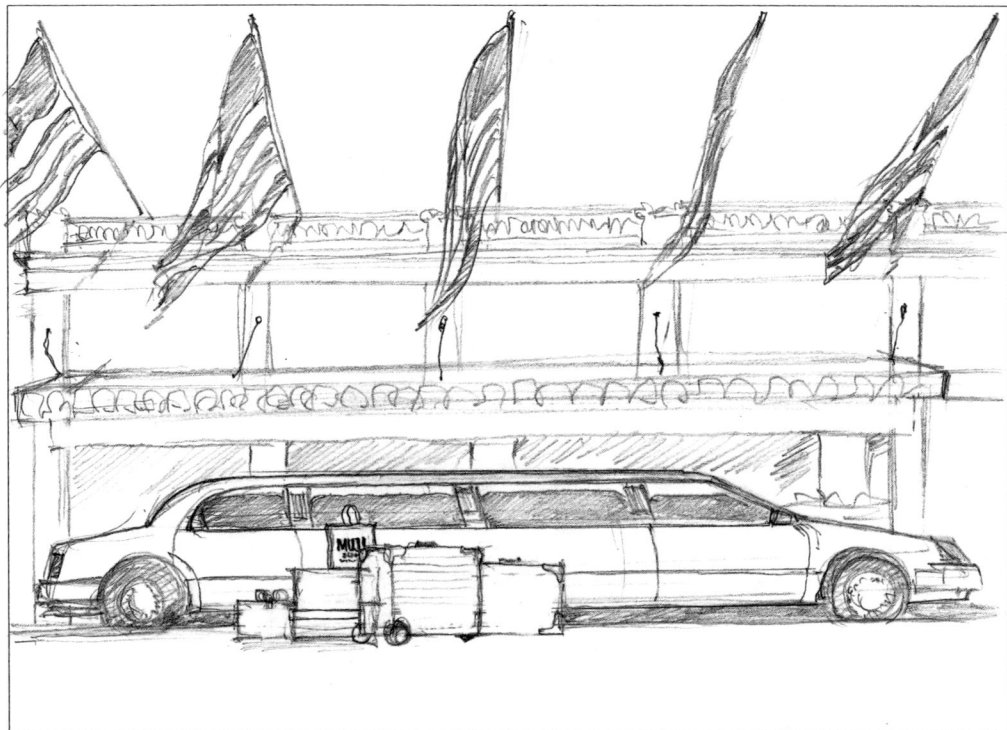

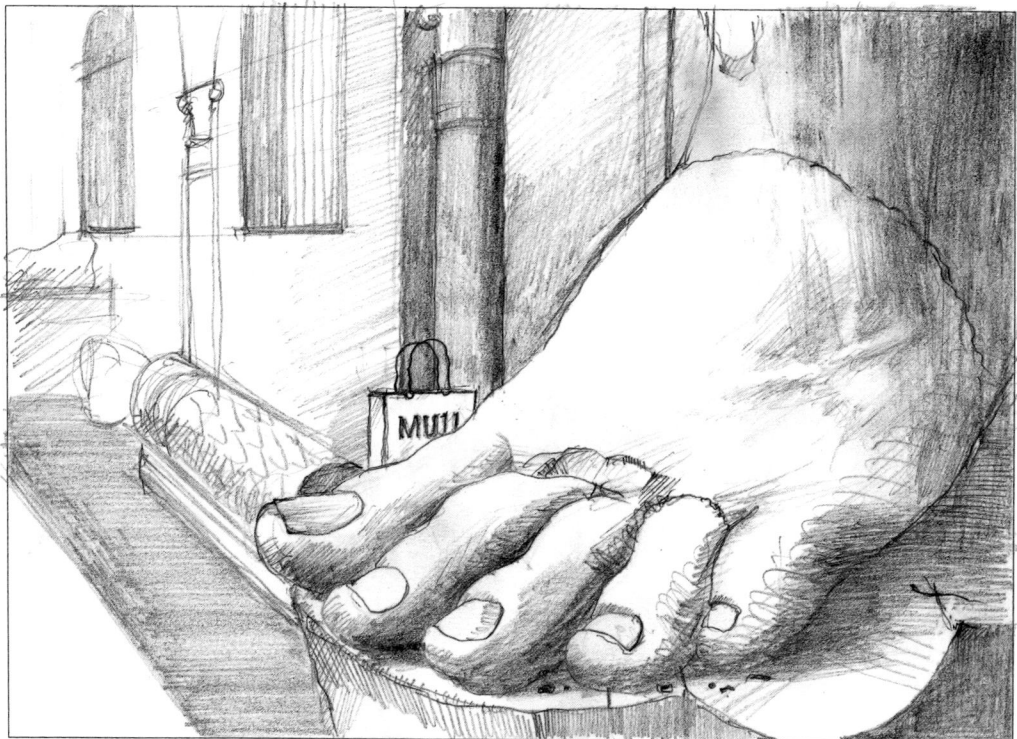

We envisioned a certain type of person wearing MUJI clothing, showcasing natural, organic colors.
Our goal was to capture the openness and fairness of the Nordic people.
The session took place in Iceland and featured individuals from different generations.

I was asked by an American friend to create an architectural plan for a large piece of land
in Lombok, Indonesia. While she would have hired an architect if the project had moved forward
in reality, she and I were free to discuss the concept on our own. The idea was to transform
a flat plane into a more natural terrain, allowing for enjoyment of the topographic undulations.

Pool.

自然と融合した ハイテク
ワークスフィア

施設は 少しづつ 増殖す…
キノコが 生えるように。

We considered what life on the island would be like if we created a lifestyle in which work and rest were not detached, but combined in a natural flow. This concept also inspired ideas for developing facilities that could harmonize with nature in the era of tourism.

ハイテク・コテージ。
（ワークスフィア）
宿泊して休んだり
使ったりする

リゾートの農工場。（オーガニックかどうかは検討するとして）
景観資源にもなる。

敷地内のレストラン。

《等高線建築》
承恩寺 新ヴィラ構想.

ルーバーの屋根
ウッドデッキ

ルーバーの屋
ルーバーの根

ウッドデッキ

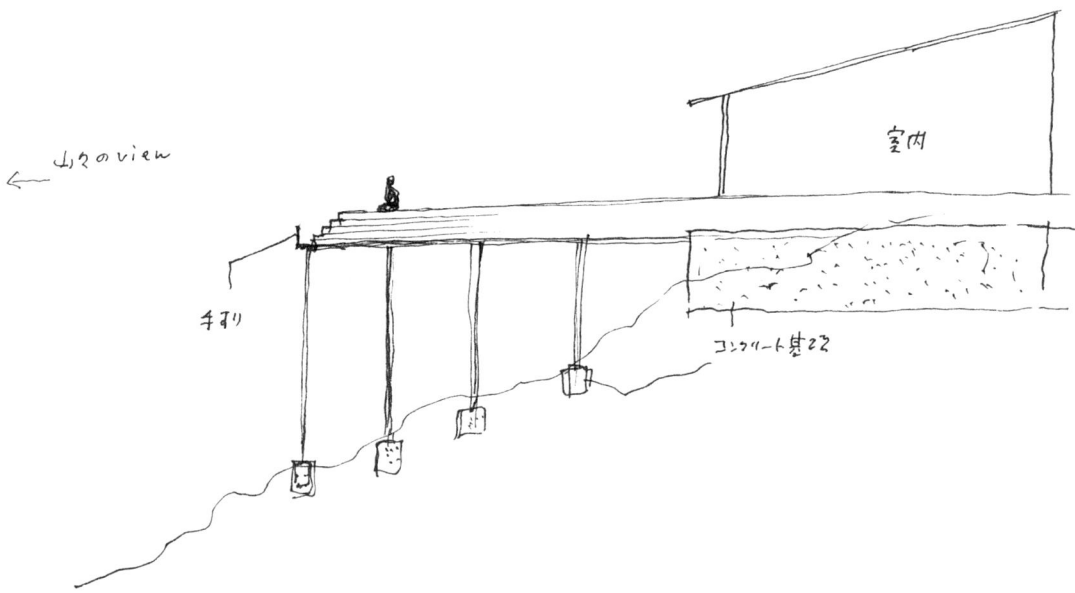

山々のview

室内

手すり

コンクリート壁22

《水平回廊, イメージ》

I met a Chinese Zen monk, Tonghua, who sought my advice about the temple lodgings under her management. Even in modern China, interest in Zen is experiencing a gradual revival. We talked about the design of the lodgings, aiming for simplicity and maintaining a connection to the natural surroundings.

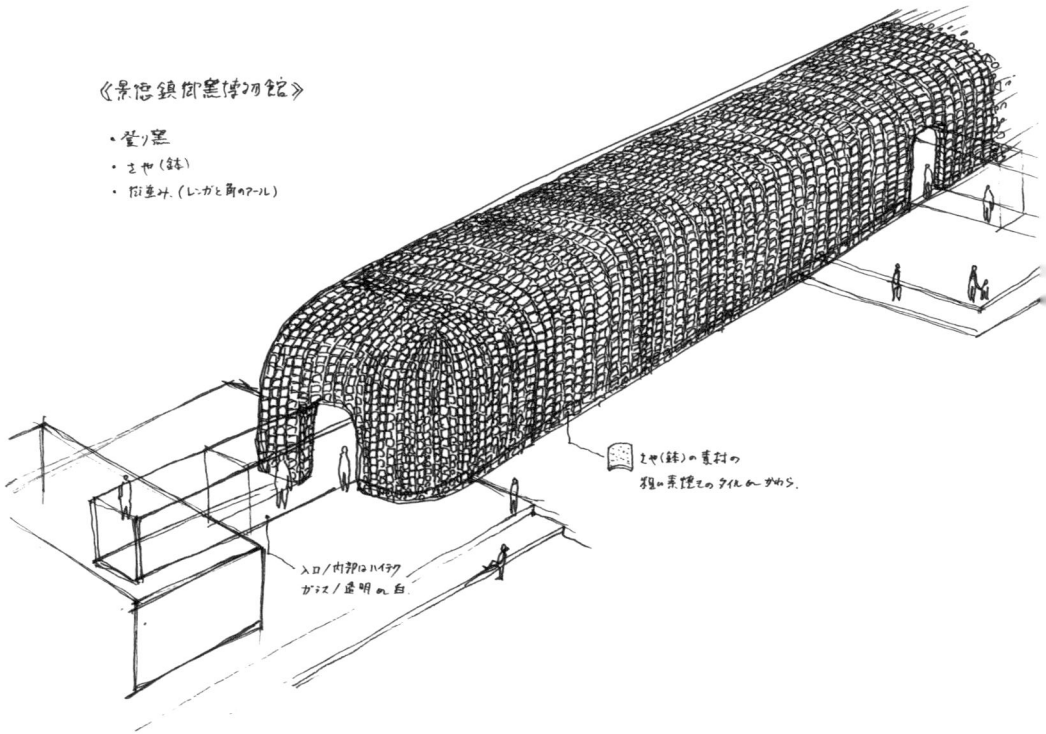

《景德鎮御窯博物館》

・登り窯
・さや（鉢）
・街並み（レンガと石のアーチ）

さや（鉢）の素材の
独の素焼でのタイルの ぬめり。

入口/内部はハイテク
ガラス/透明の白。

Jingdezhen, China, was the site of porcelain production for the emperor during the Southern Song dynasty. I drew this when I was approached by the administrative authorities of Jingdezhen, who wished to build a museum of pottery and porcelain on the site. I asked architect Hiroshi Naito to participate, and he gave a presentation, but unfortunately this plan did not materialize.

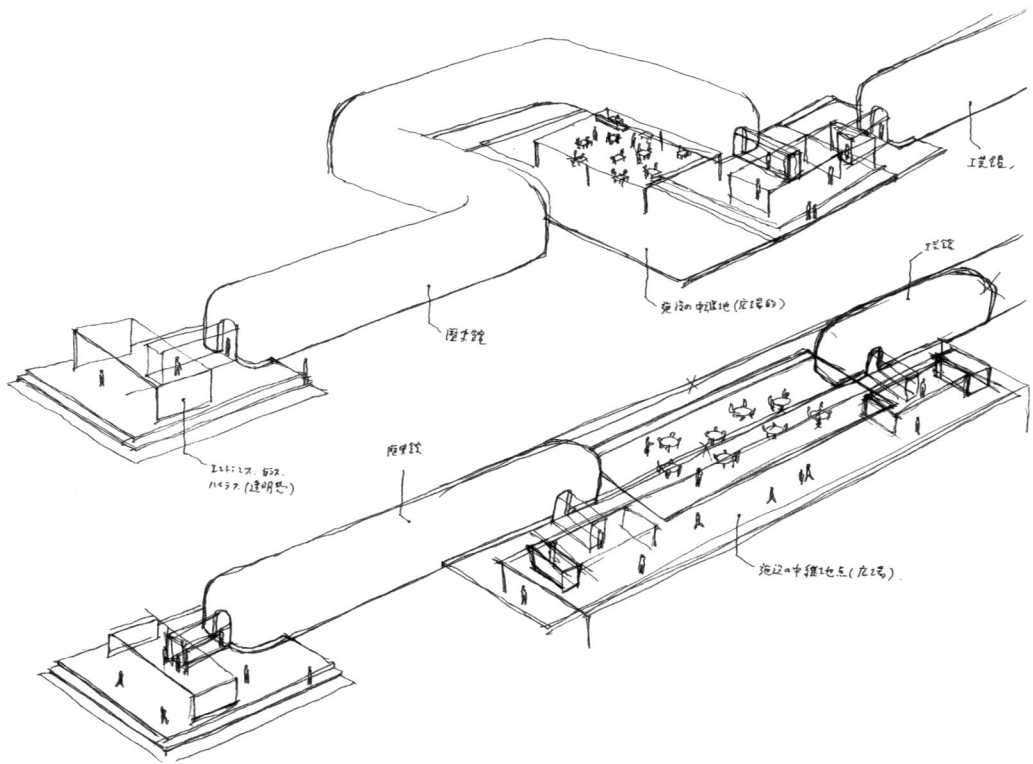

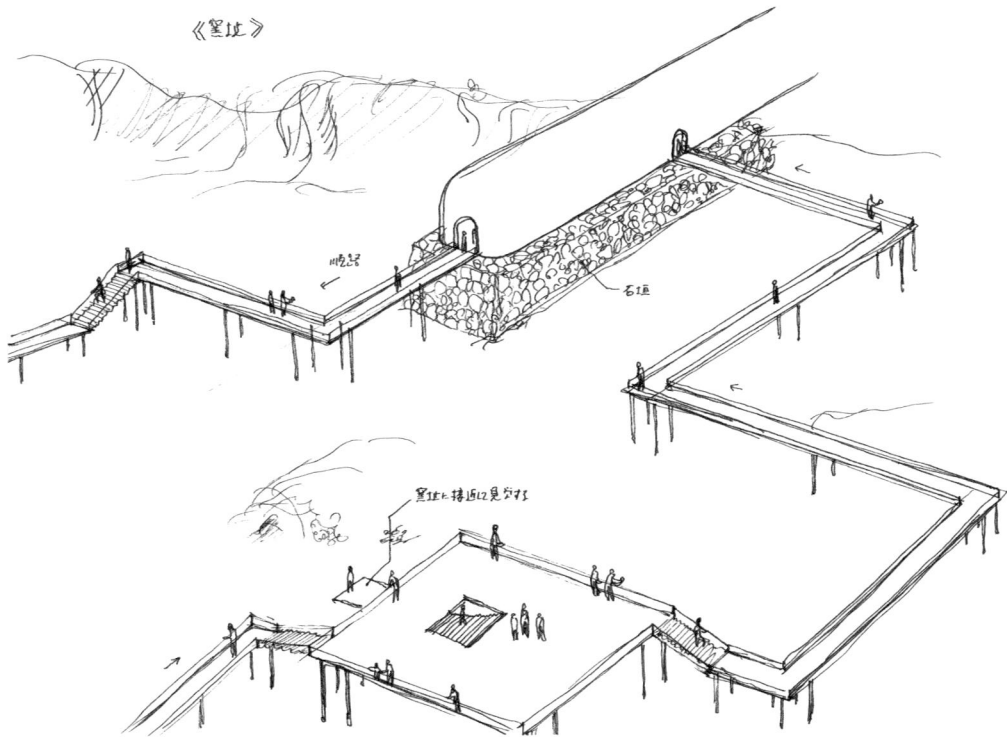

TOKYO FIBER '09
SENSEWARE

Poster for the "SENSEWARE" exhibition. In this exhibition, the medium that inspires the human creative spirit was dubbed "SENSEWARE." We liken this to stone in the Stone Age and paper, which aroused human motivation as a writing material. Here, man-made fibers are seen as a new SENSEWARE, providing creators with opportunities to make something new.

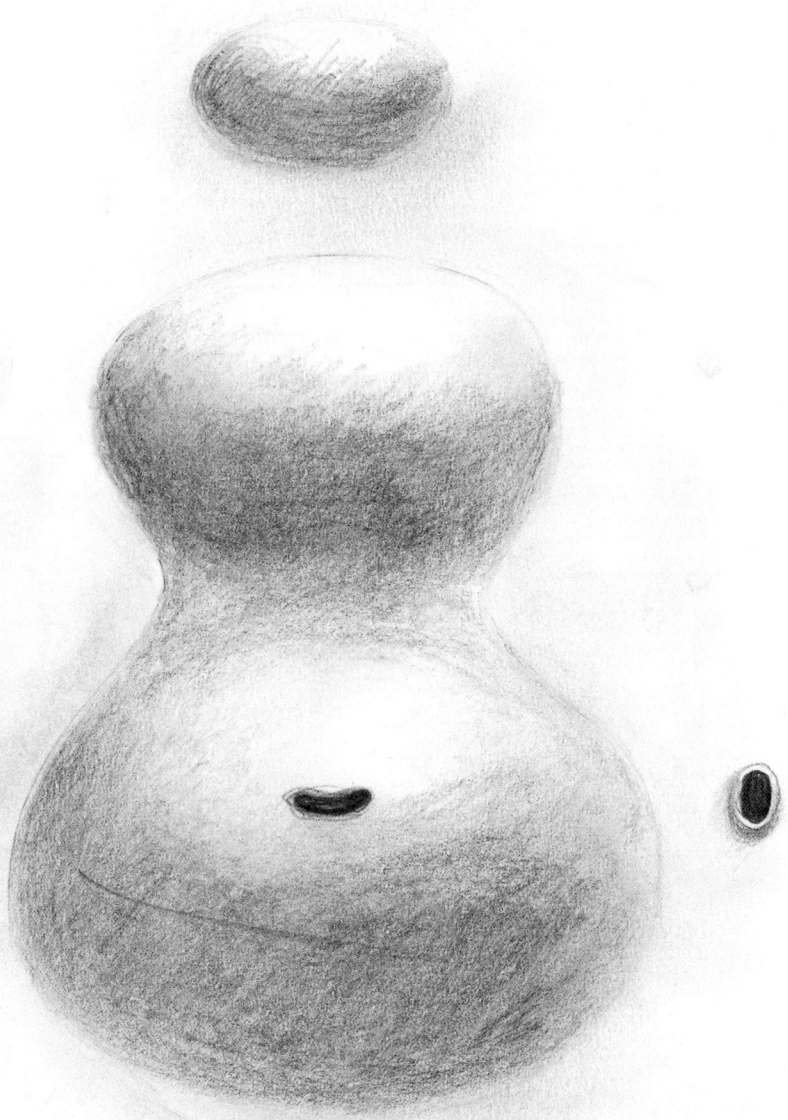

TOKYO FIBER '09
SENSEWARE

[the model of Brain and each organ]

These sketches were made at a time when I was thinking about the relationship between the sensory organs and images. Think of a human being as a ball. Our senses – sight, hearing, taste, smell, and touch – all operate on the membrane of the ball. Stimuli acquired on the membrane are then transmitted to the brain's core, where images are generated.

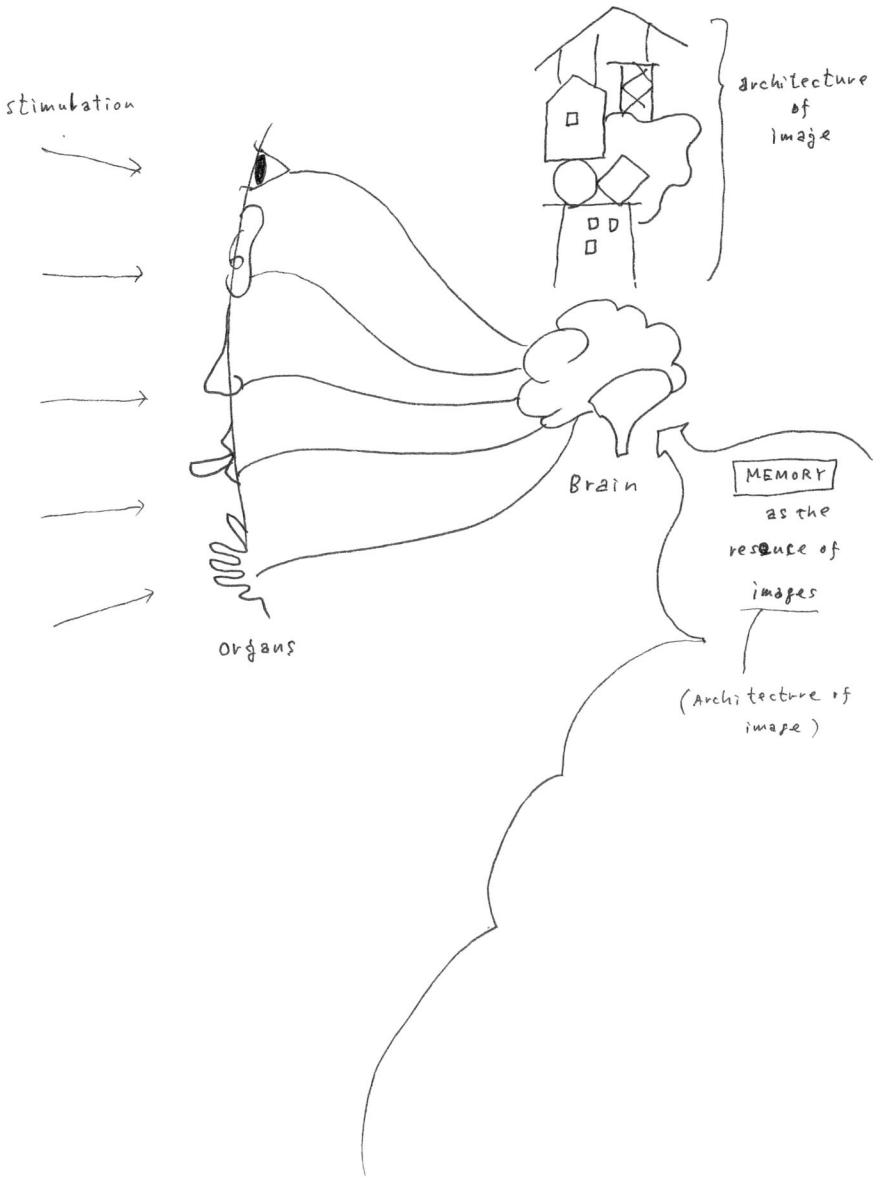

stimulation

architecture
of
Image

Brain

MEMORY
as the
resource of
images

Organs

(Architecture of
image)

The senses transmit stimuli to the brain, triggering the recall of
relevant memories from the brain's extensive storage. External stimuli
and recalled memories create an "architecture of images" in the brain.
Memory also serves as the material for these images.

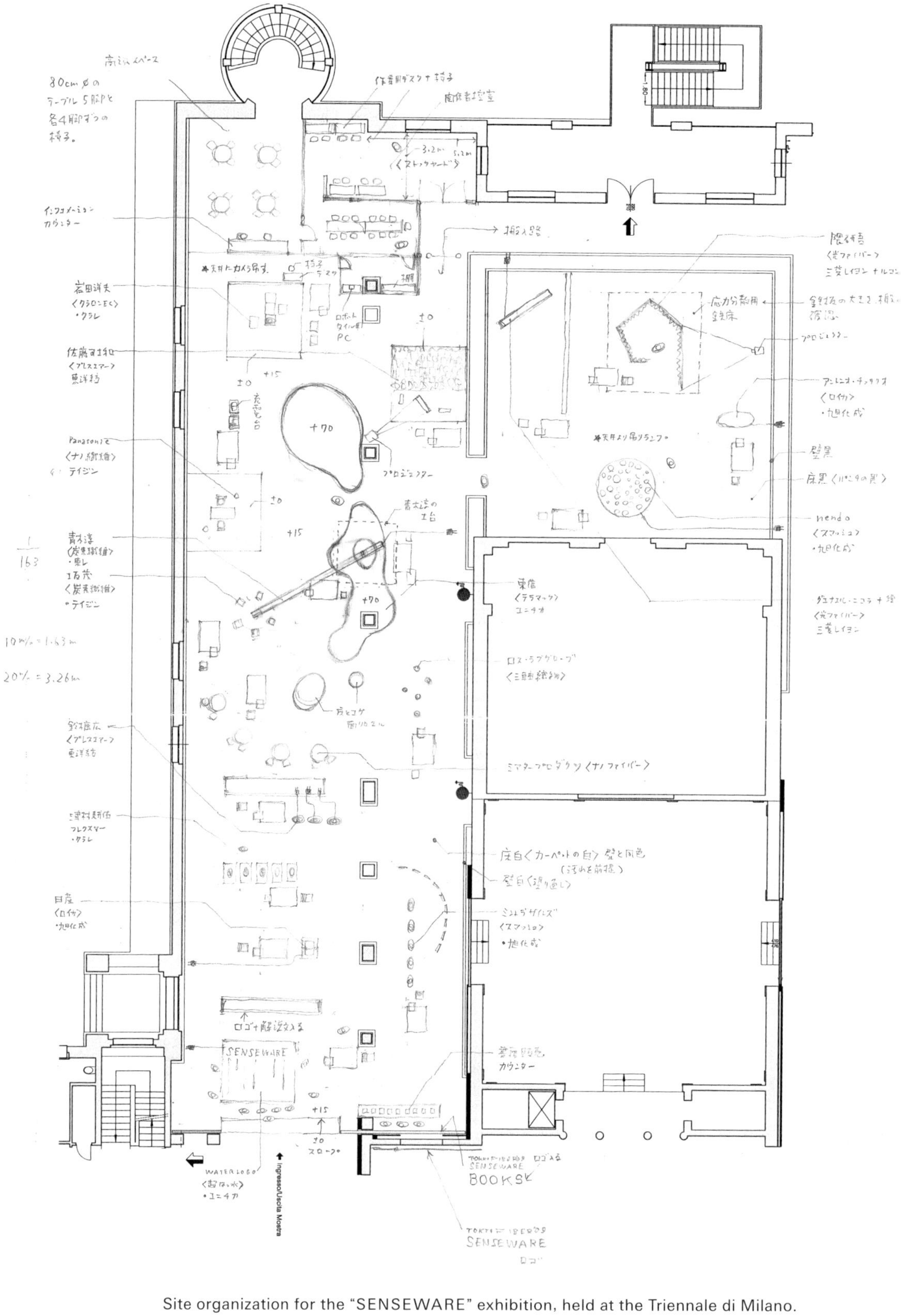

Site organization for the "SENSEWARE" exhibition, held at the Triennale di Milano.

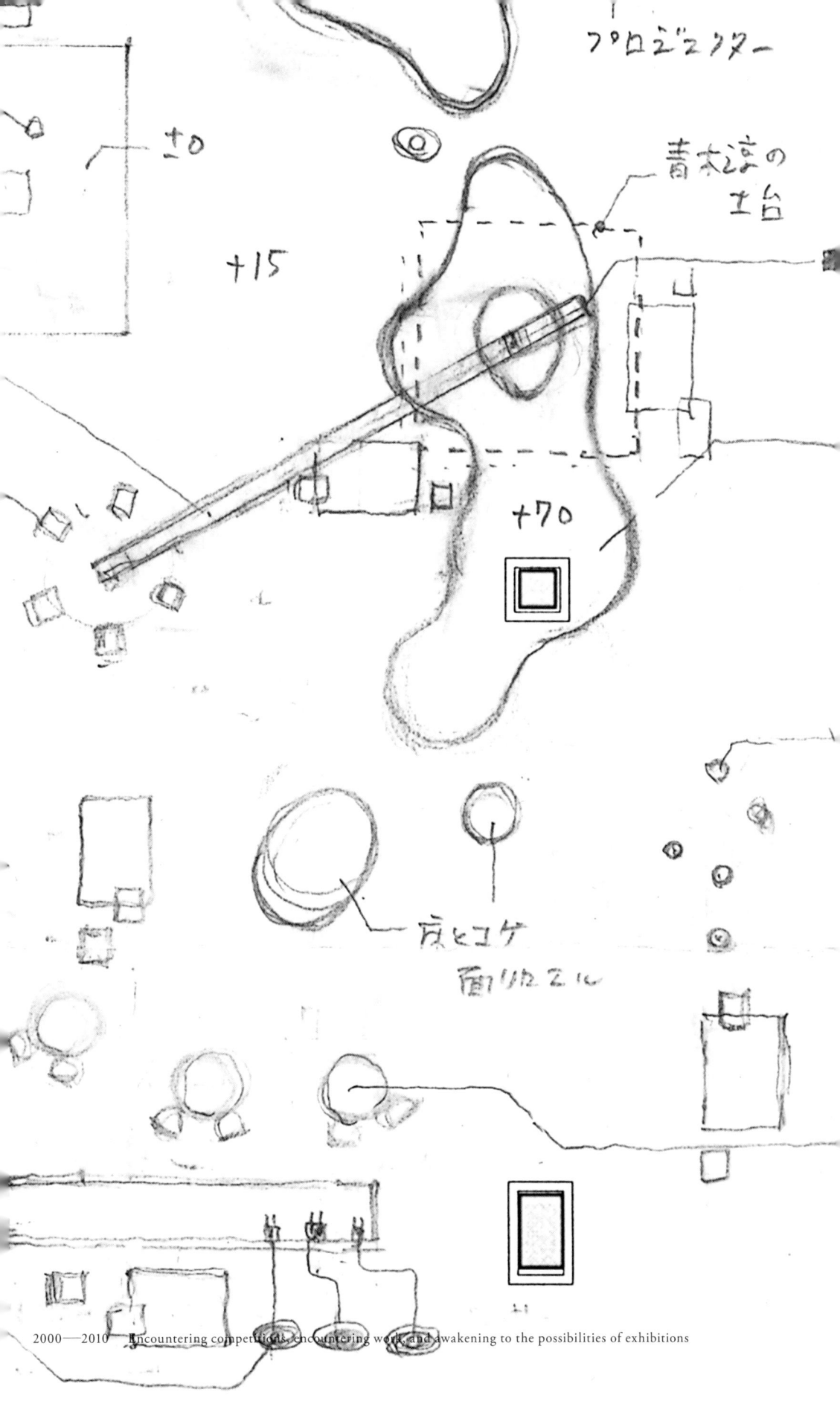

プロジェクター

青木淳の
工台

±0

+15

+70

灰とコケ
面りなそに

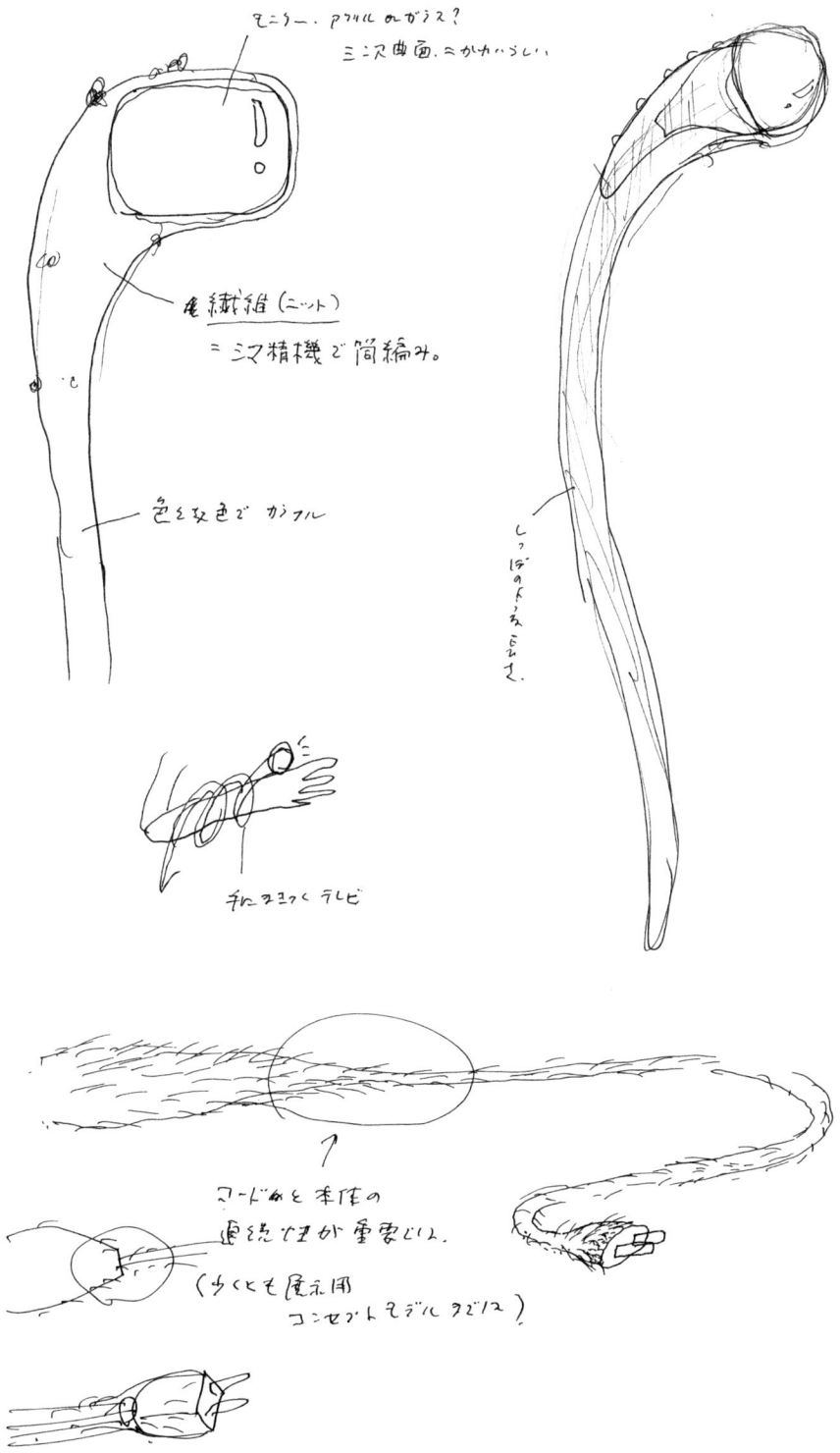

モニター、アクリルのガラス？
ミニ次曲面、ミかからしい

繊維（ニット）
＝シマ精機で筒編み。

色を変色で カブル

チにスゴツク テレビ

しっぽのような 長さ

コードめを本体の
連続性が重要どいう
（少くとも尾元用
コンセプトモデル 9212）

I collaborated with companies to generate ideas for products that stimulated the five senses.

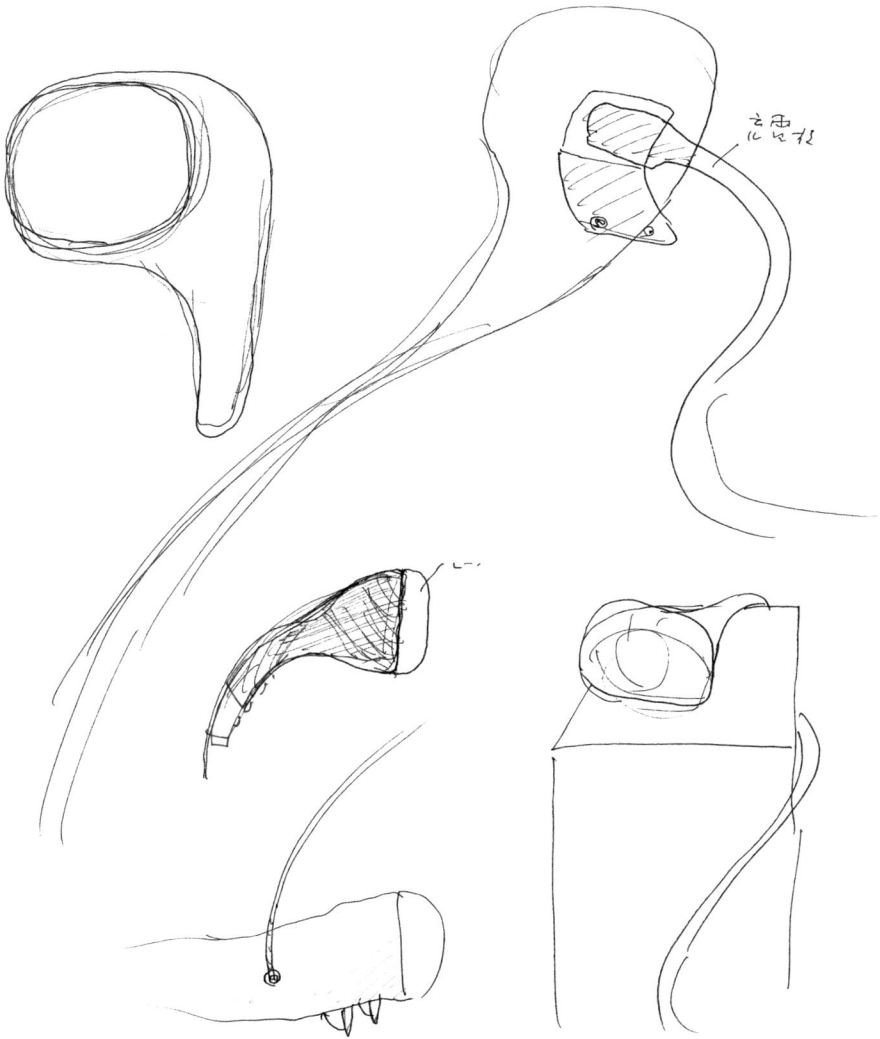

左思す

どっか動物的な / 普通の接器とは違う
接作部の感じがほしい。

ex: モのやに埋まっている スイッチの イメージ。
たとえば Fiberでおおわれていて
プラスターを触室が…とか…

《津村耕佑》フレクスター

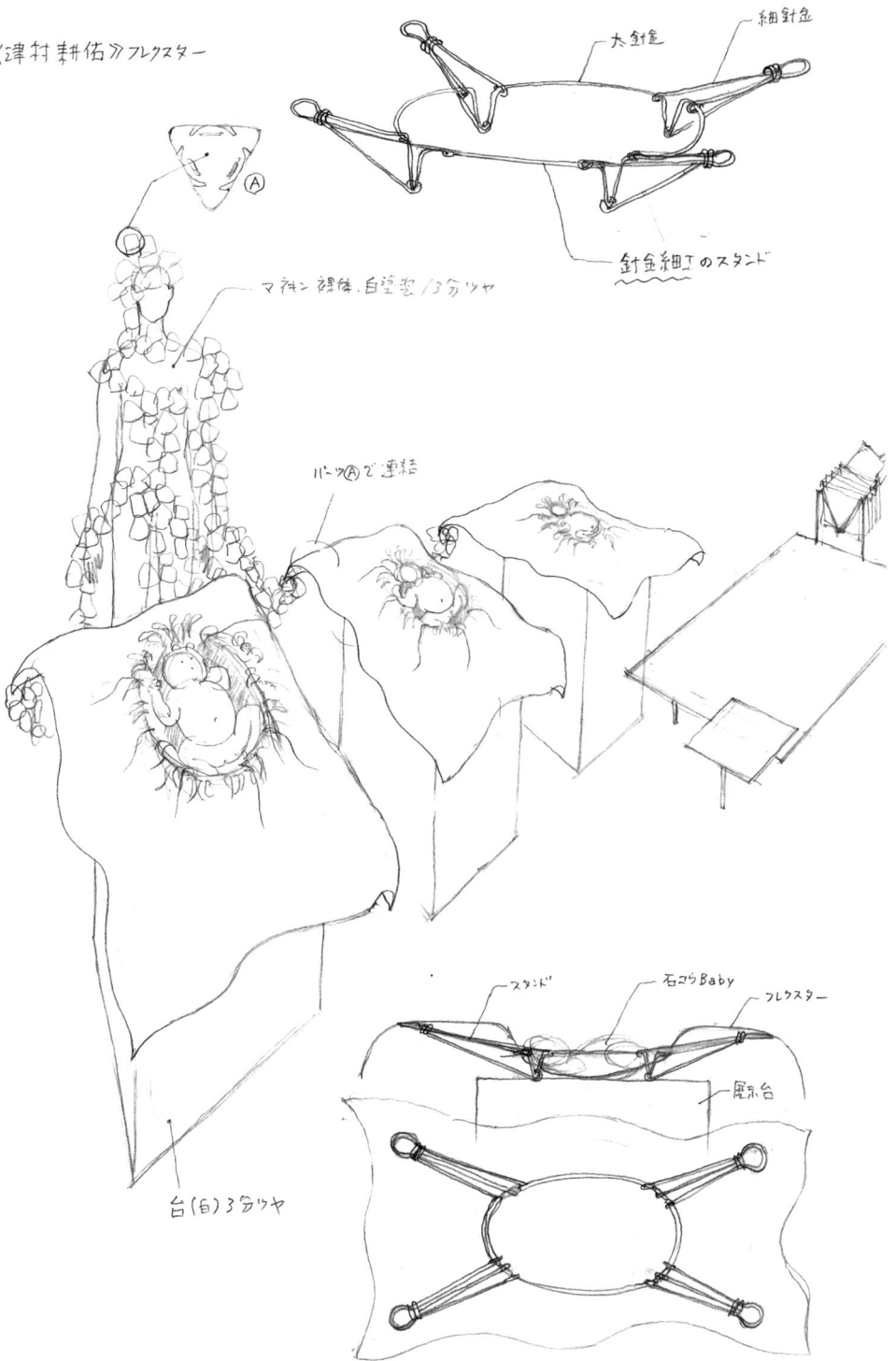

Ⓐ

大針金　細針金

針金細工のスタンド

マネキン胴体・白塗装・3分ツヤ

パーツⒶで連結

台(白)3分ツヤ

スタンド　石コウBaby　フレクスター

展示台

Sketches for the exhibition plan and moveables, resulting from
careful consideration of how best to display the creators' proposals.

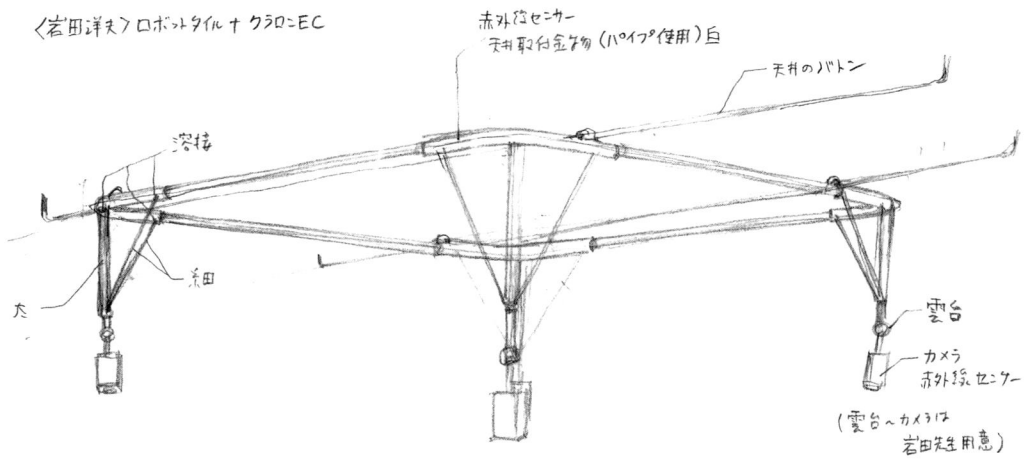

〈岩田洋夫〉ロボットタイル＋クラロニEC

溶接

細

大

赤外線センサー
天井取付金物（パイプ使用）白

天井のバトン

雲台

カメラ
赤外線センサー

（雲台〜カメラは
岩田先生用意）

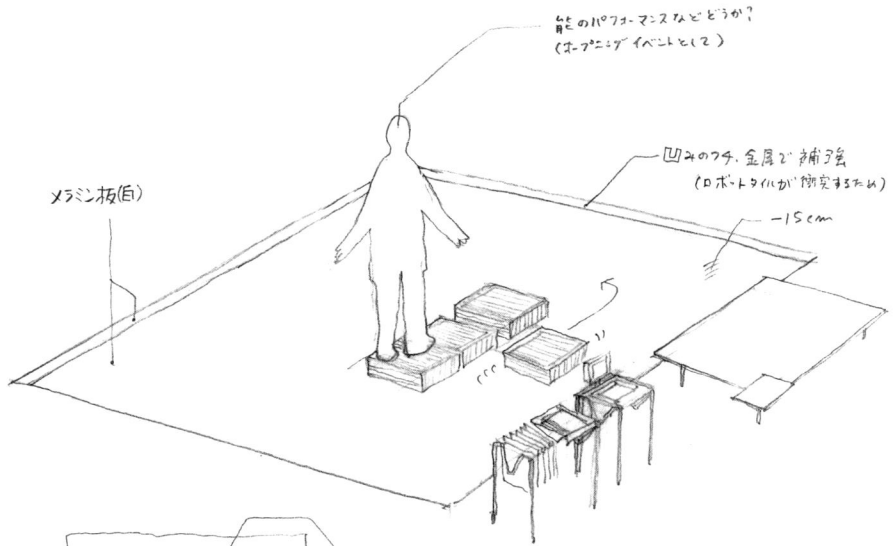

メラミン板（白）

能のパフォーマンスなどどうか？
（オープニングイベントとして）

凹みのフチ、金属で補強
（ロボットタイルが衝突するため）

ー15cm

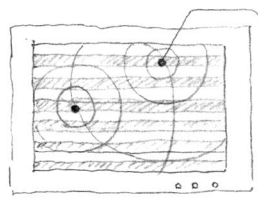

クラロニECを
指えで押すと、
モニター上に点と
波紋が現われる

布のキーボードの
ようなもの。
スイッチングデバイスの
撮影を解決する

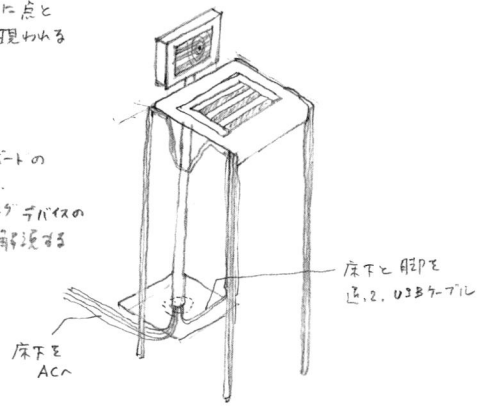

床下と脚を通、2、USBケーブル

床下を
ACへ

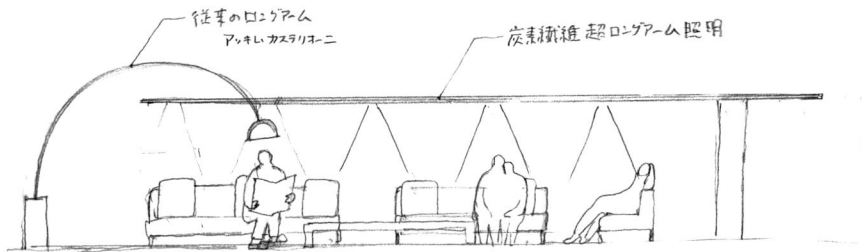

従来のロングアーム
アッキレ・カステリオーニ

炭素繊維 超ロングアーム照明

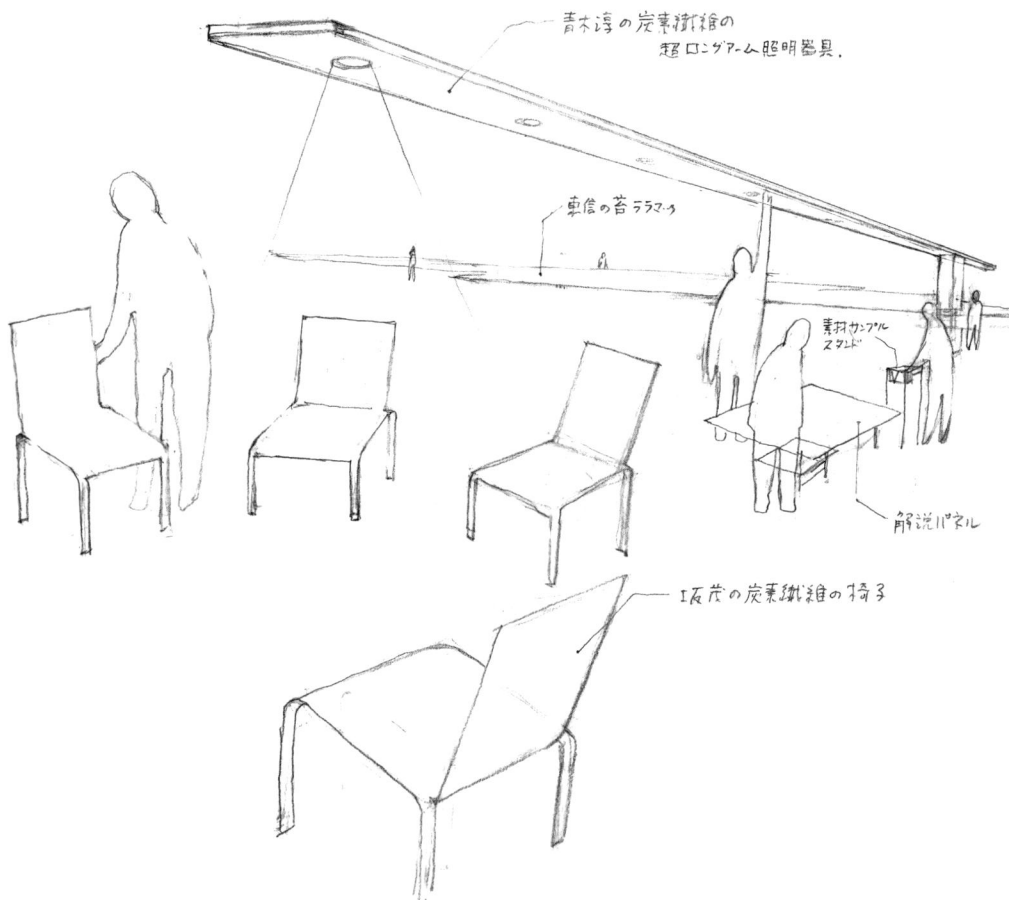

青木淳の炭素繊維の
超ロングアーム照明器具.

東信の苔 テラマック

素材サンプル
スタンド

解説パネル

工反芯の炭素繊維の椅子

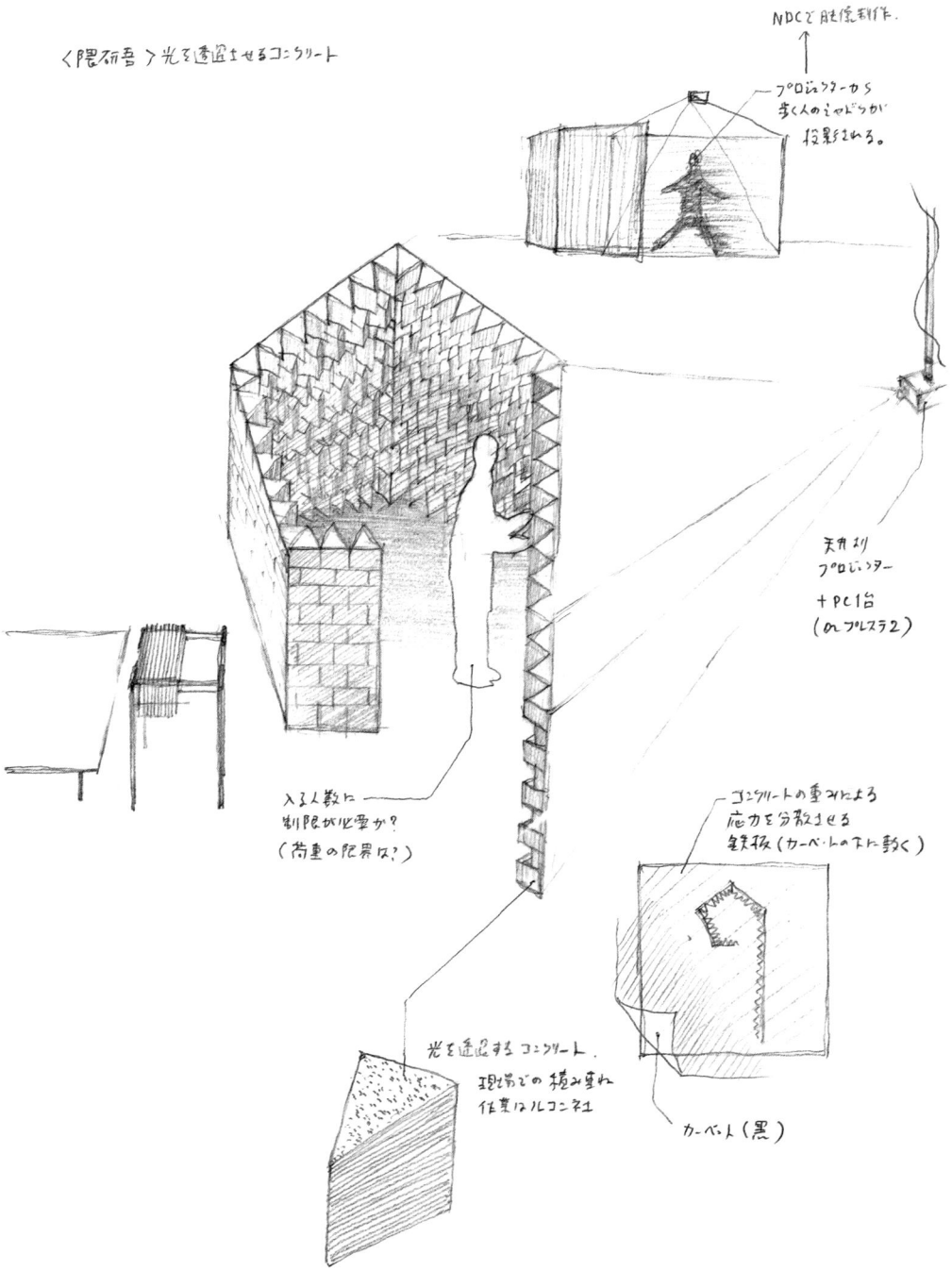

〈隈研吾〉光を透過させるコンクリート

NDCで映像制作.

プロジェクターから
歩く人のシルエットが
投影される。

天井吊り
プロジェクター
+PC1台
(のプレステラ2)

入る人数に
制限が必要か?
(荷重の限界は?)

コンクリートの重みによる
応力を分散させる
鉄板(カーペットの下に敷く)

光を透過するコンクリート.
現場での積み重ね
作業はルコン社

カーペット(黒)

〈 Panasonic 〉 拭き掃除ロボット

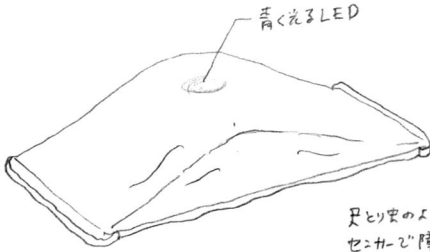

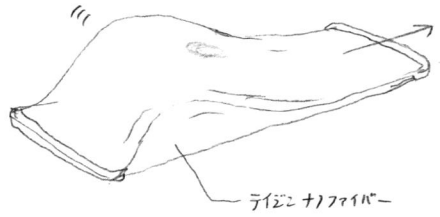

青く光るLED

テイジン ナノファイバー

尺とり虫のような動き？
センサーで障害物を感じて重きを変える。
留守中にフローリングの床をふいた拭き掃除をする。
ナノファイバーの ゴミ吸着力 / ロボットテクノロジー / 家電.

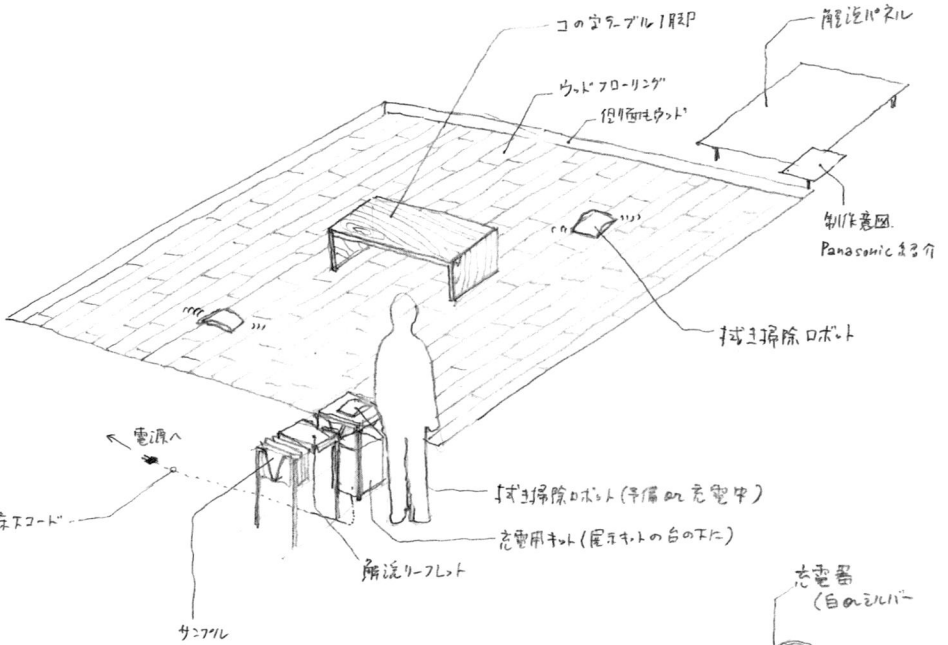

コの字テーブル１脚

ウッドフローリング

但仮面モキット

解説パネル

制作意図.
Panasonic紹介

拭き掃除ロボット

← 電源へ

床下コード

拭き掃除ロボット (予備の充電中)

充電用キット (展示キットの台の下に)

解説リーフレット

サンプル

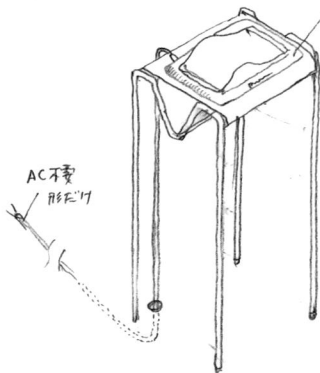

充電器

AC不要
形だけ

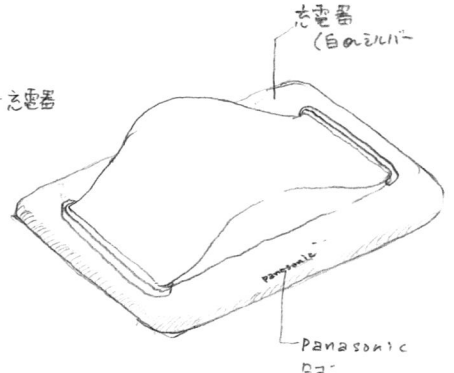

充電器
(白のシルバー

Panasonic
ロゴ

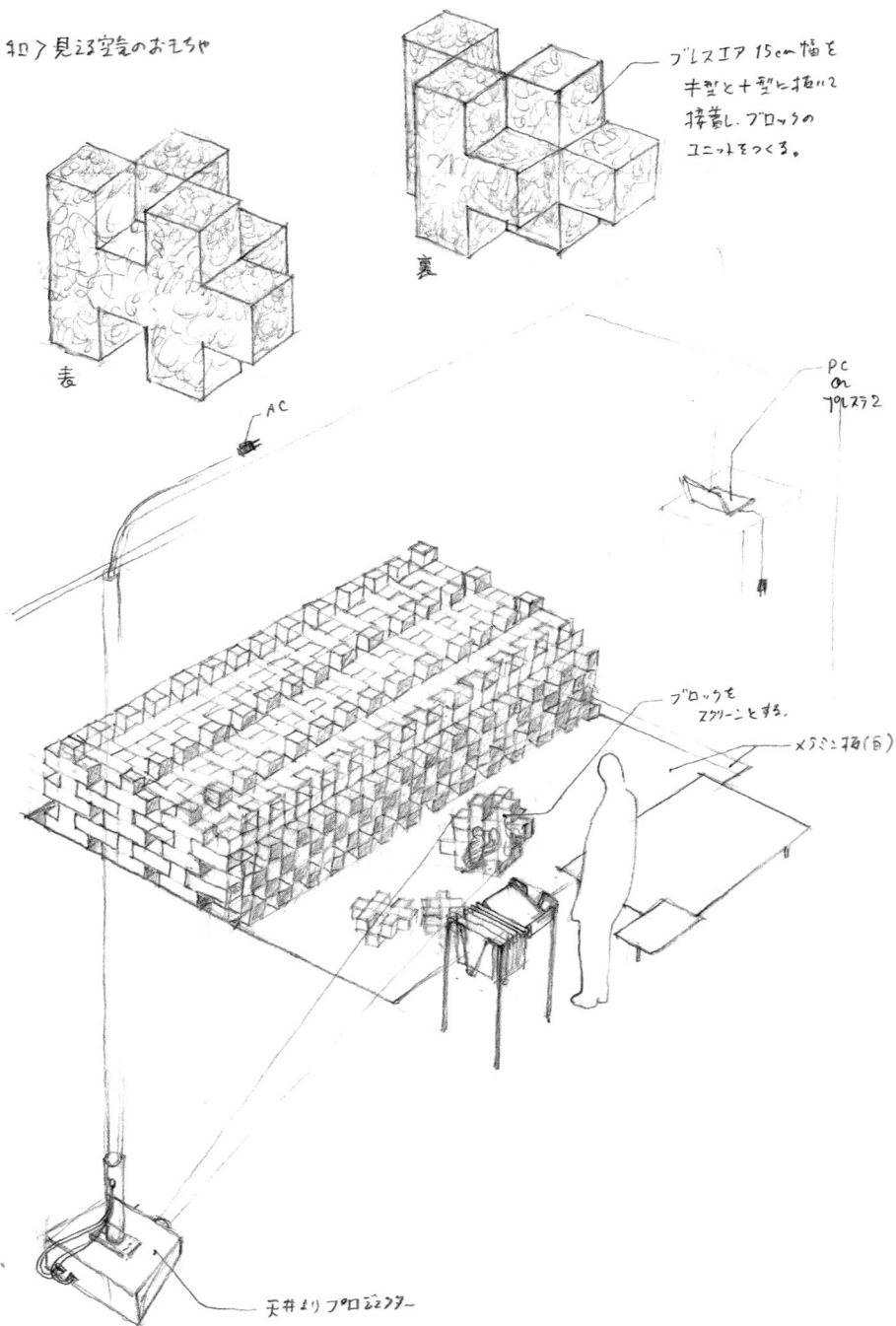

〈佐藤可士和〉見える空気のおもちゃ

ブレスエア 15cm 幅を
半型と十型に切りに
接着し、ブロックの
ユニットをつくる。

裏

表

AC

PC
on
プロジェクタ

ブロックを
スクリーンとする。

メラミン板(白)

天井よりプロジェクター

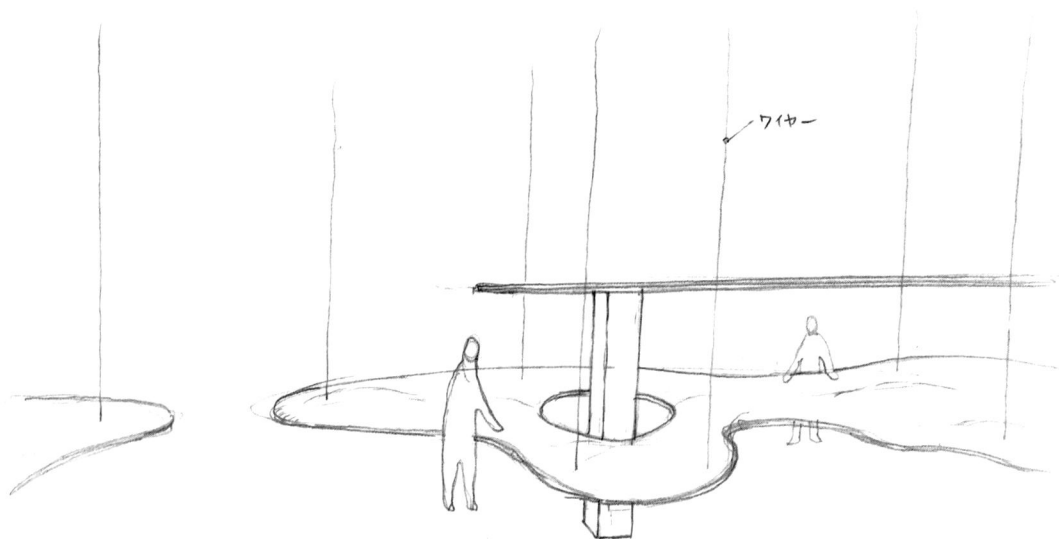

ワイヤー

青木誌.照明

+70cm

床と同じレベルに生苔を埋め込む

《Nendo》スマッシュ

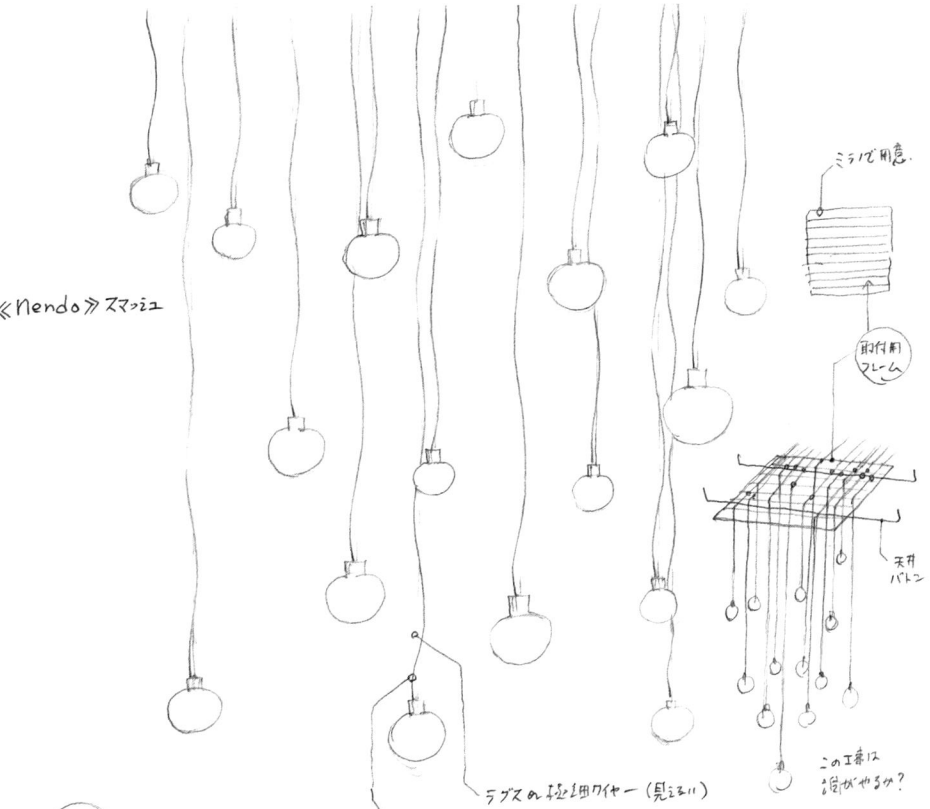

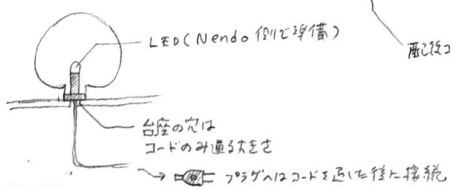

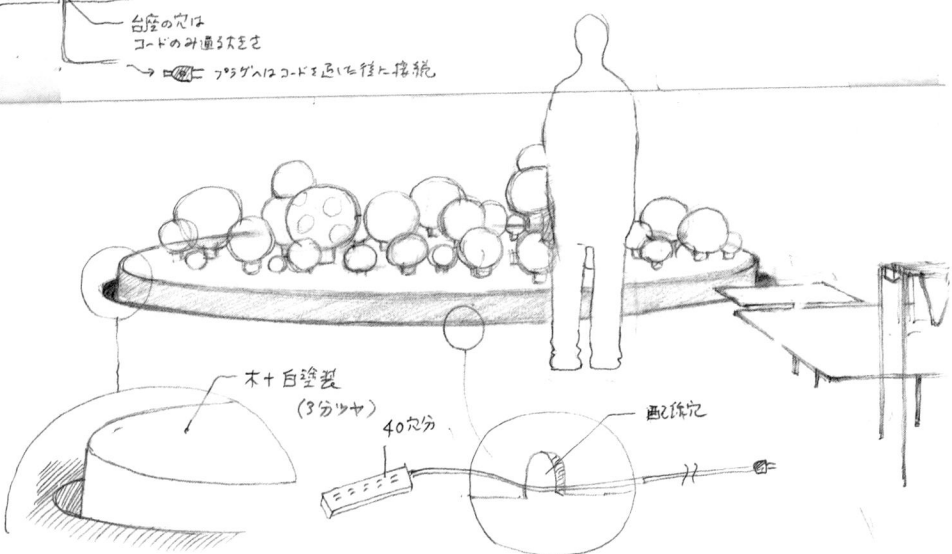

ミラノで用意

肘付用フレーム

天井バトン

この工夫は 何がやるか？

LED（Nendo 側で準備）

ラブスの極細ワイヤー（見える!!）

配役コード（見える）

台座の穴は
コードのみ通る大きさ
→ プラグへはコードを通した後に接続

木 + 白塗装
（3分ツヤ）

40灯分

配線記

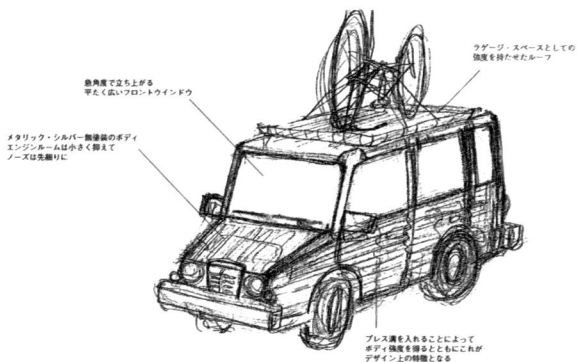

ラゲージ・スペースとしての
強度を持たせたルーフ

急角度で立ち上がる
平たく広いフロントウインドウ

メタリック・シルバー無塗装のボディ
エンジンルームは小さく抑えて
ノーズは先細りに

プレス溝を入れることによって
ボディ剛度を得るとともにこれが
デザイン上の特徴となる

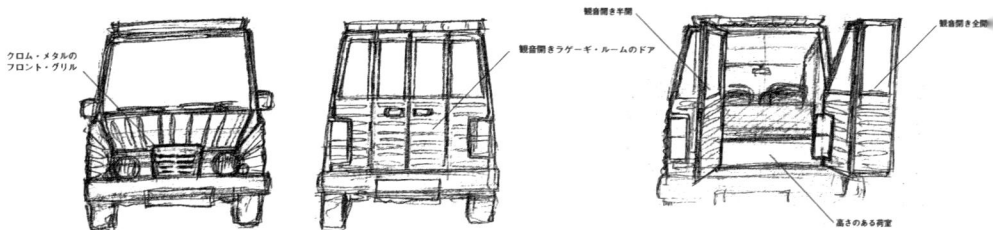

クロム・メタルの
フロント・グリル

観音開きラゲーギ・ルームのドア

観音開き半開

観音開き全開

高さのある荷室

取り替えの容易なヘッドレスト・カバー

取り替えの容易なヘッドレスト・カバー

2：居住性
外板のシンプルさに応えて、室内は落ち着きのある素材をシンプルに用いて簡潔にまとめたい。

リア・シートの備品としての
クッション

I envisioned a car that could be sprayed with a hose and scrubbed with a deck brush.
Thinking that it could be made out of aluminum or Duralumin, an age-hardenable
aluminum alloy, I made these sketches at the beginning planning stage.
If I drove, this is the kind of car I'd want.

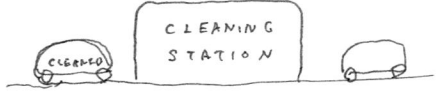

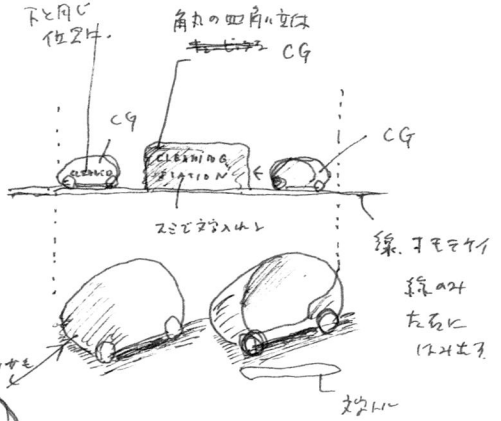

CLEANING STATION

CLEARED

CG

CLEANING STATION

CLEANED

Apparently, in Europe, cars that have abandoned a sense of speed and aerodynamic design are known as "underdog cars." I think it's fine for cars to be underdogs or losers. I don't like cars with stern expressions or bulging eyes. This is the right feeling for electric cars that cover the shortest distances quickly even at low speeds.

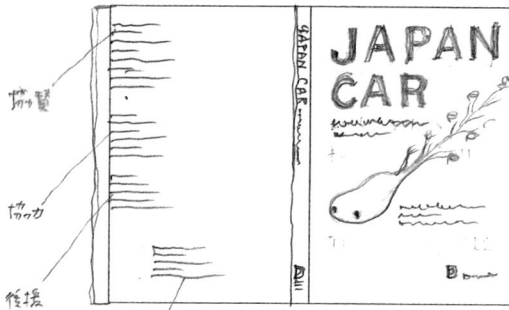

カバー表4　　カバー表1

摺り箔

ザラザラ

箔援

含浸，含糊

JAPAN CAR

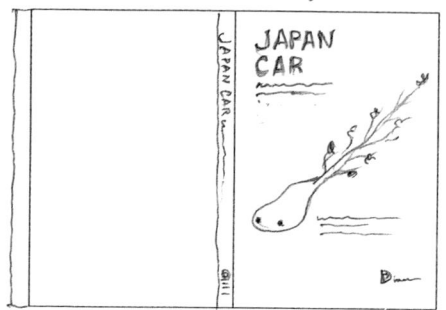

表4　　表1

JAPAN CAR

4　　　　　　　5

S. MUSEUM
アンドリュー
あいさつ

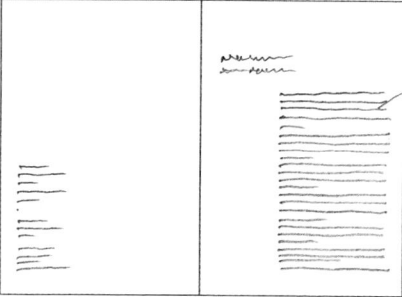

6　　　　　　　7

広告企

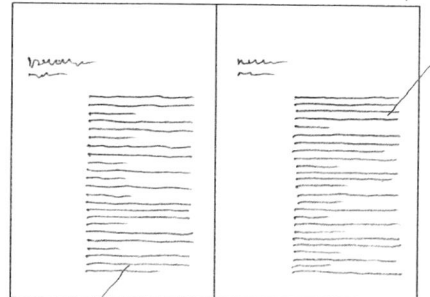

協賛，あいさつ

12　　都市（夜景）俯瞰　　13

1: Small

盆栽

都市
＋
道路の
夜景

14　　　　　　　15

魚ふ

タント

20　　　　　　　21

住宅街の
津田川度

22　　　　　　　23

ロダ

昆日

iQ

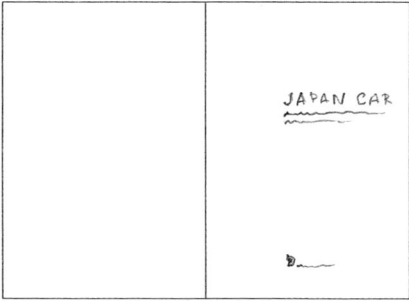

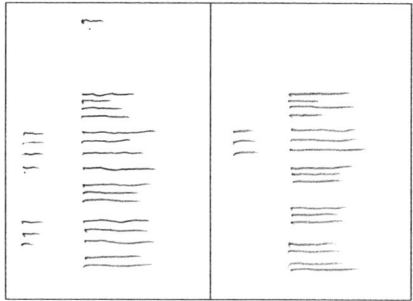

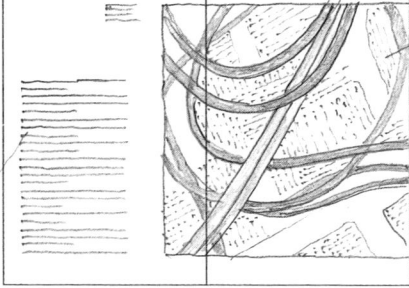

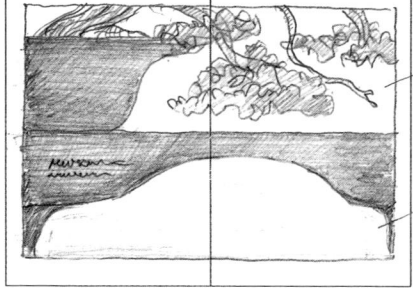

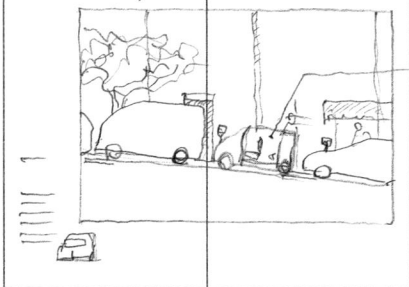

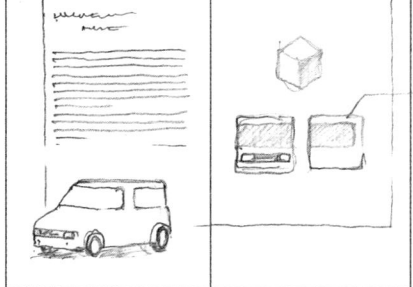

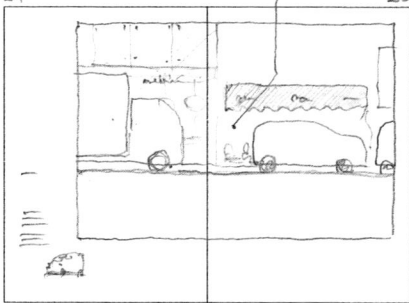

I designed the JAPAN CAR exhibition with the architect Shigeru Ban. It was held at the Science Museums in Paris and London in 2008–2009. This initiative resulted from consulting with the leaders of the design departments of Japan's main car manufacturers.

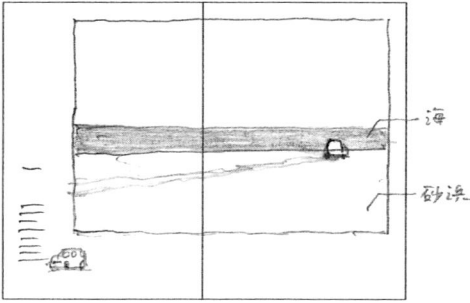

海

砂浜

ハイゼット

コペン

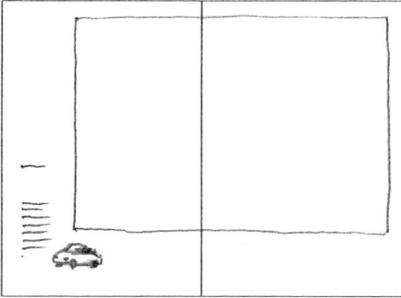

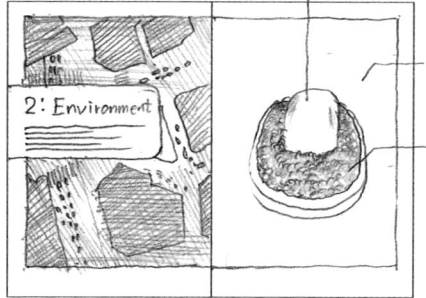

クルマ模型（i-Miev）

2: Environment

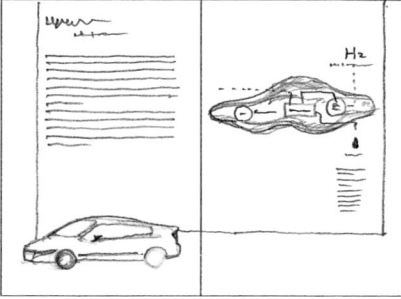

FCX

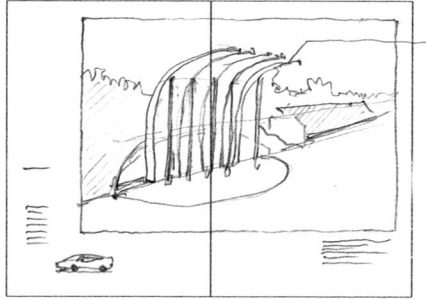

H_2

32　33　34　35

トラクター
あぜ道
田や畑

ディアテ・スジック
（デザイン評論家/英）

40　41　42　43

ユーノスロードスター

48　49　50　51

インサイト

アザラシ

56　57　58　59

i-Miev

充電口
アップ

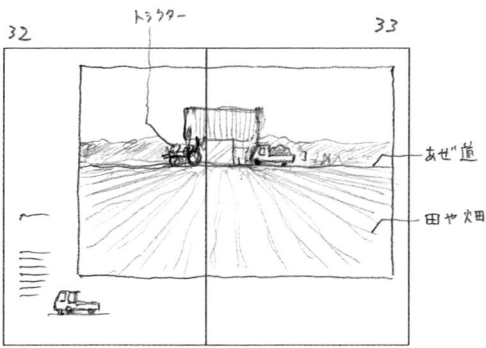

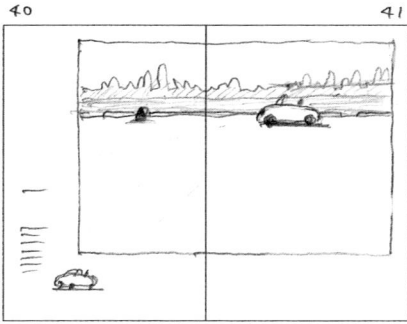

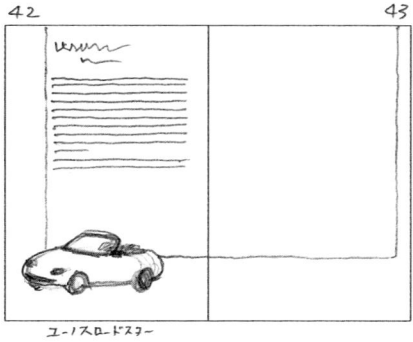

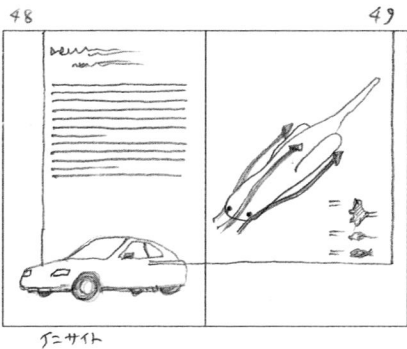

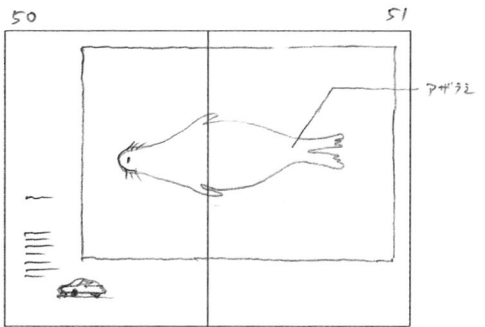

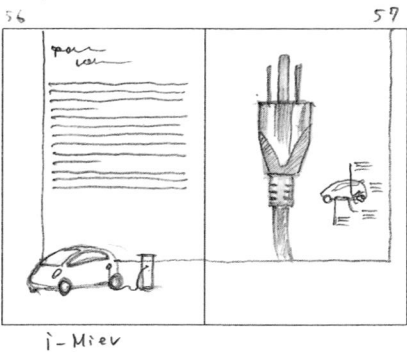

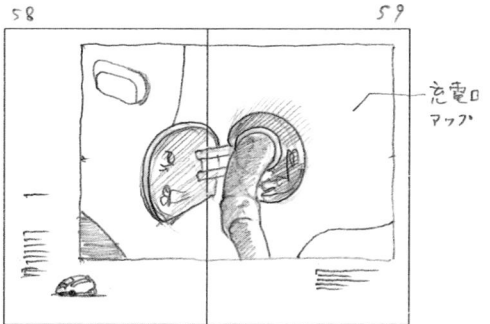

The Japanese auto manufacturers Toyota, Nissan, Honda, Mitsubishi, Daihatsu, Suzuki, and Mazda displayed pieces in the JAPAN CAR exhibition. Because of the depth of collaboration and the corporate scale of the collaborators, it required a ridiculous amount of energy to get to this point. There were three themes: Smallness, Environmental Technology and The Rise of Traveling Urban Cells. The Japanese cars of 2009 clearly looked as if they were from the future.

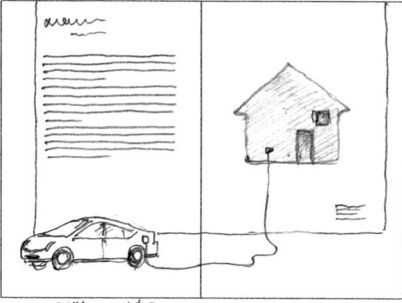

60 61

プラグイン・プリウス

62 63

茂木健一郎（脳科学者/日）

68 69

70 71

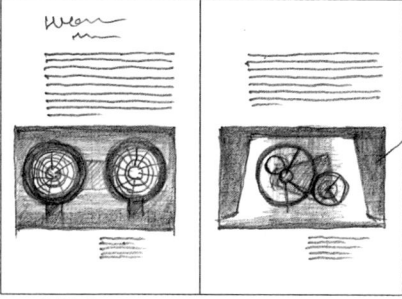

76 77

DENSO

左右とき
タコ/スピード
メーター・
裏タイニフラフ
ミョ乙

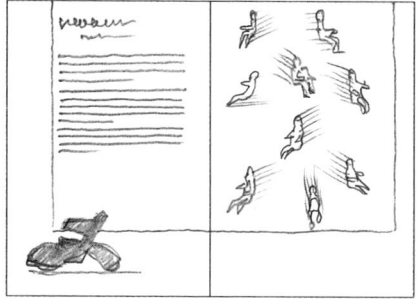

78 79

i-Real

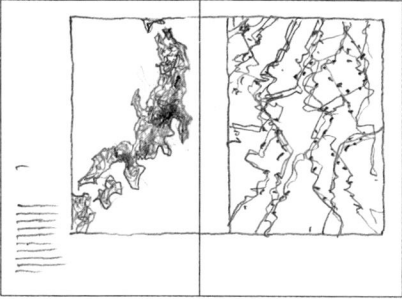

84 85

GPSが描くクルマ

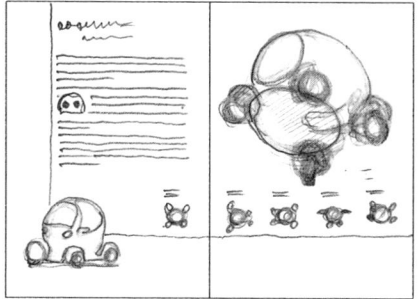

86 87

Pivo 2

In the midst of transitions such as that from to motors and from fossil fuels to electricity, the very nature of cars is changing. With this exhibition, we predicted new divisions in the car industry, led by factors like driving vs. mobile, city vs. nature, and public vs. personal, replacing the traditional demarcation between passenger cars and commercial vehicles.

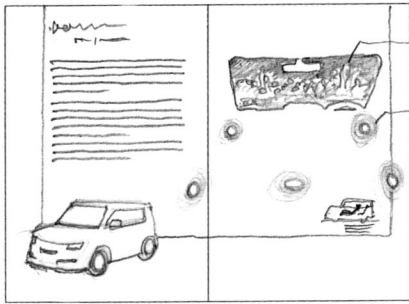

64　65

夜景
(抽象)

音
イルミネーション

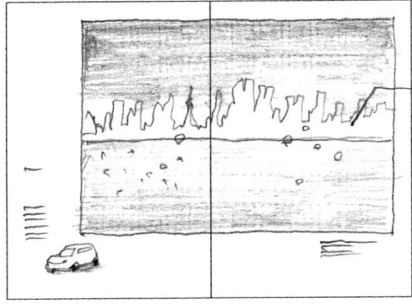

66　67

東京の夜景

6B
72　脳の血管　73

3: Mobile Cell

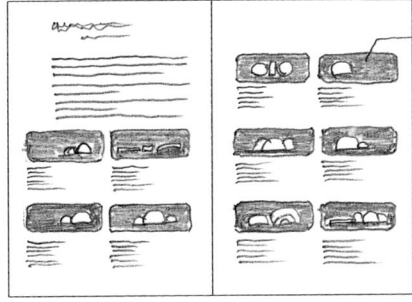

74　75

スピード
メーター
10に
絞る

80　81

コミュニケーション
のコンセプト

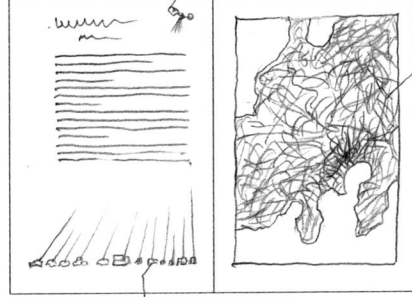

82　人工衛星　83

GPSで
とびきた
クルマ
ニ
毛細血管

HITACHI　様々なクルマ

88　89

顔の表情を読み取る
インターフェイスのロボット

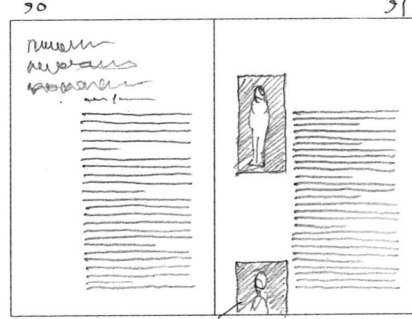

90　91

ジャン・ヌーベル (建築家/仏)

ART HOUSE PROJECT

BENESSE HOUSE
NAOSHIMA

ACCESS TO THE SETOUCHI
INTERNATIONAL ART FES. ZONE

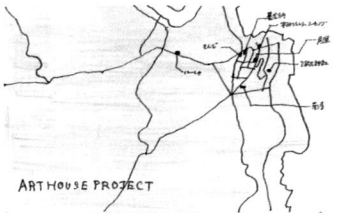

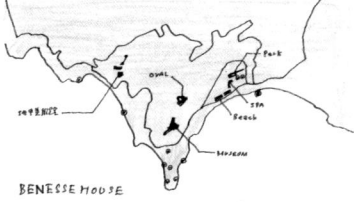

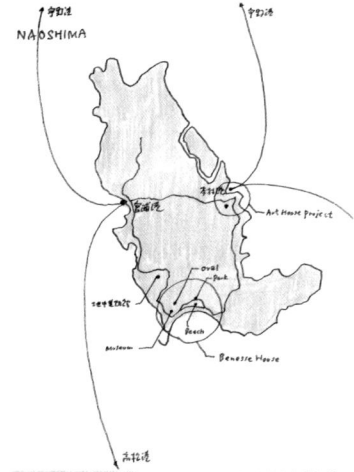

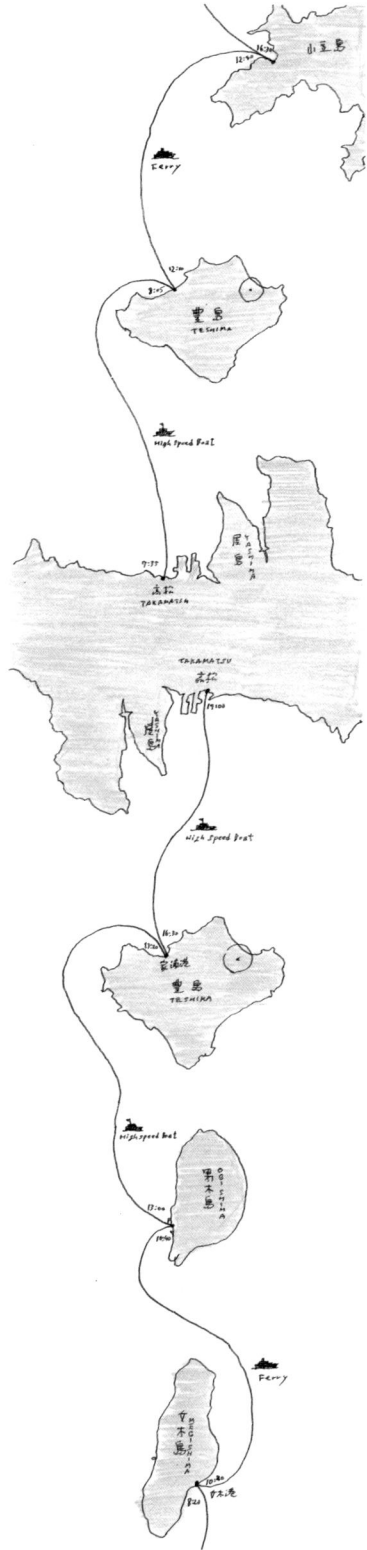

This image of islands hopping spontaneously came to mind
when I was asked to work on the Setouchi Triennale, a contemporary art festival.

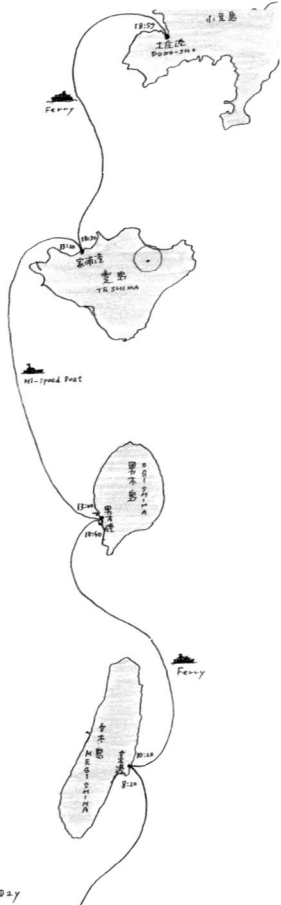

The second day (PLAN B-1)

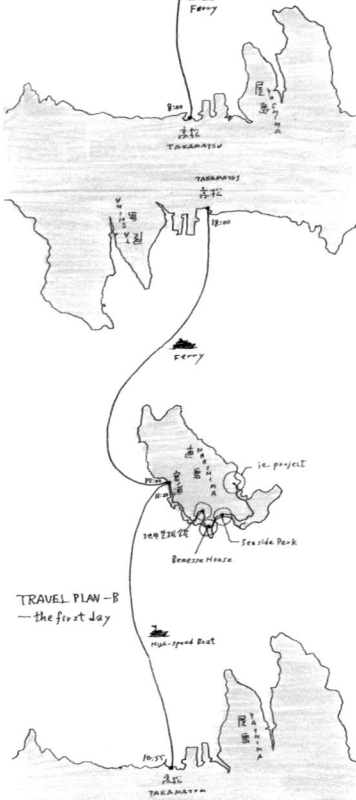

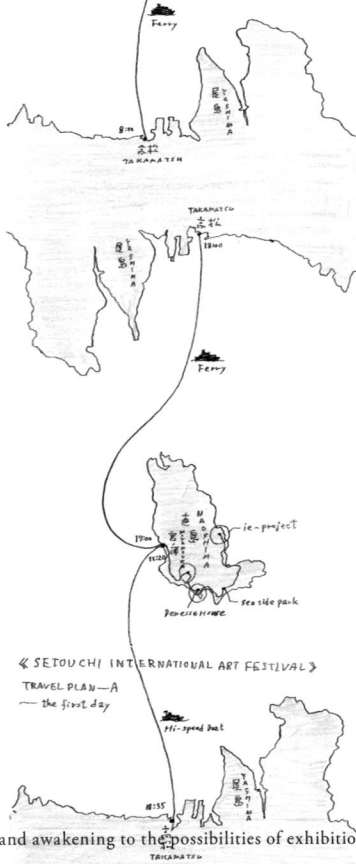

Ferry

TAKAMATSU
高松

TRAVEL PLAN-B
— the first day

Hi-speed Boat

ie-project

Benesse House
Seaside Park

TAKAMATSU
高松

CRUISE 2010

SETOUCHI INTERNATIONAL ART FESTIVAL

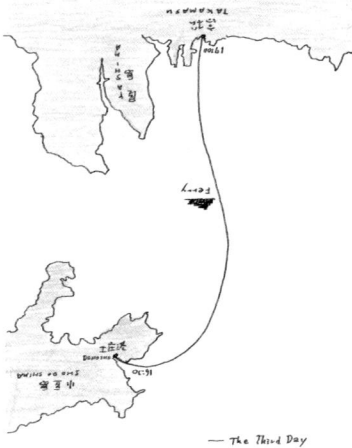

TAKAMATSU
高松

Ferry

土庄港
Dodo-sho

— The Third Day

小豆島

土庄港
Dodo-sho

Ferry

豊島
TESHIMA

Hi-speed Boat

男木島
OGISHIMA

Ferry

女木島
MEGISHIMA

The Second Day

Ferry

TAKAMATSU
高松

TAKAMATSU
高松

Ferry

ie-project

Benesse House
sea side park

《SETOUCHI INTERNATIONAL ART FESTIVAL》
TRAVEL PLAN—A
— the first day

Hi-speed Boat

TAKAMATSU

I continue to work on label design for Grace Wine in Yamanashi Prefecture.
The product, Koshu, made from a white grape variety known as Koshu, is already highly
acclaimed worldwide. This is the label design for a sparkling wine made from Chardonnay grapes.

2010—2020

HOUSE VISION, Architecture for Dogs,
journey to Earth / other worlds

People have never created architecture for anyone other than humans. Therefore, architecture made to put the scale of other animals in relation to human scale remains revolutionary. And yet people from all cultural spheres on the planet know of dogs. So what if you asked talented architects from around the world to design architecture for dogs, put together the results in actual size, and held an exhibition – and then created a site publishing the plans and construction videos, making these internationally accessible? A friend came along who was willing to finance and collaborate on this Architecture for Dogs project, and the exhibition became a reality. This book includes my sketches for this project.

Around 2010 I became interested in the concept of the house or home, that is, in the dwellings that constitute the basis of our daily life. I've always been a fan of architecture, but in this case, it was not just the architecture of home or house that interested me. I thought that enterprises and human resources that forecast the future should turn their attention to the house as a crossroads of industry, a place where many potentialities and social issues converge, including energy, travel, logistics, telecommunications, health care, community, and elder society.

So I thought if we created an exhibition for a full-size house unlike any seen before, in which business and architects and creators collaborated, there might emerge an event that would allow us to foresee the future. I rented a huge space and financed the exhibition myself. It's my theory that Japan and the rest of Asia should focus on design via the platform of the house. This concept was the basis of the exhibition HOUSE VISION, held in 2013 and 2016 in Tokyo, 2018 in Beijing, and 2022 in Seoul. I wooed exhibitors, paired architects with corporations, built more than a dozen full-sized buildings, and set admission fees. My goal was for all of the participants, industries and creators alike, to collaborate on creating an awareness of the future.

In order to advance the project, at a certain stage, I needed to draw a detailed rough sketch of the book, in order to understand the architecture and its functions and to examine how they would be presented. Only by contemplating the content through sketches while editing them into a book can I function as an exhibition director. I assume this is the same as an orchestra conductor taking a period of several months to load all of the sheet music into his or her mind.

Meanwhile, the Tokyo Olympics were held again, and something akin to ambition stirred in my mind. Once again I created a new image for the Tokyo Olympics through an abundance of sketches. I chose a selection of these sketches for this book. Because this is a global festival, an event that condenses immeasurable energy, my concern was how best to express the enormous passion of the event, akin to magma. It is the golden age of motion / action visuals, but the life of a symbol lies in its ability to still the moving world. My proposal was the runner-up.

The 2017 exhibition "NEO-PREHISTORY—100 Verbs" at Triennale di Milano was commissioned by Andrea Cancellato, director of the ADI Museum in Milan. He wanted me to collaborate with architect Andrea Branzi to create a landmark exhibition on history. While it was a great honor to team up with Andrea Branzi, an architect known for his unique intelligence and the broad range of his activities, I was also quite apprehensive about the idea of group work. However, we clicked from our very first meeting. We immediately agreed upon the idea of viewing the present from the grand perspective of ancient times. So we paired verbs, acting as metaphors for desire, with man-made tools, and decided on a proposal for an exhibition of 100 pairs of verbs & tools from the Stone Age to the present. It was a great relief to us to be able to exhibit, with the support of many of Italy's museums, precious historic artifacts. At the same time, through this exhibition, I truly recognized that the civilization in which humans transformed the environment by making tools with their hands is coming to an end.

In my work for MUJI, I have aimed to provide a global perspective on contemporary life. This has involved capturing photos of alpacas in the Andes and filming on location in Iceland on the theme of natural materials, as well as taking pictures of coral reefs and land as a unified scene in Indonesia's Raja Ampat Islands exploring the theme of Earth's colors. In 2016, accompanied by a biologist, I visited the Galapagos Islands and gazed at nature devoid of humans. Nature without humans was pure and beautiful, but this young, rough nature, despite its raw and unsophisticated beauty, felt like something was missing.

In 2018–2019, for a large-scale campaign, "Cleaning: Pleasant, Somehow," which included a TV commercial, I traveled around the world. The research was done before COVID-19 swept the globe, but development proceeded during the pandemic. Cleaning is a human activity adjacent to the activities comprising daily life, and when I lined up scenes of cleaning from around the world, I experienced strangely powerful emotions. I felt that I had created a viable and universal message that aligns with the MUJI philosophy.

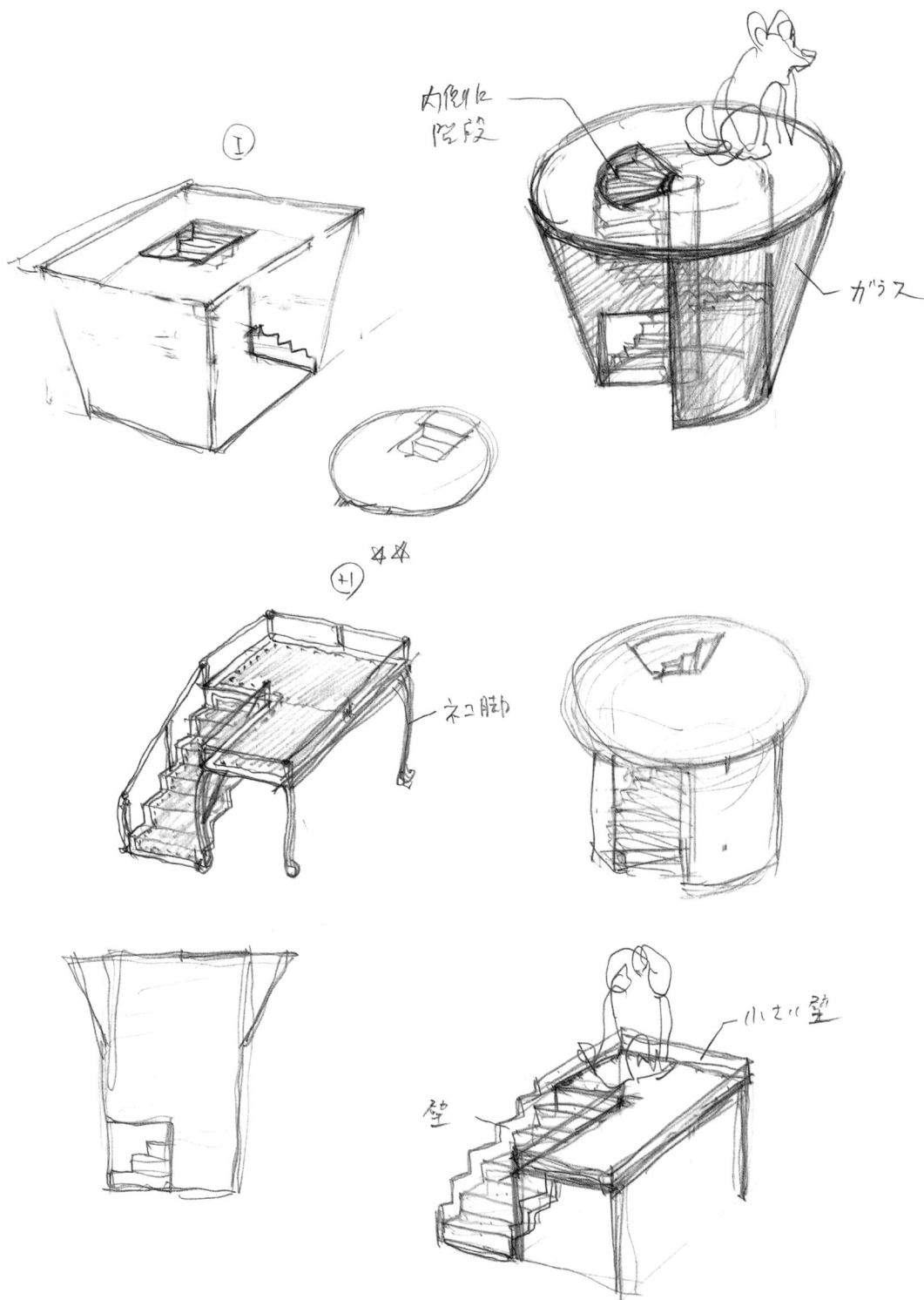

I

内側に
階段

ガラス

ネコ脚

小さい壁

壁

For many years, I had been mulling over the idea of "architecture for dogs." This is not a proposal for cute or interesting dog houses. Because architecture for non-human living beings had not been made, it was groundbreaking to seriously consider architecture on the scale of animals.

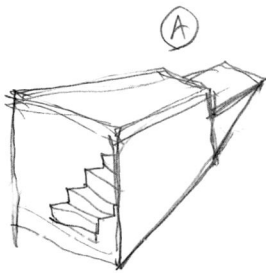

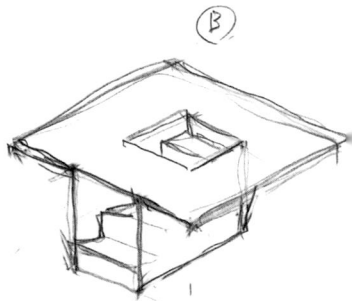

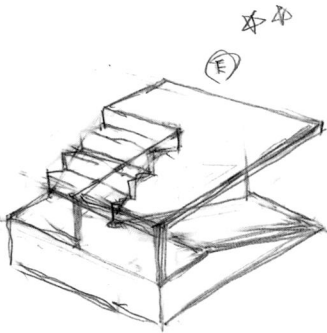

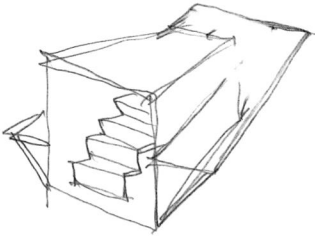

DogTower

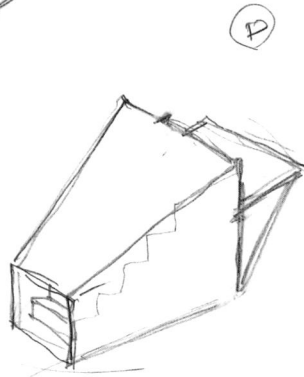

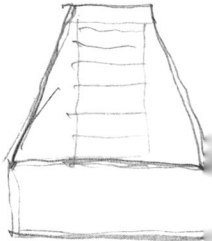

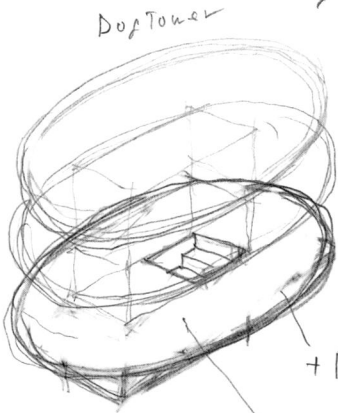

＋階屋に

階段コニット

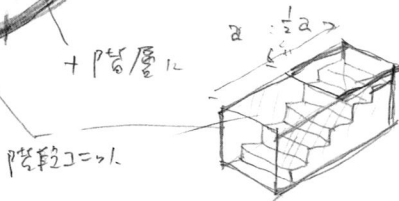

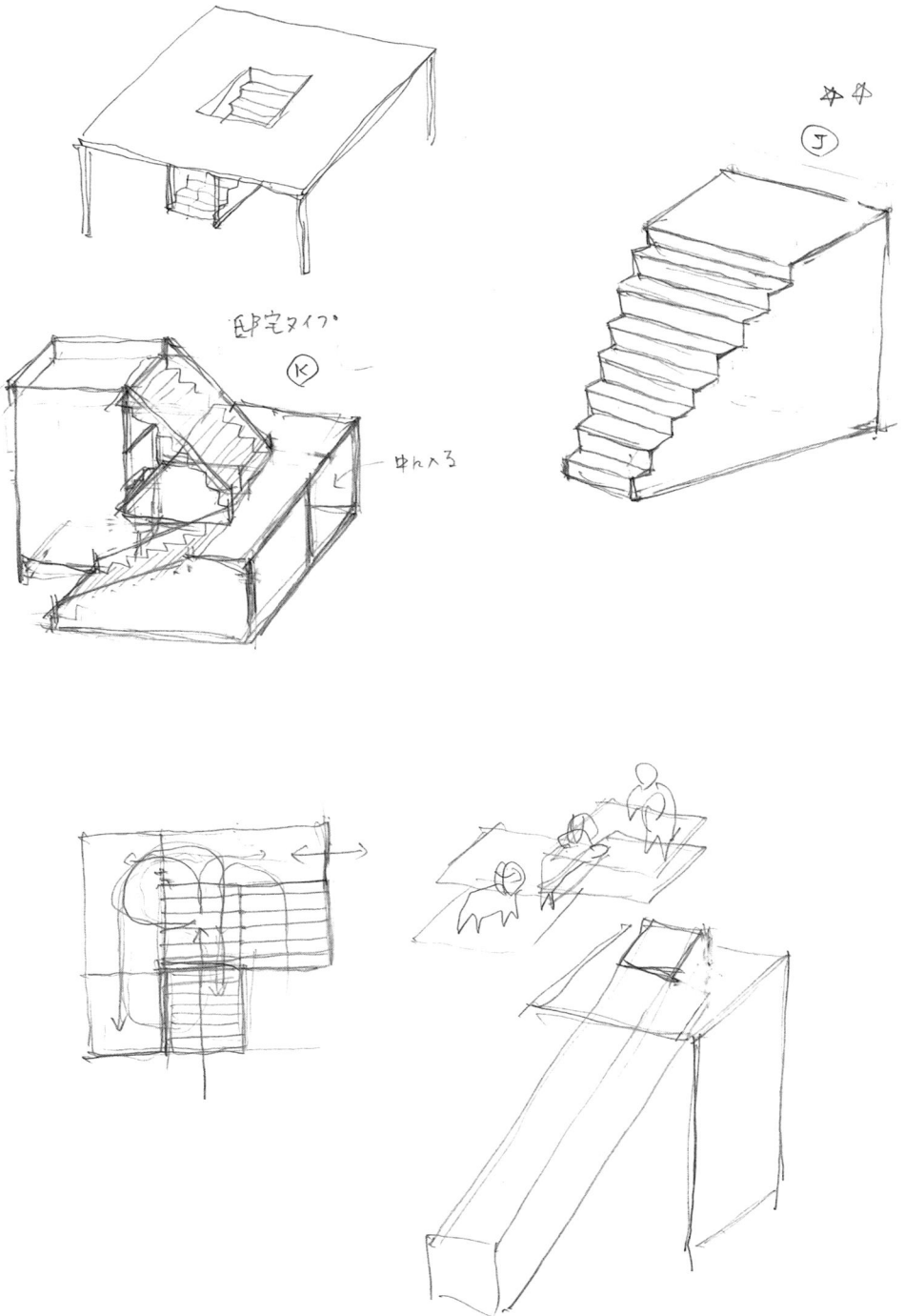

臥宅タイプ

K

中に入る

⊕ ⊕

J

Domesticated dogs originated from wolves. In order to create dogs to live side by side with humans, people created many breeds of dogs, from large to small. What kind of space can we provide for these partners who are destined to coexist in human spaces?

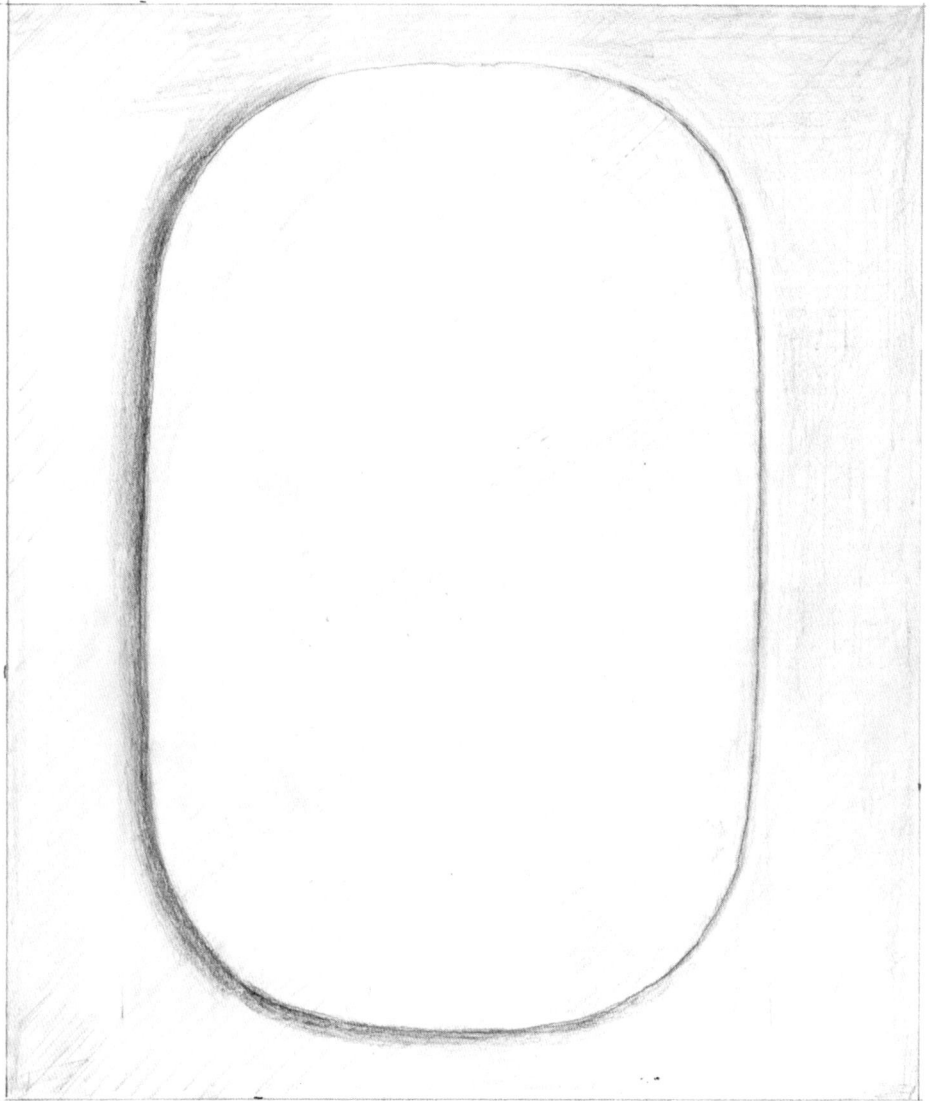

SUBTLE

Rough poster sketches for the 2014 "TAKEO PAPER SHOW, SUBTLE."
The goal was to express the concept of "Delicate or Infinitesimal."

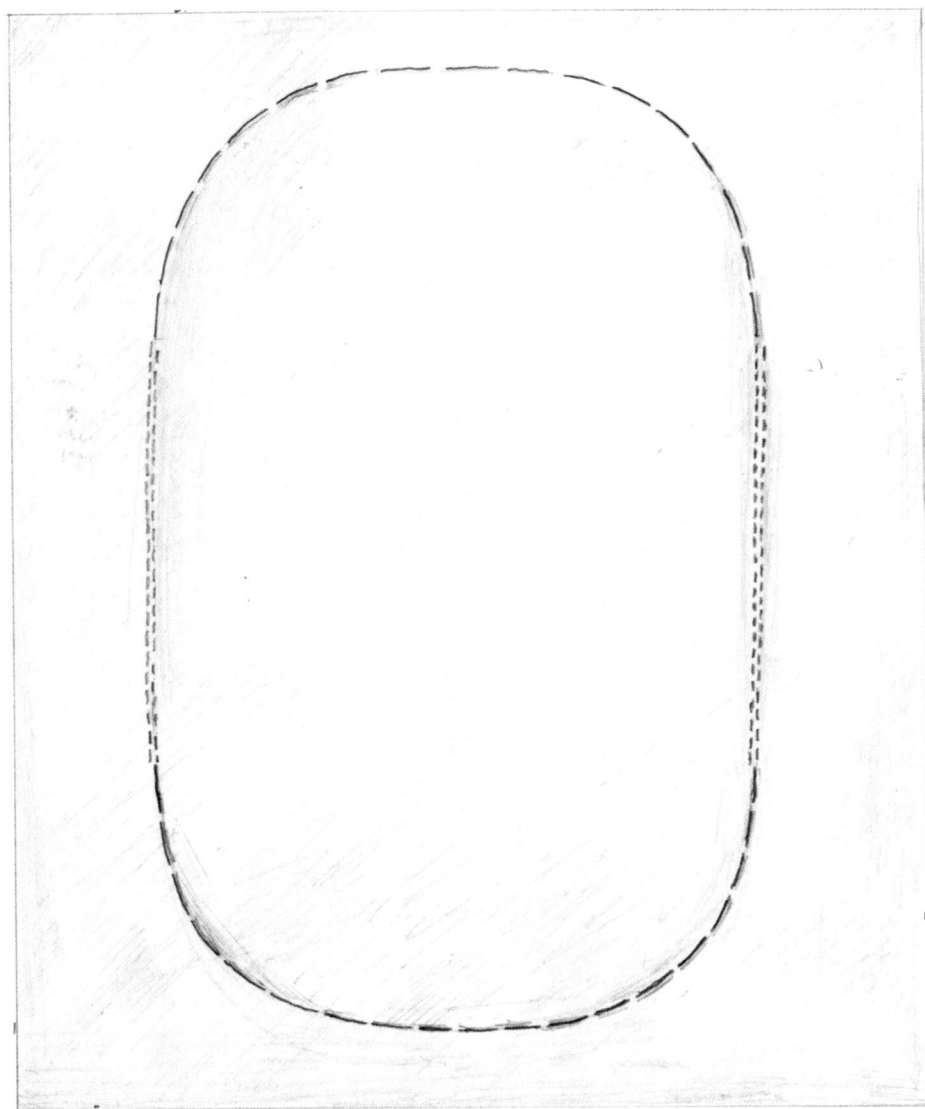

SUBTLE

ひっかける

セ刀れ目

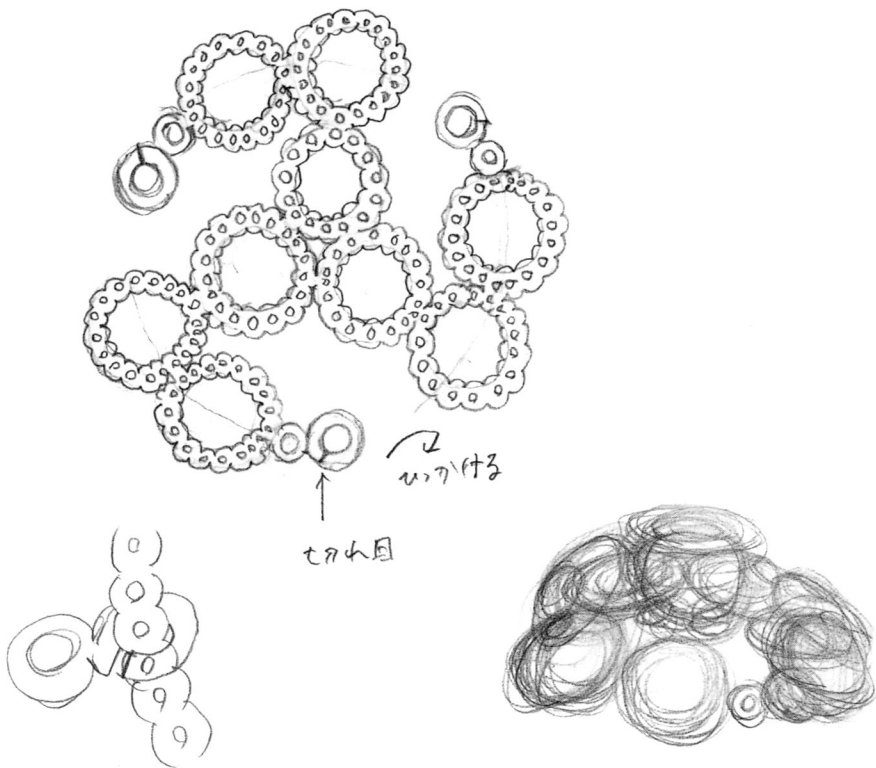

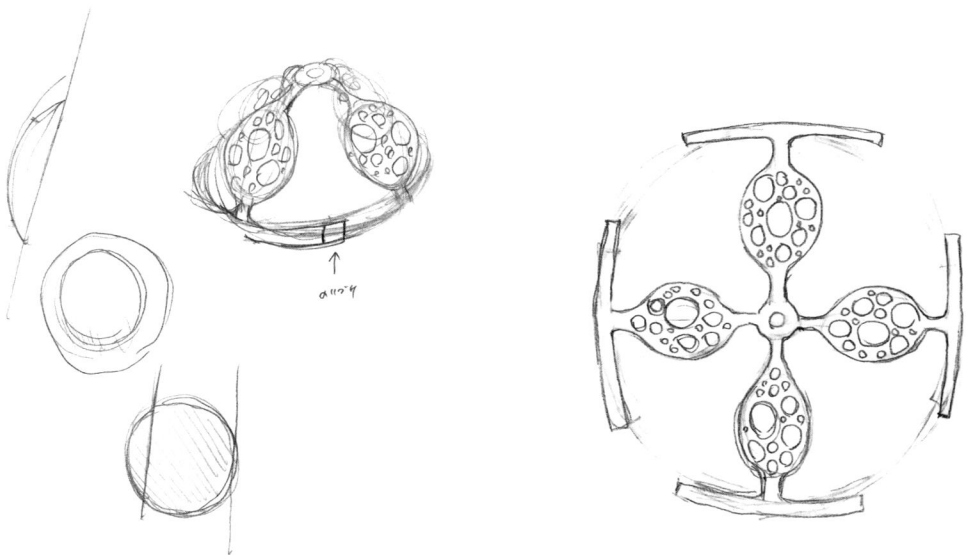

Technological advances are dramatically changing the methods and
techniques used to process paper. These sketches are for products
made with a laser cutter, which supports subtle sensitivities.

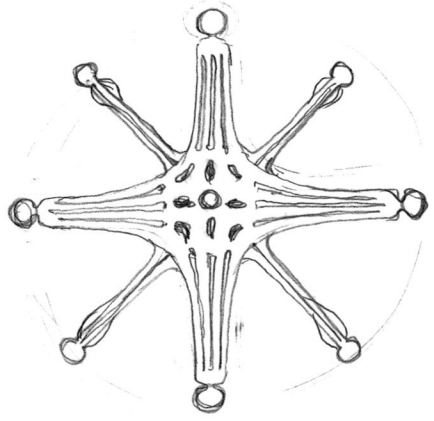
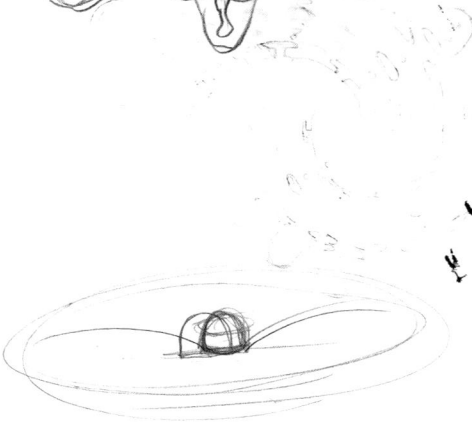

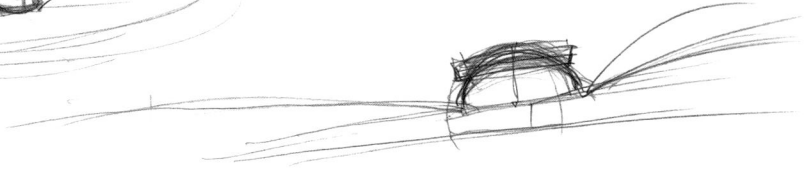

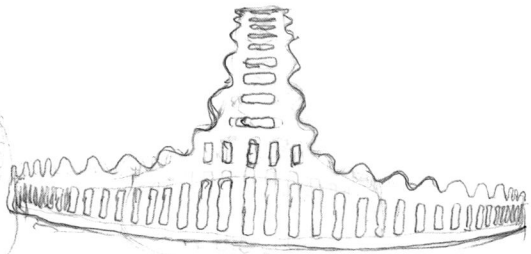

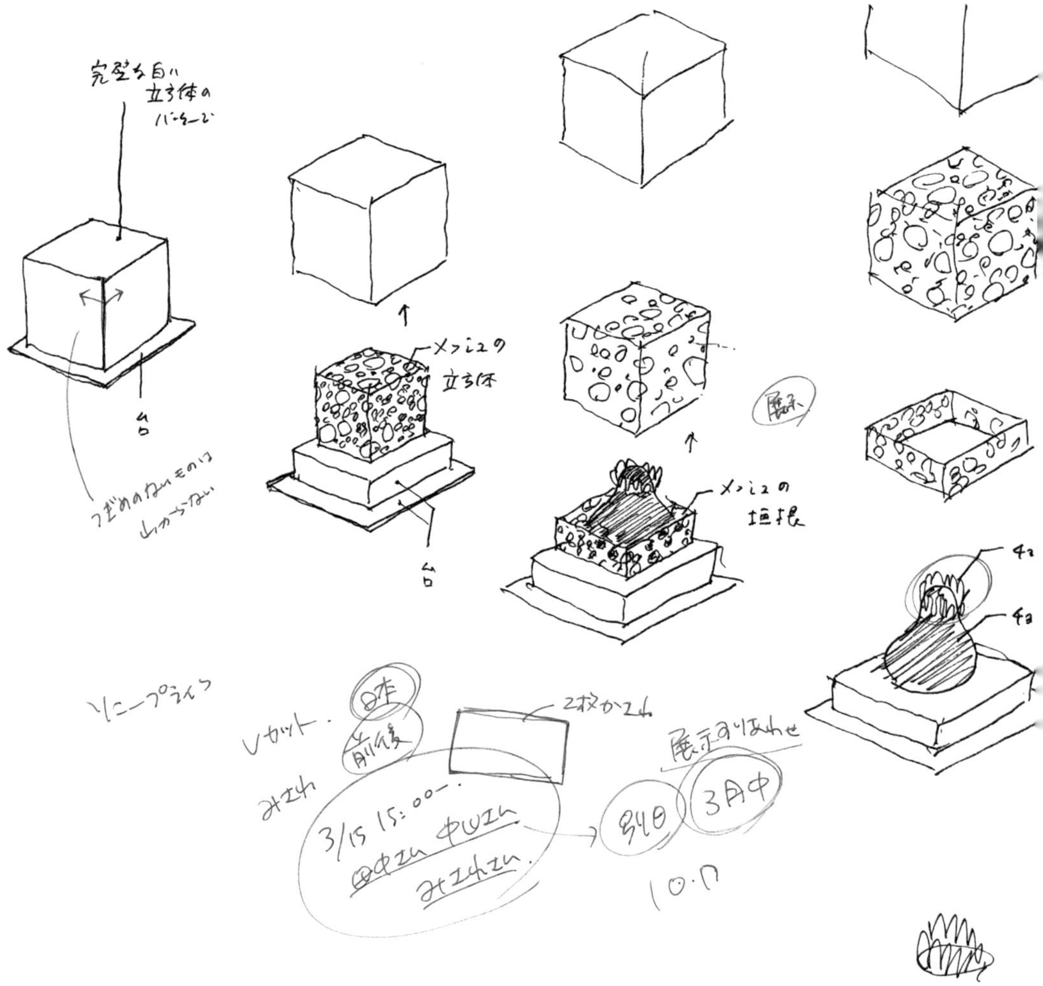

I attempted to craft a delicate paper coronet for the top of a chocolate.

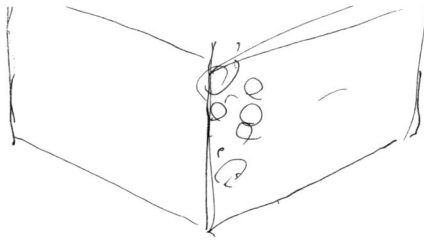

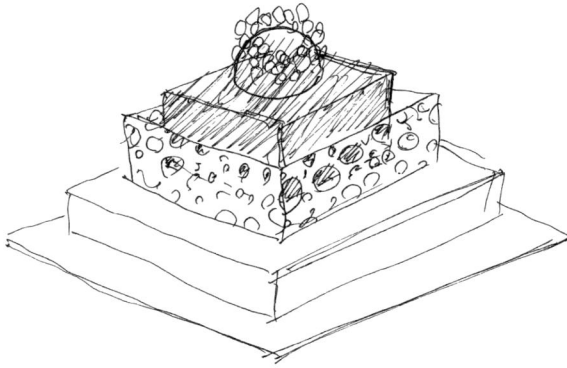

ひかりで出たく
はこの構造

東末
三光紙器さん

日本の3本の形

ユーツ・イレブン
静岡

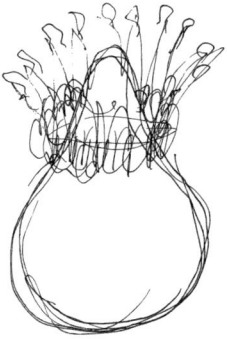

チョコレートの帽子 2018

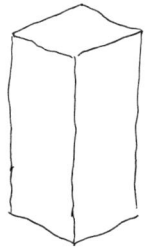

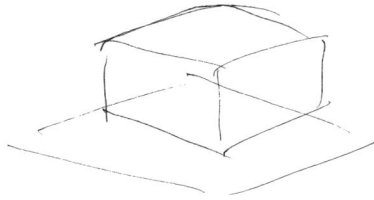

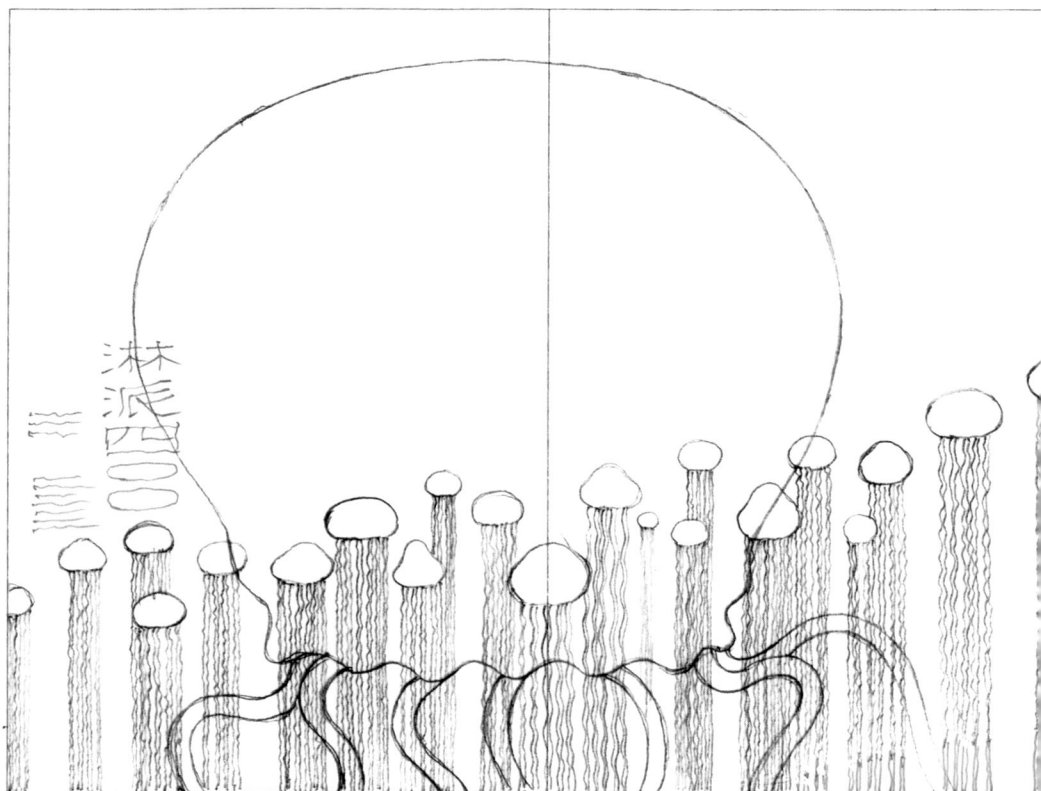

琳派400年/ポスター

海月図／下絵 2015/6/21

Poster sketches for an exhibition celebrating the 400th anniversary of
the Rinpa school of Japanese painting. It features jellyfish arranged in the Rinpa style.

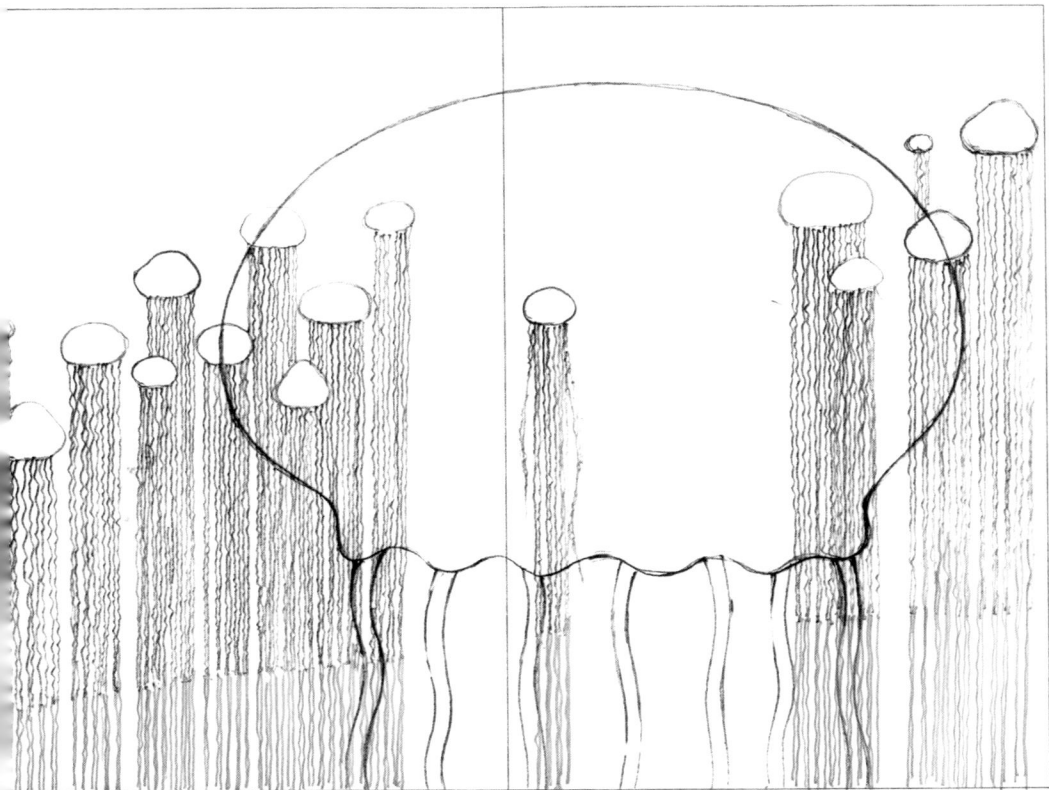

1.8倍トに. A3に 2枚.
0.1 ヘにど A3ペーパーに 描き. スキャンして 囲める.
大クラゲの 影. をどうするか?
手記に サニごとっい足す.

Rough poster sketches for the first "HOUSE VISION" exhibition in 2013.
Being a graphic designer, I aimed to create a carefully crafted poster for the event.

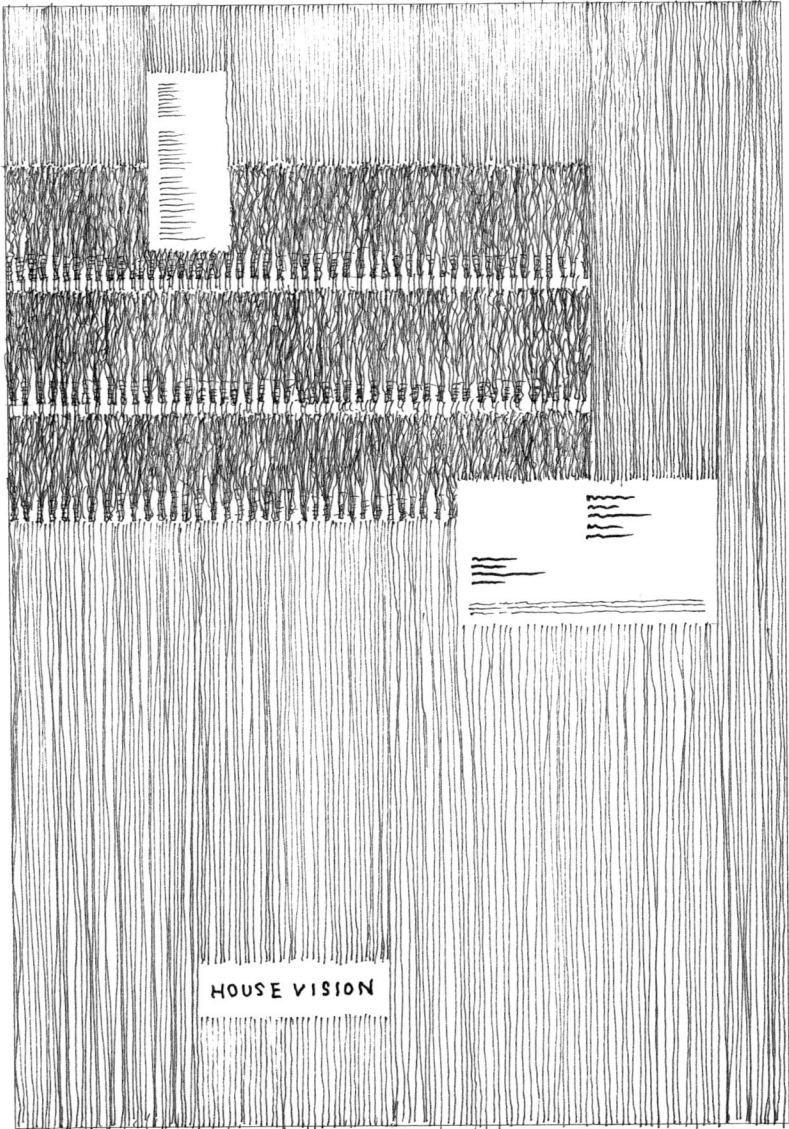

HOUSE VISION

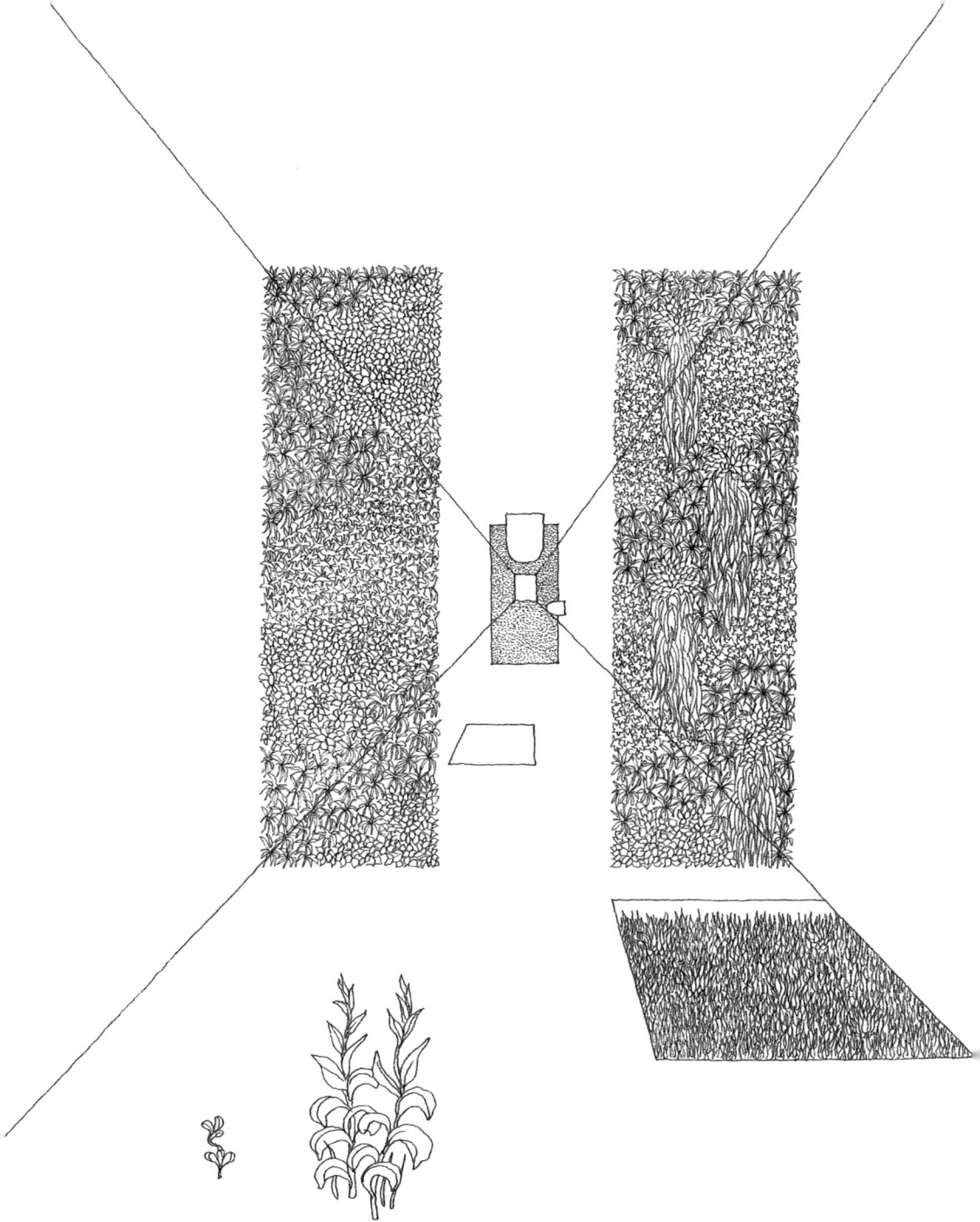

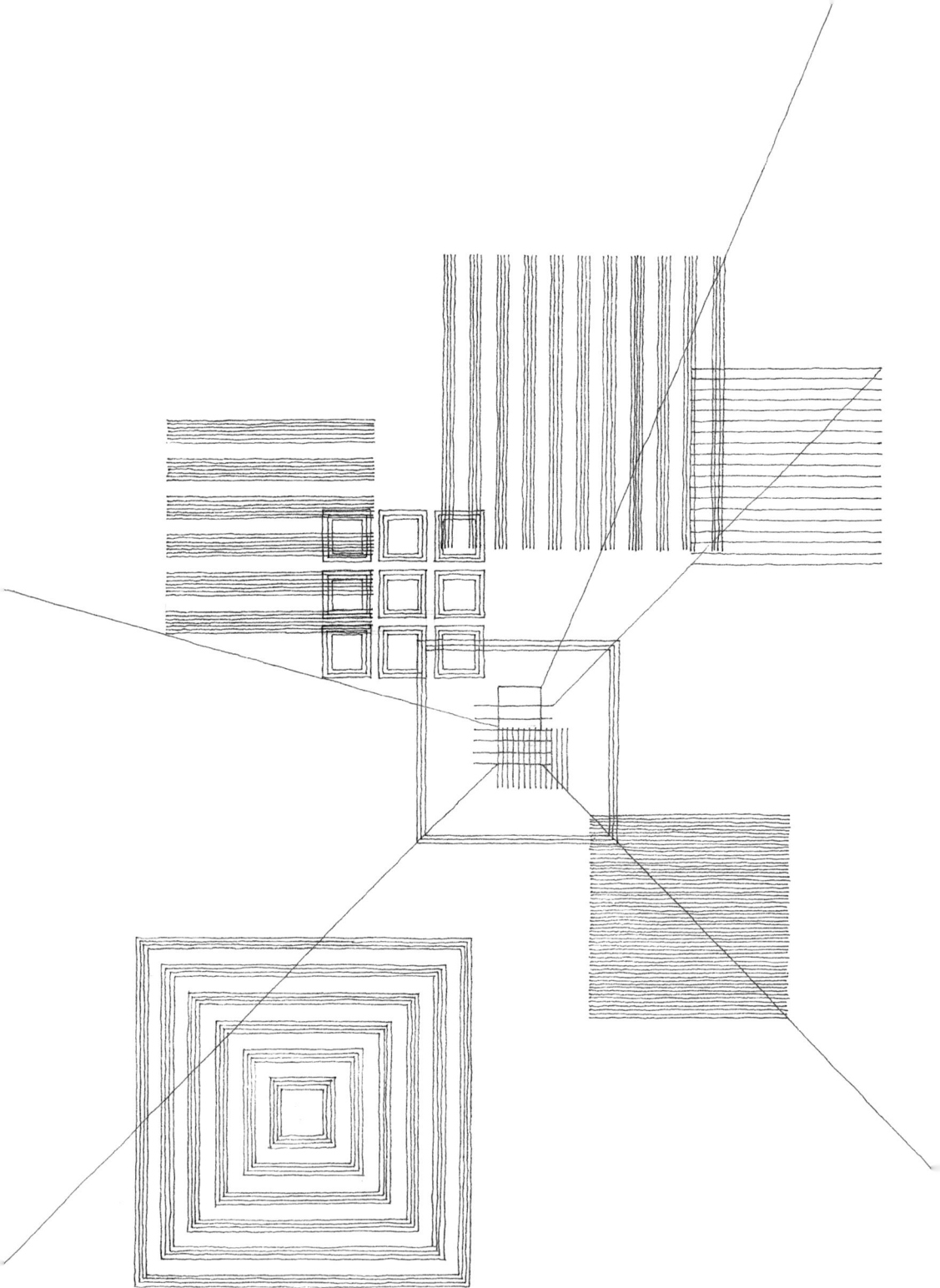

The objective was to express "home" as multiple layers of materials and textures.

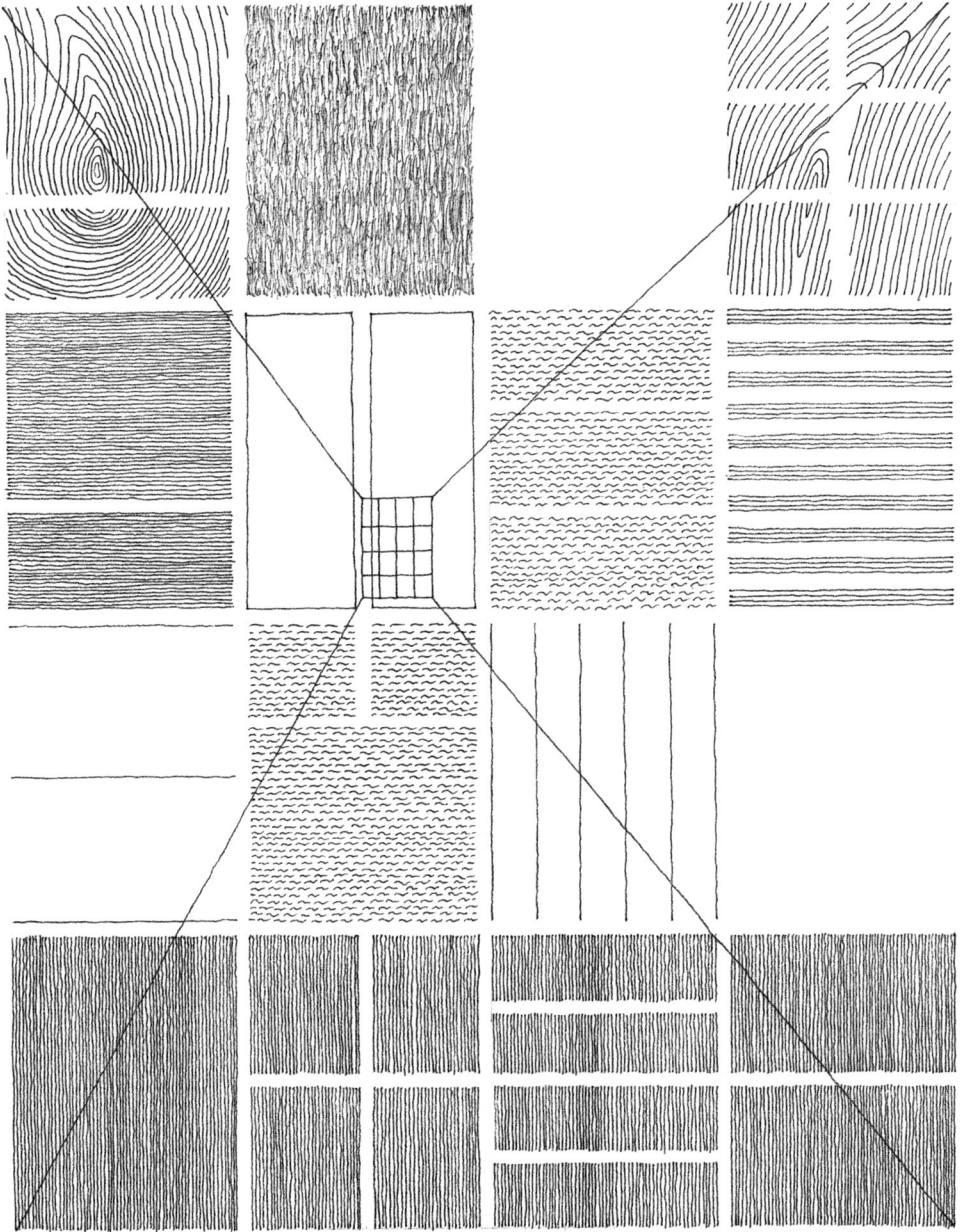

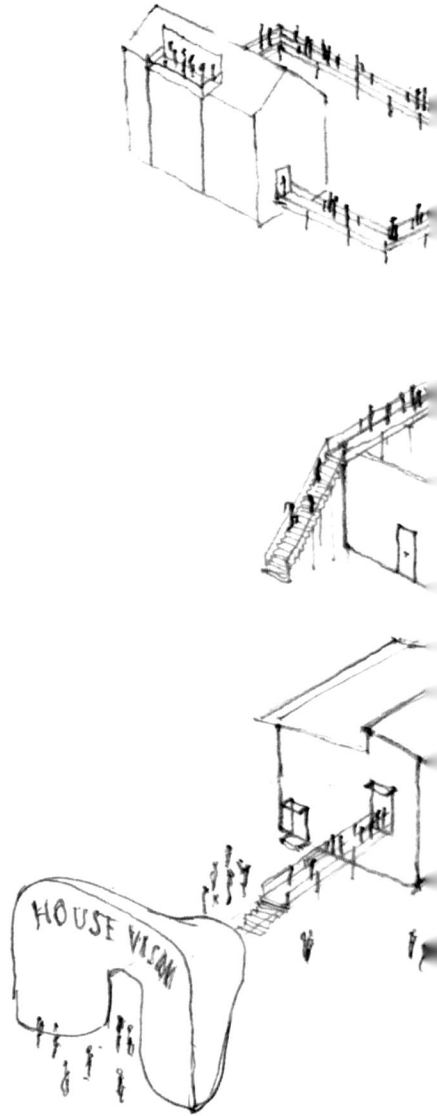

An early conceptual sketch of "HOUSE VISION." This is an effort to create an exhibition plan that would focus on infill rather than the exterior, under the assumption that "home making" is primarily renovation. I conceived a bold composition in which the audience would travel through the spaces on bridges, and never actually descend to the floor level, as the bridges would run through the centers of the houses.

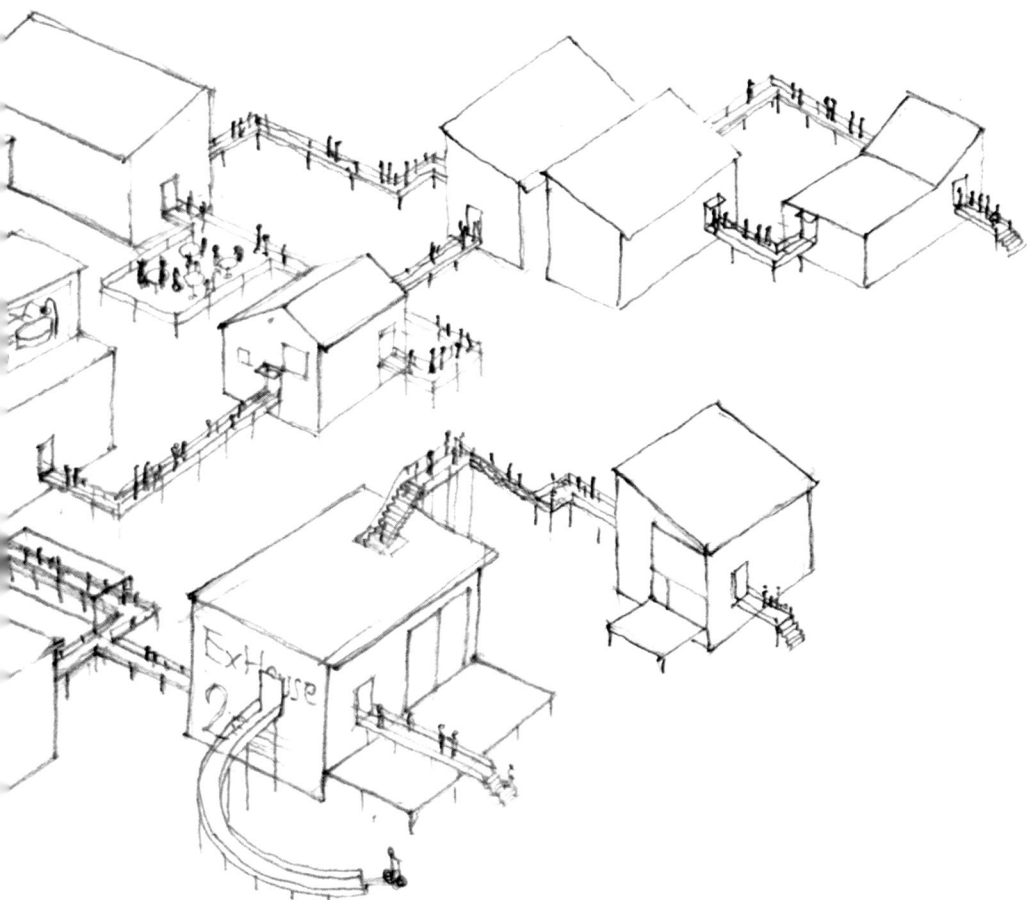

The house has a growing potential to be
an "intersection of industry," rather than a residence.

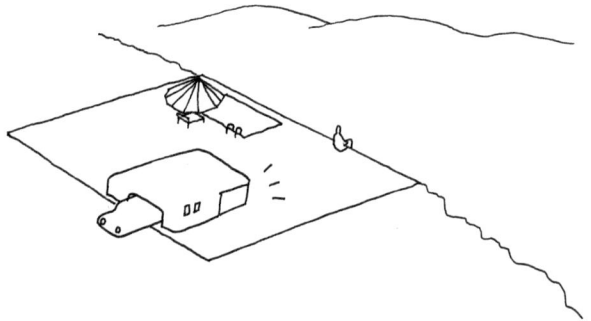

Electric vehicles serve as power sources,
bringing electricity to remote locations.

Is it truly convenient to use drones for delivery?

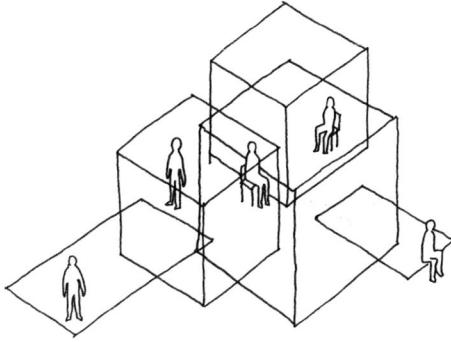

Even in the same house, the members of a family may be isolated.

Floatplanes could turn small fishing ports into airports.

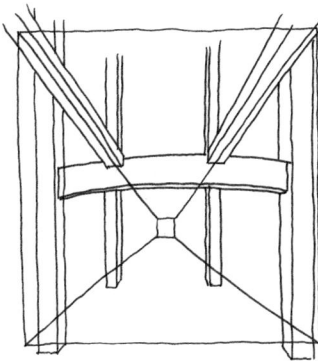

Traditional homes are a valuable future resource.

The potential is greater for the home as an "intersection of industry" rather than a residence.

A dual-residence lifestyle that means living in the city and the suburbs begins.

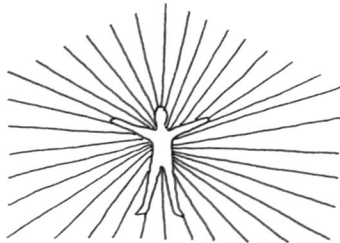

An interactive communication environment begins.

Even if living separately, family members are connected digitally.

People are shaped and nurtured by their homes.

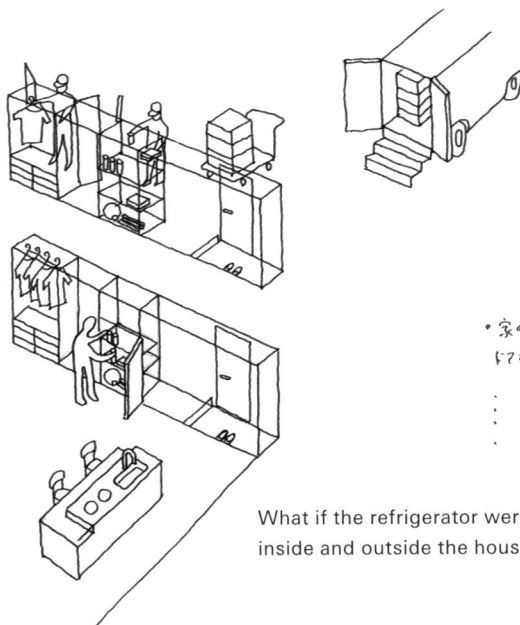

・家の 甘にもいくつの
ドアで 起限にコトる.

What if the refrigerator were accessible from inside and outside the house?

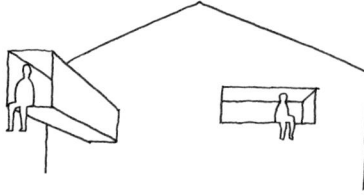

What if windows had depth?
We would live in the windows, and by the windows.

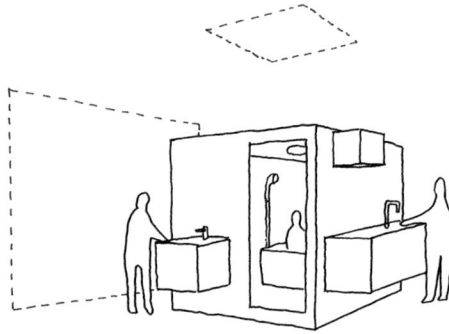

The ability to move the wet areas around
would result in drastic changes to interiors.

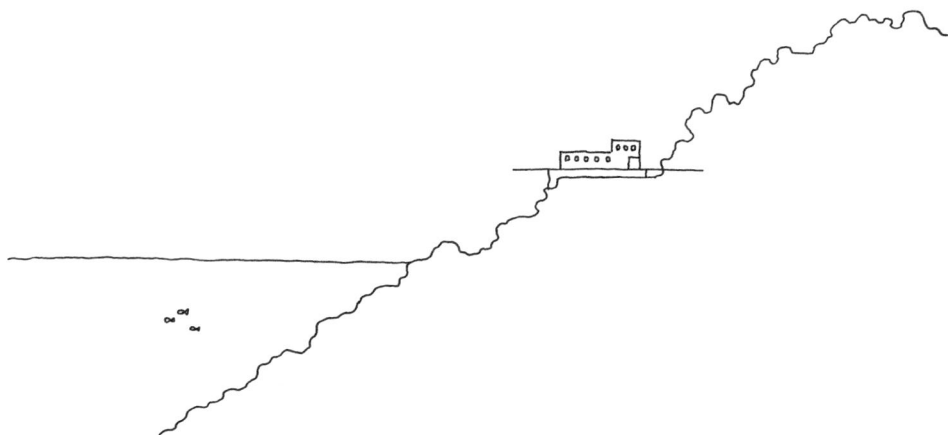

Really, where do you want to live?

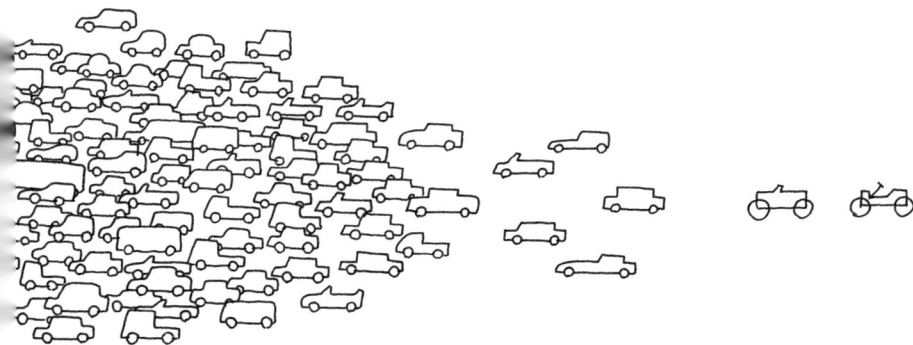

Ninety percent of cars are parked in garages, and when they're on the road, they carry only the driver.

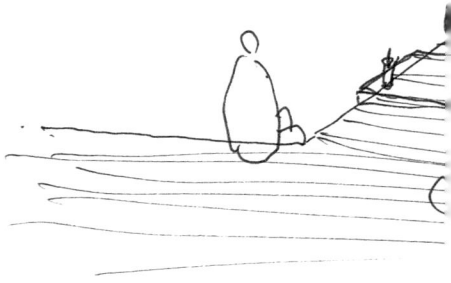

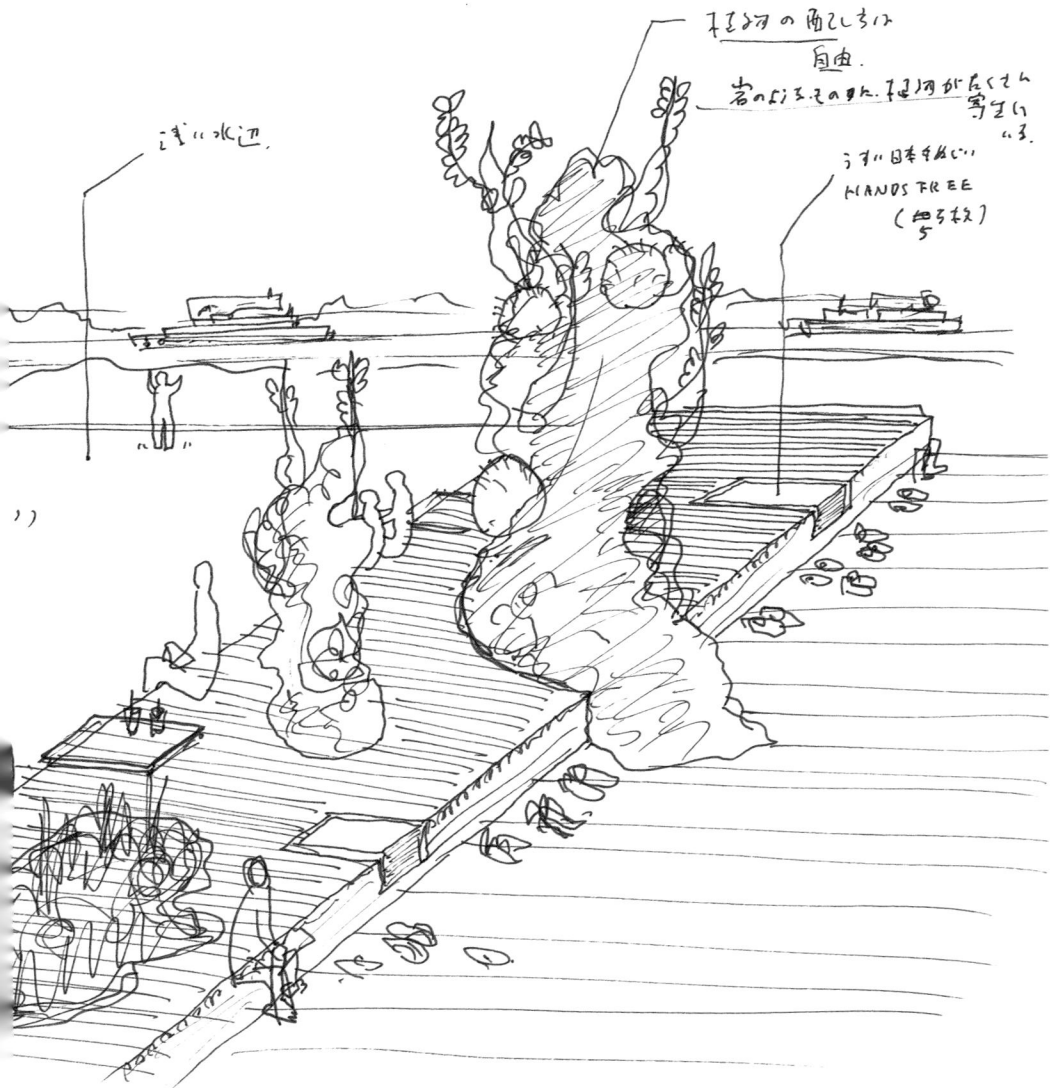

A sketch of the concept for a waterfront installation at the "HOUSE VISION 2 2016 TOKYO EXHIBITION" venue. I asked a team comprising Sumitomo Forestry, Kengo Kuma, and Seijun Nishihata to create this space. I envisaged the need for a space with a man-made waterfront and temporary plantings in 2020, when the Tokyo Olympics were scheduled to take place.

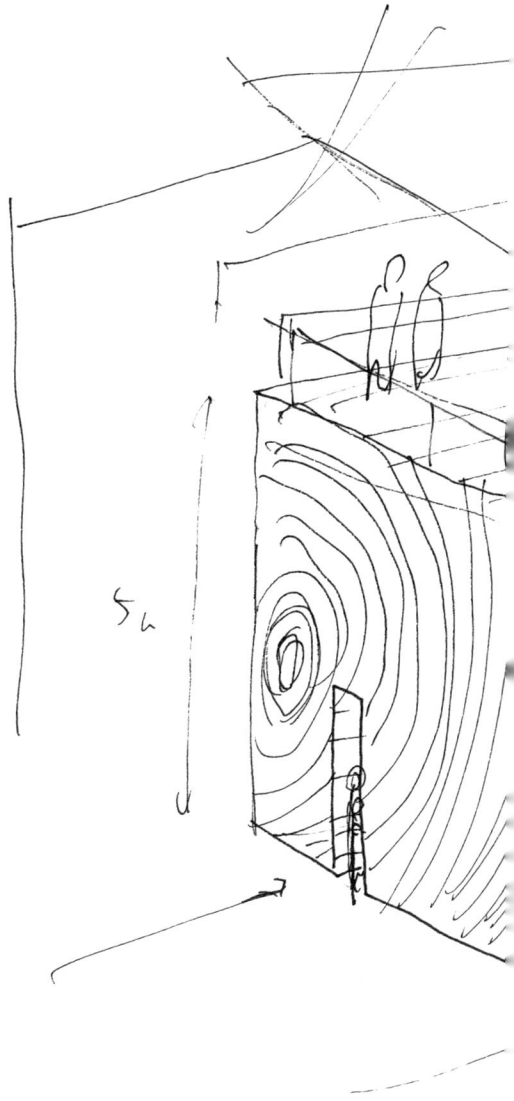

The concept was to hollow out a huge tree, create a living space inside of it and making it into a home. It was a reversal of the idea of building structures using pillars, but there isn't any such piece of lumber large enough.

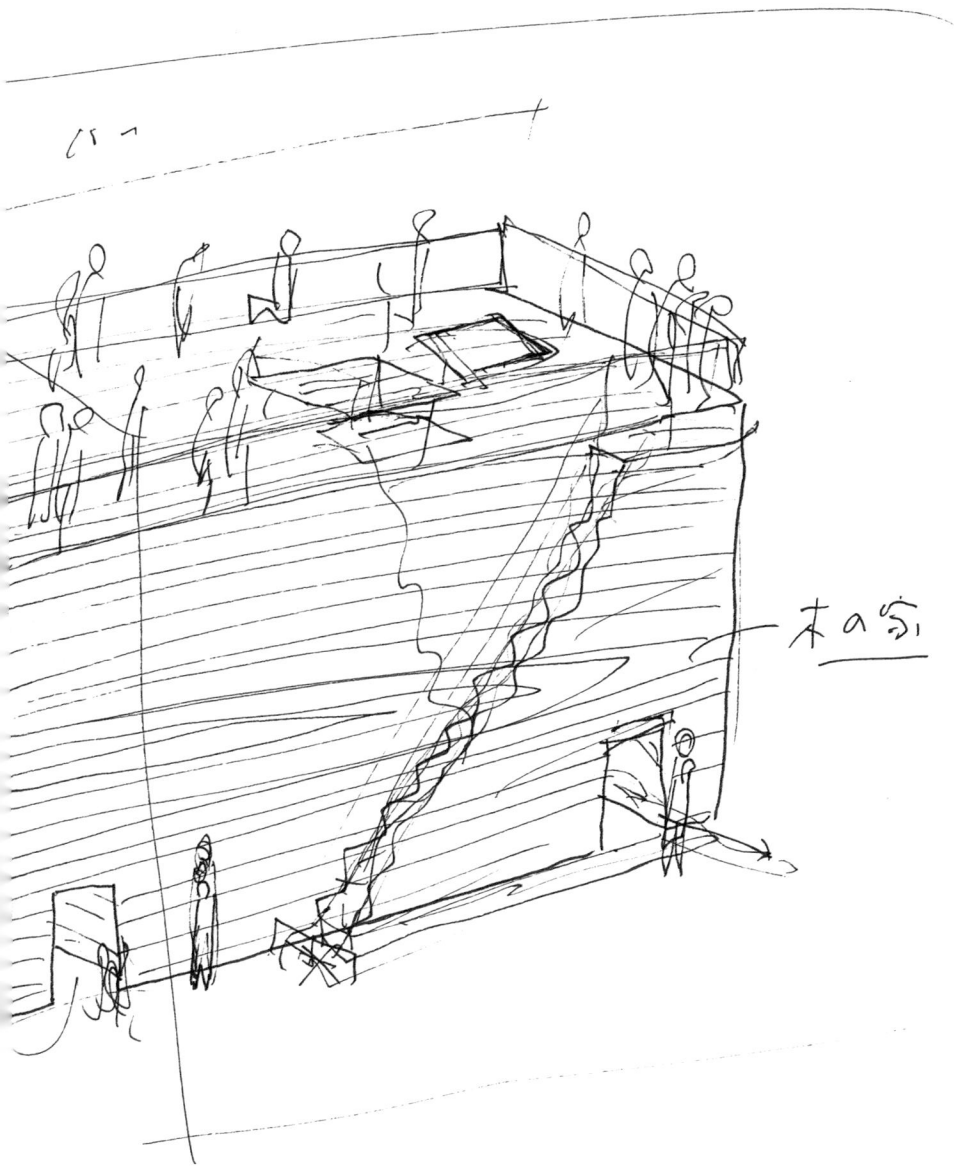

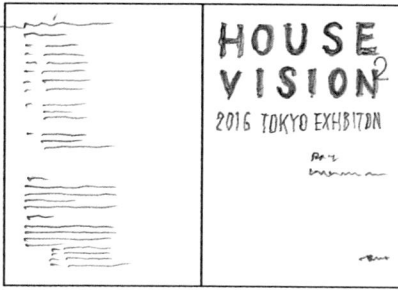

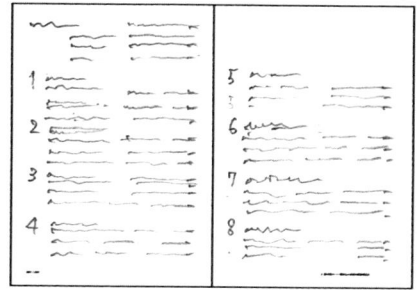

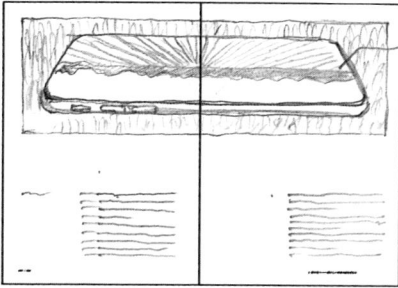

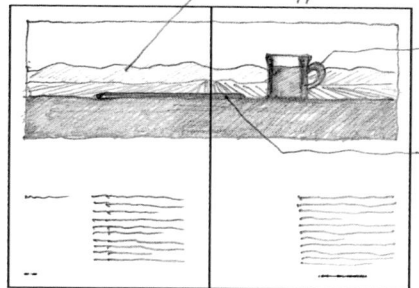

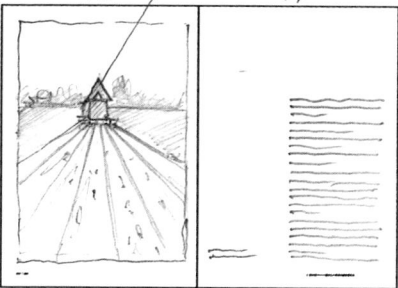

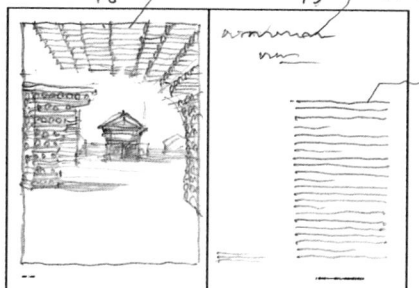

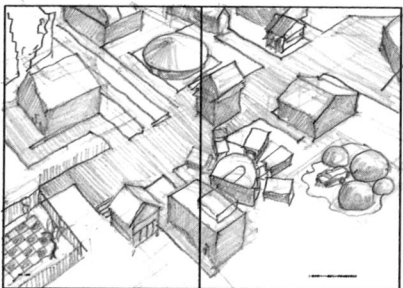

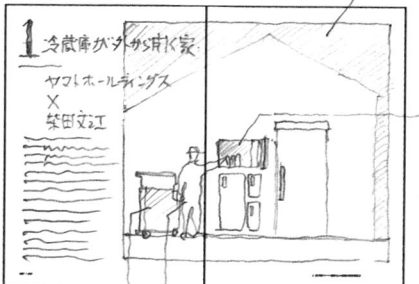

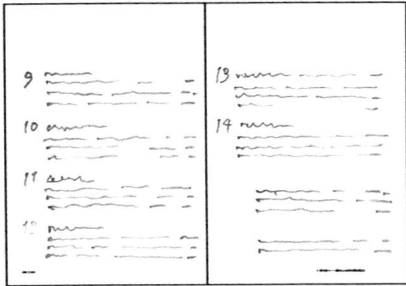
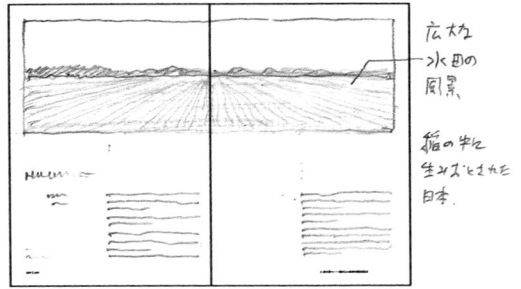

広大な
水田の
風景、

稲の粒を
生みそてきた
日本。

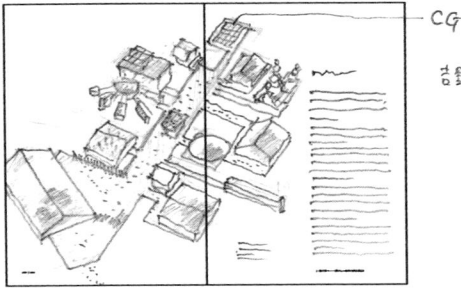
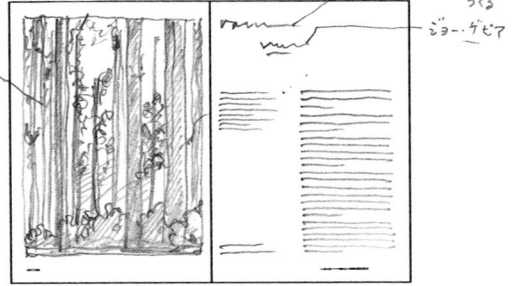

— CG

吉野の
杉材

家から浮きを
つくる
ジョーゲビア

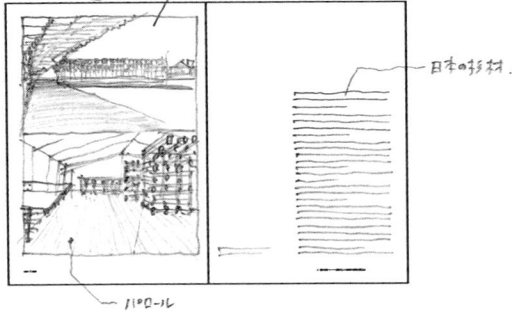
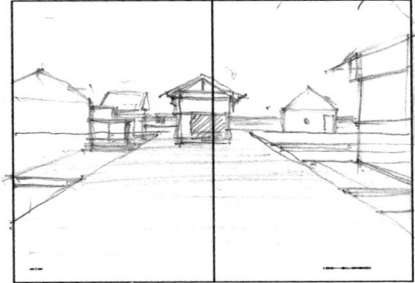

— 広場

日本の杉材.

パーゴル

全景

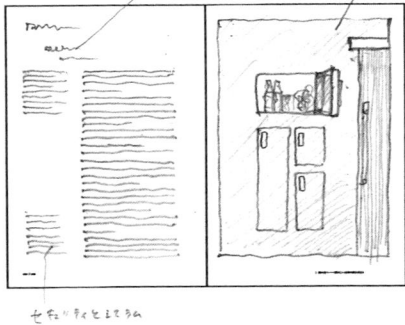
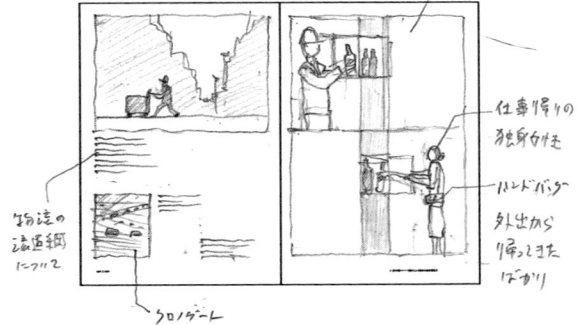

袈田文江 — CG

セチュリティとまとめる

物送の
運送網
に?ば?

クロンゲーム

仕事帰りの
独身女性

ハンドバッグ
外出から
帰ってきた
ばかり

I compiled and organized the exhibition in book form, while planning detailed information about the function and presentation of the physical structures. Orchestra conductors will shut themselves away for a period of time so as to thoroughly read the score, and concentrate on interpreting it. Conductors thus assimilate into their intuition the details of all of the instruments' parts. The work of creating these sketches resembles that process.

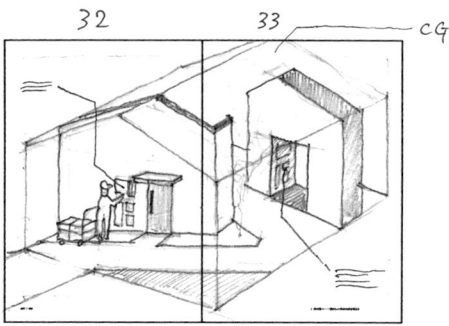

32　33　CG

ヤマトホールディングス

34　35　冷/温

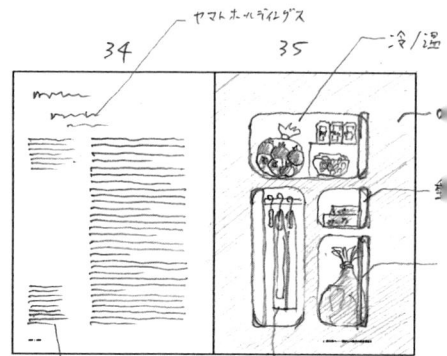

ここで差を説明する。

ランドリー

40　長谷川豪　41

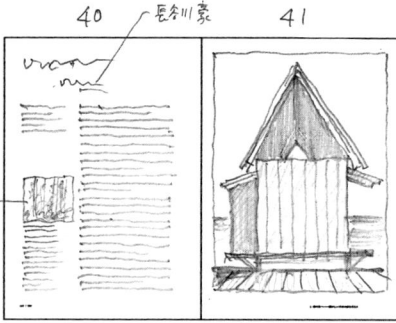

42　43

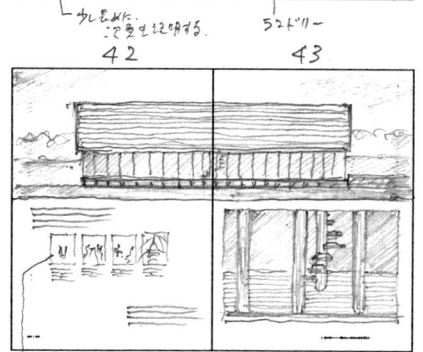

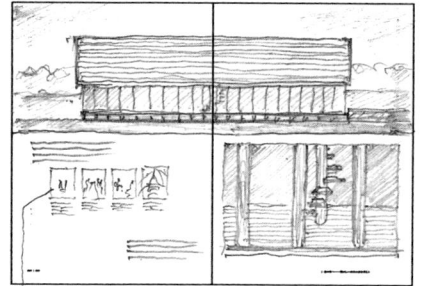

家のつかいち スケッチ (GESTとHOSTの関係)

吉野杉の材料は

HOLE VISION で

48　49

吉野杉
物流
字+CG合成
(クアルト)

CGで
物流を説明

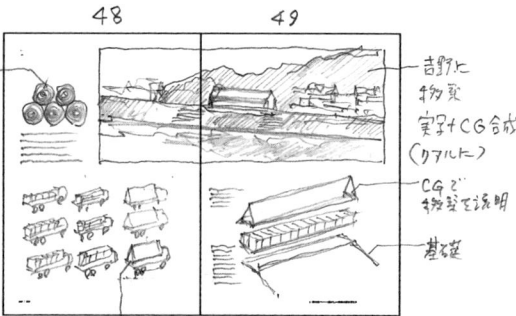

CGでトラック運搬システムを美しく

Panasonic
×
の家 3

50　51

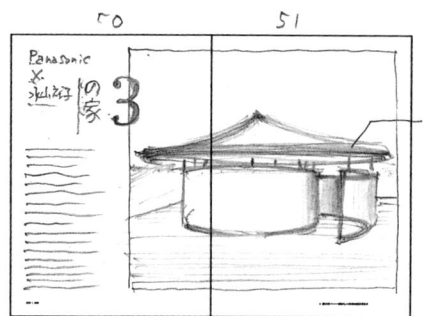

56　57

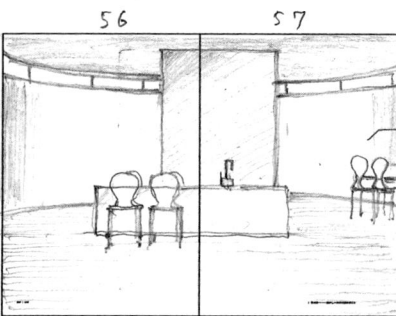

Photo

Panasonic

58　59　CG

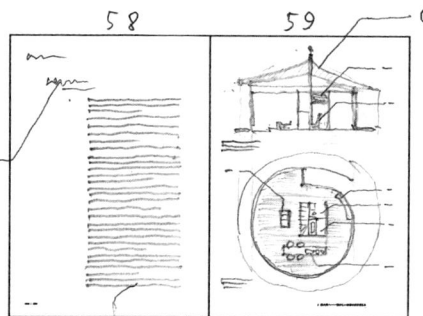

「家化」するテクノロジーについて。

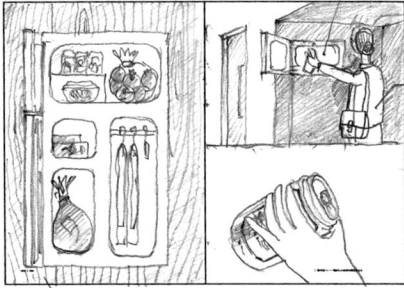

36

37 光ってる

仕事帰りの
女性。
届けている
ビールを
手にする。

Airbnb
吉野杉
大工
おる室

indoor

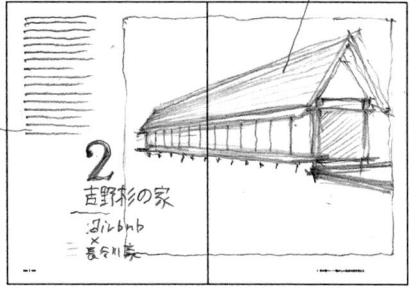

38

39 Photo

2
吉野杉の家
Airbnb
×
長谷川豪

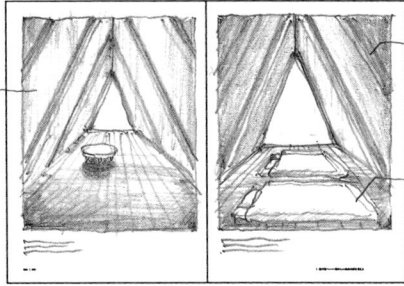

44

45

居根裏
日の出の部屋

ふとん

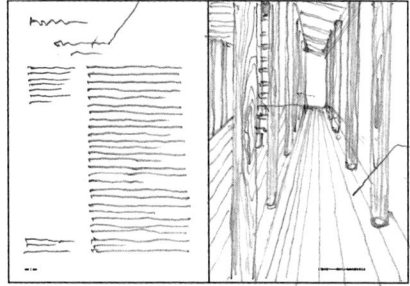

46 ジョー・ケビア

47

縁側

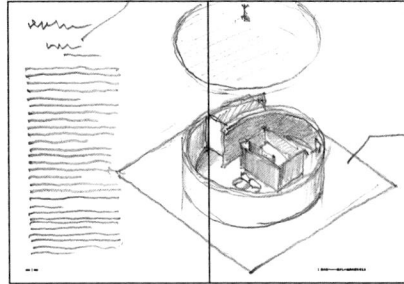

52 永山祐子

53

CG

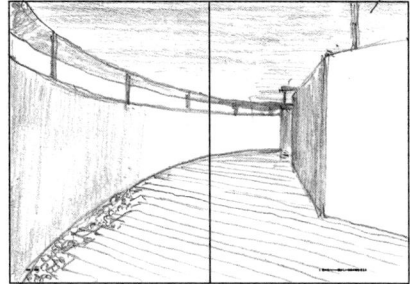

54

55 Photo.

曲面
美しく

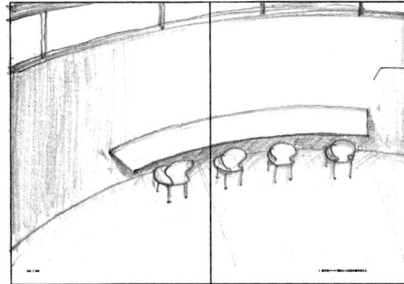

60

61

Photo
曲面
美しく

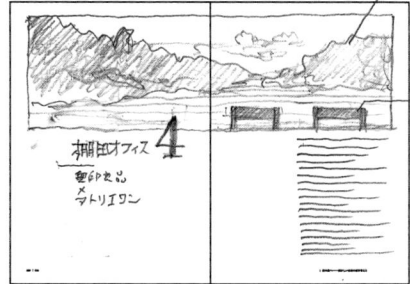

62

63 鴨川

棚田オフィス 4
無印良品
×
マトリエラン

日影になる
持子の前
(MUJ)

64   65   66   67

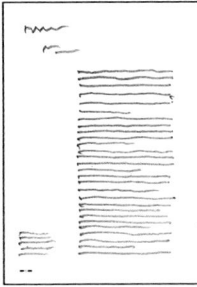   

— Photo

photo

P

72   73 — Photo   74   75

窓中合成
美しく
気持よく

5

ニューノマドの家
三起伊沢用
谷尻誠・細実

もみじ風呂入れる

エッセンシャリズム

80   81   82   83 — Photo

  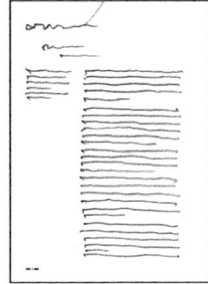 

— Photo
ベッドルーム

賃貸住宅を再定義する/藤本壮介

88   89   棚型 90   91

 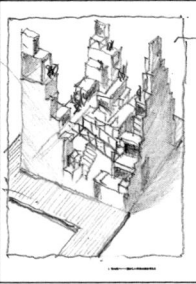 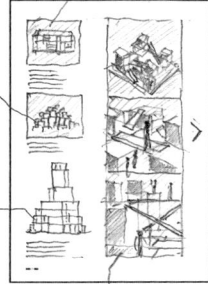 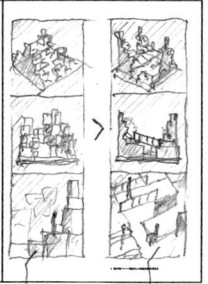

— Photo
クレーン

共用
スペースの
最大化

賃貸空間を
積み上げる
たくさんの
テラスをつなげると。

やさしい
く空間

図
賃貸住宅
マター

模型1   模型2   模型3

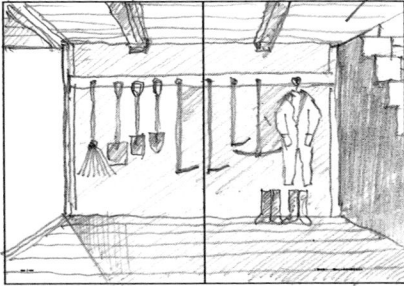

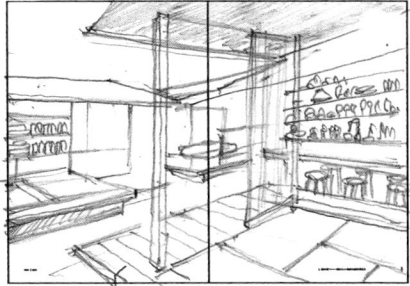

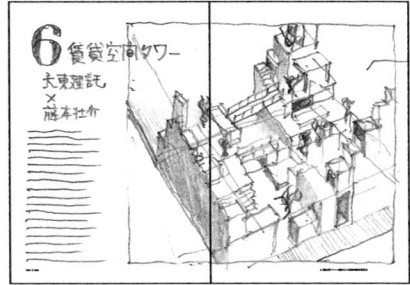

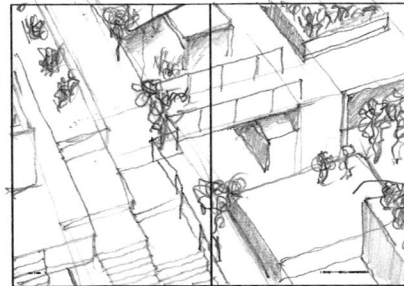

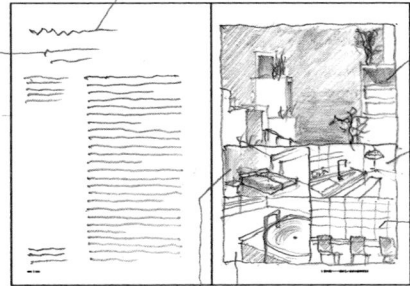

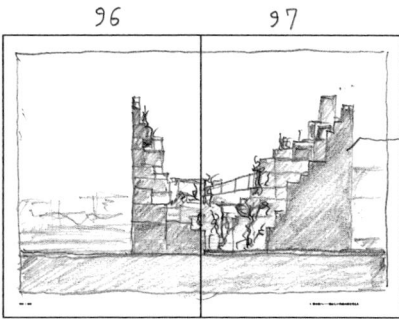

96 97

Photo

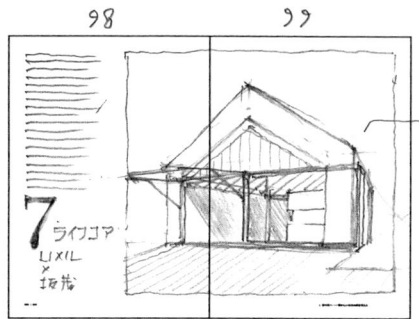

98 99

P
光

7 ライフコア
LIXIL
×
拓殖

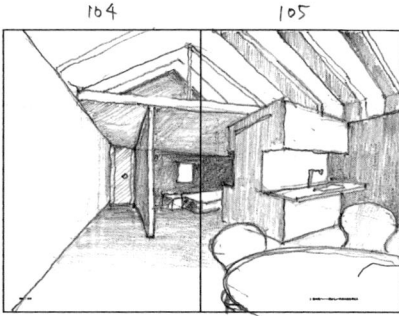

104 105

Photo

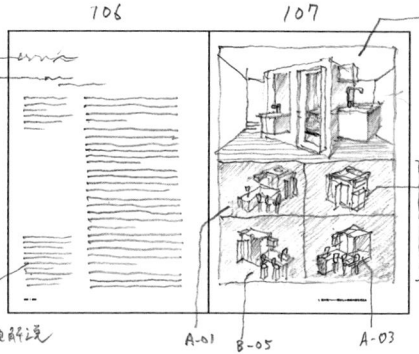

106 107

ライフコア
OASIS

LIXIL
川本丘

変更前提案

A-01 B-05 A-03

A
C
I
L

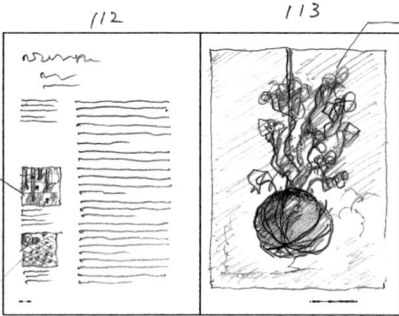

112 113

コンクリートの
木材のストック
ヤード

変形等
3次応図

クレーンで
釣り下げられる
柱材
(空中吊上げ)
Photo

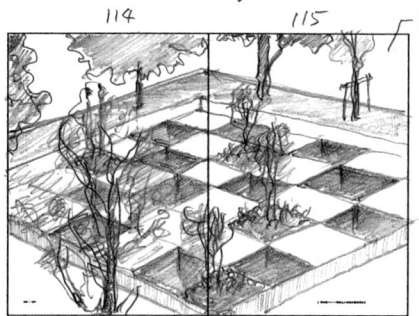

114 115

Photo

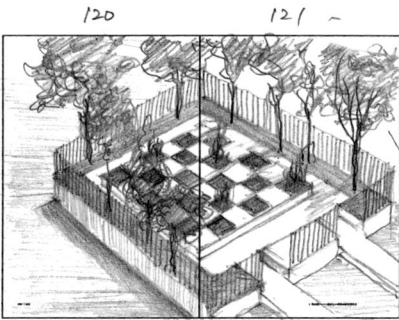

120 121 ～

引き
Photo
クレーンより

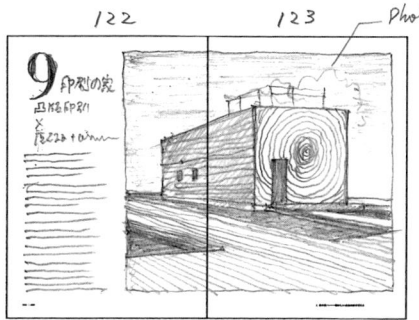

122 123

Photo

9 印刷の廃
田幡印刷
×
尾えこも＋のか～

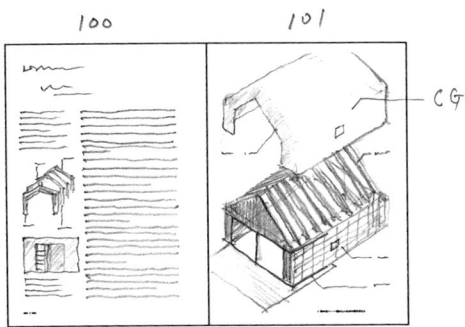

100　101　— CG

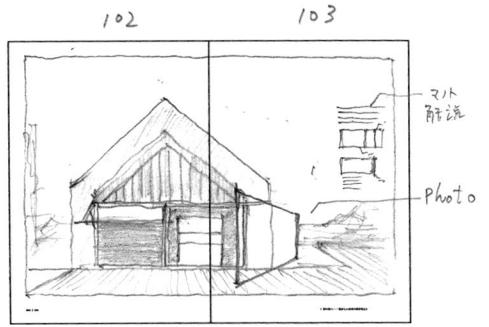

102　103

マット
紙流

Photo

108　109　— photo

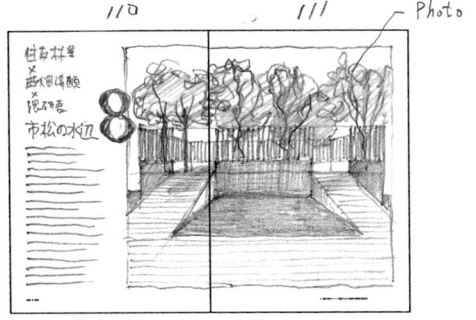

110　111　— Photo

住石林業
×
西田導師
隈研吾
市松の水辺

8

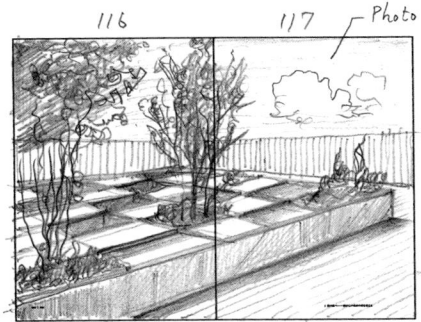

116　117　— Photo

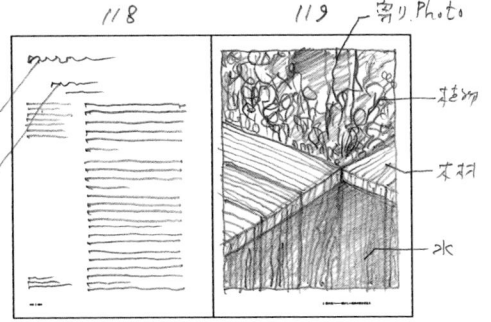

118　119　— 寄りPhoto

郡内の木の
木と水の場

住石林業
市川社長

オランダ

木材

水

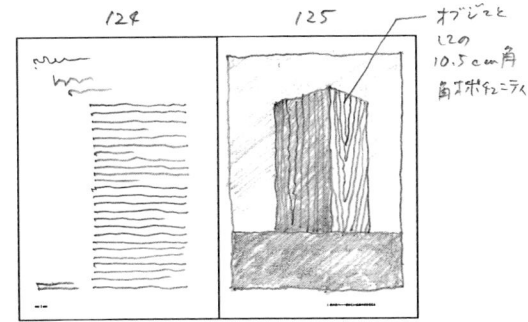

124　125

オブジェと
しての
10.5cm角
角材オポチュニティ

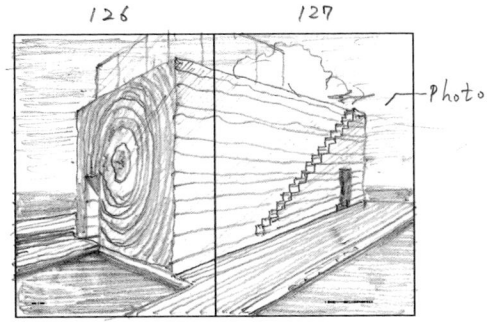

126　127　— Photo

抗木
もっと
スプガサに。

128　129　水谷君の
イラスト？

木目の迷宮
130　凸版石山中氏　131　Photo

登壇
正見枢

ライト
Photo
相の迷宮

オリジナ水木
何の言葉を
ない工片.

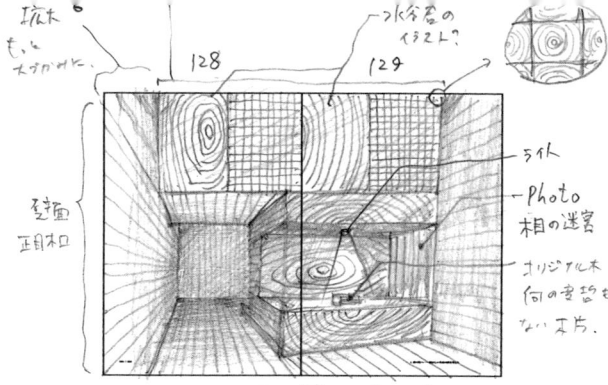

木目の迷宮をつくる　Face

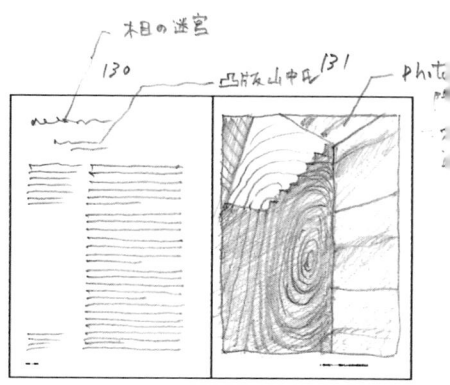

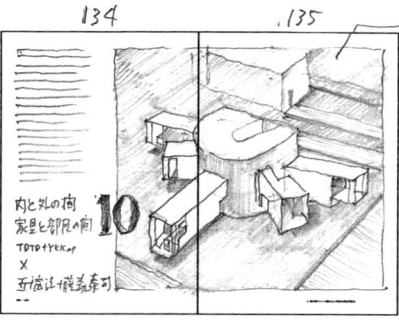

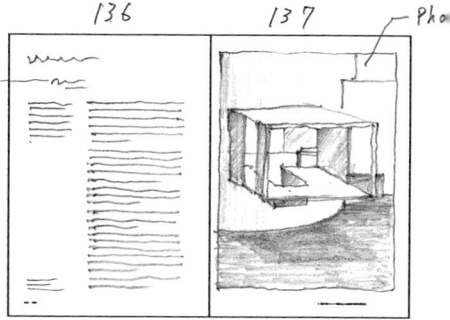

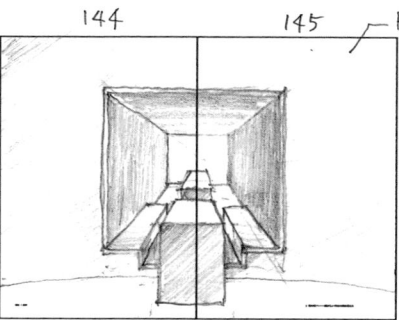

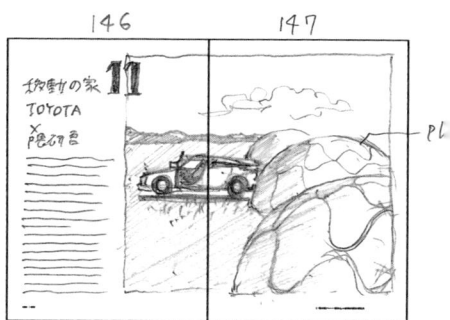

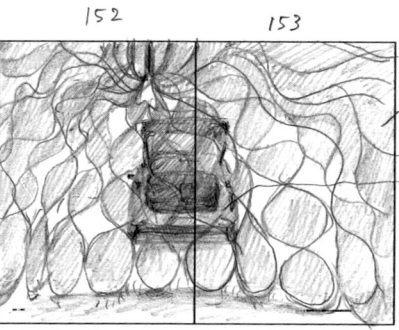

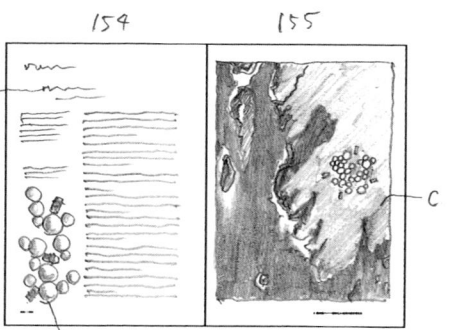

134　.135　Photo
クレーン撮影
五十嵐？

内と外の荷
家具と部屋の荷
TOYOT+YEKの
×
五十嵐江瀑義泰司
10

136　137　Photo

144　145　Photo

146　147
移動の家 **11**
TOYOTA
×
隠岐羽君
Pl

152　153
photo
テント内動から
外を見る
クルマ
リア1ゴニの
荷室あけ
透過

154　155
TOYOTA
C
クルマ＋テント＝空間拡張

132　　　133　　　会場Photo
クレーン

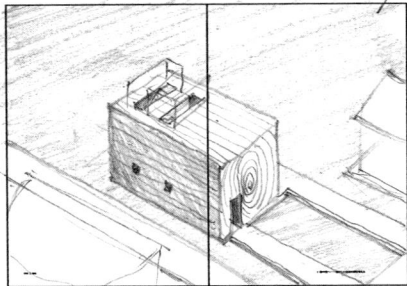

140　　　141　　　CG

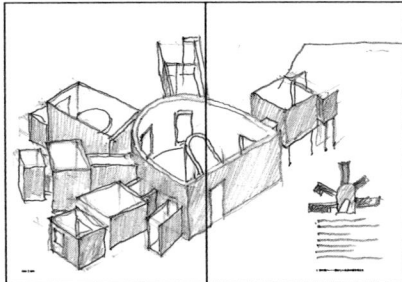

138　　　139　　Photo

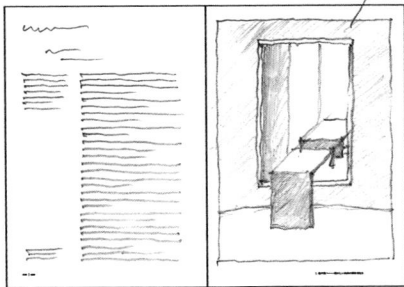

142　　　143　　Photo
TOTO
トKKAP

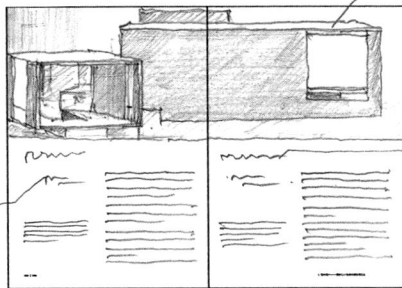

148　　　149
PIHV
プリウス
遠景
Photo(ロケ)
累界

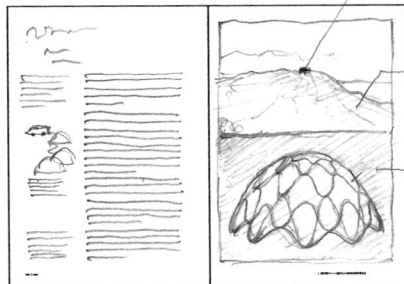

テーマ：UP
炭素循環の
吸着力をみがした
治水構造の
Photo
事前撮影

150　　　151　　Photo
クレーン

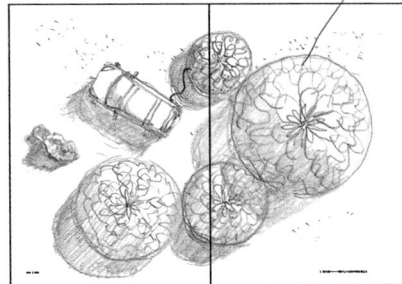

156　　　157
Photo
クルマは
背骨に
スタイリングを
見せたい.

158　　　159　　Photo
電波の家 12
CCC
×

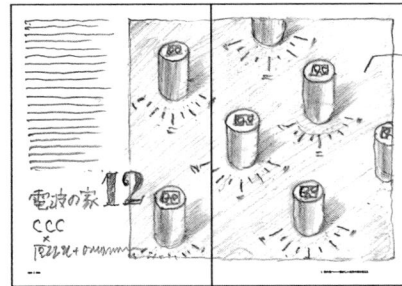

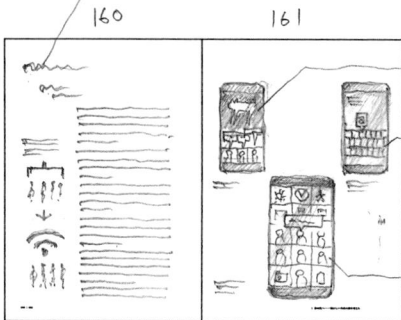

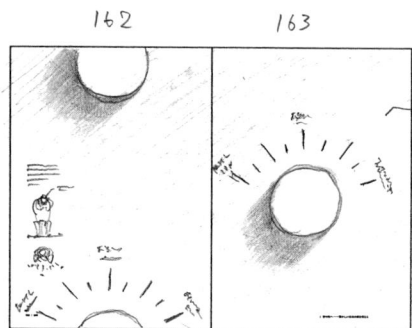

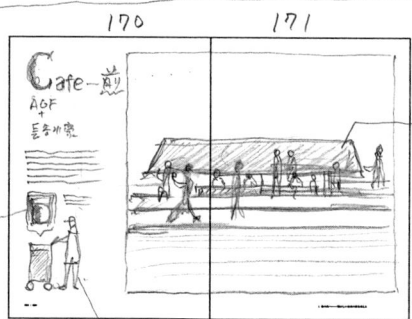

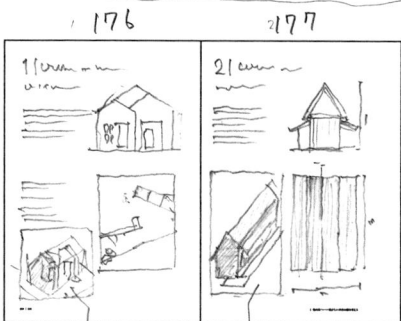

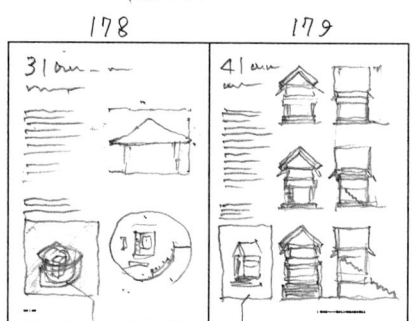

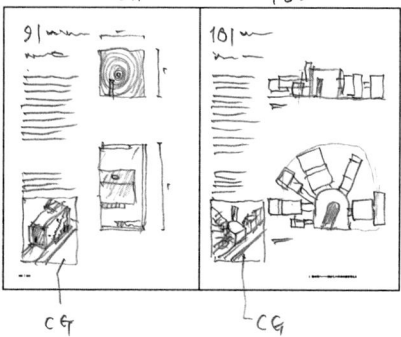

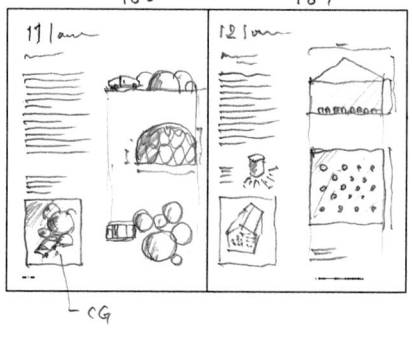

人を軸とした UI

160 161 162 163

写真の共有と4セット

文字入力画面

〈CG〉

画面

P

コント① 168 169 170 171

Photo
たけし(田中)

Photo
おばあちゃん(田中)

Photo
おじさん(太田)

コント②

Cafe 煎り
AOF + 喜多加奈

Photo 角版

Photo サンプル

Ph
A
IC
CA

176 177 178 179

1|cm～ 2|cm～ 3|cm～ 4|cm～

CG CG CG CG

184 185 186 187

9|cm～ 10|cm～ 11|cm～ 12|cm～

CG CG CG

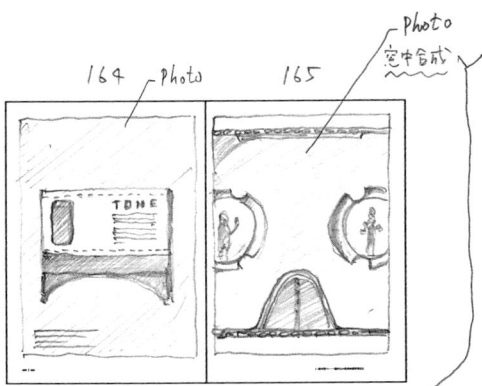

164 — photo 165 — photo 室内合成

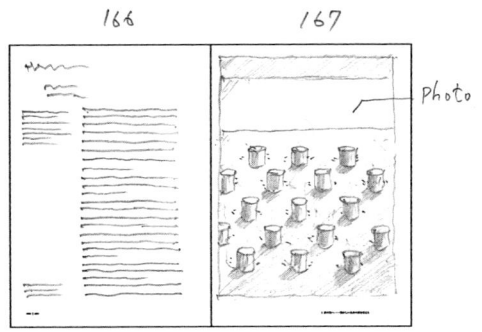

166 167 — Photo

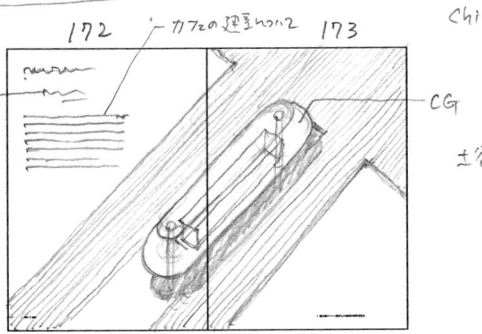

172 — カフェの建築かな？ 173 — CG

China HOUSE VISION 174 175

土谷さん

北京
シンポ
ミラノ他

ベニス
ビエンナーレ
CHINA
HOUSE
VISION
Photo

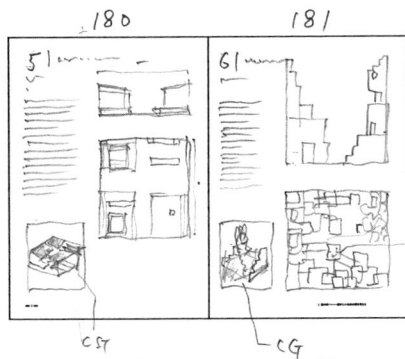

180 181

5 | 6 |

CSヤ CG

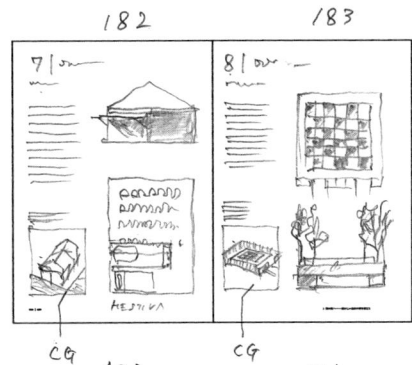

182 183

7 | 8 |

HESTIKA

CG CG

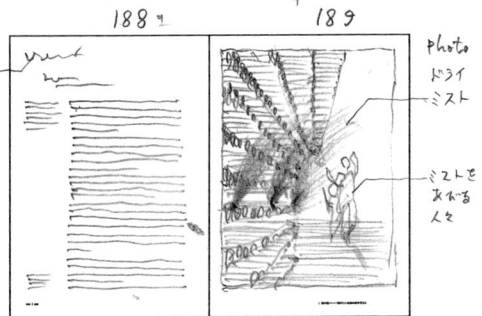

188 ¶ 189 — Photo
ドライ
ミスト

ミストを
あびる
人々

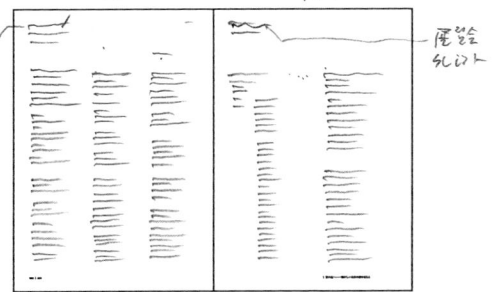

190 191

図版 図版
セレクト

尾崎
セレクト

Wheat | France

小麦
Wheat

種
Seed

パン
Bread

パン
Bread

パン
Bread

Wheat | Italia

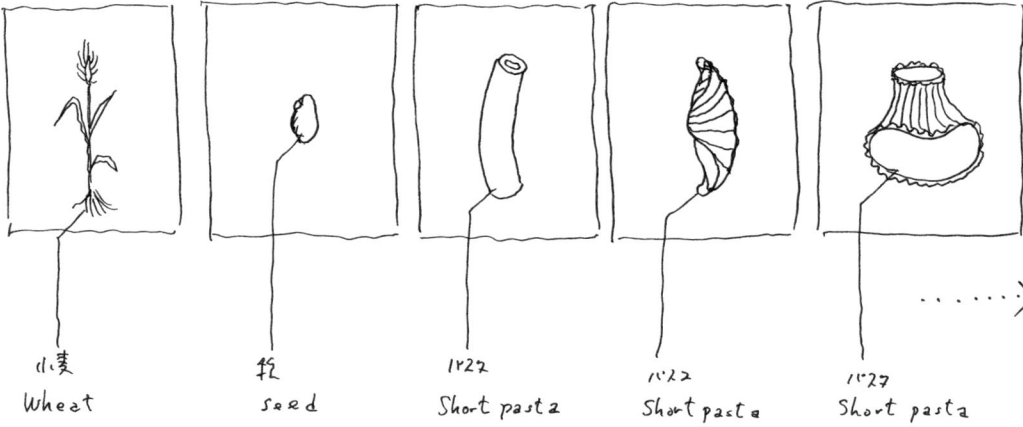

小麦
Wheat

種
seed

パスタ
Short pasta

パスタ
Short pasta

パスタ
Short pasta

Corn | India

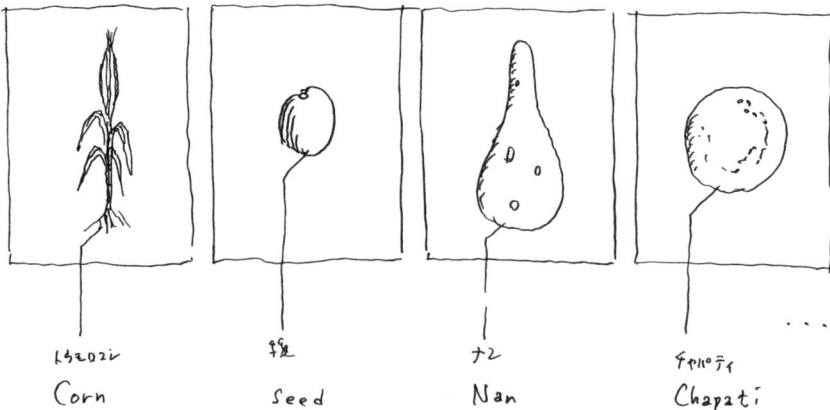

とうもろこし
Corn

種
Seed

ナン
Nan

チャパティ
Chapati

Sorghum | China

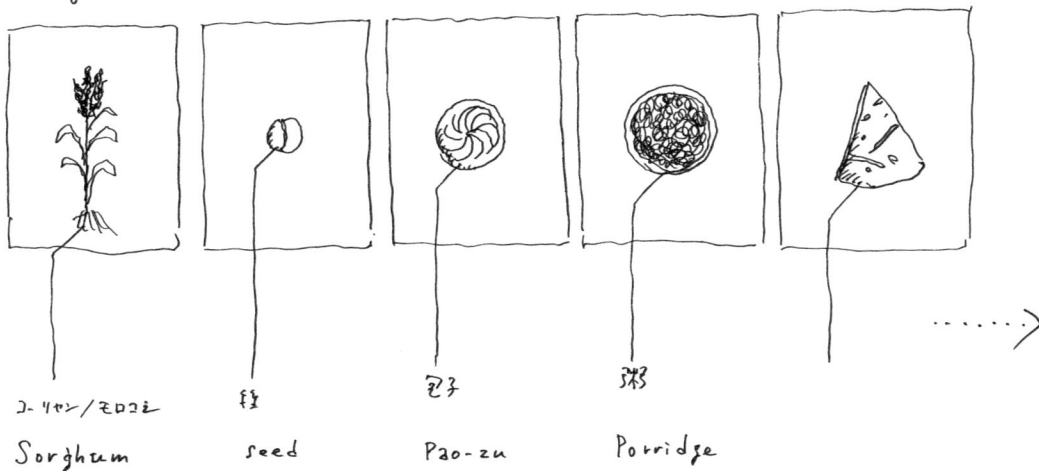

コーリャン／モロコシ
Sorghum

穀
Seed

包子
Pao-zu

粥
Porridge

Rice | Japan

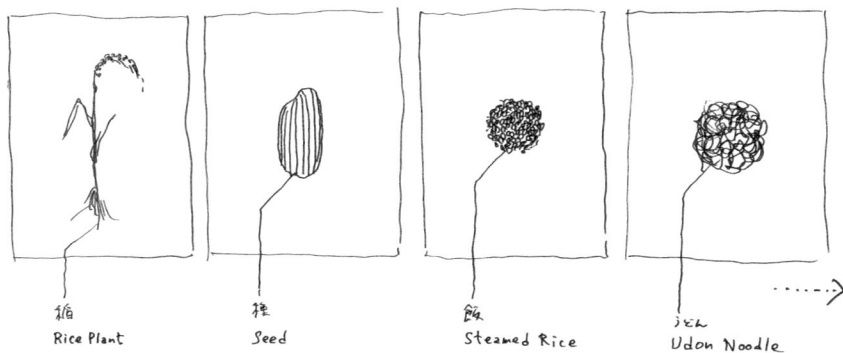

稲
Rice Plant

種
Seed

飯
Steamed Rice

うどん
Udon Noodle

I was invited to an exhibition celebrating the renewal of
the London Design Museum, and made these sketches of my proposed idea.
Under the title, "STAPLES," I sketched staple foods from around the world.
After grinding grains into flour, what kinds of foods do we invent?
This is one approach to the origins of creativity.

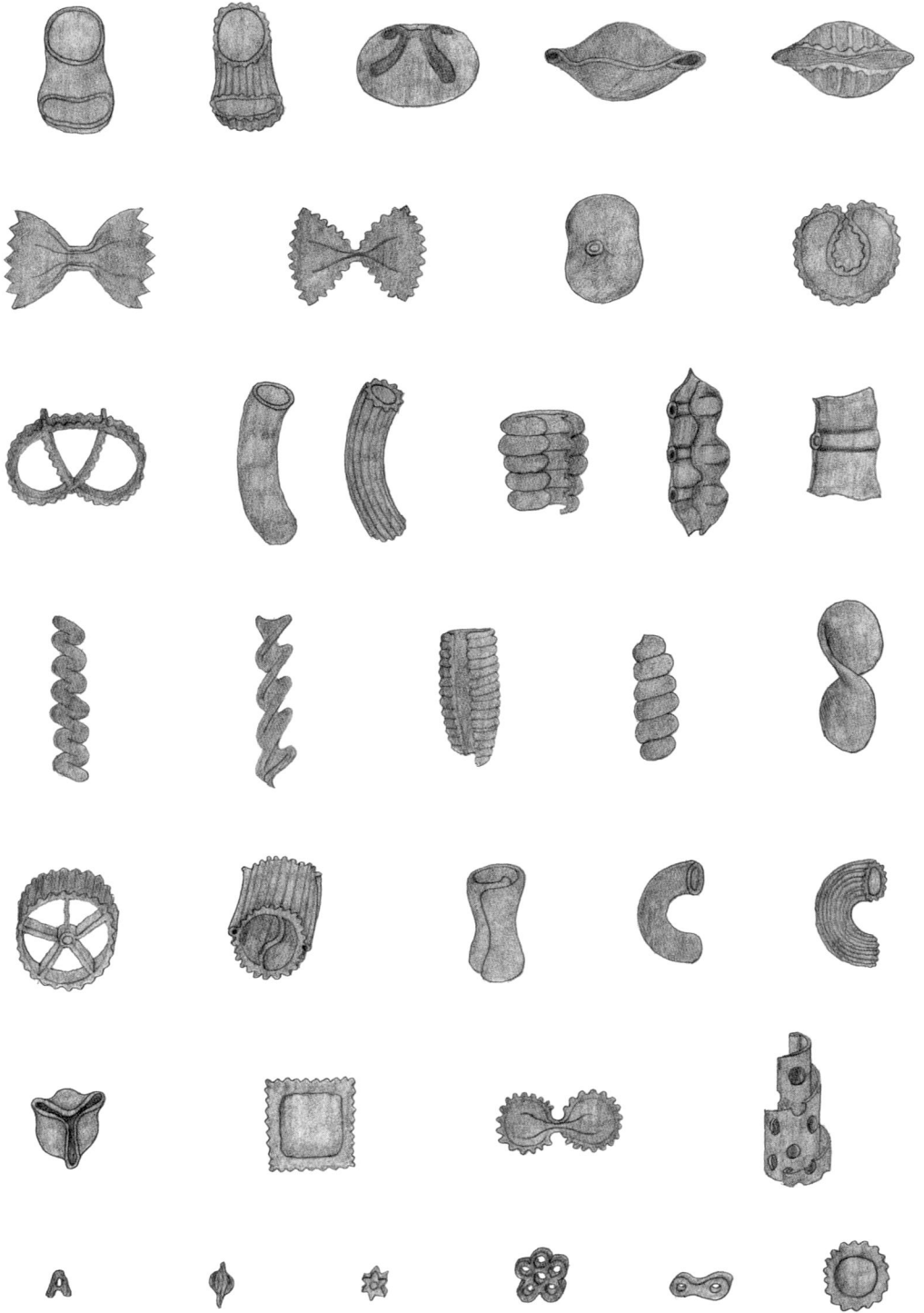

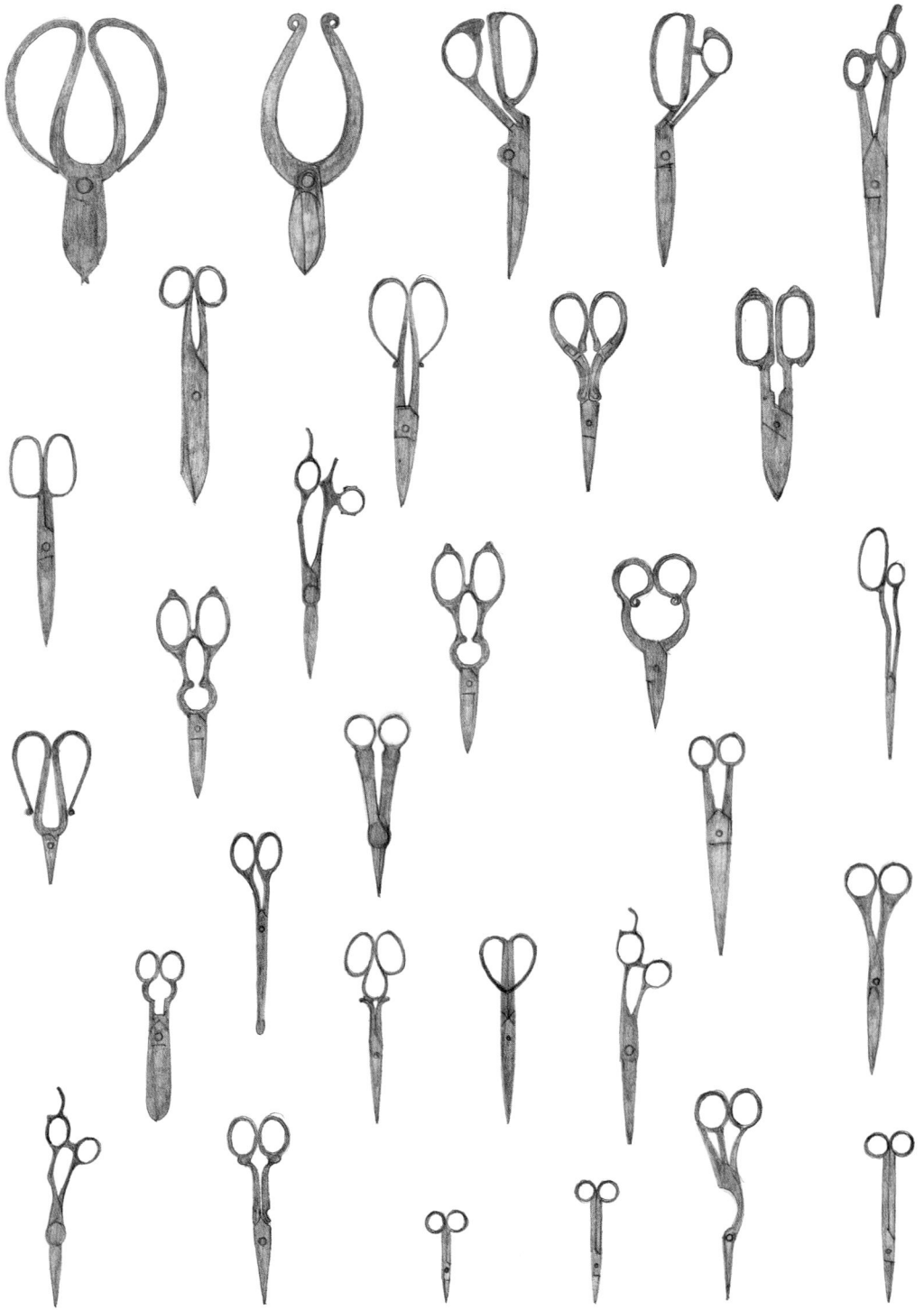

In 2020, Tokyo was set to host the Olympics for a second time.
Despite concerns about overshadowing the spectacular 1964 Olympics,
once the decision was made the necessary steps were taken.

A designer's thoughts about a goal are simple.
I wanted to express the intensity of the energy appropriate to this global event.

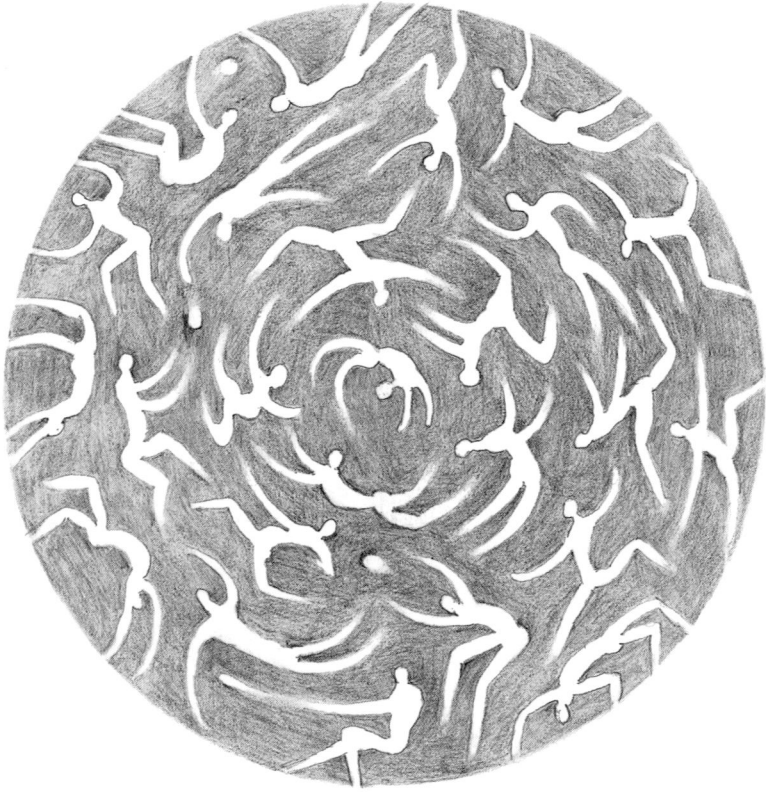

Wanting to express the torrent of a more planetary energy, an overwhelming energy like magma on the move, or lava pouring out, I scribbled these sketches of images that flashed across my mind while I was traveling in a taxi.

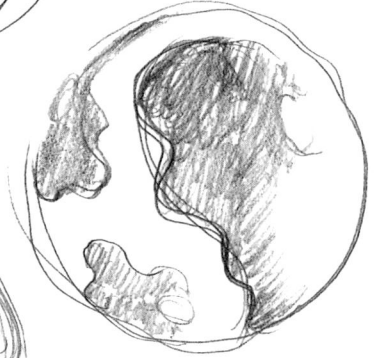

2010—2020   HOUSE VISION, Architecture for Dogs, journey to Earth / other worlds

Bodies moving at high speed above the surface of a planet-like globe. Intrigued by the round shapes of the irregular white blobs, I sketched them over and over again.

As I drew, I got the feeling that something was beginning to appear.
It wasn't yet clear where these sketches would converge.

The final form: The Earth, Japan, an inundation of energy.
In the end, I developed it and completed it as a sphere.
This effort garnered second place in the competition to design the Olympic emblem.

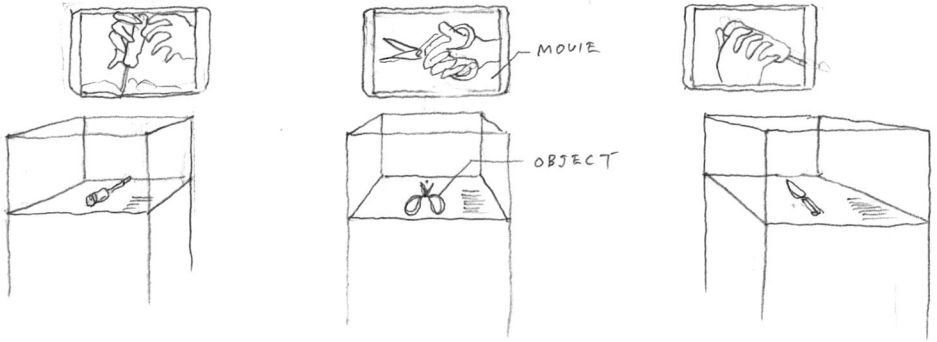

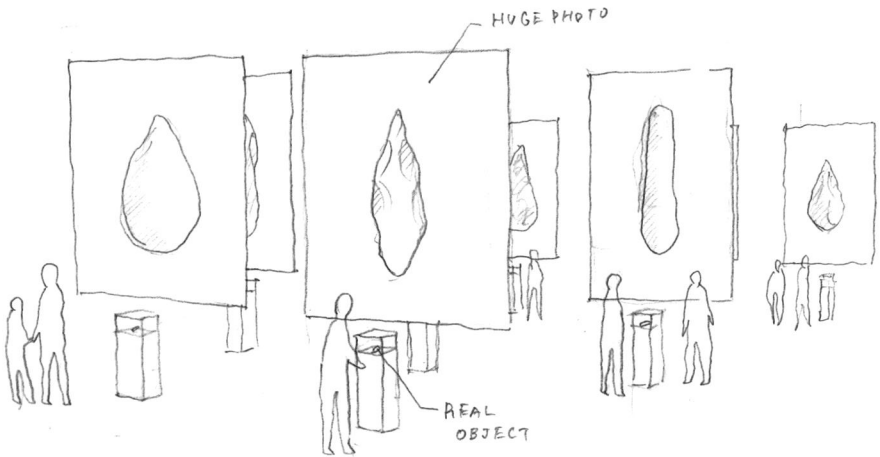

These are early sketches for the exhibition held in 2017 at the Triennale di Milano Museum,
"NEO-PREHISTORY: 100 Verbs." This was my first collaboration with the architect Andrea Branzi,
but from the very beginning, we were on the same wavelength. We created an exhibition with
a sweeping view, traveling back to prehistoric times, of the Stone Age through to the modern day.
For this purpose, we chose 100 verbs as metaphors for human desires, and their matching tools, as pairs.

Photo (Various Sizes)
hanging from the ceiling.
fixed on the floor.

Real Object

Rocks like as the "Stone Henge" (Projection Mapping)

DESIGN AFTER DESIGN
100の動詞　人間はこんな風に世界を変容させてきた
100 verbi – l'umano ha cambiato il mondo cosi' ….

石器はタイプごとに
ひとつの展示台に ひとつずつ置いて。
できるだけ多数を見せる。
その前に動詞のプレートが立つ

●石器時代以前　● Prima dell' eta' della pietra.	1	ある	加工していない石		1個。
●石器時代 (旧石器時代／新石器時代)●Il L'eta' della pietra (Eta' Paleolitica/periodo neolitico)	2	持つ	石斧　旧石器12点		フランチェスカさんと連絡とりあって 30個くらいの石器を選ぶ (原サイズでリードする)
	3	打つ	石棒　中石器		
	4	叩く	石斧		
	5	つくる			
	6	壊す	石棒		

These are notes on the process according to which we chose the tools to correspond to the verbs.
We paired up verbs and artifacts. We procured the display items by borrowing them
from a number of Italian museums and art museums, and also brought some from Japan.

誰に9抒
合に30合

7 潰す	石棒			
8 刺す	石鏃			
9 射る	石鏃			
10 殺す	*アイスマンの武器			
11 投げる	*ブーメランと投げ槍	aborigini — lancia aborigini		
12 煮る △	縄文土器	Jomon Pottery from JAPAN		
13 死ぬ	*イタリアの墓石と木の頭	石の墓	木彫	

農耕と定住のはじ

2010—2020   HOUSE VISION, Architecture for Dogs, journey to Earth / other worlds

#				
14	恐れる	ストーンヘンジ 恐れると同時だ。恐れさせる。	Dolmen or Stone henge	Projector
15	食べる	*パプアニューギニアのカトラリー？	sticks from PAPUA NEW GINIA	
16	飾る	玉器	台北 胡宮博物館 stone object from CHINA	
17	愛する △	玉器	Magatama from JAPAN	
18	耕す	鋤・鍬	鋤	
19	切る メリる	*ロンバルディアの鎌	れ゛ぃ゛を゛ひとつ	
20	紡ぐ △	糸紡ぎ	ひとつ"	

●農耕と定住の時代● L'era di sistemazione della dimora fissa e dell'agricoltura

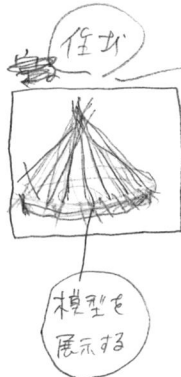

住む

模型を展示する

As tools evolve, so do desires. Evolved desires require new tools. In this way, tools and human desires coevolved. To our minds, this is in fact mankind's genuine and pure history.

4

21	溜める △ 器類	日本 pottery 縄紋土器		酒や小麦を運ぶ 船に穴があいていた。 ← anfora from ITALIA
22	分ける △ 枡			フランチェスカさんが おしいくれる recipiente
23	測る ＊天秤			ballance grande conpaso
24	運ぶ △ 筏／丸太舟			アシで作られたボート (シチリアのシラクーザの) 博物館にある。 piroga siracusa 昔空のなり船 (コンティキ号)
25	戦う ＊矢の先とスーダン のブーメラン			3つの 展示台。
26	住む 閉じる ＊鍵			3つでひとつ
27	踊る △ 仮面			Mack from AFRICA

ひとつづつ

「ムーデ」博物館（ミラノ）
からかりエか
ブランツィさんも？つくらい
もいる。

2010—2020　HOUSE VISION, Architecture for Dogs, journey to Earth / other worlds

42	航海する △ 探検する	羅針盤＊＊中国が起源だが？		中国の羅針盤
43	観測する	＊ガリレオの道具をセットで		個別に展示、
44	奏でる	楽器		琴
45	研究する	＊ガリレオのガラス機器（温度計）		
46	交換する	＊ギリシャの貨幣？		first coin of Greece "Drakma"
47	撃つ	機関銃		火縄銃. (イタリア"
48	覚える 学ぶ	辞書・教科書		百科事典 イタリア

49 仕立てる 切る	針／はさみ	JAPAN	JAPAN	
50 慈しむ (子供と 生き物)	人形）			
51 養生する	＊薬箱セット	box of Medicine		
52 働く 考える	背広／鞄／靴	レオポルドの手書きの詩		
●産業革命以降● I Post rivoluzione industriale 53 計画する	＊メタボリズムの模型(NDC手配)	architecture Model		
54 発明する	電球,真空管,トランジスター	Edison's light		
55 稼ぐ	＊金の延べ棒(1本のみ)	Gold		
働く				

仕立てる
学ぶ
考える

建てる

ミース・ファレンスワースロース

56	賭ける	スロットマシン		slot machine
57	汚す／染する	煙突		Pink plastic glove,
58	座る	キャスレリオーリ／コルビジェ／イームズ／ヤコブセン／ウェグナー	520製造	
59	蹂躙する	*戦車(はりぼて)とバズーカ・ベスパ		バズーカベスパ レンバ22 リアナル
60	攻撃する	*手榴弾		
61	料理する	テーブルウエア調理器具		
62	開発する	*巨大トラクターの車輪		huge tire of Tractor.

Desires don't necessarily evolve in a good direction.
The desire to dominate, sloth, cunning, and brutality all coevolve with tools.

10

63	ドライブする	*ランボルギーニ	ランボルギーニ
64	~~治療する~~ 手術する	注射器/医療機器	tools for Dentist
65	~~差別する~~ 無視する	鉄格子の扉	ハクセイのネワ／ミヤネルヒ・か ダイトとか
66	抹殺する	*ガスマスク	
67	逮捕する	手錠	
68	流行する	~~衣服~~	SONY WALKMAN
●コンピュータと大量破壊兵器の時代● l L'era delle macchine per l'uccisione di massa e il computer	69	~~生産する~~ 製造する	*巨大スクリュー (はりぼて)	huge propella of huge oil tanker

70	汚染する	煙突		
71	移動する	新幹線・飛行機		飛行機の ファーストクラスの シートか トルトーナ・755の 新幹線の座席.
72	淫する 麻薬する	注射器		真空パックされた 注射器
73	降伏する	白い旗		white flag
74	絶望する	原子爆弾		Atomic Bomb 模型を作る(トリフェアレ)
75	威嚇する	ミサイル		トマホーク 模型を作る
76	測定する クロノメトレ	時計・計測機器 ストップウォッチ		クロノグラフ

256 | 257   DRAW

77	装う	ジュエリー・香水・化粧品			
		fashinale		CHANEL 5°	
78	記念する	建築		サッカー world cupのトロフィー	
79	祝う	シャンペン・シャンペングラス			
80	対話する	携帯電話・ブルーベリー フリザ		NOKIA	
81	精緻化する	Mac Book Air		iMac	
82	買い物をする	スーパー・コンビニ			
83	旅行する	スーツケース			

98	依存する	アマゾンポスト・iPhone 初音ミク		iPhone ——初音ミク
99	共有する 遠隔操作する	Facebook・Twitterのアイコン Remote Controle 折り紙ロボット		リモートコントロールされる 極小折り紙ロボット
100	凝縮する（ナノ化する一極小化する） 極小化する	ヘッドマウントディスプレイ 傷の上にモニタリング用にプリントされたセンサー		傷のようにプリントされたセンサー。
101	連繋する	iPhone		iPhone Facebookのうにか iPadになる
102	自己組織化する	自動運転車		タフのiPhoneの画面をさがって鳥の群のようすを
103	同調する	ロボット ハーバート大学		多数が集まって図を再現する。モニターで表現。

As tools become more complex, so too do verbs.
To control remotely, to survive, to masquerade, to miniaturize, to self-organize.
At the very end, we placed the verb "to reproduce." The corresponding tool
is a holograph of an artificial heart beating in the air.

家族の繁栄篇（FAMILIES / FAMILY TREE） 全体で 90～120秒

[同一単位が増殖していく様子 / 異なる単位と競い、バランスしていく様子]

土から
→ F1

房えが。

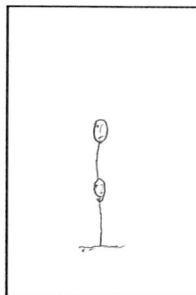

さらに
Ⓐ

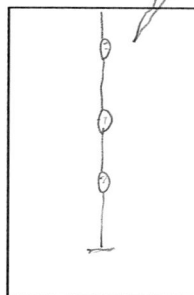

上らた.
→ FO → E

→ F1
房えが

叫んど工増こる

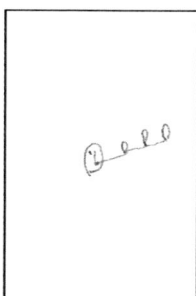

増える
Ⓑ

叫えど

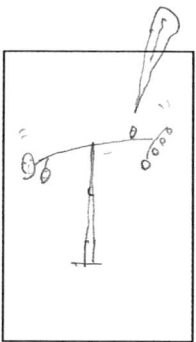

→ F1
Ⓗ バランスが

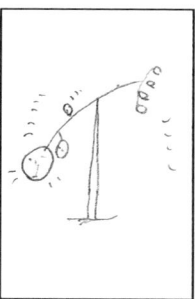

こわれる

もどす.

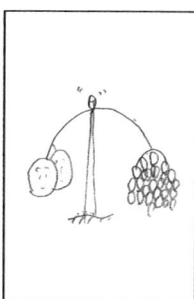

無理がまじる
互

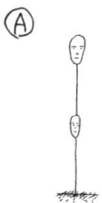

Ⓐ

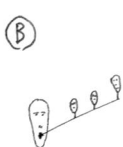

Ⓑ

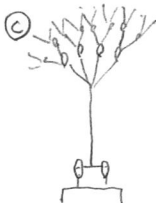

Ⓒ

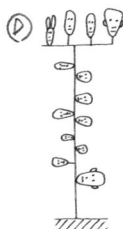

Ⓓ

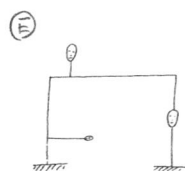

Ⓔ

Ⓕ

描に花が　　　　　ここえ、　　　　ここえ、　　　Ⓓ さらに子番に
→ FO

④へで増える　　ひとりが　　　よろけれそろと　　ⓒ どんどん増える
→ FO → FI　　　　　　　　　　　　　　　　　　　　　　→ FO

均衝する　　土台に　　　ひとつ積み　　ふたつ積み　　３つ積み
→ FO → FI

Ⓖ　　Ⓗ　　Ⓘ　　Ⓙ　　Ⓚ

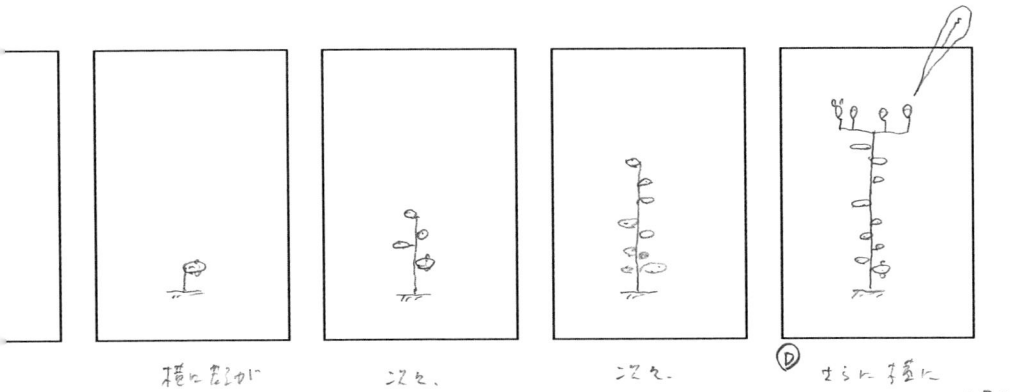

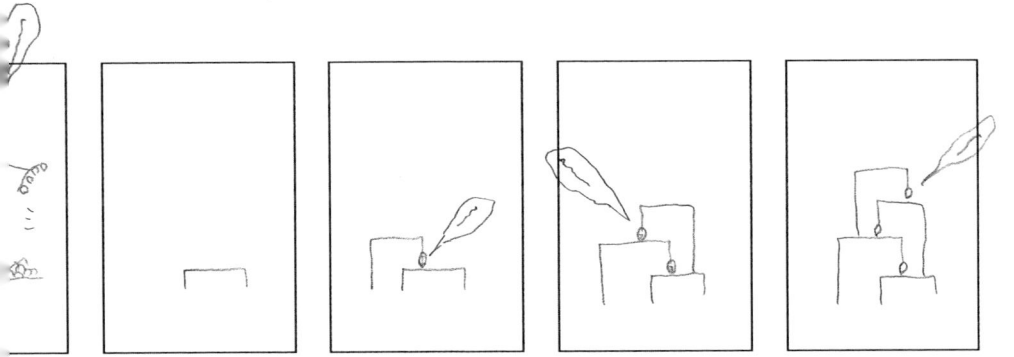

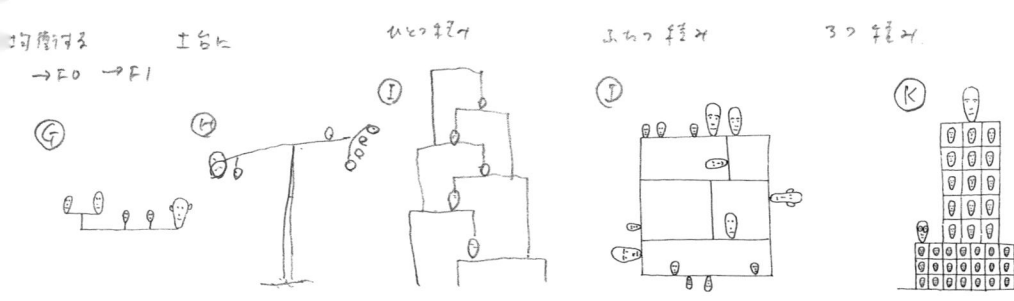

Storyboard for the animated short film of Andrea Branzi's book, *GENETIC TALES*.

③ 集団と集合篇 （GROUP and CATEGORY） 90秒でループ

[いかなる組成によって集団ができるか。いかなるカテゴリーに分かれていくか]

 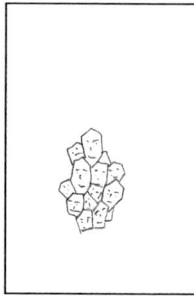 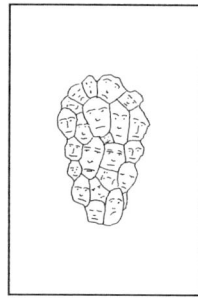 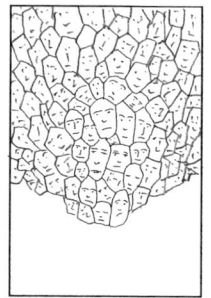

1サカ1らが   増殖し.   Ⓐ サオスオリになり.   岩になる   ひ

→ F1   →FO   →F

se つぶれる〜

  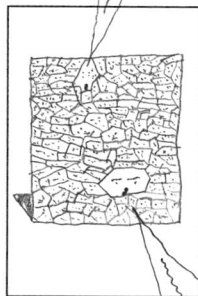 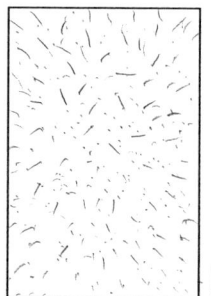

分裂をはじめ   Ⓒ せめぎあい   圧殺されて.   破裂する   Ⓓ

                          se   →FO

se 部室風に

 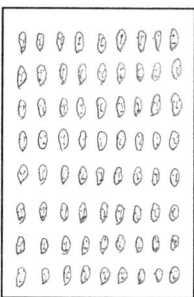  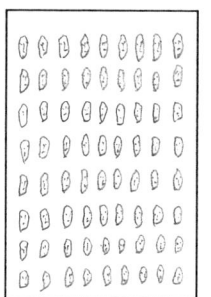

Ⓕ → ヘアスタイルの様々 → 平均化し → Ⓖ ヒゲ族になり. アフロ風に → 元にモドリ → Ⓗ

 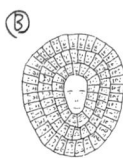   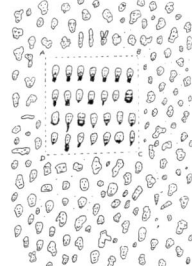 

Ⓐ   Ⓑ   Ⓒ   Ⓓ   Ⓔ

(ORIGINAL)

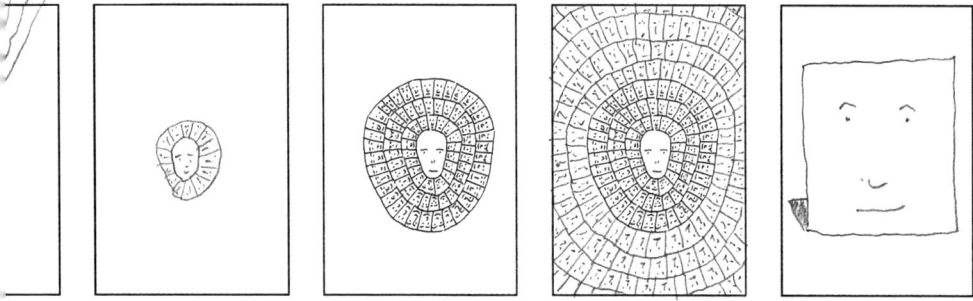

号令風に

増えはじめ   Ⓑ 大きくなり.   世界を埋めつくす.   1人占めだったものが
→FO → FI

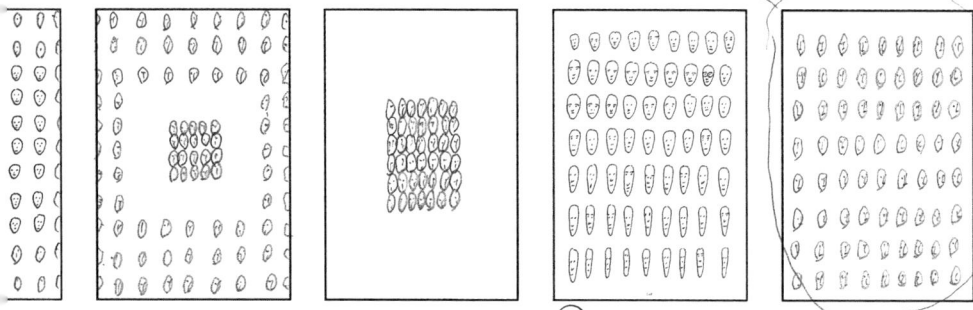

集団になり.   待たされる → Ⓔ 散開して個性化し → 平均にもどる

se
オバケ風に.

se
プリミティブに

マフィア風に
se

→ ループ
→ FO

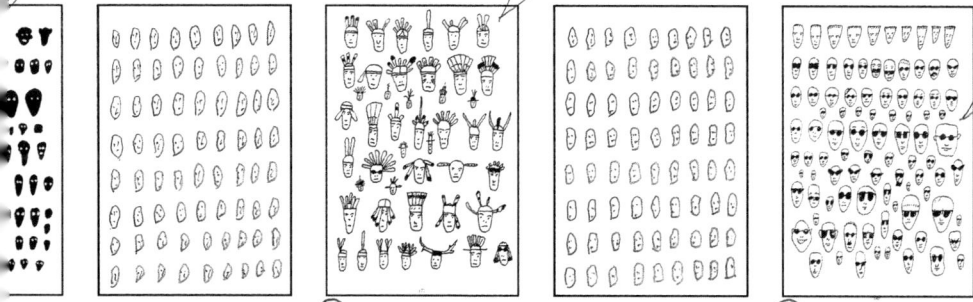

あり → 元にもどり → Ⓘ まるまるの頭上装飾 → 元にもどり → Ⓙ サングラス族になる

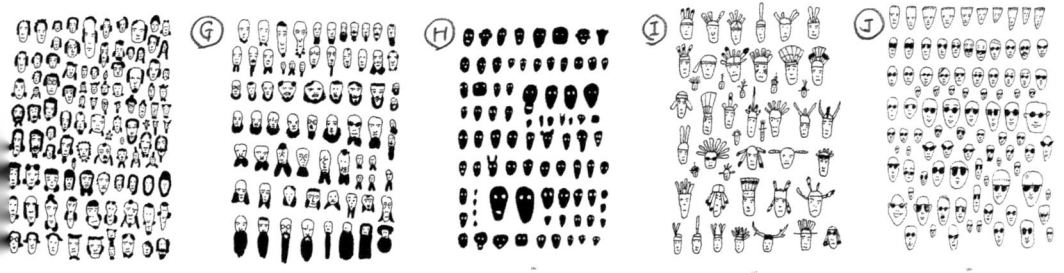

群集篇 (Crowds) 全体で 90秒 ゲループ

[人が増加し、互いの益をせめぎ合うことの矛盾と向題を VISUALIZE する]

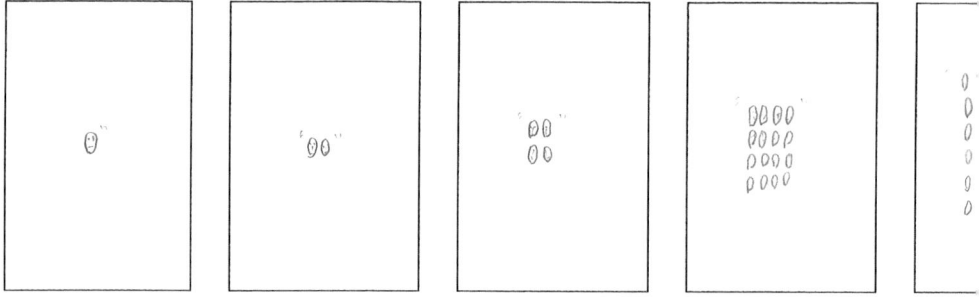

→Fi   ————→ 倍増 ——→ 増殖

Ⓟ   Ⓔ

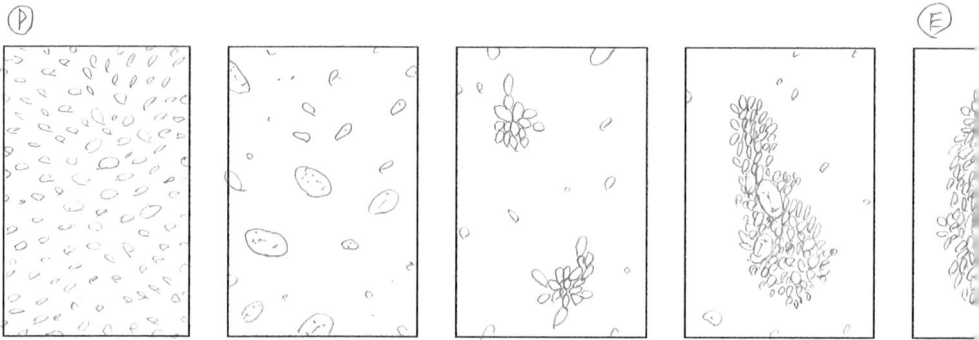

破裂   ————→ 拡散   中心化・核化
(Se)

Ⓖ   Ⓗ   逆もする   Ⓘ
                              逆でする

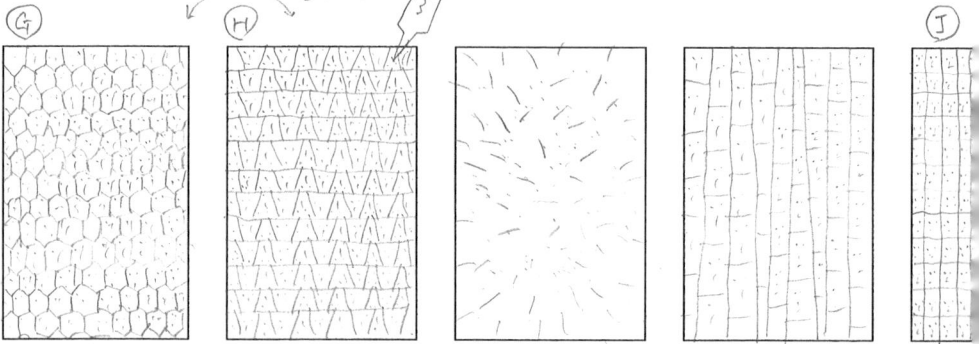

→ 6角高密化 六角形   → バラバラとなり   → 再び構造化され   均質に
                              (Se)

Ⓐ   Ⓑ   Ⓓ   Ⓒ   Ⓔ

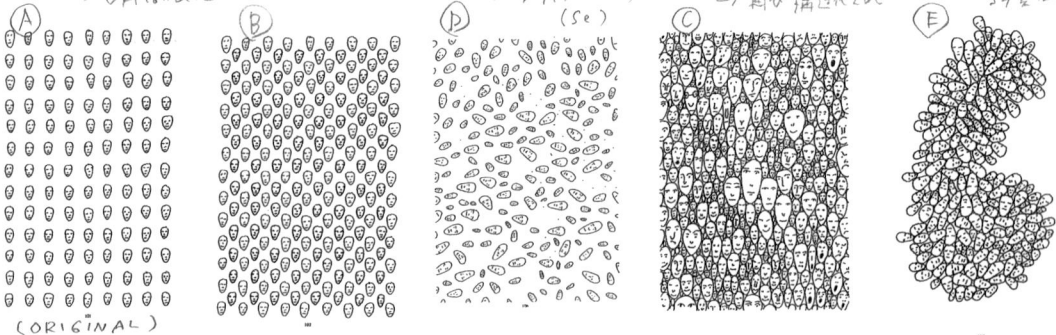

(ORIGINAL)

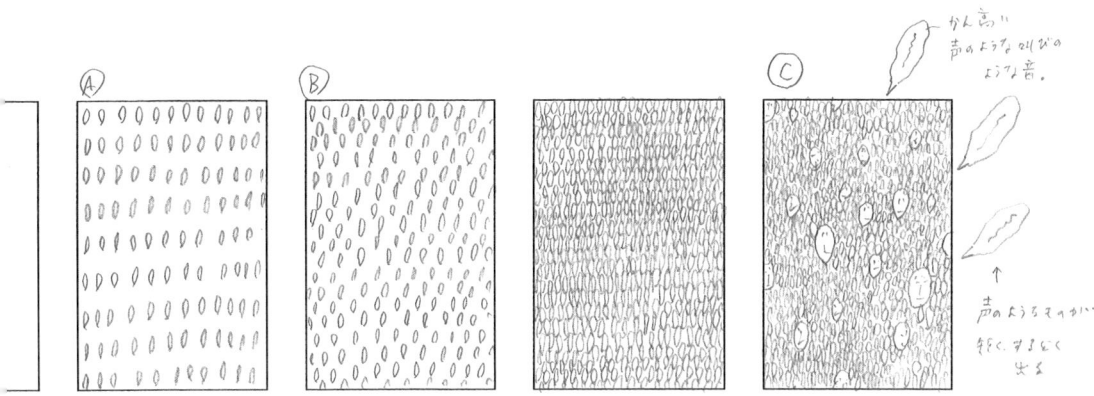

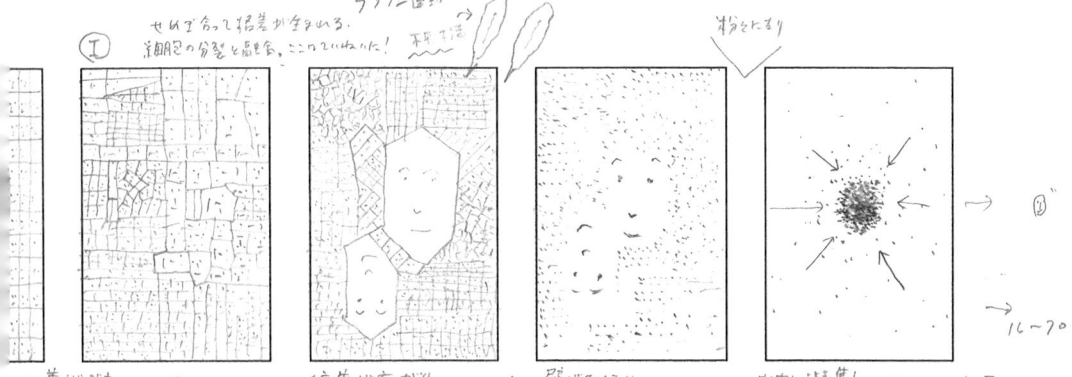

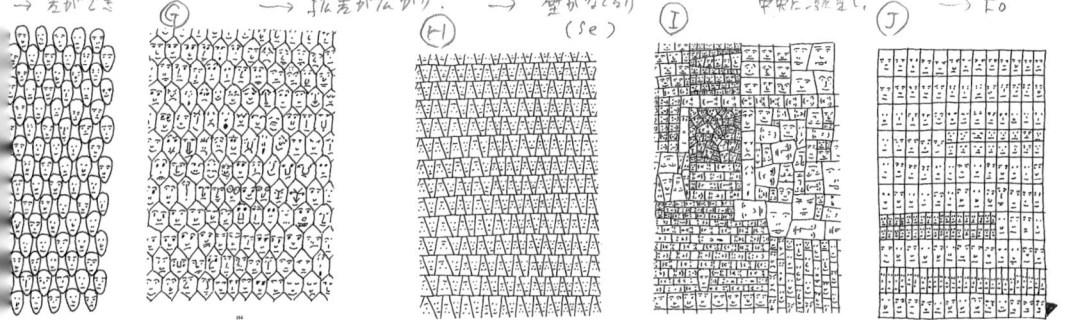

56 稼ぐ
guadagnare

金の延べ棒
lingotto d'oro

57 働く
lavorare

製造する
fabbricare

大きなスクリュー（模型）
grande elica

58 賭ける
giocare d'azzardo

スロットマシン
slot machine

汚染する
inquinare

ピンク色のプラスティック製手袋
guanti di plastica rosa

59

建てる
costruire

53

ミース　ヴァンデルローエの高層建築
grattacielo
Mies Van Der Rohe

54 計画する
progettare

メタボリズムの都市模型
modello della citta'-metabolism

...Edison/ transistor

ランジスター

撃つ
sparare

機関銃
...ucile

30cm くらい

51 養生する
curarsi

薬箱セット
farmacia portatile

52 考える
pensare

レオパルディの詩。
インフィニティー手稿
manoscritto poesia
"L'Infinito" di Leopar...

27 戦う
conbatt...

pugnale ...
+ clave

49 切る
confezionare

針／はさみ
forbici italiane
e forbici orientali

50 慈しむ
affezionarsi

人形
bambola

王定
解ぼう学の本

39 書く
scrivere

アナトミアの手書き本を探す！
小野...

38 競う
competere

多様な球体ボール類
palla

王定
王冠を探す
支配する
重要 33 regnare sovrano

椅子／王冠さやつきの王の剣
王座は
NO.
trono + spada con fodero

40 味わう
gustare

カトラリー
set posate antiche

多様な書籍
ダビンチのマニュスクリプト
マニュスクリプト手写本／
小野業照著書(MOA)
manoscritti di
codice leonardo/Tofu

ダ'ウィ'ウチ生理.

奴隷の足かせ.

34 服従する
obbedire

足枷 時代不詳
catene ai piedi

30 梳く
pettinarsi

櫛
pettine

31 食事する
mangiare

原始カトラリー
posate primordiali

やめる 41 楽しむ
divertirsi

エジプトのゲーム
senet gioco
antico egitto

36 遊ぶ
giocare

2~3cm

古代のサイコロ
dadl

記録する 王定
探す
ヨーロッパの
35 他の時代の投
scrivere (piu' studiare)

中国の竹本
bamboo book from china

ヨーロッパ...
...んし脇
...ん工脇を
王にしてみる

28 閉じる
chiudere

所有する
所有する chiudere

3つの鍵（ローマ時...
3 chiavi

32 酩酊する
ubriacarsi

牛の角の器
bicchiere di corno

王定
フくしコ゛ツクないけ'NO
どこかで王定す。

37 装う
vestirsi

王定
王定

ガラス玉の首飾りと農耕モチーフのブローチ
collana + spilla

トァの歴史...
ちょび X

やめる

このタイプのもネタレス（ヒとポ玉）

→ブローチを探す.

11/26

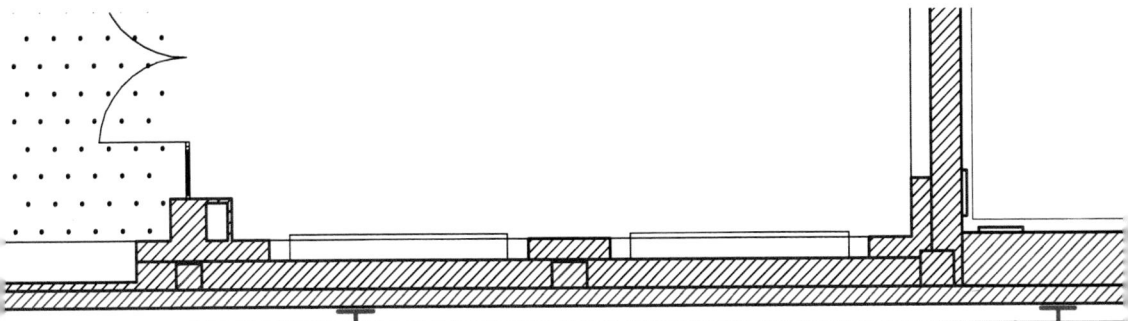

17 祭る まつる 把る
ornarsi

16 食べる
alimentarsi

12 投げる
lanciare

何年も前から、
同じ入る形の
ブーメラン
投げる

11 殺す
uccidere

18.9cm 青銅

石刀
posate cannibaliche

パプア
ニューギニア

石鏃
boomerang
+ lancia aborigeni australia

矢と刃
青銅器時代

玉器(中国製)
stone object
from china

玉器

ベネラーレ

(ひすい)

pietra

50cm

ire

青銅器時代初期

18 愛する
amare

胎児のような形
神秘的なものに
特別な心を
よせる。
曲玉

死ぬ
mor05
morire

14

始まり

13 煮る
cuocere

殺す
ascia di oetzi
石斧

magatama
from Japan

10cm

ローマ2000年前
の居住民

喜石

stele + testa in legno

縄文土器
ceramica di Jomon

24 分ける
condividere

19 耕す
arare

3

杯
ciotole per il cibo

15 祈る
pregare

②

ヴィーレンドルフのヴィーナス
venus di willendorf

25 量る
misurare

20 住む
abitare

26 運ぶ
trasportare

物差し(秤?)
bilancia

22 紡ぐ
filare-tessere

丸木舟
piroga

プリミティブな住居の模型
modellino di
abitazione primitiva

糸紡ぎ
fuseruola

丸太舟

分銅

29 踊る
danzare

23 溜める
contenere

仮面
3 maschere

器類
recipiente Jomon

29と30の間、もうひとつ タイ付加す

Sketches for a MUJI corporate ad campaign.
Andean people and alpacas. The copy reads, "Humanity: Warm?"

The Raja Ampat Islands of Indonesia are a hotspot of biodiversity located where the Indian and Pacific Oceans meet. Where a coral reef is visible in crystal clear water, the photo captures both land and sea in a single image. We are intrigued by the colors of the Earth.

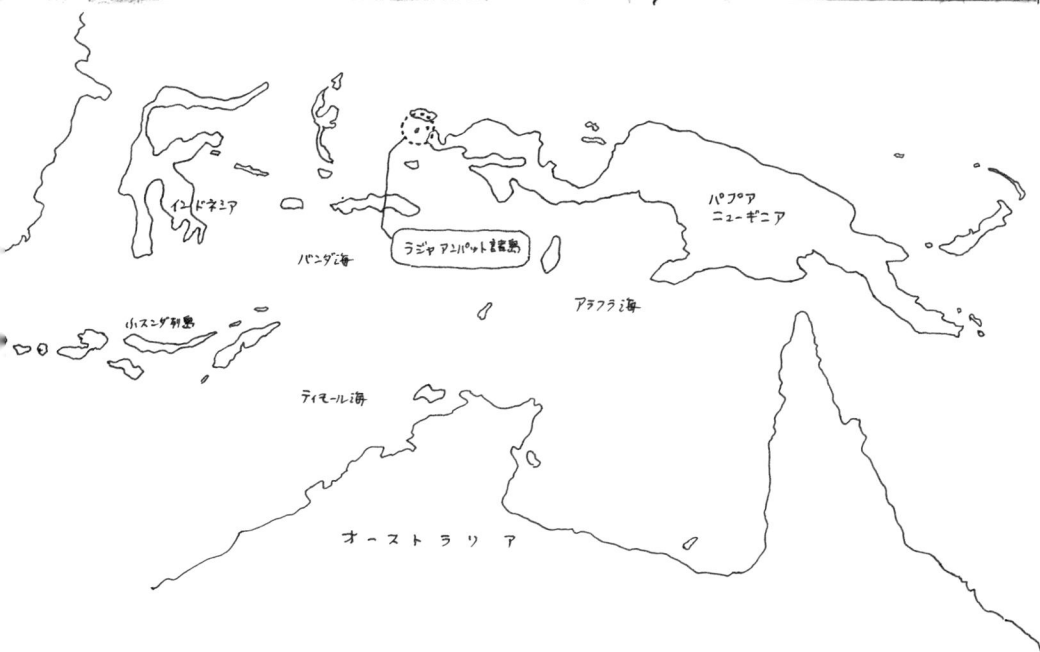

インドネシア

パプア
ニューギニア

バンダ海

ラジャ アンパット諸島

スンダ列島

アラフラ海

ティモール海

オーストラリア

20 (月)   8:40

21 (火)   9:25

22 (水)   10:08

23 (木)

24 (金)   6:59

25 (土)   8:31

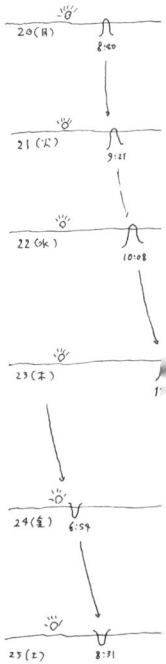

A sketch noting the timing of high and low tides so as to capture the moment
when the water's surface will be at the ideal position between sea and land.
It was an astounding coral reef that reminds us that there are forests in the sea as well as on land.

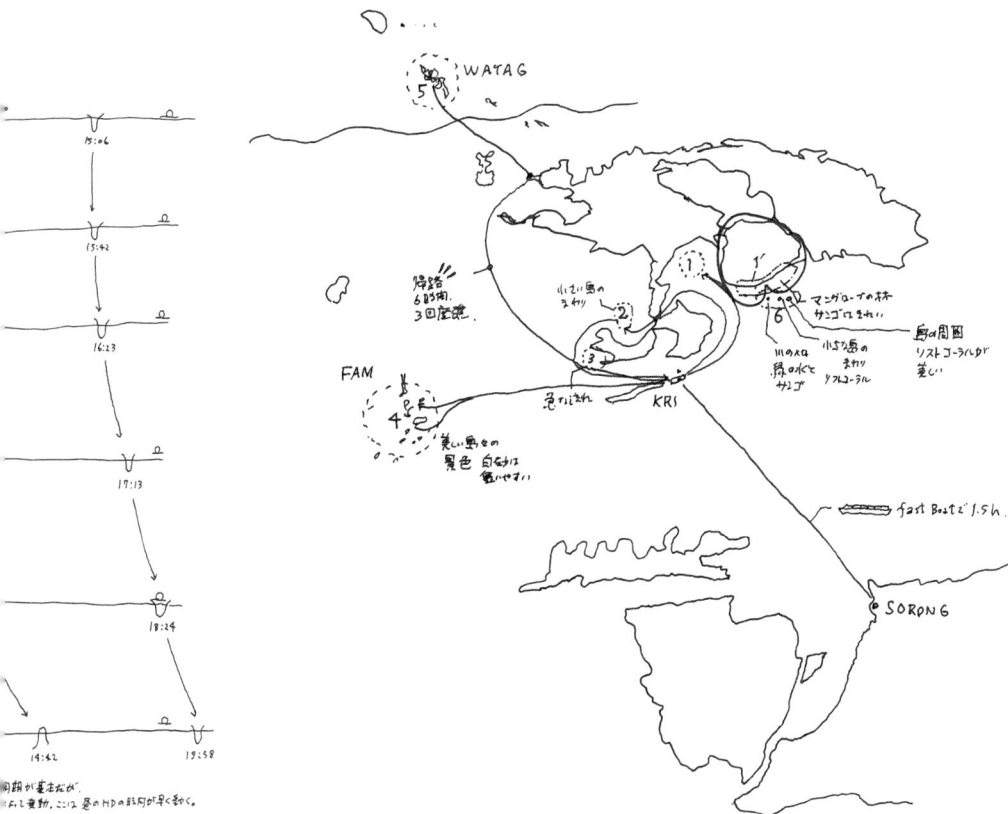

新聞を読む女
日本家屋 + MUJI

A woman reading a newspaper.
Even though it's somehow a charming scene, it was never used in a project.

新聞を読む女
住居 + MUJI

新聞を読む女
ホテル + MUJI

I visited the Galapagos Islands, the birthplace of evolutionary theory,
to undertake a project on the theme of evolution and originality.
I was thinking about a form of advertising that involves traveling to unknown places
and sharing the experience with patrons. I was also thinking about the Earth
and the environment. A biologist accompanied us on this research trip.

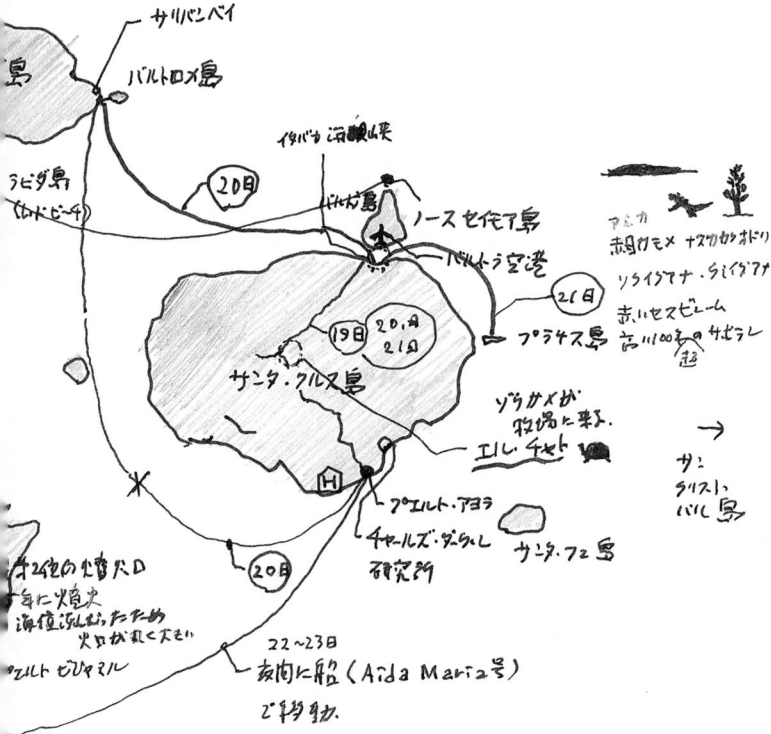

ヘベサ島

マルチェナ島

サリバンベイ
バルトロメ島
島

ラビダ島
（カトビーイ）

20日

イサバラ海峡峡

バルカ島
ノース セイモア島

バルトラ空港

21日

19日 20日 21日

プラチス島

サンタ・クルス島

ゾウガメが
牧場に来る
エル チャト

サ：
クリスト
バル島

プエルト・アヨラ

H

チャールズ・ダーウィン
研究所

サンタ・フェ島

オ24号の燈台入口
また燈火
海底沈んだため
火口が丸く大きい
プエルトビリャミル

20日

22～23日
夜間に船（Aida Maria号）
ご移動。

アメリカ
赤足カモメ ナスカカツオドリ
ソラインアナ・ライグアナ
赤いセマビーム 長川100多の サボテン
超

フロレアナ島

エスパニョーラ
島

21日／プラサス島

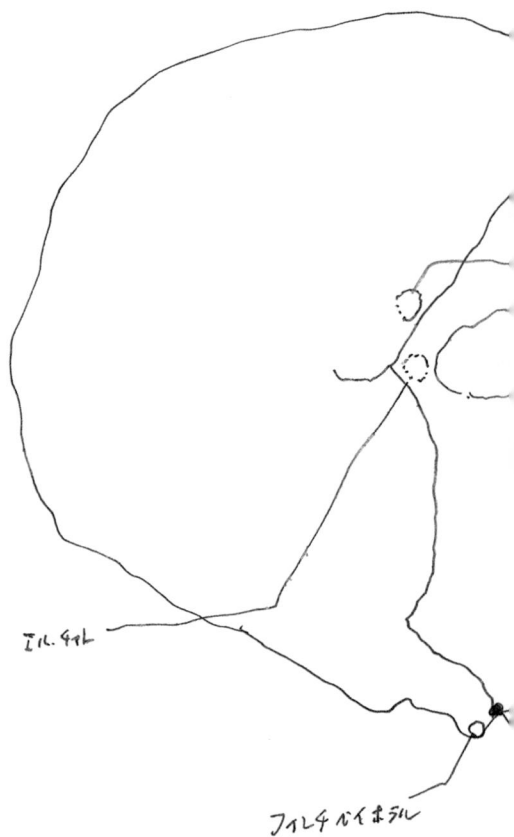

エル. タイレ

フィレ チ ベイ ホテル

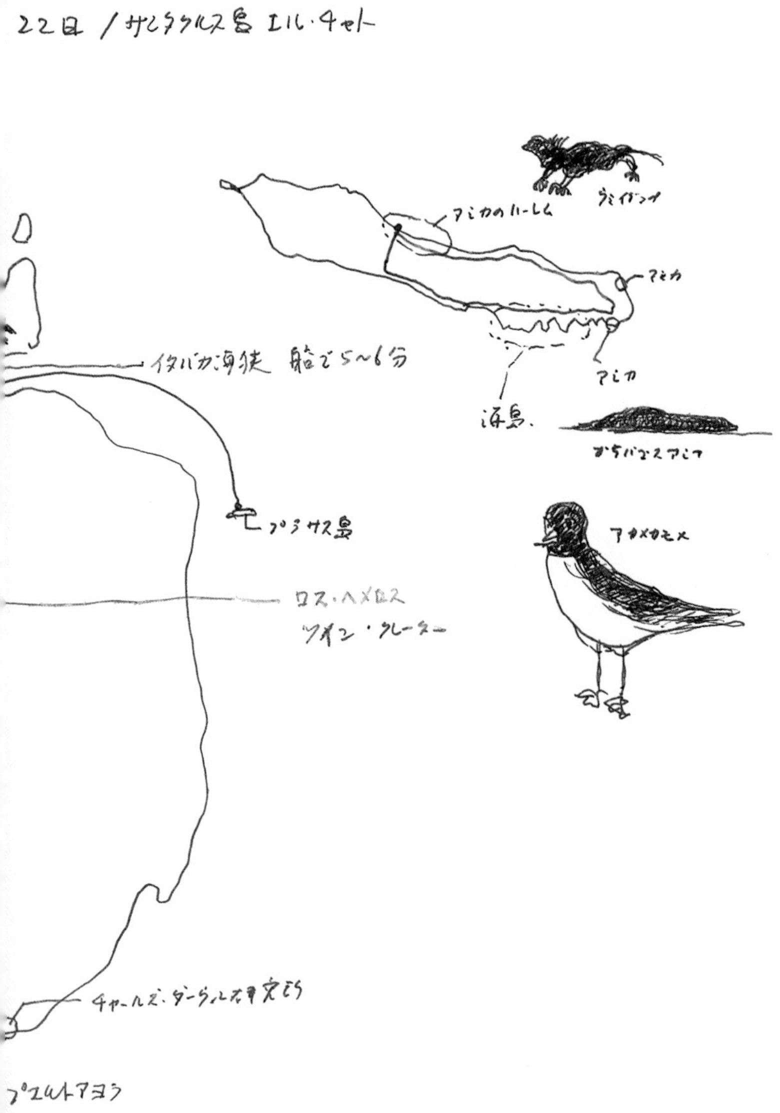

22日 / サンタクルス島 エル・チャト

アビカのハーレム　ウミイグアナ

アビカ

イダバガ海狭　船で5〜6分

浮島.

アビカ

うちなみるアビカ

アカメカモメ

プラサス島

ロス・ヘメロス
ツイン・クレーター

チャールズ・ダーウィン研究所

プエルトアヨラ

［4つの海流とがラパゴス］

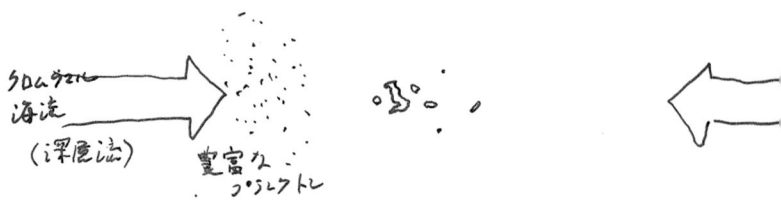

パナマ
海流
（暖流）

がラパゴス
アシカ

クロムウェル
海流
（深層流）

豊富な
プランクトン

がラパゴス
ペンギン

豊富なプランクトン

がラパゴス
オットセイ

ペルー海流
（寒流）

The Galapagos Islands are young islands.
As the islands are uninhibited by natural predators,
the animals that drifted ashore evolved freely and independently.

パナマ

コスタ
リカ

コロンビア

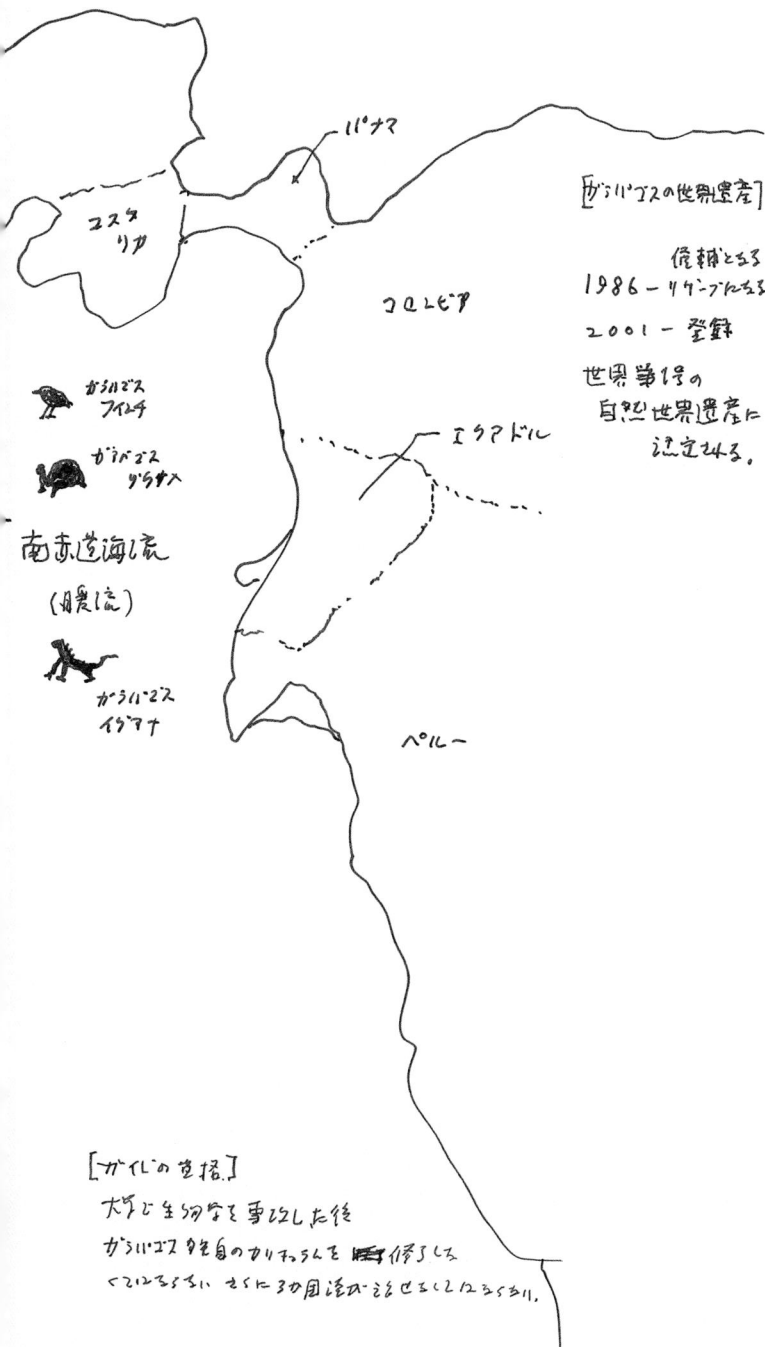

[ガラパゴスの世界遺産]

危機とする
1986 ─ リケーブになる
2001 ─ 登録
世界第1号の
自然世界遺産に
認定される.

ガラパゴス
フィンチ

ガラパゴス
グラナス

南赤道海流
(暖流)

ガラパゴス
イグアナ

エクアドル

ペルー

[ガイドの支援]
大学と生分けを手ていした後
ガラパゴス独自のカリフォルムを 修了した
くているること さらに3カ国活が送せることになること.

23日 / イザベラ島 / シエラネグラ火山・ディレトレラ湾
24日 / イザベラ島 / プンタモレノ付近。

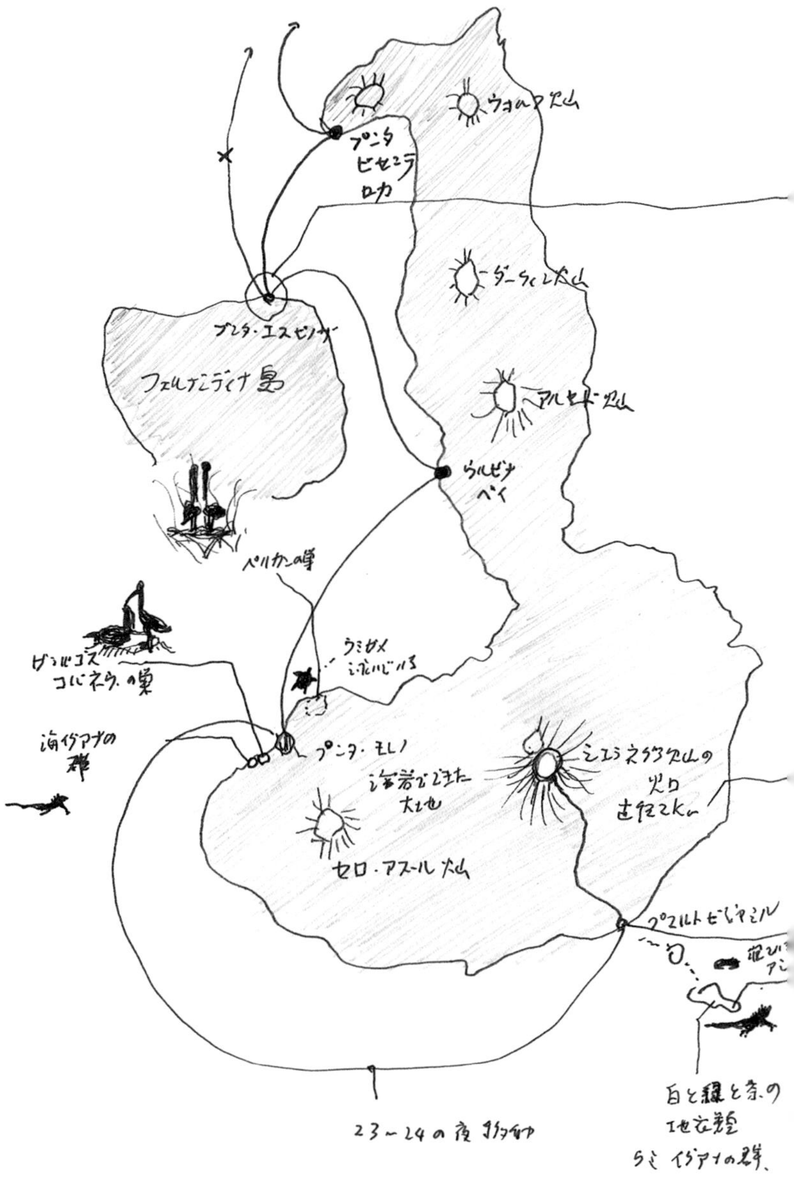

23〜24の夜移動

282 | 283   DRAW

25日/フェルナンディナ島

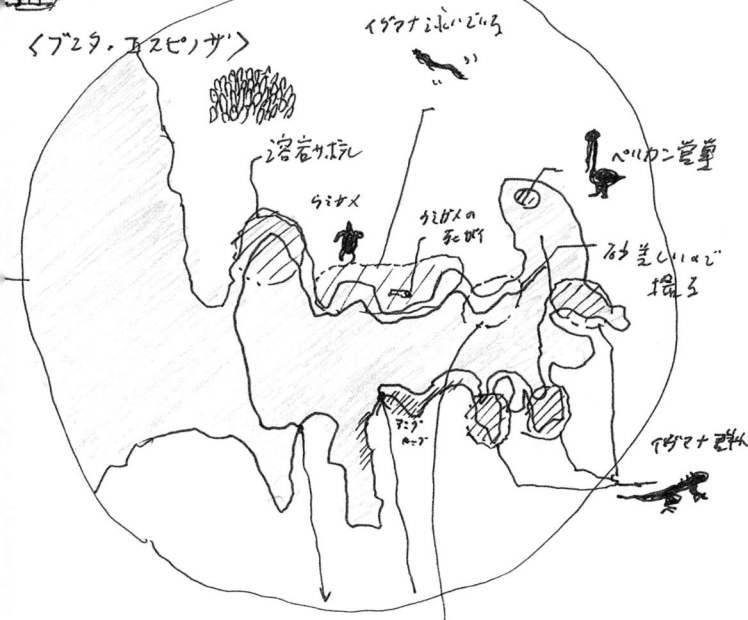

〈ブンタ・エスピノザ〉

イグアナ泳いでる

溶岩カバネ

ラミサメ

ウミガメの産卵

ペリカン営巣

砂差しいらで撮る

イグアナ群れ

〈新しいるう〉
るんなりちいの砂

溶岩の破片

骨の不発方

サンゴの破片

貝の破砕片

豪雨のため
あまり全景見ず
しかし少しの晴れ間を撮る

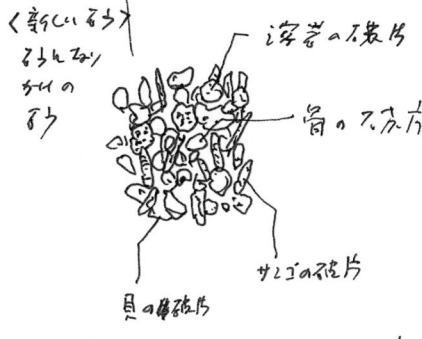

ティントレラ島
Tintoreras

そちの5%は岩石(鉱物)
あとの50%は動物の死骸
骨/貝から、サンゴ
破片である

The sand on these islands is very young.
It's made up of bits of coral, lava, seashells, and animal bones.
Because the particles are still relatively large, the origins of the sand are easy to discern.

25日 / イベペる島　ブ2フ・ピセ2テ・ロカ

切り立た岩壁.　．かラスの カーサ．ミ3 の トリス

ブンタ・ビセラ・ロカの岩壁

島

意外と目玉がてつい
アオアシカツオドリ

とび：タヨマミ
カフエレッ

Neither the animals nor the birds are afraid of people.
The birds fly nearby to take a look at us.
The toddling fledglings do not run away. We feel as if we've become invisible.

26日/ ~~供六言島~~ サンティアご島

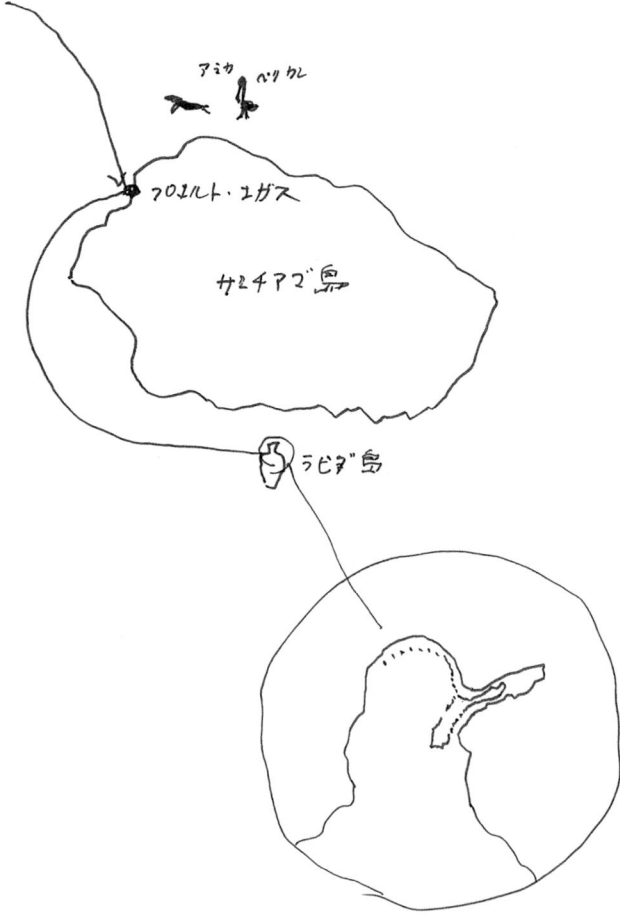

アミカ　ペリカレ

フロェルト・ユガス

サンチアご島

ラビヅ島

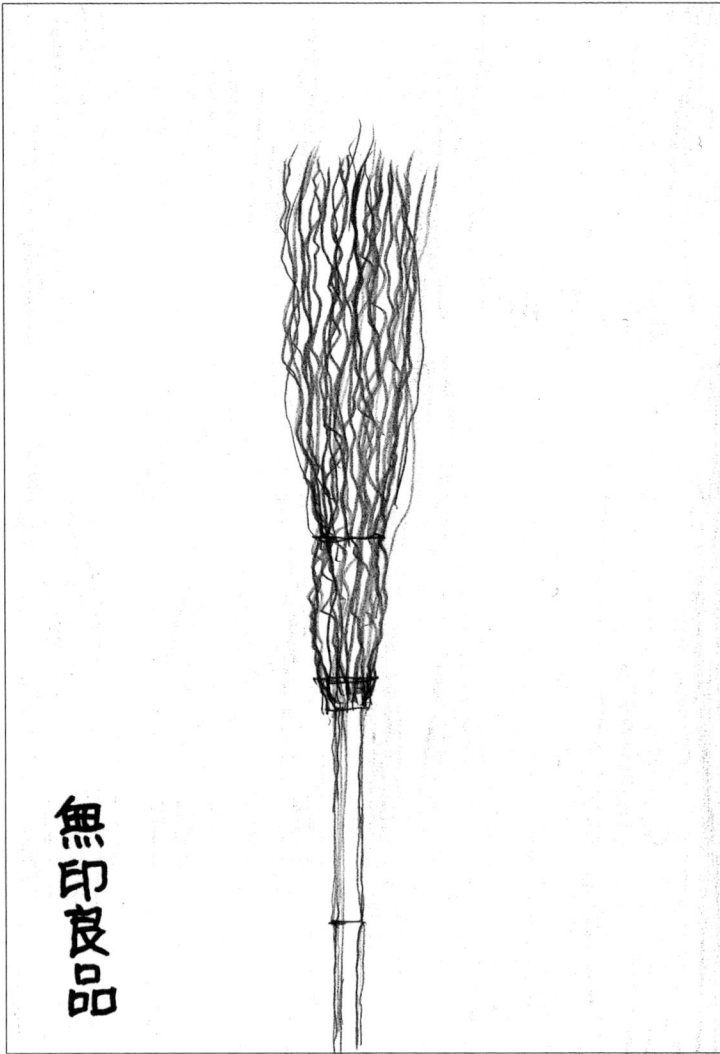

無印良品

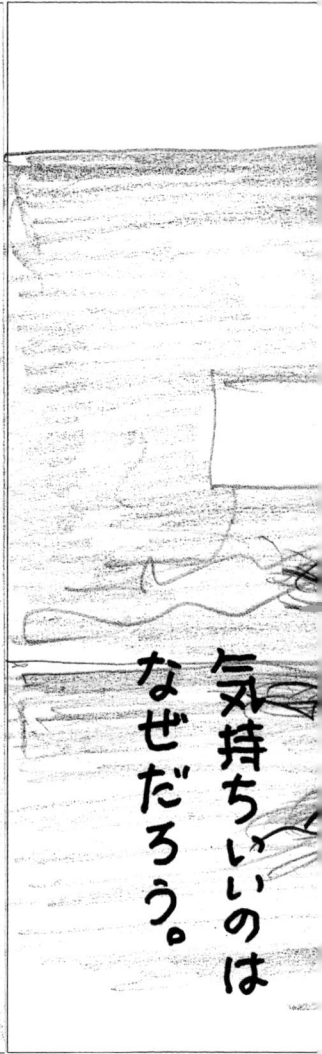

気持ちいいのは
なぜだろう。

As I gathered scenes of cleaning from around the world, I found the assemblage to be quite moving.
I got the idea of actually going out and shooting these scenes, and putting them together into a video.
I was able to turn the lingering question of why this was "pleasant, somehow" into a message.

清掃車／中国

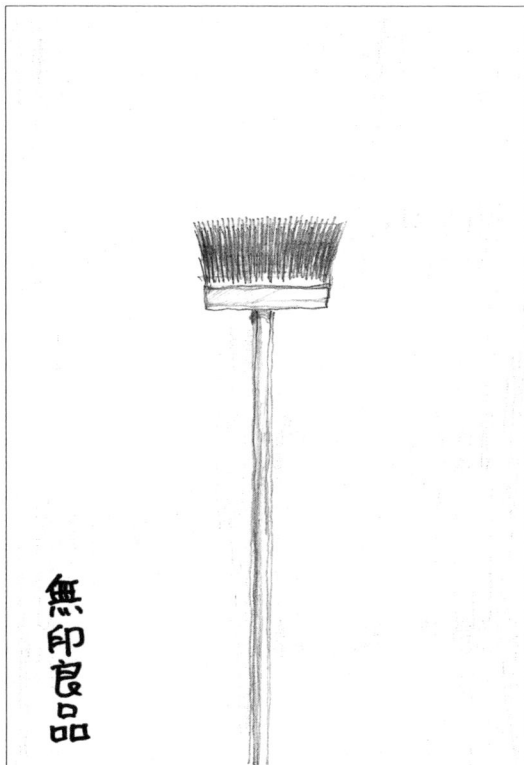

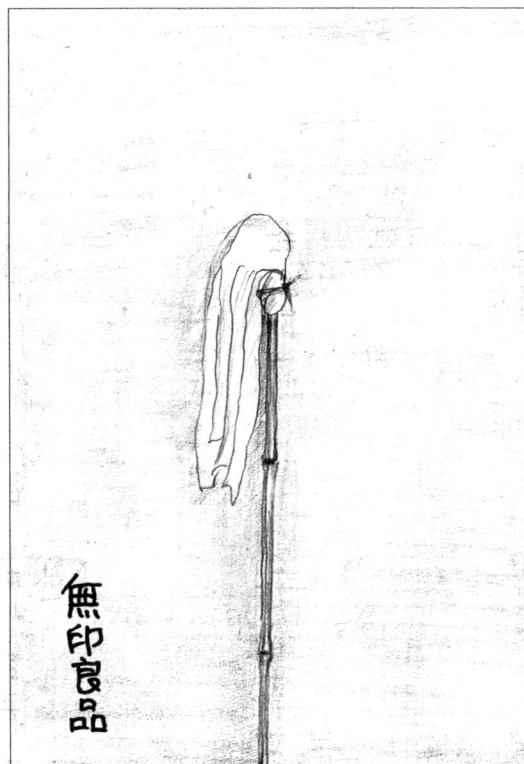
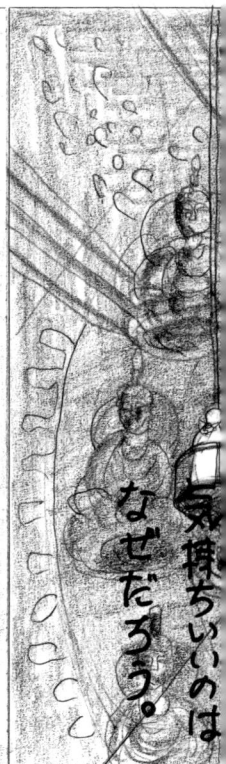

2010—2020   HOUSE VISION, Architecture for Dogs, journey to Earth / other worlds

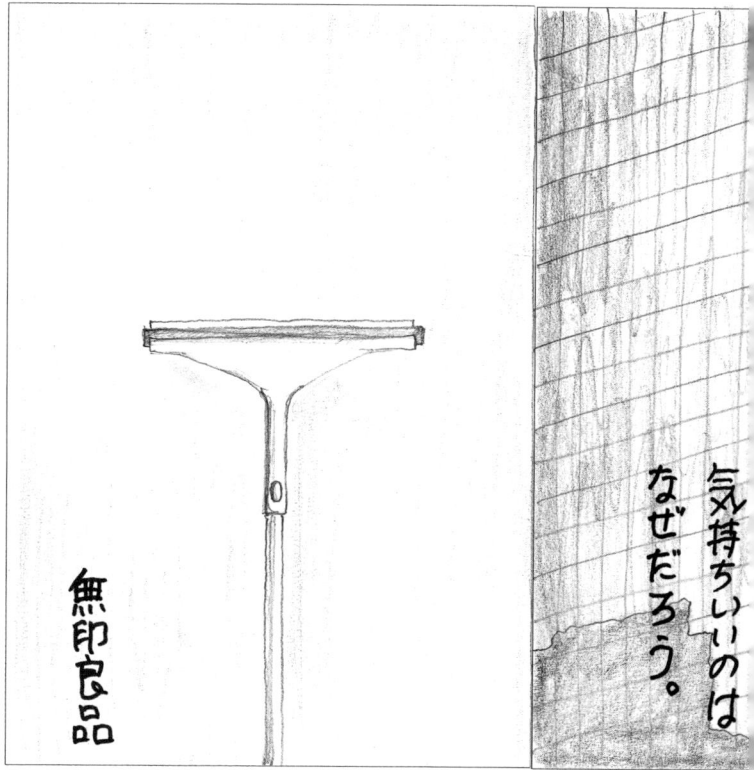

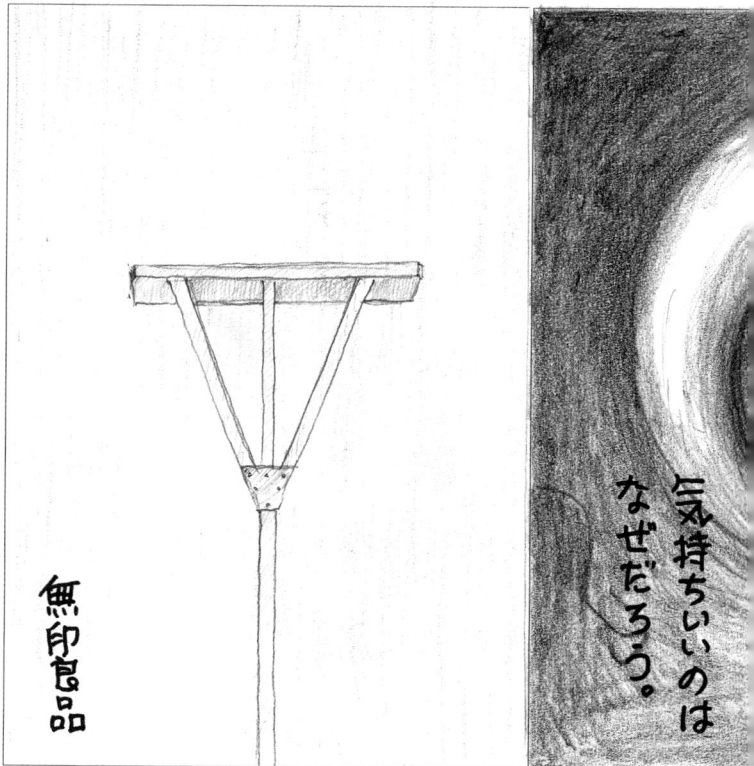

2020—

GLOBAL / LOCAL,
contemplating the Japanese archipelago

In 2023, I had an opportunity to direct the TAKEO PAPER SHOW after a hiatus of nine years. TAKEO is not a paper manufacturer, but a paper trading company that plans paper products, monitors the paper market, has paper made by manufacturers, and manages the production and distribution of paper products. The TAKEO PAPER SHOW is an essential event that helps find new paper markets and deepens relationships with creators and designers. I have been involved in this project for 35 years, since around 1988. This project is similar to HOUSE VISION, where I form an orchestra and act as its conductor, inviting many creators to participate in the exhibition and make a book to complete the job. The 2023 exhibition focused on "packaging," which was entering a new phase due to changes in technology and logistics. The exhibition's theme was an exploration from two perspectives: "function" and "laughter." I believe this exhibition serves as one compilation of my work concerning paper. As society has changed, so has MUJI, both in terms of the nature of its ideology and the scale of its development. Forty years after its inception, MUJI stands at an important milestone. In times like these, it is vital to take an honest look at the state of daily life in the world and reexamine our lifestyles from a more practical and local perspective.

For the 2025 Osaka-Kansai Expo, architect Shigeru Ban has arranged for me to act as the general producer of the Blue Ocean Dome, a pavilion that will address the issue of marine pollution. Three domes, one large and two small, will cover the themes of circulation, oceans, and wisdom, respectively. The central ocean dome will feature a 10-meter-diameter ultra-high-definition hemispherical LED screen that showcases the story of the sea. The Expo may not necessarily be warmly received in Japan, particularly given the sluggish state of the economy. Nonetheless, if there's an opportunity to spread the wings of imagination, whatever the circumstances, I'm up for the challenge. A 100-meter-wide dome screen has already appeared in Las Vegas. With this project, I hope to demonstrate that excitement can be created without relying solely on a grandiose scale, but also through imagination and creativity.

Meanwhile, over the past ten years, I have developed a specific interest in lodging facilities such as hotels and *ryokan*. There was a global shift from settling down to moving around, and a significant industry was developing around the pleasure of moving across countries and cultures. The more I stepped out into the world, the more I felt that it was possible to utilize the cultural sphere of Japan and the special geographical features and potential of the Japanese archipelago as future resources. Although 67% of its land area is covered by mountains and forests, Japan rushed towards an existence as a factory-like industrialized nation, but I think it's about time for us to clean up the land and focus on the country's intrinsic possibilities.

For several years, while Covid-19 spread worldwide and made it difficult to travel abroad, I visited hidden places of interest and accommodations around Japan, and, using videos, photos, and brief texts, I presented them in a subtle manner on a website I created called the "High-resolution Tour." As of this writing, I have visited over 60 locations. These formed my basic research, and around 2020, work entailing creative direction for inns and hotels began to gather momentum.

This comprehensive supervisory work covers a broad range of communication tools and customer service techniques, ranging from emblems, logos, photographs, videos, and key visuals to architecture, space, materials, furniture, uniforms, and dinnerware. In a sense, I can finally work in a position to which I've always wanted to apply myself. It is important to be attentive to the local climate and environment and to carry on traditions, but when I consider these factors as resources for the future, and think of the many architectural talents I can invite to work on these projects, my heart sings with excitement.

On the other hand, I launched a conference called "Setouchi Inter Local Design Conference" to explore the possibilities of new tourism and businesses in the Seto Inland Sea with influential business people and entrepreneurs in Hiroshima and Okayama. This conference is designed for the free and open expansion of imagination, brainstorming about not only accommodations, but also, for example, new architecture that floats on the sea or "the sea floating on the sea." At the same time that we optimize the allure of local regions, we can also design travel that encompasses sea, land, and sky, including individual aerial transportation, and sense an exciting future. As I travel around Japan, one of the regions where I see great potential for tourism is in the Seto Inland Sea and the Kii Peninsula. In these areas, the allure of the plate tectonics of the Japanese archipelago is evident, and I sense the roots of the Japanese aesthetic sense, born out of respect for the transcendent presence of nature. The Seto Inland Sea is not an ocean separating Shikoku, Honshu, and Kyushu, but a truly inter-local medium connecting them. The existence of hundreds of uninhabited islands here itself seems to me to be an untapped opportunity. The year of my writing, 2024, saw a major earthquake on the Noto Peninsula on the eastern side of the main island of Honshu; the threat and the blessing of nature always go hand in hand. Historically, Japan has been sensitive to the threat of nature and sought to find wisdom in it. I think the future of my work lies beyond gazing at the oceans and mountains of Japan and East Asia and considering hotels, inns, and residential spaces as mirrors of these environments. This book may be a grand sketch toward the realization of that future.

a

b

↓

0.9 a

b

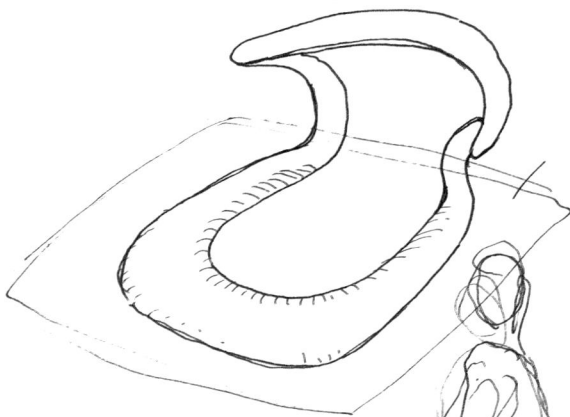

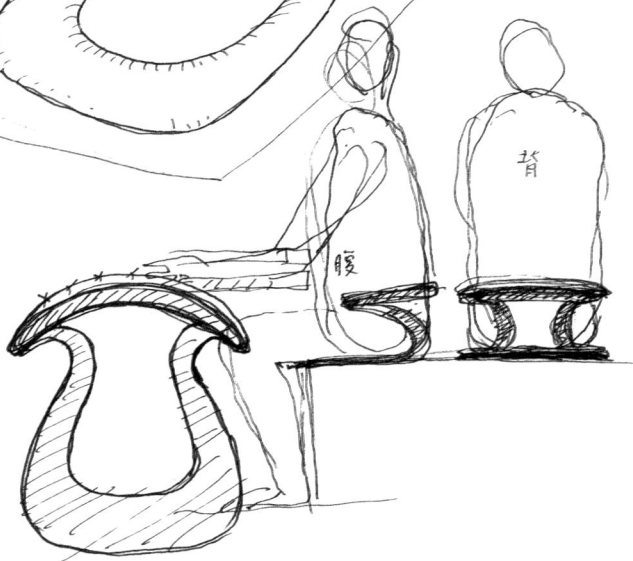

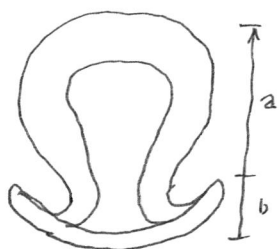

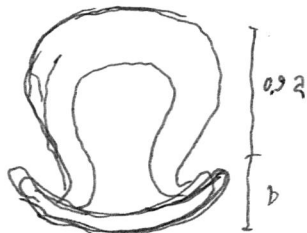

Given the opportunity to
design furniture for my own use,
I designed this legless chair for my study.
I gave it the name TATAMIZA,
and actually use it.

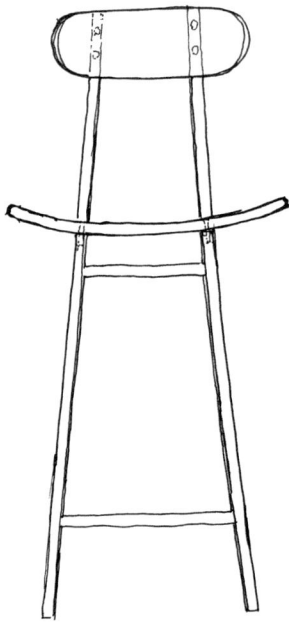
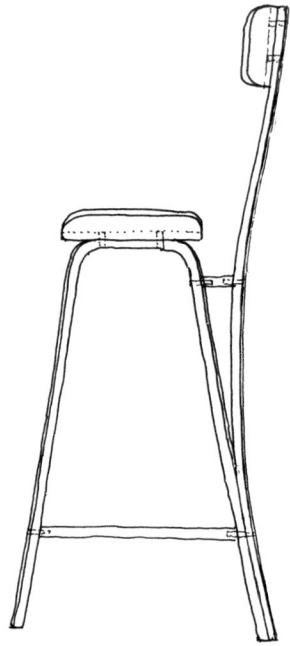
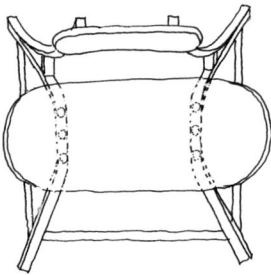
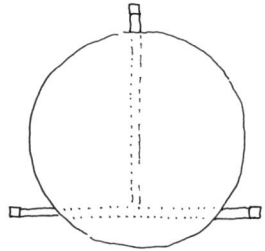
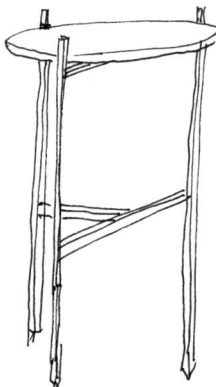

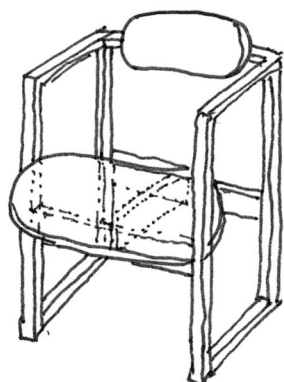

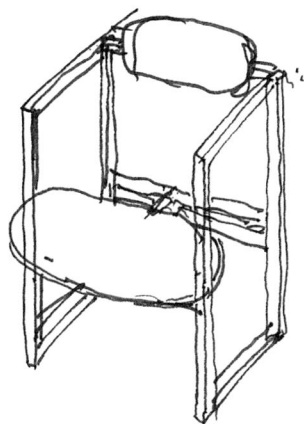

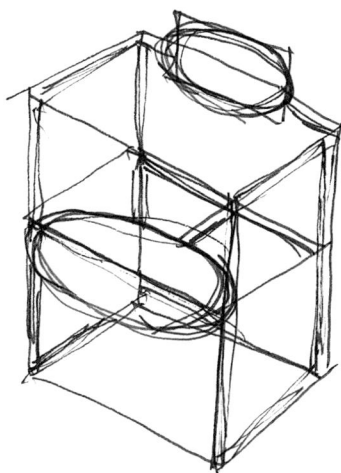

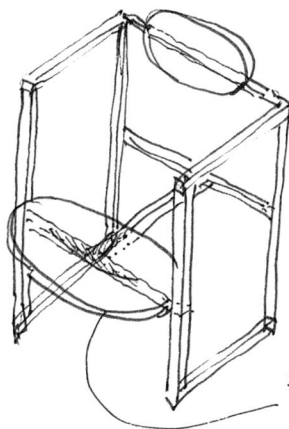

I worked with the manufacturer of TATAMIZA,
Hida Sangyo, to design SUWARI, a series of chairs
distinguished by the structure of their legs,
designed especially for placement on tatami mats.

この仕霊も少し上
も少し??

16th SHACHIHATA
New Product Design Award

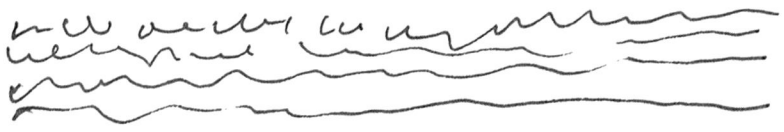

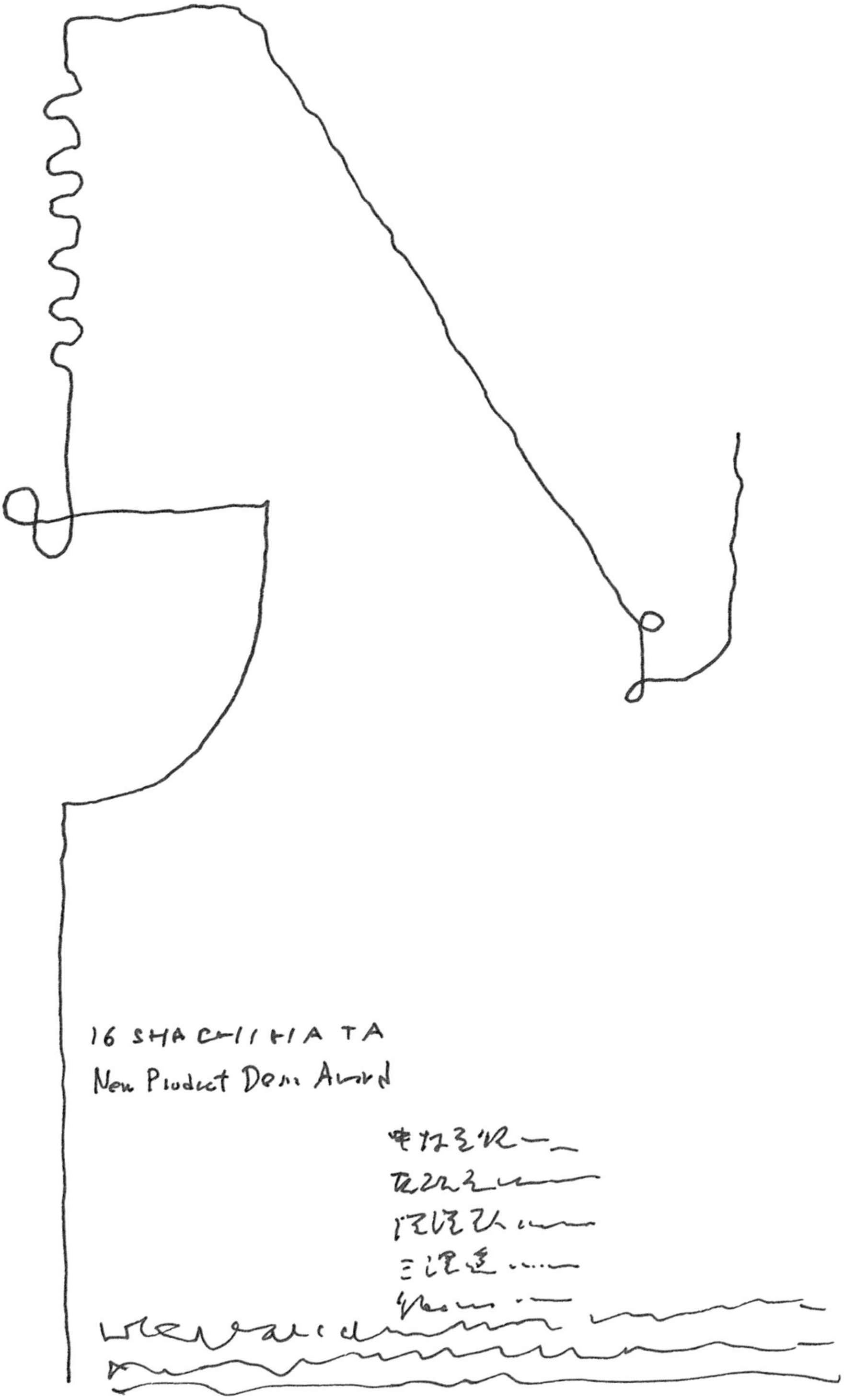

A sketch for the Shachihata New Product Design Competition poster.
Following pages: rough book design for "TAKEO PAPER SHOW 2023."
I conceived the exhibition organization using a book as the medium.

160   1

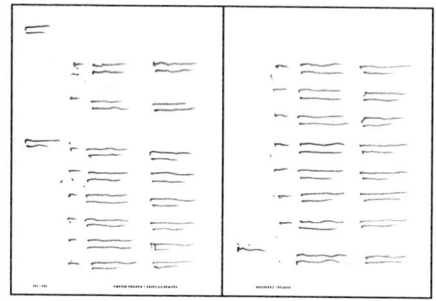

2   3

→ 紙と環境

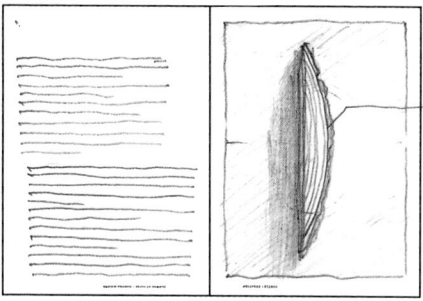

パルプ
原料となる
木片。

8   9

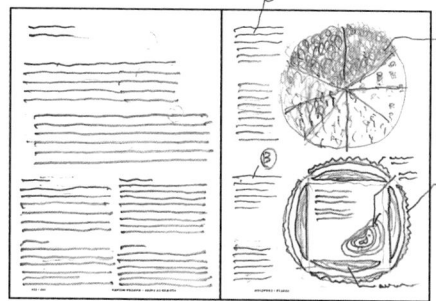

大体 8

加工

10   11

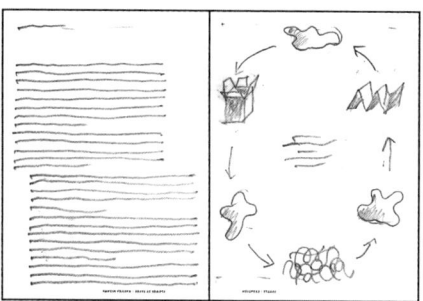

16   17

水分量

マテリル

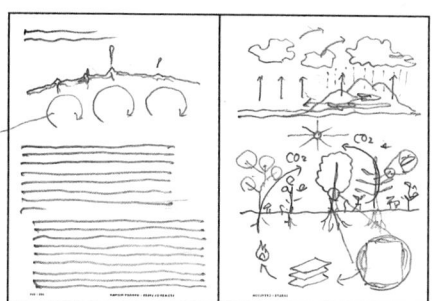

18   19

CO_2

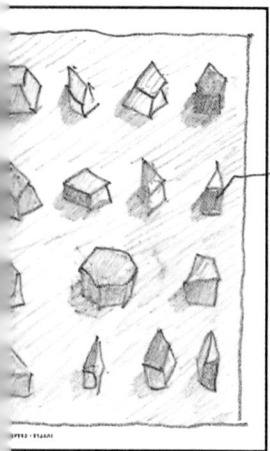

バラバラ
15ピース

結合

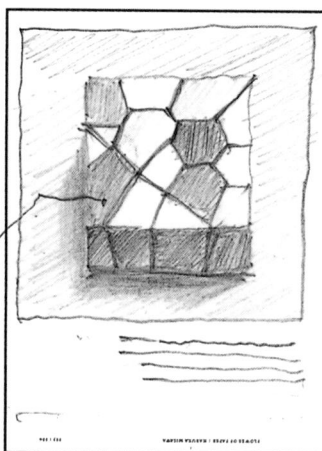

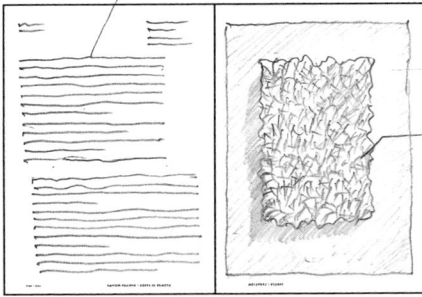

しわしわの
何も
君にいろい
ない。

4 5 6 7

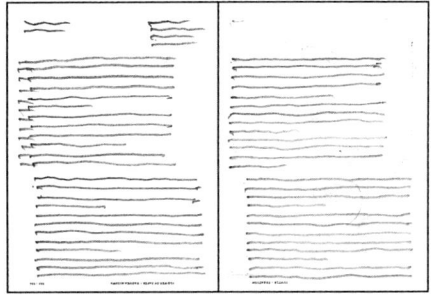

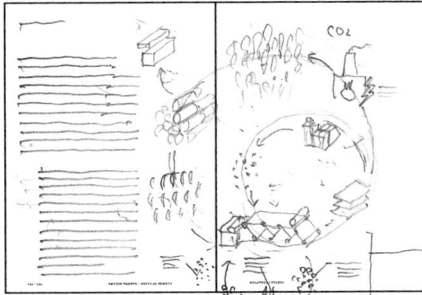

CO_2

右ページ
ご経画
経画

ここ重要。

12 13

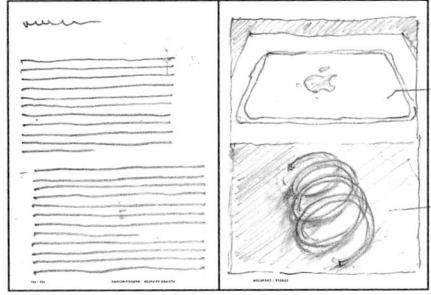

iPhone
パッケージ
photo

佐藤君の
ラセン。

15

石君

うすまさの
ボール

photo

20 21

サントリーのペット、つぶして3~4個。

余白

22 23

ーストロー

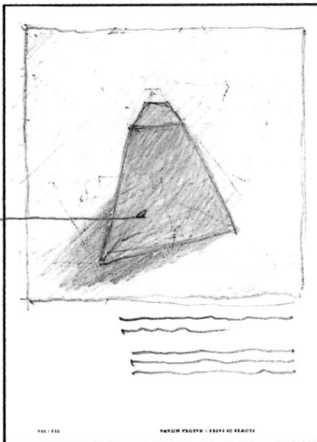

銀紙
展開

オレンジ
多断面
ジュース

(プリントとして
組立て)

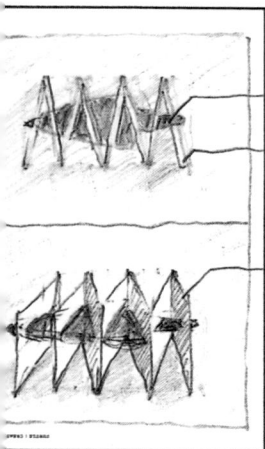

やじり
気包紙

箱ナシ
内紙のみ
で撮影

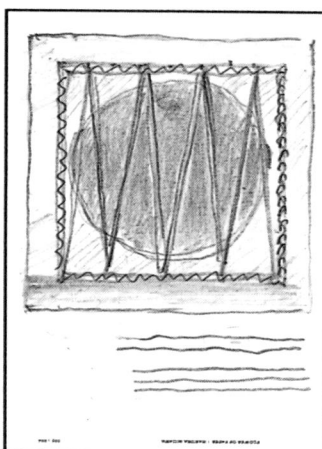

茶代

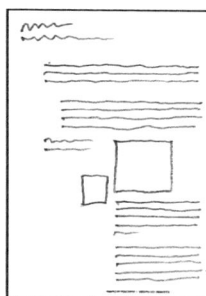

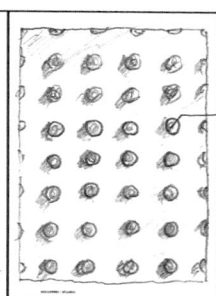

圧縮
ビースの数々

40 41

1ピース

ほぐし始め

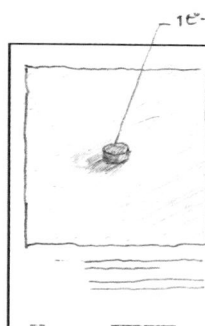

42 43

石川

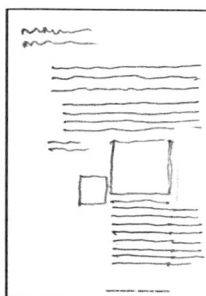

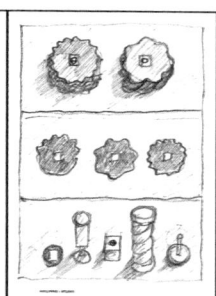

48 49

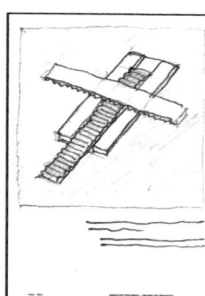

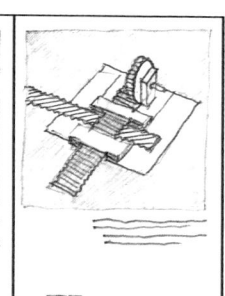

50 51

NEW
塗り紙

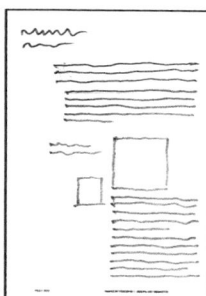

56 57

刷毛

筆

58 59

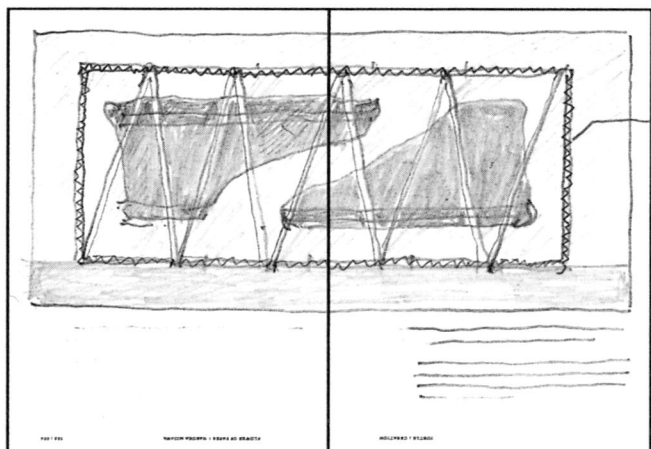
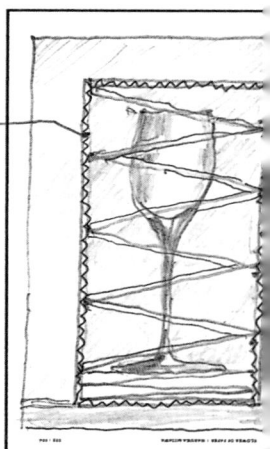

ファイン
プレート白

なぐし中間　　　完成したしいの美

図は
後で考る

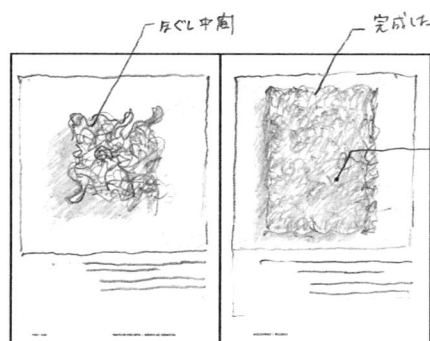

44　　　45

パッケージへの応用（TPS）

アルミ

ふくらみ

圧縮後

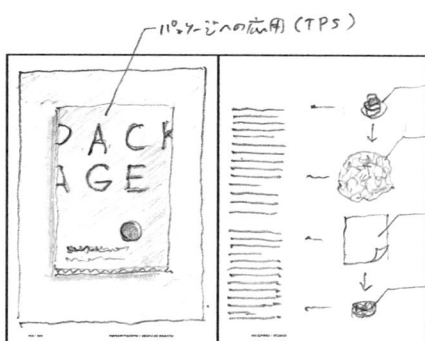

46　　　47

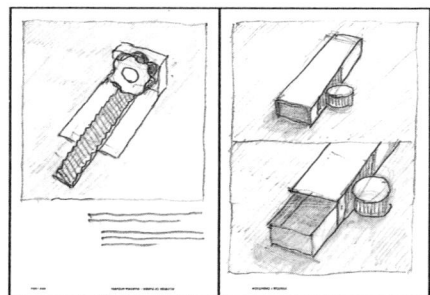

52　　　53

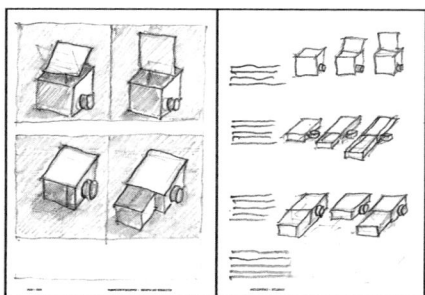

54　　　55

糸

裂り目

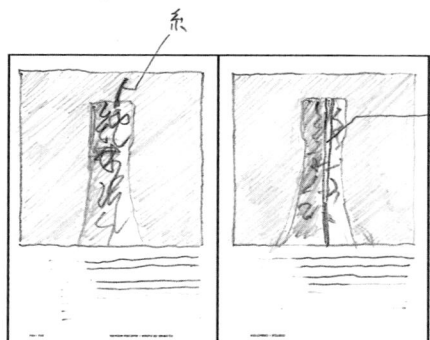

60　　　61

塗る
とれのる

皮とろる
パッケージ

62　　　63

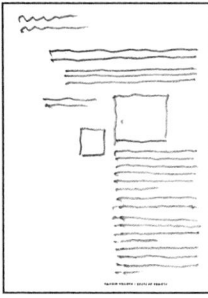   

TPS 2018 Preciousの パンフレット

古地図・海図

永宝

96　　　97　　　98　　　99

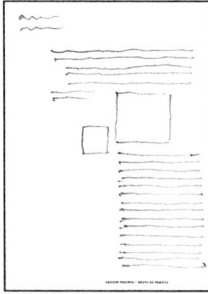 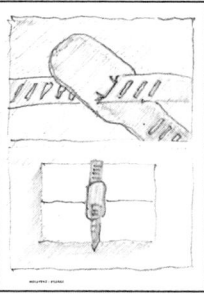 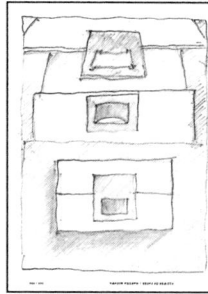 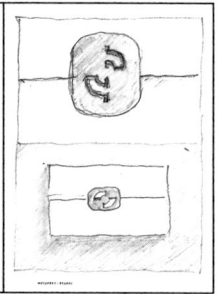

NEW
ラッパー

104　　　105　　　106　　　107

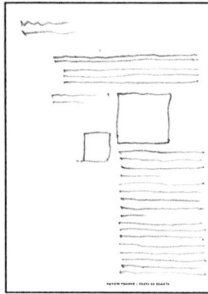 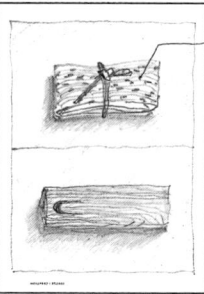 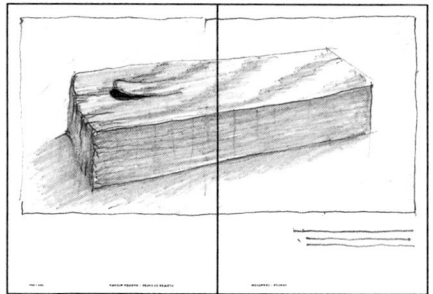

狩引?

経木

112　　　113　　　114　　　115

 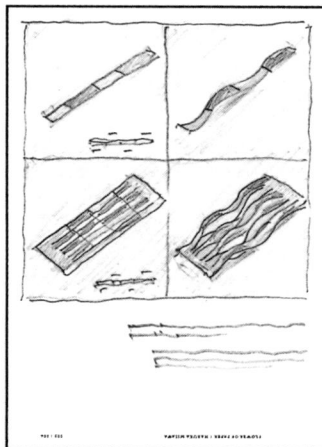 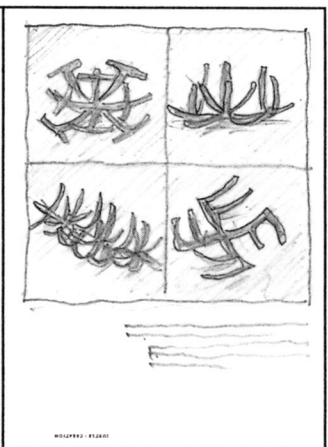

坂本龍一の記事
JAPAN TIMES

100　　　101

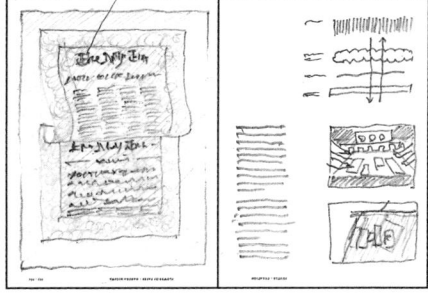

古いNew York Times

102　　　103

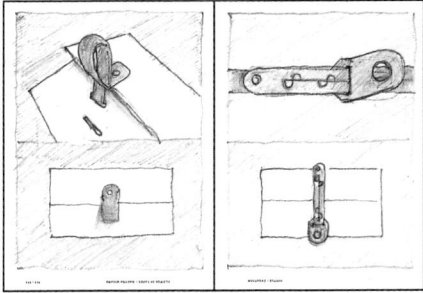

108　　　109

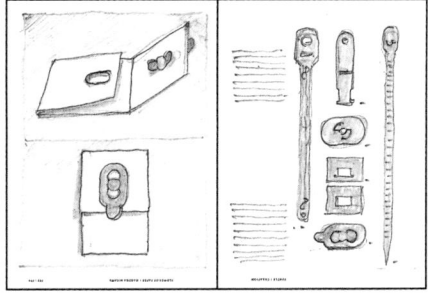

110　　　111

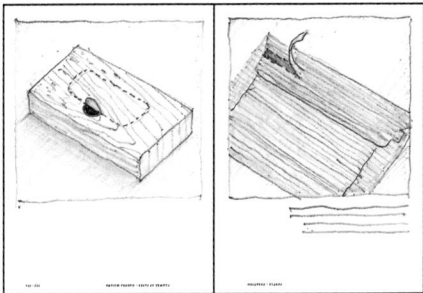

116　　　117

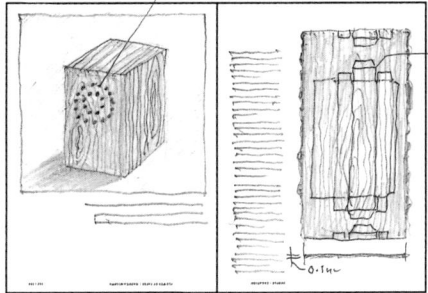

ミシン目のレタトの
小穴のボキャブラリー入れて見ては？

0.1㎜
スライスの
木の上に.
展示図
入れて
みては？

118　　　119

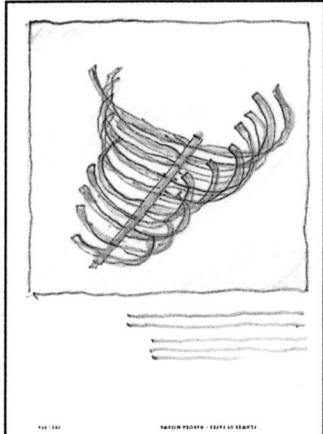
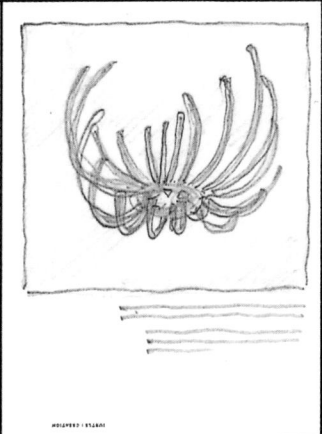

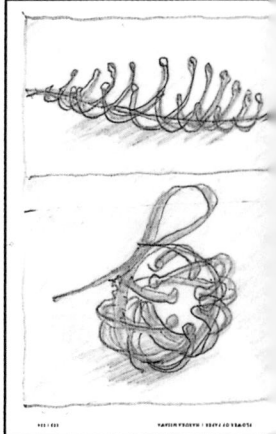

1:【宇宙の循環】

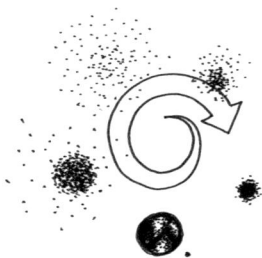

2:【マントル対流】

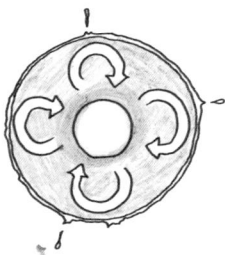

5:【大気大循環】

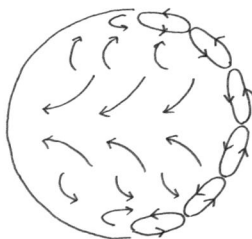

6:【水の循環】

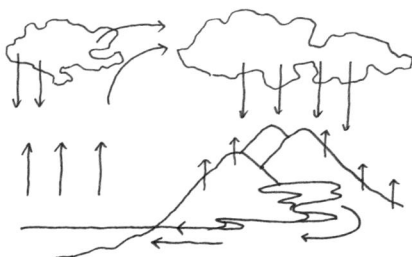

3: 【プレート（地殻）循環】

4: 【海洋大循環】

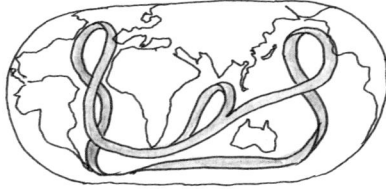

7: 【森林循環】

O_2 | CO_2

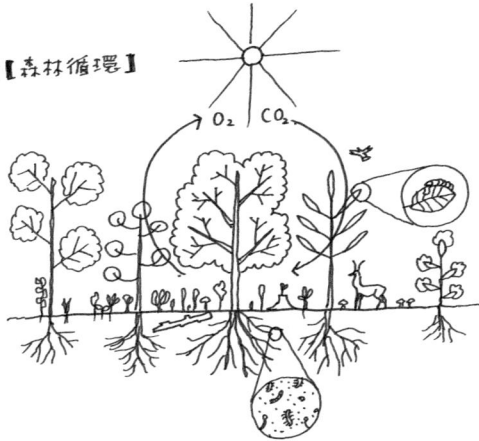

8: 【人体の循環】

I drew an image of circulation.
The circle of transmigration is the primordial
image of life and the universe.

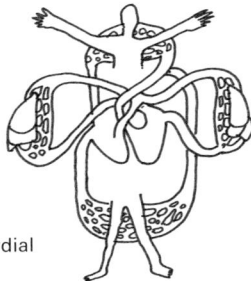

PLASTIC OR PET
(TRANSLUCENT / TRANSPARENT)

WATER DROP
SCREEN by
PLASTIC / PET

ENTRANCE

TSUKUBAI 2025

SHISHIODOSHI 2025

INTRODUCTION
MONITOR OR PANNEL

EXIT

STAGE

seat

SHOP

MONITOR
OR SCREEN

MONITOR OR SCREEN

WATER BAR

STRAGE

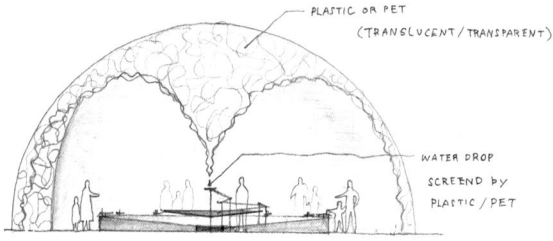

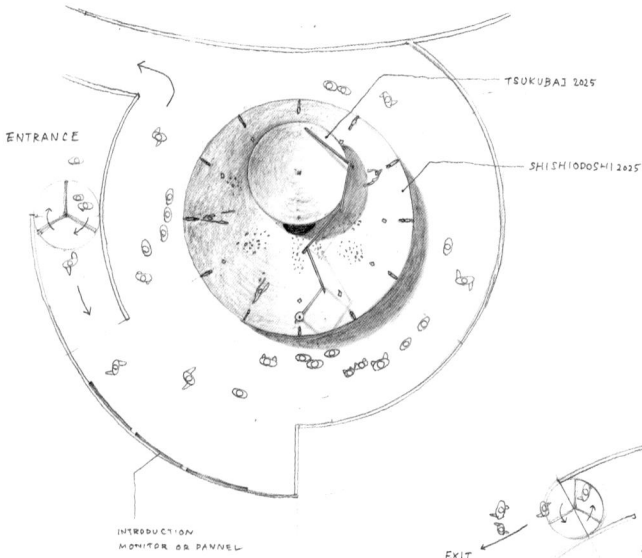

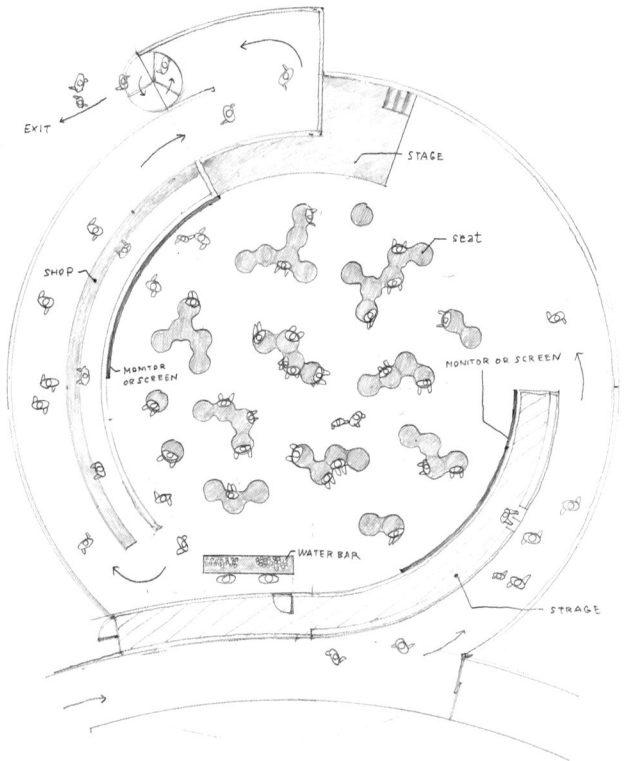

The architect Shigeru Ban approached me to produce a pavilion at the "EXPO 2025."
He designed three domes, one of paper, one of carbon fiber, and one of bamboo.
I was in charge of the exhibition content.

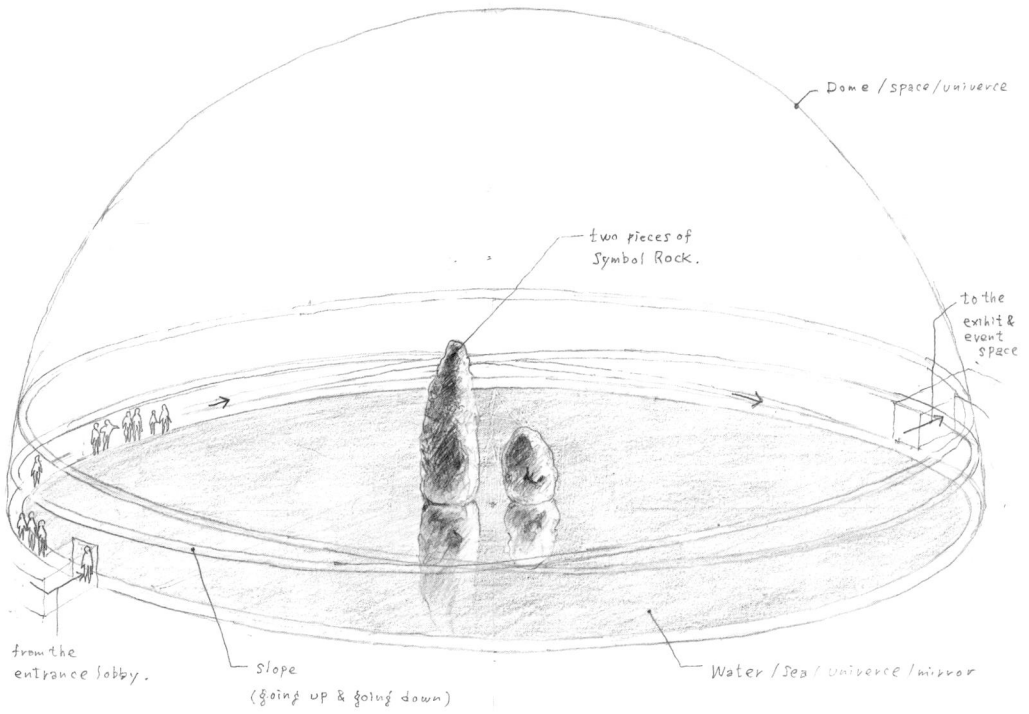

Dome / space / universe

two pieces of
Symbol Rock.

to the
exhibit &
event
space

from the
entrance lobby.

Slope
(going up & going down)

Water / sea / universe / mirror

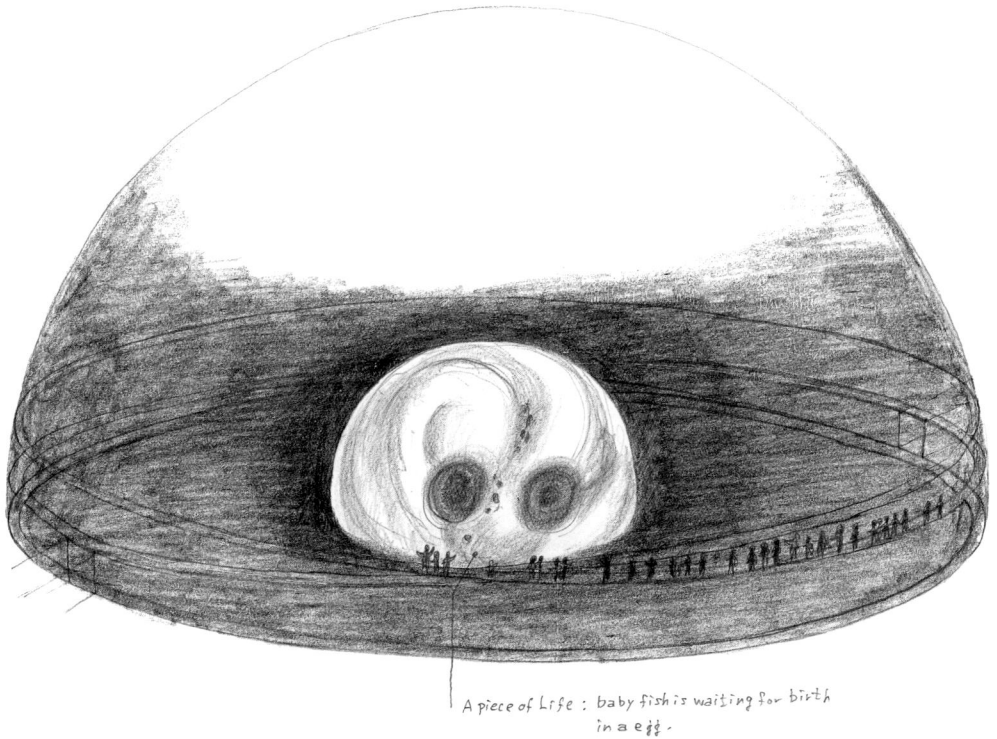

A piece of Life : baby fish is waiting for birth
in a egg.

The theme of the pavilion is marine plastic pollution. The concept involves projecting images onto a hemispherical high-definition LED screen with a diameter of over ten meters.

「BECOMING」素描／CG る。

「BECOMING」素描／CG る。

物体を独立状が形成されいく。
反り曲部から窩素の心が形成されいて

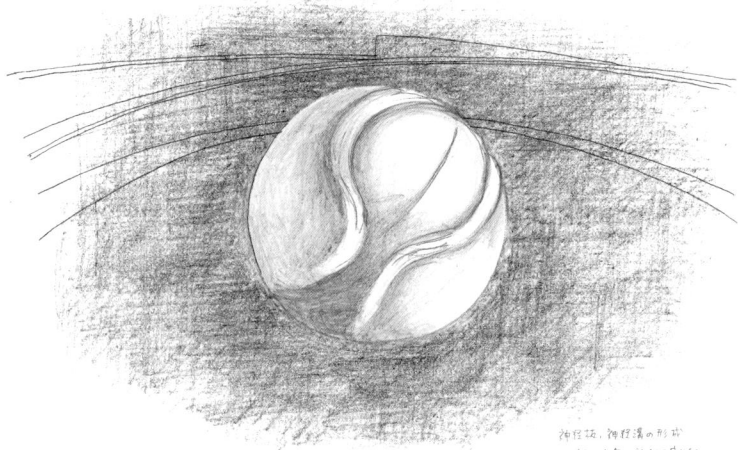

神経坂、神経溝の形成
このあたり、生命の神秘を感じるくーった。

生物の「かたち」が形成されいくる

The rhythm of the crashing waves occurs eighteen times per minute, the average respiratory rate of a human being. The composition of human blood and seawater are very similar. We have an ocean inside us.

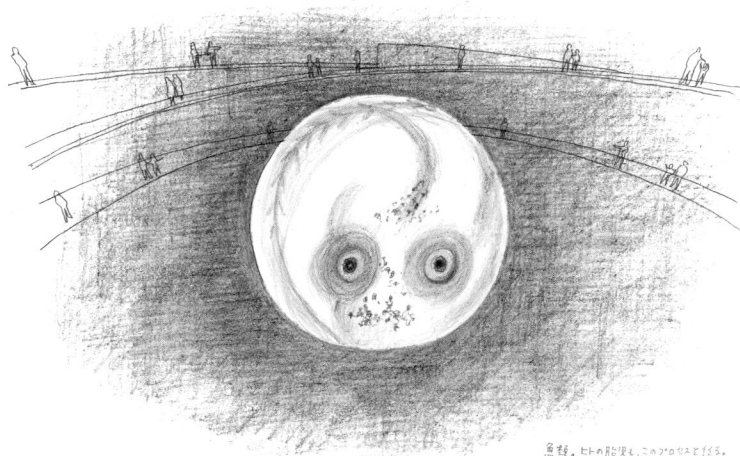

魚群。ヒトの胎児も、このプロセスをたどる。

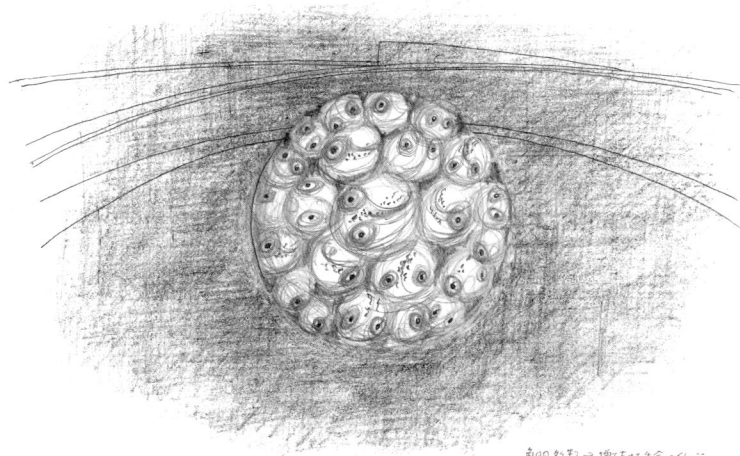

意明カ初 → 増殖する生命のイメージ

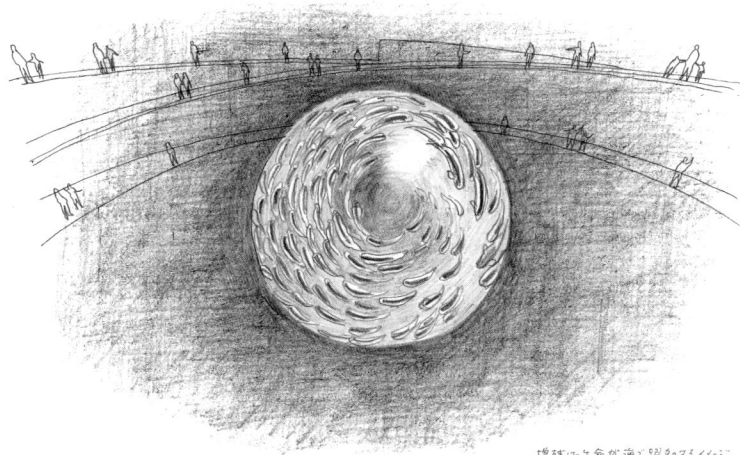

増殖した生命が海に回帰するイメージ。
群作 → 生命の輝きを表現する。

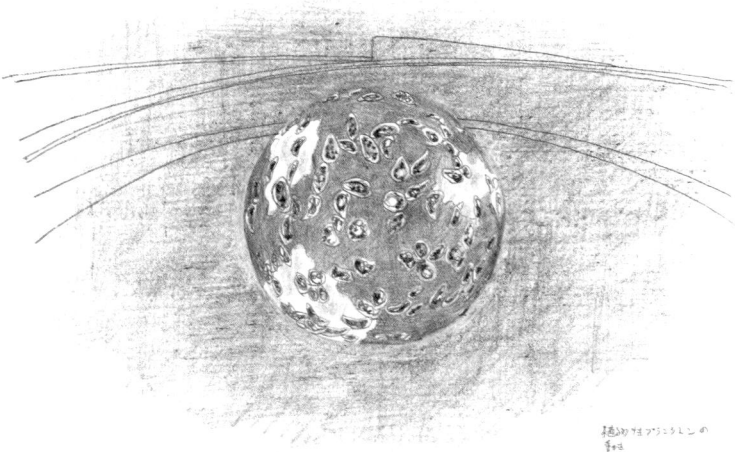

珪藻（植物プランクトン）の
動き。
100μm

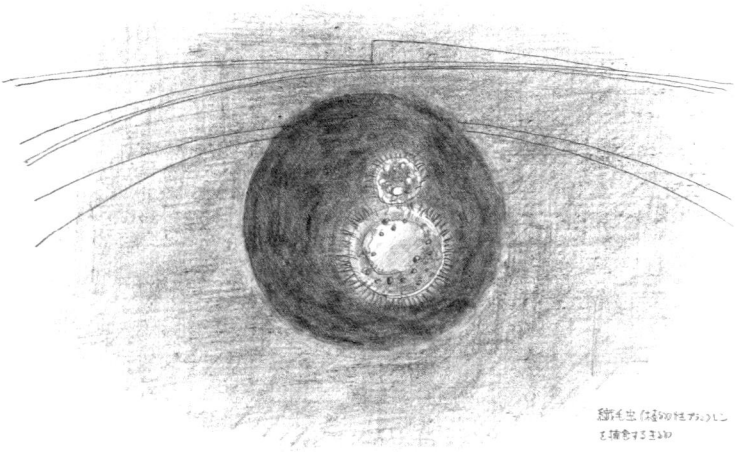

繊毛虫（植物性プランクトン）
を捕食するもの
80μm

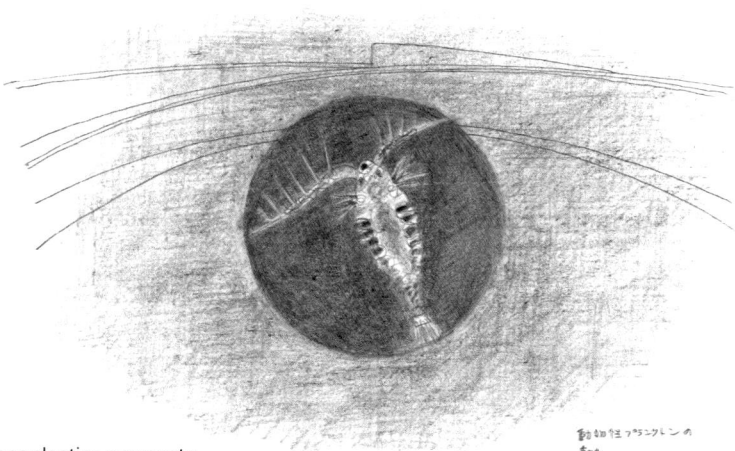

動物性プランクトンの
動き。
200μm

Micro- and nanoplastics permeate
every stage of life and their intricate processes.

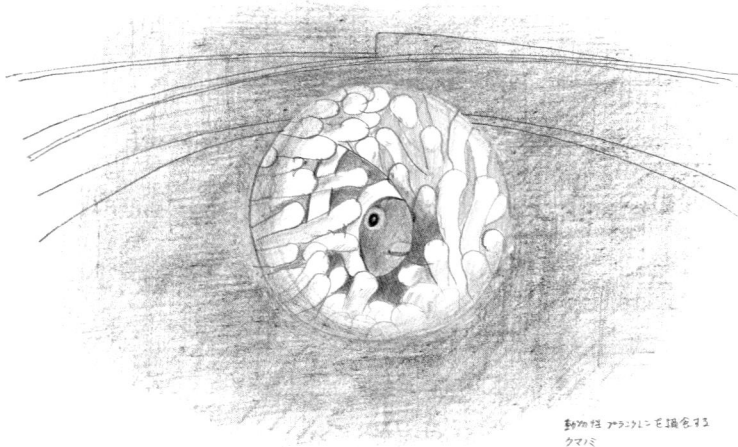

動物性プランクトンを捕食する
クマノミ

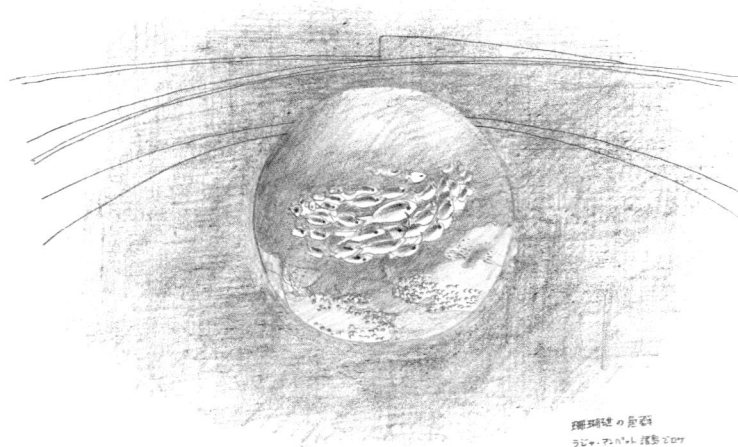

珊瑚礁の魚群
ラジュ・アルバート 運動ブロ7

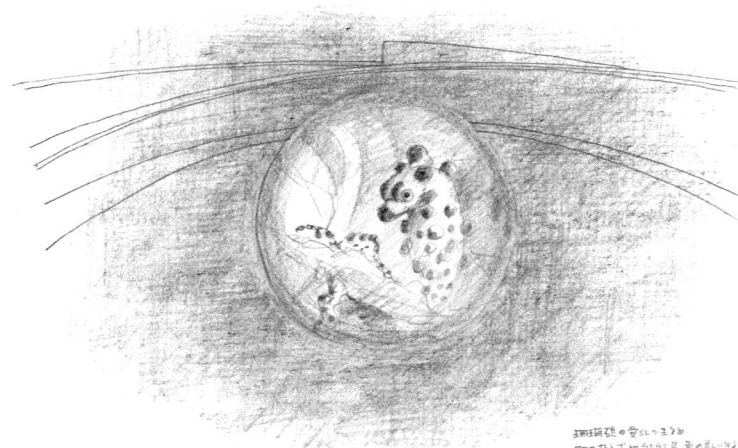

珊瑚礁の会にいする
クマのオトゴヤうとらし君 色のまいもの

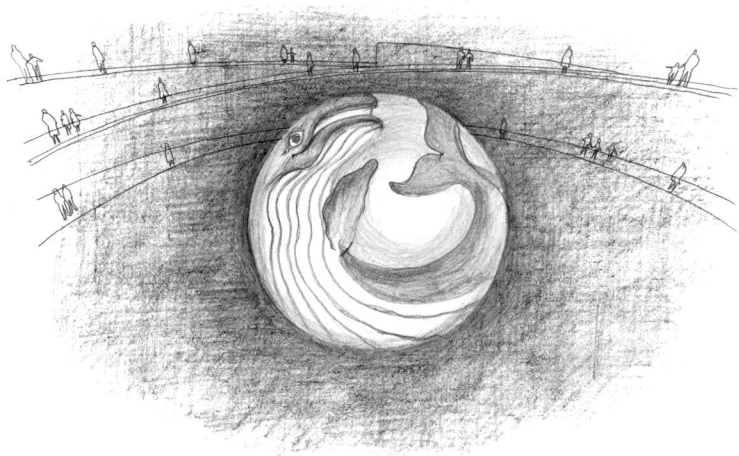

クジラの眼のアップに
ボコっと泡が出るタイミングと
ペルガイルのうちゅーの開くが出現.

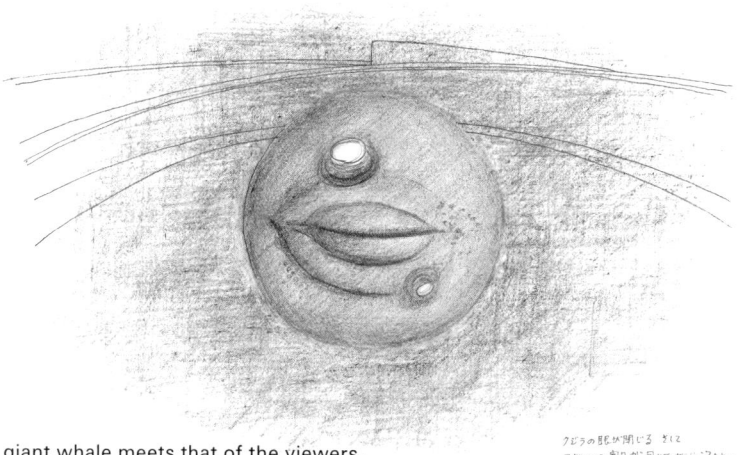

クジラの眼が閉じる さきに
マクリューの 開口 が回りらが ニアると.
マクリューは うれのある生気と 前やかる者

The gaze of a giant whale meets that of the viewers,
as if they're making eye contact with the living organism called Earth.

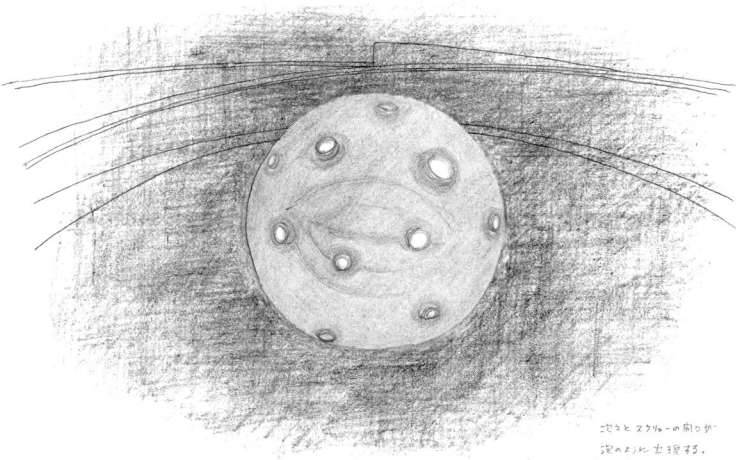

泡々とスクリューの周りが
泡のように去現する。
書ういい 音、赤、鉄、クローとイエロー

まびんだい泡のような閉ロ。
書、舌、鉄、クローイエローの流色
自然の色がこめれていく。

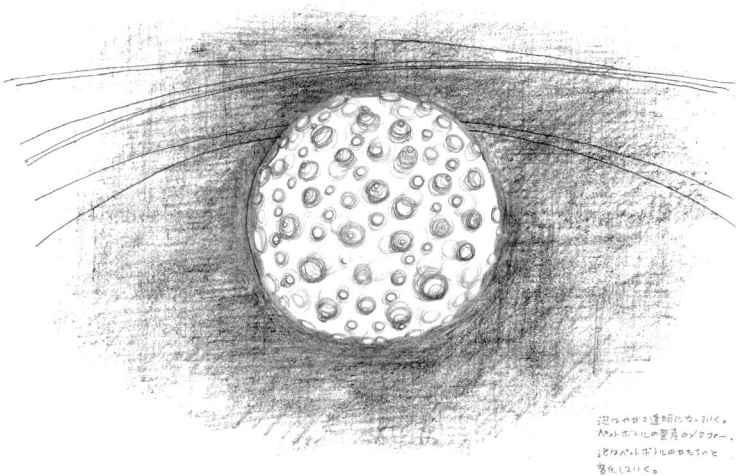

泡つやがて透明になっていく。
ペットボトルの書店のメタファー、
泡をペットボトルのかたちへと
書化していく。

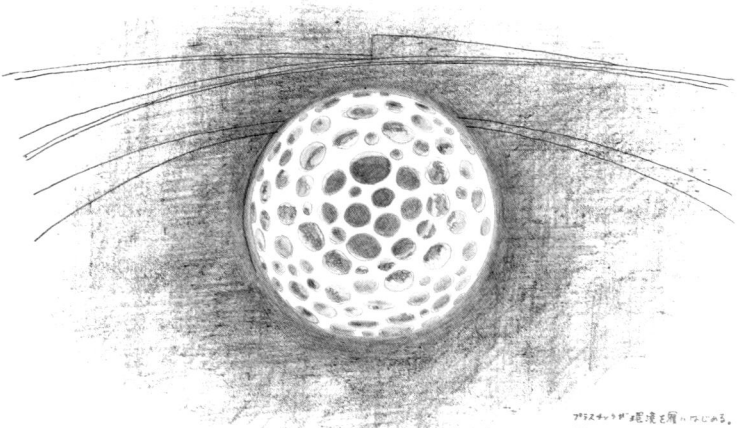

プラスチックが硬度を増しはじめる。
網の目をイメージさせるかたちが、
からだ中の頭蓋組織「クレーンブレーホール」を
包みはじめる。

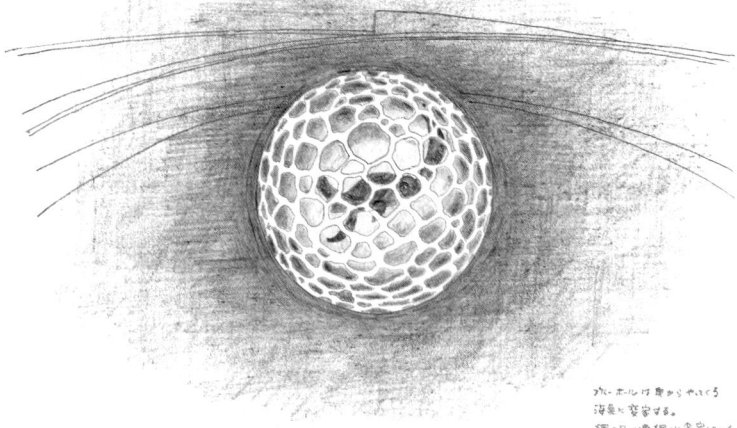

クレーンホールは魚からやってくる
海鳥に管管する。
網の目は漁網へと管管していく。

漁網に絡まる海鳥。
太陽の光をさし込みっつぷいで。

青い海の中を漂ぎえる海亀。
絡み恵調をかきまりつつ。

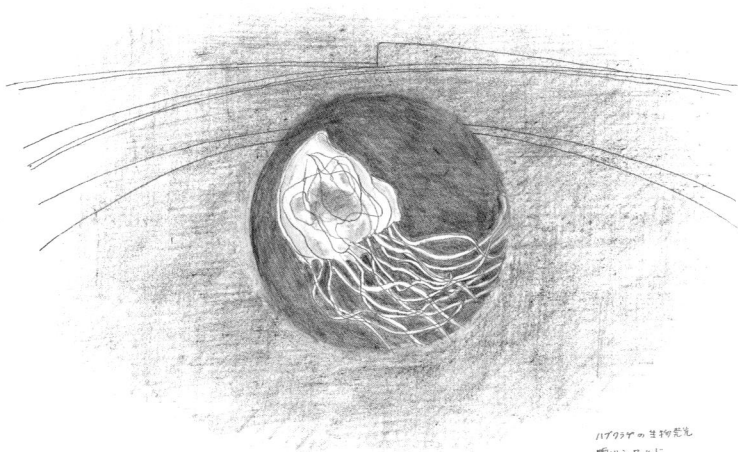

ハプタシアの生物発光
腸川ミューワールド

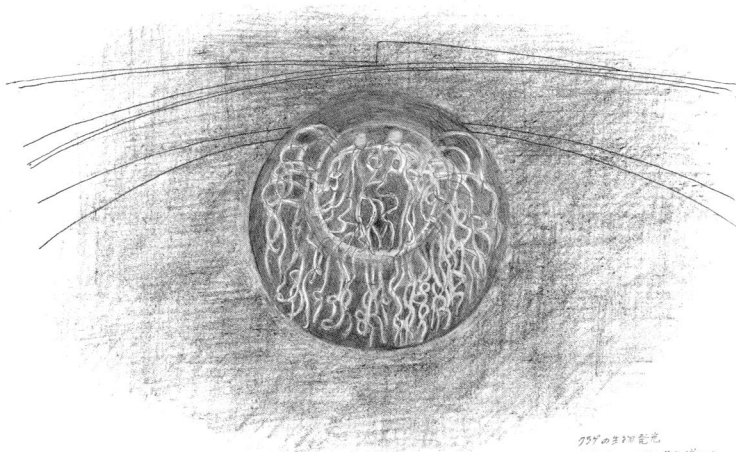

クラゲのまわる発光
水深2700mでの発光（青い）

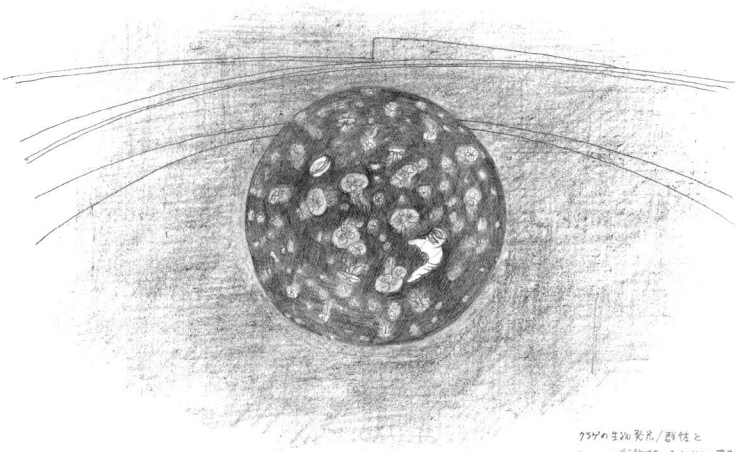

クラゲの生物発光/群性と
その中を浮遊するペットボトルの破片と
キャップ

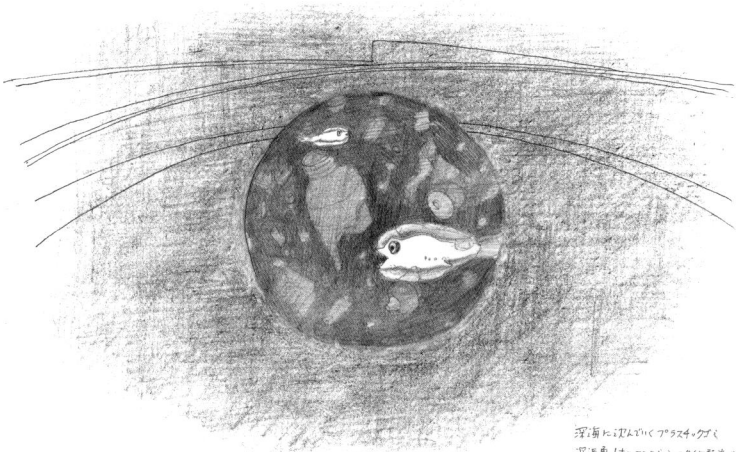

深海に沈んでいくプラスチックと
深海魚(オニアコウ)の生物発光で
照らし出される

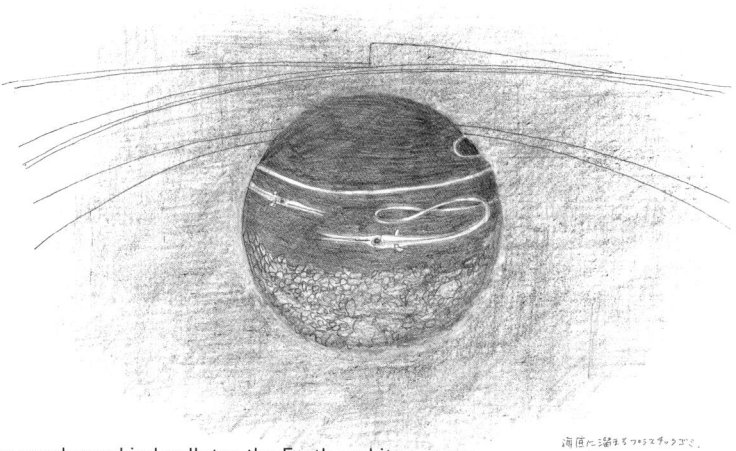

海底に溜まるプラスチックゴミと、
深海魚(ミギラナギ)がよる所囲にいる。

No matter how much mankind pollutes the Earth and its oceans,
nature simply continues to accept it in silence.

ミヤウナギが去った後にジュウモンジダコが現れる。
ゆっくり踊るように回転する。

ジュウモンジダコは、って行く。遠ざかってつつ海に潜る。
下がる何かがせりよってくる。

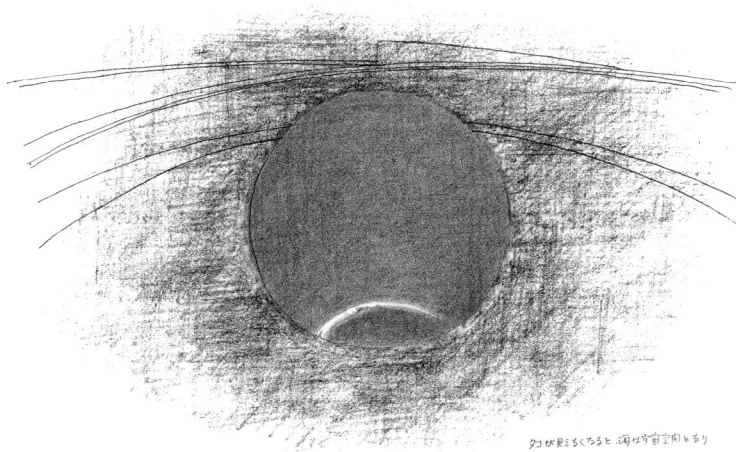

タコが見えなくなると、海は守宙空間となり
夜明けの地球がせりよってくる。

I was honored to receive Poland's Jan Lenica Prize.
A commemorative exhibition occupied the entire ground floor of
the National Art Gallery of Poznan. This is the initial sketch for
the exhibition poster. On the following page is a side view of
what is meant to be a three-dimensional face.
The exhibition was titled "Make The Future Better Than Today."
When I created this drawing, I did so with a sense of anger in my heart.

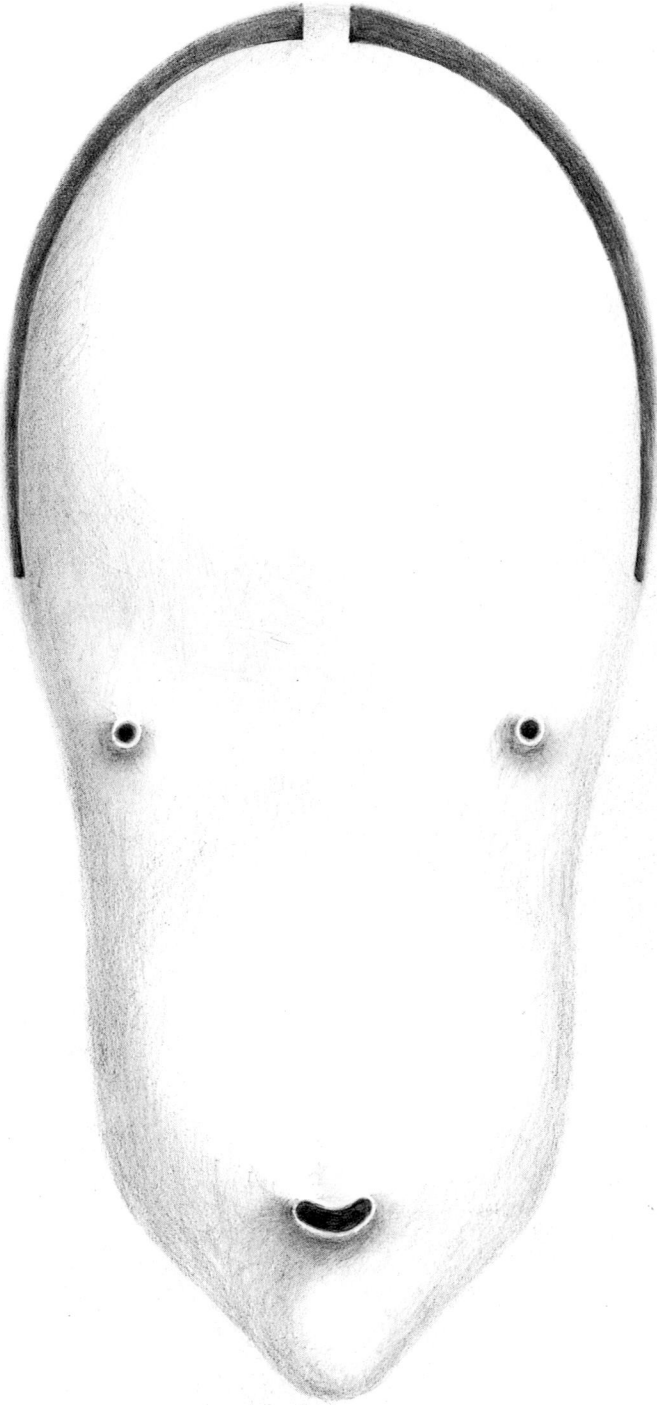

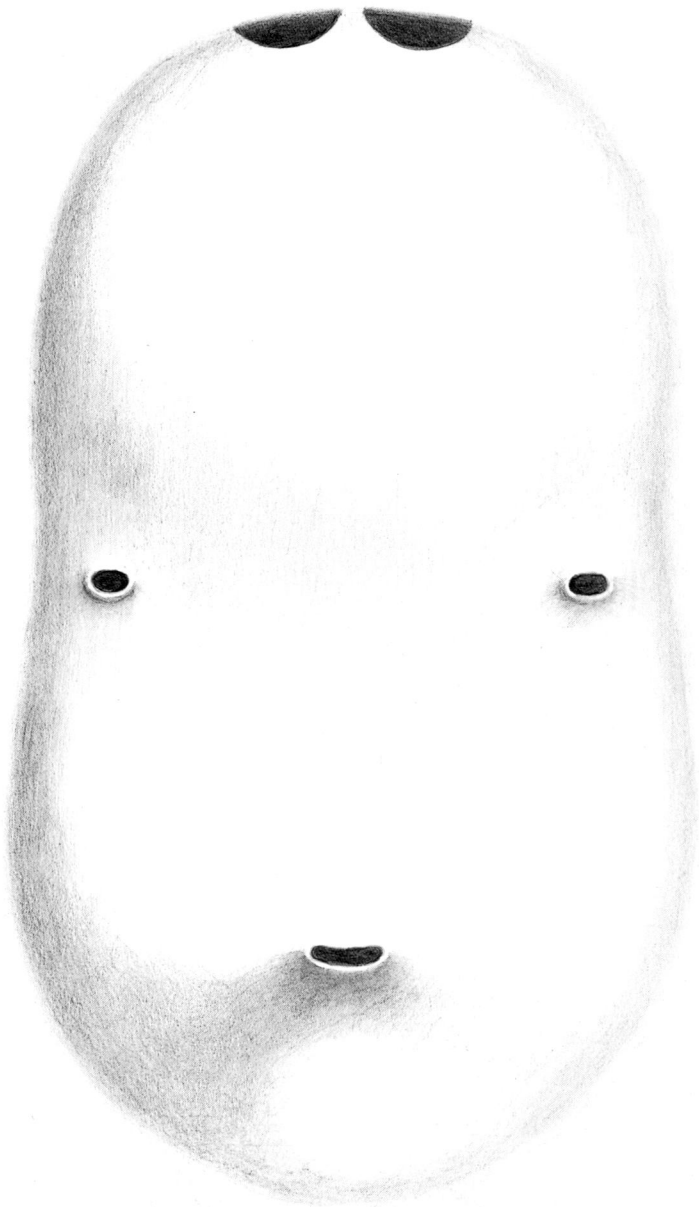

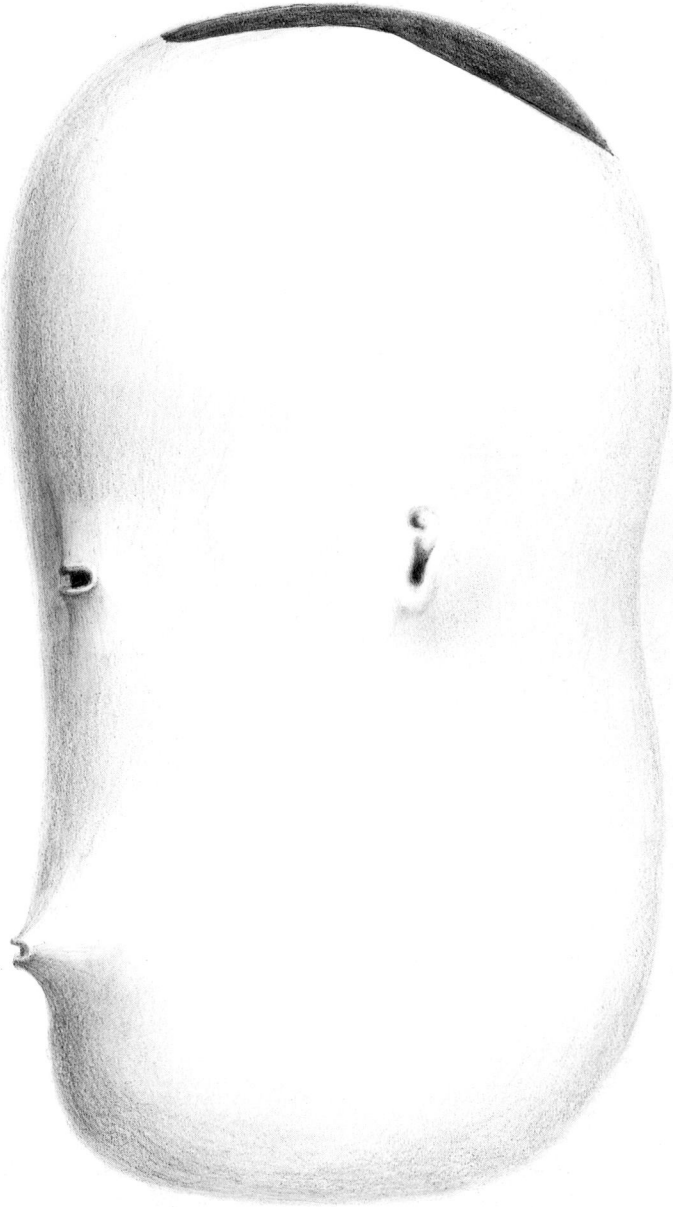

GLOBAL / LOCAL, contemplating the Japanese archipelago

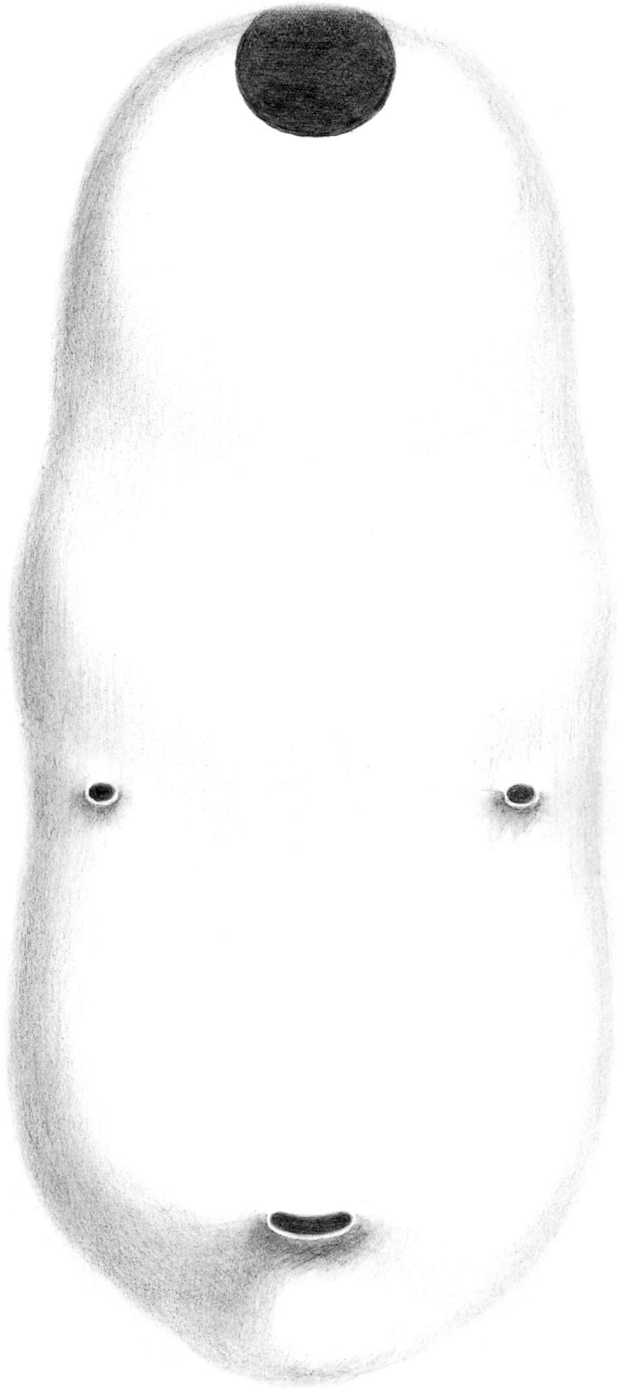

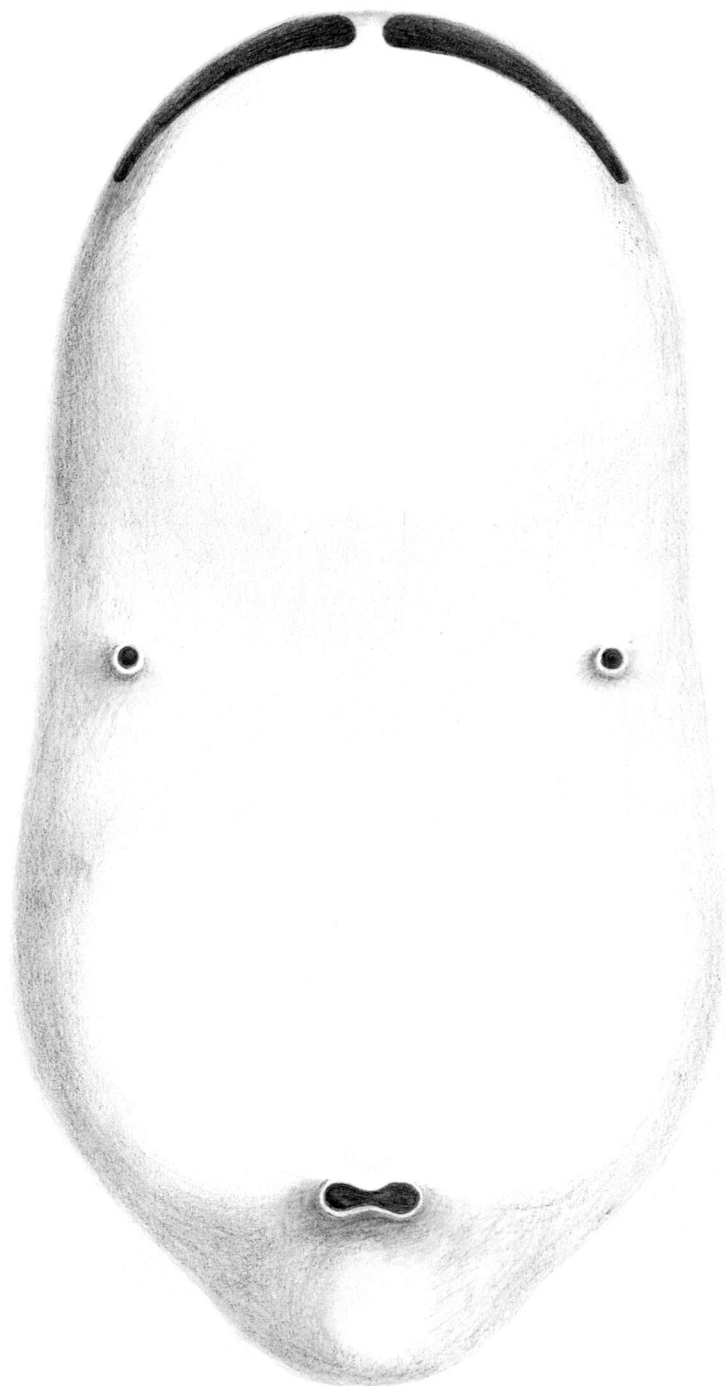

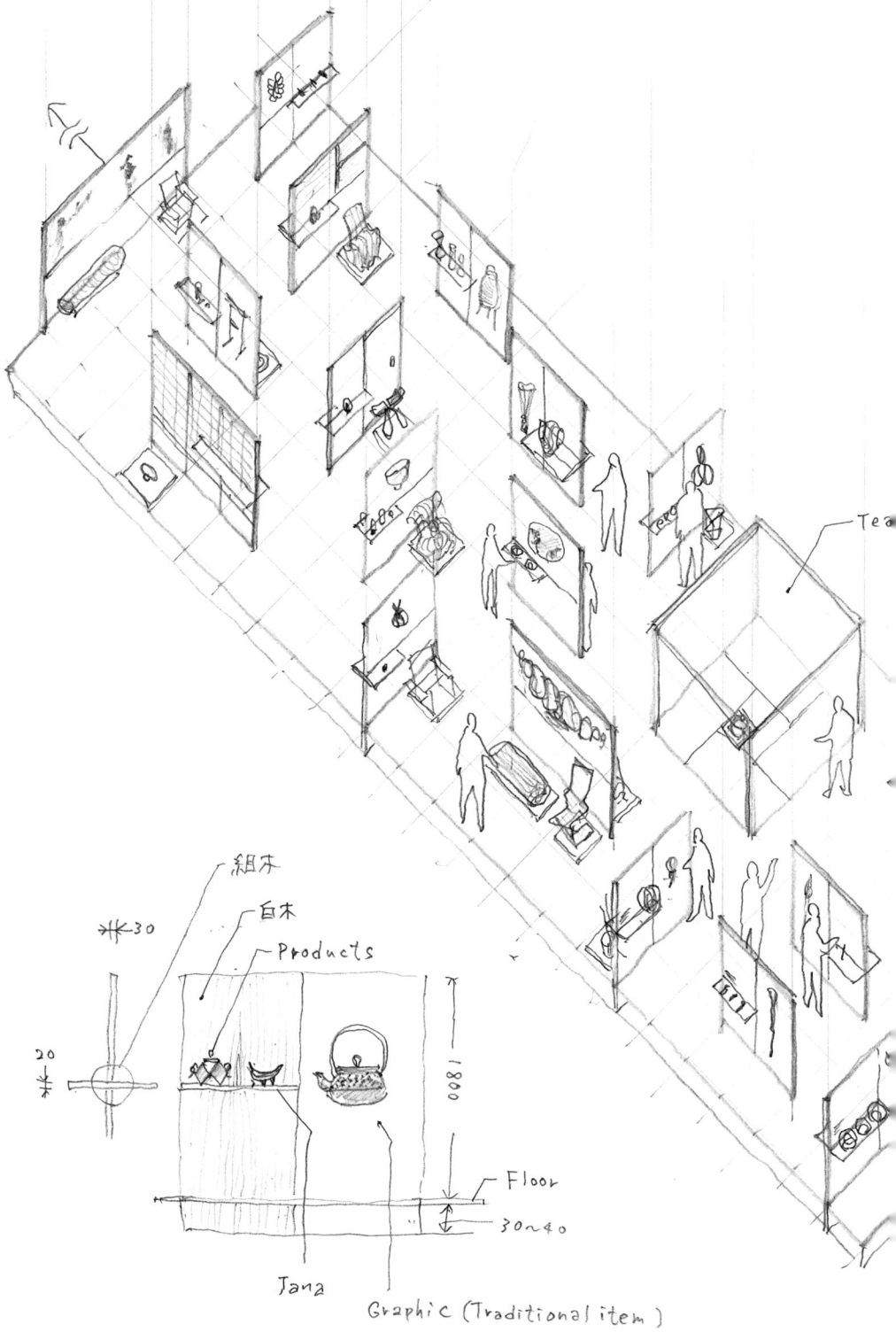

組木

白木

Products

├ 30

20

1800

Floor

30〜40

Jana

Graphic (Traditional item)

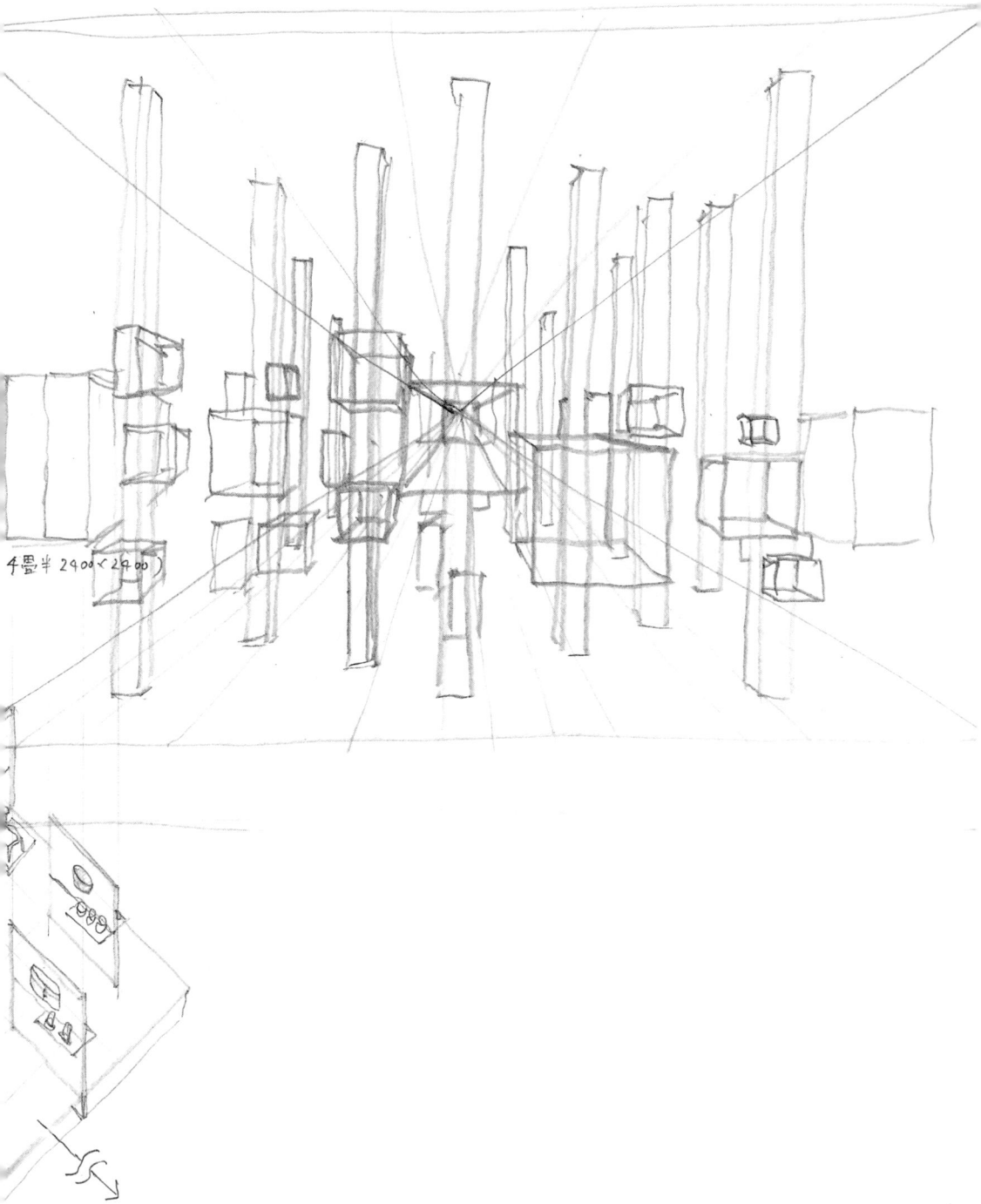

4畳半 2900×2900

Sketch for the exhibition space for
"ORIGIN of SIMPLICITY—20 Visions of Japanese Design" at the
ADI Design Museum in Milan in 2024. The themes were classified into
twenty pillars and the exhibits distributed accordingly. Rossella Menegazzo,
an expert in Japanese design, curated the exhibition. I drew these rough sketches
quickly during a meeting. Sketches for posters are on the following pages.

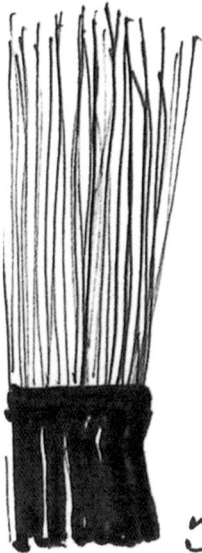

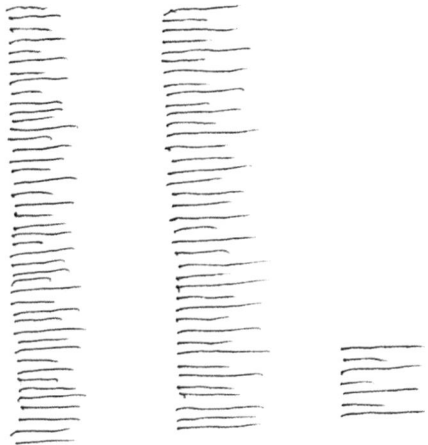

ORIGIN of SIMPLICITY
20 Visions of Japanise Design

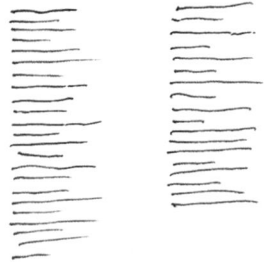

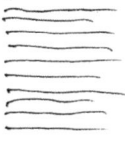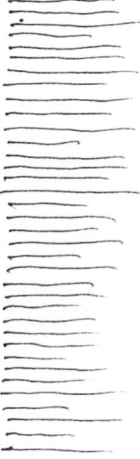

ORIGIN of SIMPLICITY
20 Visions of Japanese Design

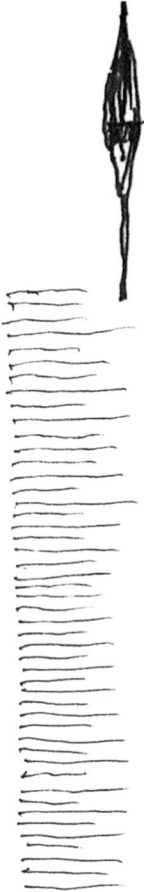

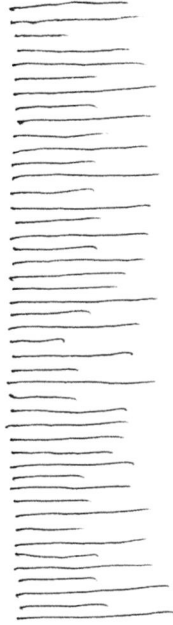

ORIGIN of SIMPLICITY
20 Visions of Japanese Design

ORIGIN of SIMPLICITY
20 Visions of Japanese Design

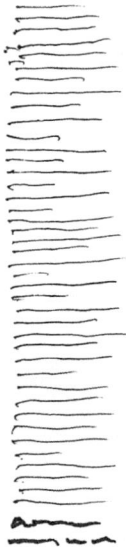

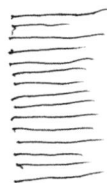

Rough sketch for the poster for Setouchi Triennale 2025. Diving platform idea.

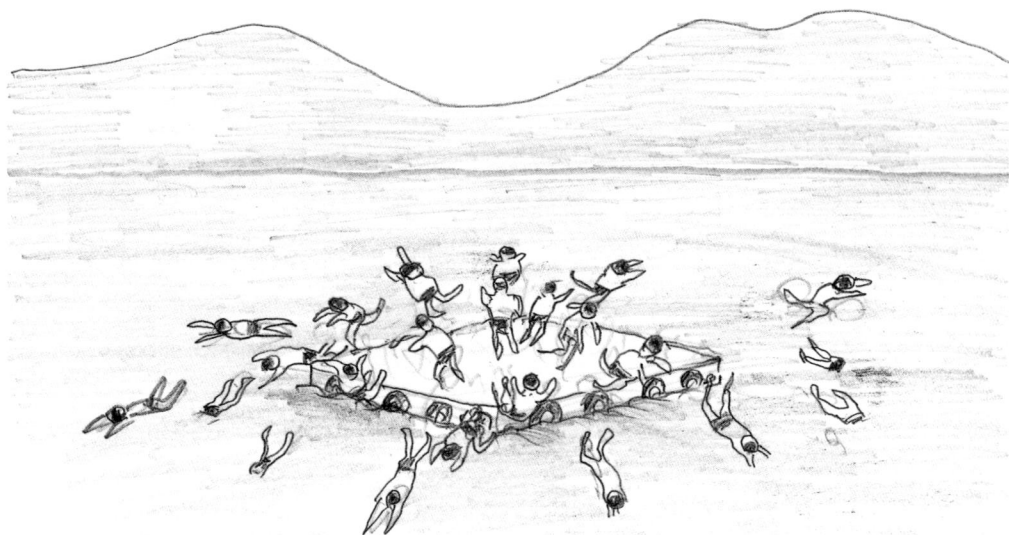

The members of the winning team in a traditional cutter boat race raise their oars in unison. I also sketched them raising their oars on land.

【小値賀島/五島列島】

Embarking on the High-resolution Tour Project ignited
a dedicated focus to every corner of the Japanese archipelago.

【熊野カルデラ図皿】

I HOTEL SHIP 諸和

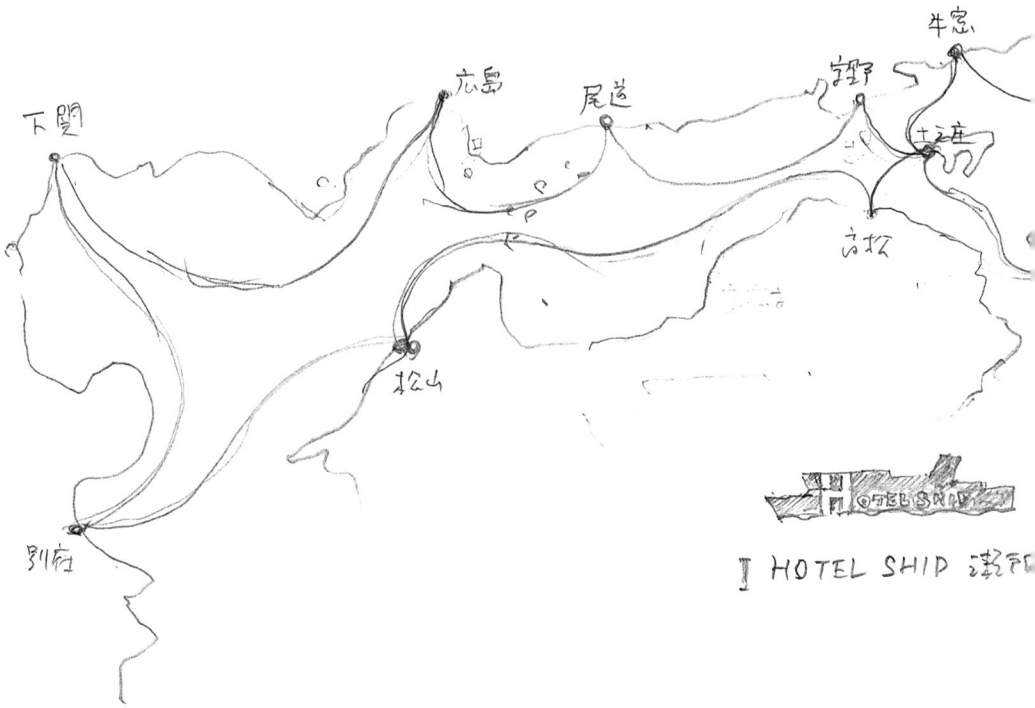

A small fishing port can be compared to an airport;
we imagine and envision aquatic aircraft operated by
a "peninsular airline" transporting people to their destinations,
and a ferry that, with accommodation features, becomes a hotel.

神戸

堺

構想【

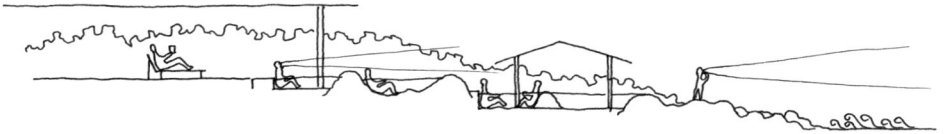

岩場へと自然に抜ける面白さ。

Hot springs act as creative receptacles that draw on topographic and climatic features.

RYOKAN

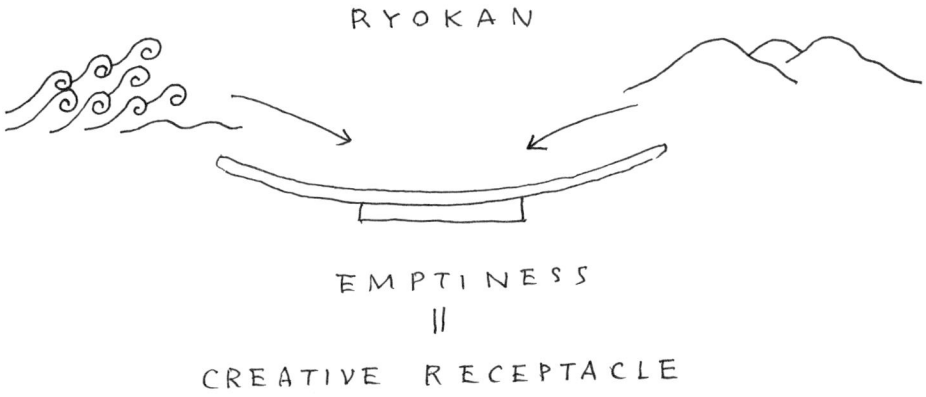

EMPTINESS
||
CREATIVE RECEPTACLE

HOTEL

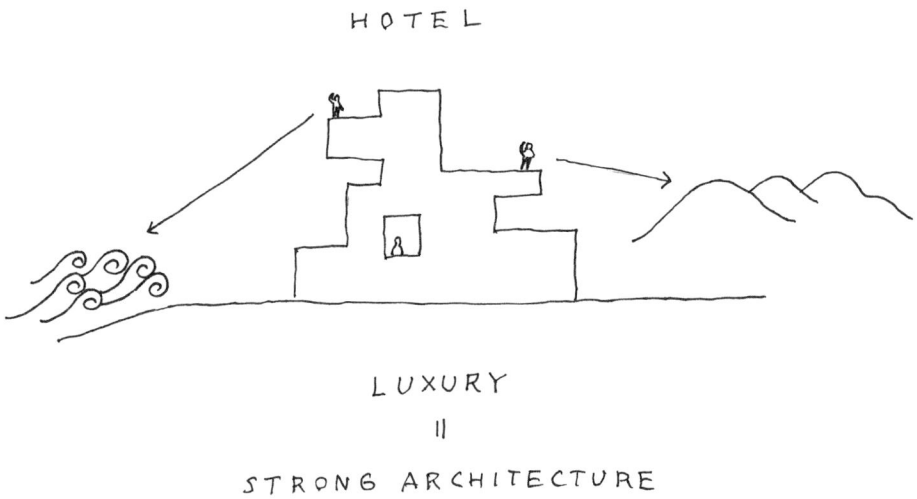

LUXURY
||
STRONG ARCHITECTURE

Ryokan act as mirrors, reflecting the environment and the surrounding nature.

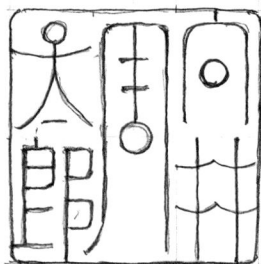

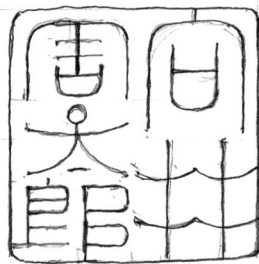

〔森羅万象の射影りとしての文字〕

↑
黒部分が朱
太陽残像、回帰像より
線は全て曲線、なめらかに。

←

↑
コンクリートポエトリー 声振り より「あ
精密に印で再現する。

白文

18mm

18mm

MU
KAI
SHU
TARO

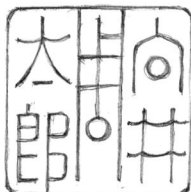

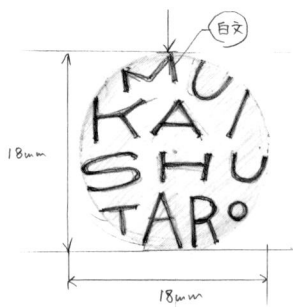

Design of a seal commissioned by my mentor teacher, Shutaro Mukai.
With the image of my mentor in mind, a man who was also a practitioner of
concrete poetry, I decided to design it as a bridge-shaped seal.

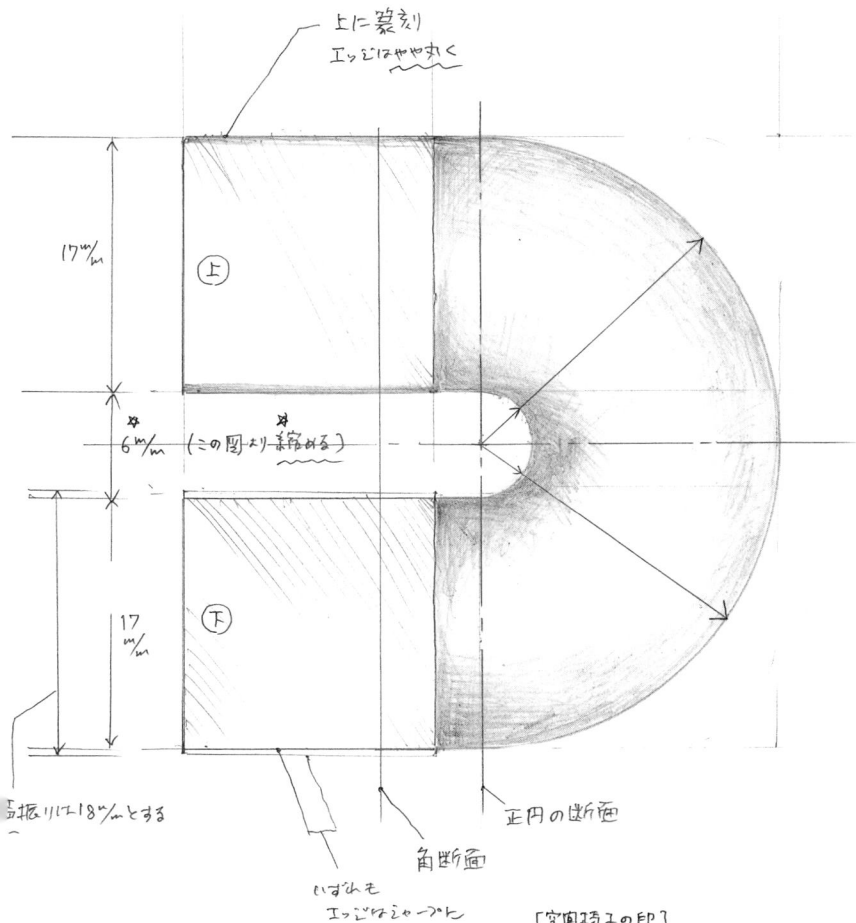

上に篆刻り
エッジはやや丸く

①17ᵐ/ₘ

上

6ᵐ/ₘ（この図より縮める）

①17ᵐ/ₘ

下

正円の断面

角断面

いずみも
エッジはシャープに

振りは18ᵐ/ₘとする

[空間椅子の印]

50m/m

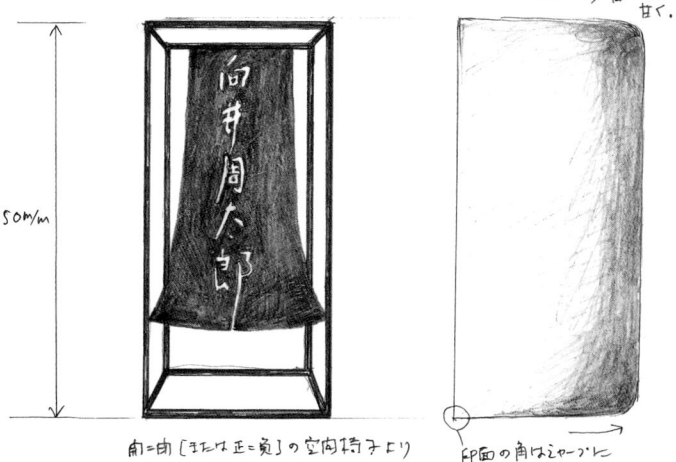

角=曲 [または正=負] の空間椅子より

印面の角はシャープに

苦に向って
甘く。

Trust Your Drawing!

Lars MÜLLER

Throughout human history, people have used drawing as a means to depict what they see and visualize their thoughts – from prehistoric cave drawings to contemporary design concepts.

The authorship of a drawing belongs exclusively to its creator. To exchange this for the promises of artificial intelligence would mean sacrificing the authenticity of the sketch and the pride of its maker.

Drawing and thinking are interdependent. In the process of drawing, an idea takes on an immediately visible physical form so that it can be examined, corrected, and developed further.

A designer's knowledge makes up a personal spiritual universe that serves as a source of inspiration and creativity from which insights and ideas are born. As they discover the world with delight and curiosity, explore natural phenomena, and come to an understanding of human needs and achievements in technology and civilization, designers store up and reflect on this learning in order to produce effective communication and good design.

In the texts he has written for this book, Kenya Hara demonstrates keen powers of observation and an enduring thirst for knowledge, and yes, also a fine sense of humor, as he describes a career that began with drawing. With the discipline and dedication of a draftsperson, he is today devising complex solutions for cultural and social events by first lending them distinctive form as drawings and then expanding on these concepts to produce large-scale, forward-looking exhibitions and installations.

This detailed look at Kenya Hara's design world along with the book's title serve as a powerful reminder never to underestimate the technique of drawing.

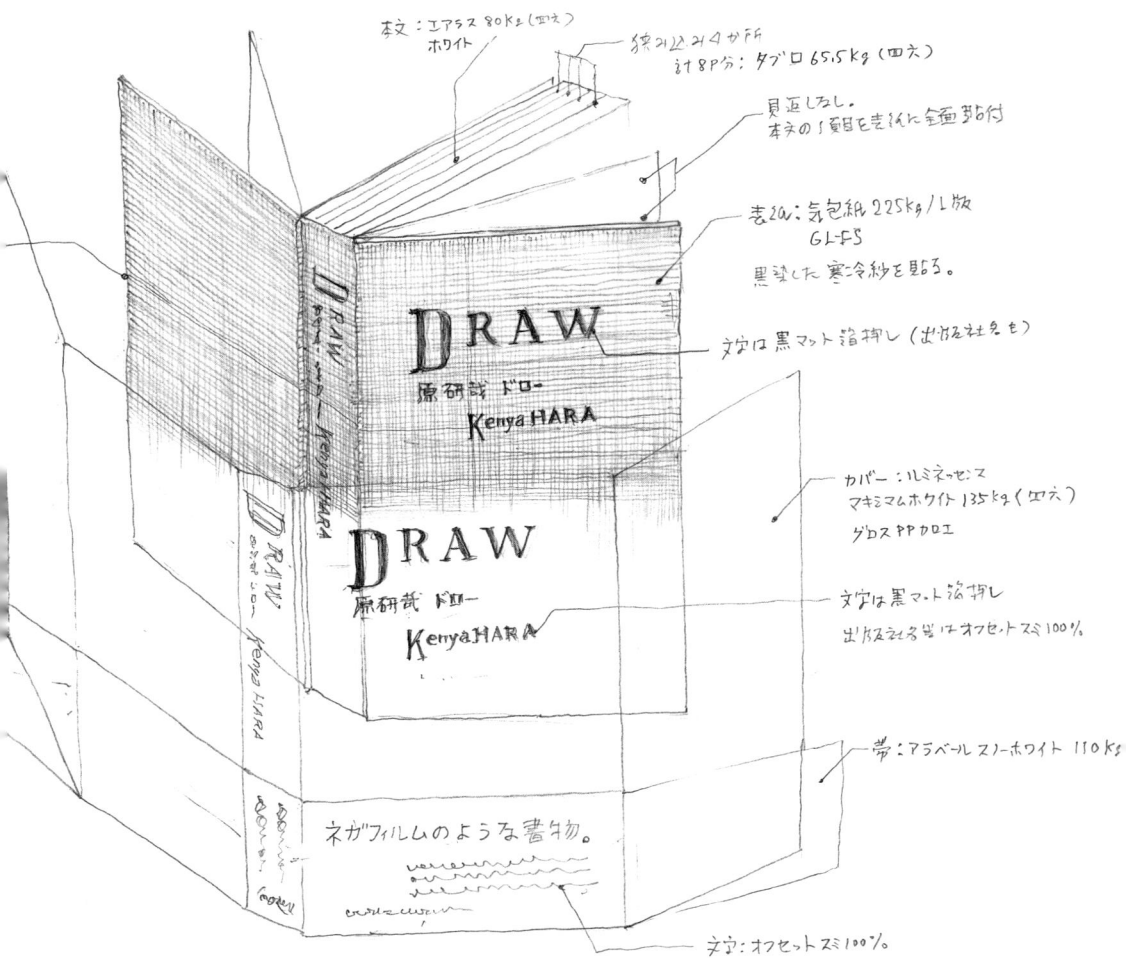

本文：エアラス 80kg（四六）
ホワイト

狭み込み4ヶ所
計8P分：タブロ 65.5kg（四六）

見返しなし。
本文の1頭を受けた鋼釘貼付

表紙：気泡紙 225kg/L版
GL-FS

黒染した寒冷紗を貼る。

DRAW

原研哉 ドロー
Kenya HARA

文字は黒マット箔押し（出版社名も）

カバー：ルミネッセンス
マキシマムホワイト 135kg（四六）
グロス PP カロエ

DRAW

原研哉 ドロー
Kenya HARA

文字は黒マット箔押し
出版される号はオフセットスミ100%

帯：アラベール スノーホワイト 110kg

ネガフィルムのような書物。

文字：オフセットスミ100%。

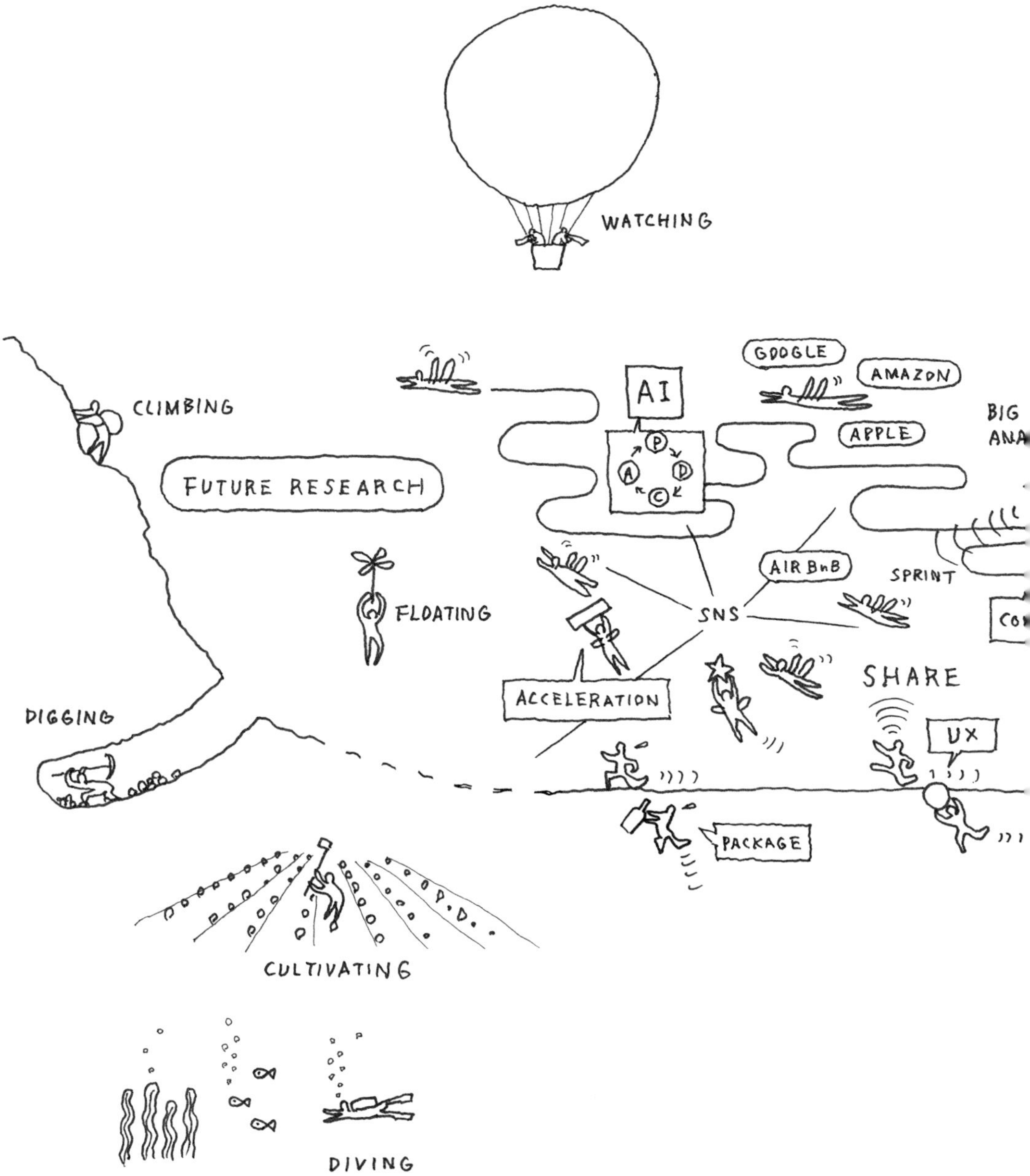

WATCHING

CLIMBING

FUTURE RESEARCH

FLOATING

DIGGING

AI

P
A   D
C

GOOGLE

AMAZON

APPLE

BIG
ANA

AIR BnB

SNS

SPRINT

CO

ACCELERATION

SHARE

UX

PACKAGE

CULTIVATING

DIVING

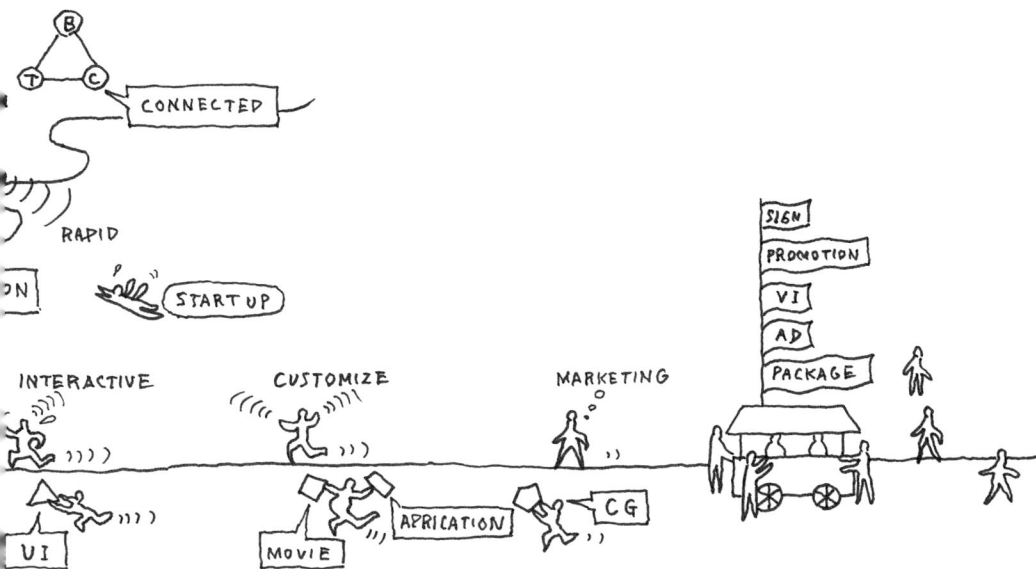

This illustration, read from right to left, symbolizes the
evolution of technology and the changing nature of design.
In the past, it was enough to offer design as a service in a variety of fields.
However, as technology and society continue to change,
the nature of design is becoming more diversified and multifaceted.

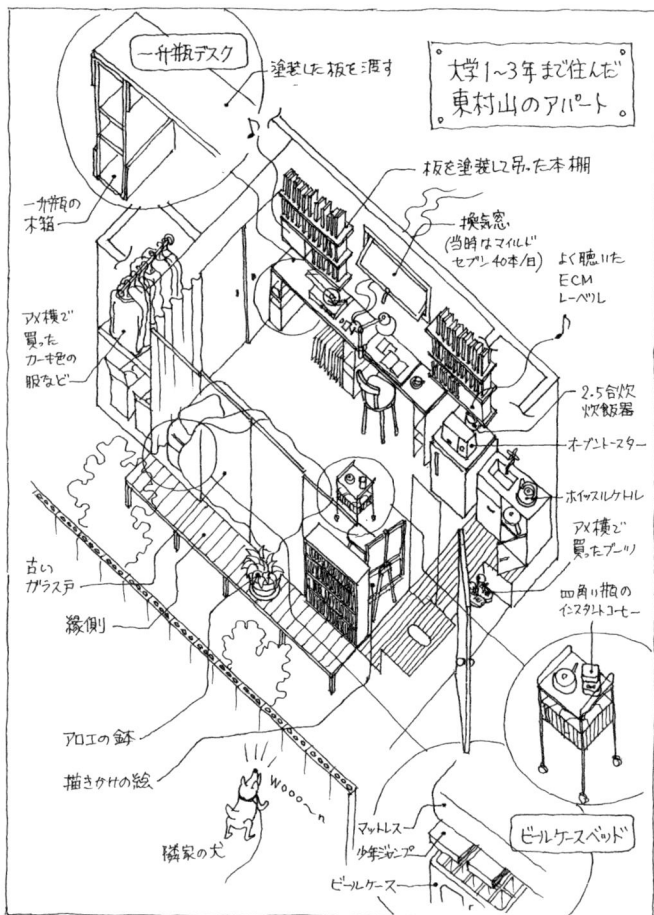

DRAW

First published in 2025

Author	Kenya Hara
Editorial concept	Kenya Hara, Lars Müller
Book design	Kenya Hara + Tomoko Nishi
	Hara Design Institute, Nippon Design Center, Inc.
Translation	Maggie Kinser Hohle, Yukiko Naito
Proofreading	George MacBeth
Publishing	Lars Müller Publishers
	Zurich, Switzerland
	www.lars-mueller-publishers.com
Printing	SunM Color Co., Ltd.

My apartment in 1977,
when I entered university.
I drew it by hand for
a magazine project.
I still remember it
surprisingly clearly.